Calendar of Music and Musicians

ADELE P. MANSON

The Scarecrow Press, Inc.
Metuchen, N.J., & London
1981

Library of Congress Cataloging in Publication Data

Manson, Adele P   1916-
  Calendar of music and musicians.

  Includes index.
  1. Music--Chronology. I. Title.
ML161.M16   780'.9   80-27614
ISBN 0-8108-1395-5

TABLE OF CONTENTS

PREFACE

Today one has only to touch a button to hear any kind of music around the clock. This Calendar of Music and Musicians can provide a useful frame of reference, bringing to listeners new biographical data not only on performers, composers, and conductors, but also on music scholars and those engaged in the production and publication of music.

The Calendar aims to provide librarians, teachers, music clubs, and broadcasters both a ready-reference tool and a means for planning exhibits, programs, and announcements. A more comprehensive and updated music calendar adds new names as well as enlarges existing biographical data.

With such a wealth of material to choose from, the problem of selection is space. While one could add many times more entries, space in one volume is limited, but an attempt has been made to provide a sample cross-section of musical styles and periods, nationalities and genres. Only the principal entry on a particular day and year is traced in the index; secondary figures or titles are omitted, such as an opera in which a singer is making a debut.

As a basis for the selection of performers, composers, conductors, and the works performed, recent Schwann Record and Tape Guides, the Schwann Artist Issue, and Gramophone Classical Catalogues were used, as they are readily available in record shops and on major library shelves. These list compositions that include the newest works of present-day composers as well as those of past centuries. These listings provide a good source of selection, and, because they are so well used, the spellings of personal names and composition titles are those employed here. A number of cross-references are included for variable spellings, however.

The Title Index includes also the composer's name and the date (generally the premiere). Only symphonies or concertos that have distinctive subtitles are found in the index, and they are in quotes, e.g.: "Apocalyptic," Symphony no. 8 (Bruckner): 18 Dec

v

1892.   Lacking such a distinctive designation, such forms can be found by tracing the dates in the personal-name index.   The name index is arranged chronologically under each entry.

Often as variable as name spellings are dates themselves. The authoritative source for the dates used here was the sixth edition (1978) of Baker's Biographical Dictionary of Musicians.   The dates were painstakingly researched in it; the Russian dates are given in new-style calendar form.   Corporate entries and some artists or composers not listed in Baker's are incorporated from Marion Cullen's Memorable Days in Music. Other standard bibliographic sources are cited in the list of Sources Consulted.

For earlier centuries often the only sure date available is a death date, with only an estimate of the composer's age.   In other cases a baptismal date is the only record of birth, and therefore this date is listed.   An attempt has been made in the first chronological entry to include a person's nationality and place of birth, and perhaps also to add a phrase of interest.   Premieres, debuts, inventions, or other important events are part of the chronology.

The close of the sixteenth century marks the approximate beginning of the real development of instruments and instrumental music in the Western world.   With this evolution comes a subsequent rise in virtuosi, quite in contrast to the earlier vocal polyphony.   Moreover, as printing and literacy spread, the documentation became markedly better, so that it is easier to locate exact dates about a modern composer than, for example, William Byrd or Georg Telemann.   While most of the dates in this compilation range from the eighteenth century to the present, the earliest date is that of the churchman Philippe de Vitry and the latest, in mid-1980. De Vitry belonged to a very small minority in his time that was literate and kept precise records.

Since music is international, political history often acts upon the arts.   Composers and artists have fled oppression or sought a better livlihood, and in their migration have changed their names; so German born Georg Friedrich Händel becomes English-style George Frideric Handel.   This resettling has been on no greater scale than in our own time, when thousands entered the United States from Europe since the late 1930's--to our great musical gain.   One of the most recent examples is famed Soviet cellist Mstislav Rostropovich, who with his wife, singer Galina Vishnevskaya, sought asylum here in 1978 when they were stripped of their Soviet citizenship.   Composers miraculously survived Hitler's concentration camps, and in such a prison French composer Messiaen composed and with fellow prisoners performed his Quatuor pour la fin du temps. In World War I Paul Wittgenstein lost his right arm at the Russian front and made the most of his situation by commissioning, and thereby creating, a body of piano music for the left hand.

One can see the transmission of culture--families nurturing their children to carry on their traditions, whether in making violins

vi

in Cremona or by involving one's children in a jazz group, as Dave
Brubeck has done. In this transmission, the Bach family leads all
others, having provided outstanding musicians in a corner of Germany for more than two centuries. The artists themselves range
from millionaire conductor Thomas Schippers to ex-convict Huddie
"Leadbelly" Ledbetter, an American folksinger.

I am especially indebted to several of the Kent State University Library staff: Kenyon Rosenberg for his suggestions and ad-
vice, Dr. Neal Edgar for his help and encouragement, and Judith B.
McCarron of the Music Library. If this volume provides the im-
petus for a curious listener to pursue a lead, then it will have given
enjoyment and usefulness. For this compiler, it has already done
that.

Adele P. Manson
June 1980

SOURCES CONSULTED

American Society of Composers, Authors and Publishers. The ASCAP Biographical Dictionary of Composers, Authors and Publishers. New York: Crowell, 1948, 1952, 1966.

Bager, Robert, and Louis Biancolli. The Concert Companion. New York: McGraw-Hill, 1947.

Baker, Theodore. Baker's Biographical Dictionary of Musicians. New York: Schirmer, 1978.

Chase, Gilbert. America's Music. New York: McGraw-Hill, 1966.

Chilton, John. Who's Who of Jazz. Philadelphia: Chilton, 1972.

Cullen, Marion. Memorable Days in Music. Metuchen, N.J.: Scarecrow, 1970.

Feather, Leonard. The Encyclopedia of Jazz in the Sixties. New York: Horizon, 1966.

_____. The New Edition of the Encyclopedia of Jazz. New York: Horizon, 1960.

_____, and Ira Gitler. The Encyclopedia of Jazz in the Seventies. New York: Horizon, 1976.

Gramophone Classical Catalogue. Kenton, Harrow: Gramophone Publications Ltd., 1977, 1978.

Grove's Dictionary of Music and Musicians, Eric Blom, ed. New York: St. Martin's, 1954.

Musica AEterna. Program Notes for 1971-1978. Third volume. New York: Musica AEterna, 1978.

Schwann Artist Issue. Boston: Schwann, 1976.

Schwann Record and Tape Guide. Boston: Schwann, 1977-1978.

Slonimsky, Nicholas. Music Since 1900. 3d ed. New York: Coleman-Ross, 1949.

Thompson, Kenneth. A Dictionary of 20th Century Composers, 1911-1971. New York: St. Martin's, 1973.

Thompson, Oscar, ed. The International Cyclopedia of Music and Musicians. New York: Dodd, Mead, 1975.

Who's Who in Opera. New York: Arno, 1976.

CALENDAR
OF MUSIC
AND MUSICIANS

JANUARY 1

1585   Giovanni Gabrieli is appointed second organist at St. Mark's Cathedral in Venice, with his uncle, Andrea Gabrieli, at the first organ.

1602   Hans Leo Hassler is appointed chamber organist to the court of Rudolf II at Prague, an honorary position.

1782   Johann Christian Bach dies in London, aged forty-seven, the youngest surviving son of Johann Sebastian Bach.

1791   (Franz) Joseph Haydn begins his first visit to London to fulfill his contract with orchestra conductor Johann Salomon to compose six symphonies and conduct them from the piano. So well are they received that he later composed a second set of six symphonies.

1874   Hugo Leichtentritt, German-American musicologist and music lecturer at Harvard University, is born in Pleschen.

1878   Edwin Franko Goldman, American bandmaster, is born in Louisville, Kentucky

1879   Johannes Brahms conducts the first performance of his Violin Concerto in Leipzig, Joseph Joachim, soloist.

1889   Alexander Smallens, Russian-American conductor, is born in St. Petersburg. He was principally a theatrical conductor.

1891   Antonin Dvořák begins his professorship at Prague Conservatory.

1892   Artur Rodzinski, Polish conductor, is born in Spalato, Dalmatia.

1900   Xavier Cugat, Spanish-American dance-band leader and song composer, is born in Barcelona.

1908   Gustav Mahler accepts the post of principal conductor at the Metropolitan Opera in New York, and makes his debut directing <u>Tristan und Isolde.</u>

3

1915   The first issue of <u>Musical Quarterly</u> appears, edited by Oscar
        Sonneck.

1920   Suzanne Juyol, French mezzo-soprano, is born in Paris.

1923   Milt Jackson, American jazz vibraphonist with the Modern
        Jazz Quartet, is born in Detroit.

1930   Werner Heider, German composer, is born in Fürth; he is
        also a conductor and pianist.

1940   László Sáry, Hungarian composer and a member of the Buda-
        pest New Music Studio, is born in Györ.

1941   Mario Del Monaco stars in <u>Madama Butterfly</u> in making his
        professional debut, in Milan.

1942   Carlos Chávez's Piano Concerto receives its premiere, in
        New York City, with Eugene List, soloist, and Dimitri Mi-
        tropoulos conducting the New York Philharmonic Orchestra.

1953   Ernest Bloch's <u>Suite hebraïque</u> is given its premiere, in
        Chicago.

1977   Roland Hayes dies in Boston at age eighty-nine.

1978   A new United States copyright law goes into effect, giving
        composers greater benefits.

JANUARY 2

1732   Franz Xaver Brixi, Bohemian church organist and composer,
        is born in Prague.

1780   Johann Ludwig Krebs dies, aged sixty-five, in Altenburg,
        Germany. A former pupil and assistant to J. S. Bach, he
        wrote a fugue on the name B-A-C-H ("H" is German for note
        B; "B" is for B-flat).

1837   Mily Balakirev, Russian composer and member of "The Five,"
        is born in Nizhy-Novgorod.

1843   Richard Wagner conducts the premiere of his opera <u>Der flie-
        gende Holländer</u>, in Dresden.

1859   Mily Balakirev's <u>Overture on the Theme of Three Russian
        Songs</u> is first performed, in Moscow.

1889   Tito Schipa, Italian tenor, is born in Lecce. He began his
        musical career as a composer.

1890   Julian Gayarré dies at age forty-five in Madrid, where he had
        established a singing school.

1901   Torsten Ralf, Swedish tenor, is born in Malmö.

1904   Peter Jurgenson dies at age sixty-seven in Moscow. He be-
        came a good friend of Tchaikovsky as well as his publisher;
        their correspondence was later published.

        James Melton, American tenor, is born in Moultrie, Georgia.

1905   Sir Michael Tippett, English composer, is born in London.
        He writes his own libretti for his vocal works.

1913   Robert Elmore, American composer and organist, is born in
        Ramapatnam, India. He taught organ in Philadelphia after his
        graduation from the University of Pennsylvania.

        Gardner Read, American composer, teacher, and writer on
        music, is born in Evanston, Illinois.

1914   Italo Montemezzi's finest opera, L'Amore dei tre re, receives
        its American premiere at the Metropolitan Opera, Arturo Tos-
        canini conducting.

1915   Karl Goldmark dies in Vienna, aged eighty-four. A cantor's
        son, he began as a violinist pupil of Joseph Böhm in Vienna.

1941   Mischa Levitzki dies in Avon-by-the-Sea, New Jersey, aged
        forty-two. A concert pianist, he had studied with Dohnányi
        in Berlin.

1955   Glenn Gould makes his United States debut in a piano recital
        in Washington.

1977   Erroll Garner dies in Los Angeles, aged fifty-five. His jazz
        piano playing earned him the sobriquet of "The Man with Forty
        Fingers."

JANUARY 3

1785   Baldassare Galuppi dies in Venice at age seventy-eight.

1789   Giuseppini (Josephine) Grassini makes her opera debut in
        Italy, later joining La Scala in Milan.

1806   Henriette Sontag, German soprano, is born in Coblenz.

1836   Friedrich Witt dies in Würzburg, aged sixty-five.

1843   Gaetano Donizetti's opera <u>Don Pasquale</u> has its premiere, in Paris.

1850   Giuseppina (Josephine) Grassini dies in Milan, aged seventy-six.

1868   Moritz Hauptmann dies in Leipzig, aged seventy-five.

1878   Johannes Brahms's First Symphony receives its American premiere, in Boston.

1897   Paul Dukas's Symphony in C is first performed, in Paris.

1908   Mary Garden introduces the opera <u>Louise,</u> at New York's Manhattan Opera House.

1909   Victor Borge, Danish pianist and humorous entertainer, is born in Copenhagen.

1917   Pierre Dervaux, French conductor and composer, is born at Juvisy-sur-Orge.

1921   Newton Strandberg, American pianist, organist, and teacher, is born at River Falls, Wisconsin.

1925   Wilhelm Furtwängler makes his American debut at Carnegie Hall conducting the New York Philharmonic Orchestra.

1926   Nell Rankin, American mezzo-soprano, is born in Montgomery, Alabama.

1931   Lily Pons makes her debut singing in <u>Lucia di Lammermoor</u> at the Metropolitan Opera in New York City.

1942   Julius Conus dies in Malenki, Soviet Union, at age seventy-two.

1944   David Atherton, English conductor, is born in Blackpool.

1956   Alexander Gretchaninov dies in New York City at age ninety-one.

1967   Mary Garden dies in Aberdeen, Scotland, at age ninety-two.

1975   Milton Cross dies in New York City at age seventy-seven.

JANUARY 4

1710   Giovanni Battista Pergolesi, Italian composer, is born at Jesi.

1874   Joseph Suk, Czech violinist and composer, son-in-law of
        Antonin Dvořák, and grandfather of violinist Josef Suk, is
        born in Křečovice.

1881   Johannes Brahms conducts the premiere of his Academic
        Festival Overture at the University of Breslau, which had
        conferred on him an honorary doctorate. The program also
        includes the premiere of his Tragic Overture.

        Gaetano Merola, Italian conductor and impressario, is born
        in Naples.

1886   Die Meistersinger von Nürnberg, by Richard Wagner, re-
        ceives its Metropolitan Opera premiere, Anton Seidl conduct-
        ing.

1889   Das Rheingold of Richard Wagner receives its American
        premiere at New York's Metropolitan Opera, Anton Seidl
        conducting.

1893   Manuel Palau, Spanish composer and conductor, is born at
        Valencia.

        Saint-Saëns's opera, Samson et Dalila, has its American
        premiere in New Orleans.

1895   Michel Andrico, Rumanian composer who for many years
        accompanied Georges Enesco, is born at Bucharest.

1910   Parks Grant, American composer and teacher, is born in
        Cleveland, Ohio.

1937   Grace Bumbry, American mezzo-soprano, is born in St.
        Louis, Missouri.

1938   Jussi Bjoerling gives his first New York City concert. With
        his father and two brothers, he was a member of the vocal
        Bjoerling Quartet.

1961   Gunther Schuller's jazz ballet Variants is produced in New
        York City for the first time.

1966   Malcolm Williamson's children's opera Julius Caesar Jones
        is premiered, in London.

1969   Paul Chambers dies in New York City at age thirty-three.

        Arthur Loesser dies in Cleveland, Ohio at age sixty-four.

JANUARY 5

1778   Fortunato Santini, Italian composer and collector of a notable
       music library, is born in Rome.

1871   Frederick Shepherd Converse, American composer, is born
       in Newton, Massachusetts.

1880   Nikolai Medtner, Russian pianist and composer, principally
       for piano or voice, is born in Moscow.

1884   Gilbert and Sullivan's comic opera Princess Ida has its pre-
       miere in London.

1893   Friedrich Blume, German musicologist and editor of Die
       Musik in Geschichte und Gegenwart, is born in Schlüchtern.

1904   Erica Morini, Austrian-born violinist, now resident in New
       York City, is born in Vienna.

1906   William "Wild Bill" Davison, American jazz cornetist and
       leader, is born in Defiance, Ohio.

1912   Wilhelm Backhaus makes his American debut as piano soloist
       in Beethoven's Emperor Concerto, with the New York Sympho-
       ny Orchestra.

1917   Reginald Smith-Brindle, English composer and teacher, is
       born in Bamber Bridge.

       Wieland Wagner, grandson of Richard Wagner and director
       of the Bayreuth Festival, is born in Bayreuth.

1931   Alfred Brendel, Austrian pianist and Beethoven interpreter,
       is born in Wiesenberg.

1932   Maurice Ravel's Concerto in D for the left hand, is performed
       in Vienna; Paul Wittgenstein, who commissioned the work,
       is soloist.

1941   Marc Blitzstein's short opera No for an Answer is produced
       in New York City.

1953   Philippe Entremont makes his American debut in New York City.

1961   Easley Blackwood's Symphony no. 2, commissioned by the G.
       Schirmer music firm for its centenary, has its premiere in
       Cleveland, Ohio.

1962   Ross Lee Finney's Second Piano Quintet is performed in Los
       Angeles.

1970   Roberto Gerhard dies in Cambridge, England, aged seventy-
       three.

1973   Pierre Boulez's ... explosante/fixe, which includes a set of
        computers, is performed in New York City.

1974   Lev Oborin dies in Moscow, aged sixty-six.

1976   Georges Migot dies in Levallois, France, aged eighty-four.

1979   Charles "Charlie" Mingus dies in Mexico City at age fifty-
        six.

JANUARY 6

1755   Karl Heinrich Graun's opera Montezuma is produced in Berlin.
        Its French libretto was written by Frederick the Great.

1838   Max Bruch, German composer, is born in Cologne.   His
        most popular work, Kol Nidrei, for cello and orchestra, was
        composed for the Jewish community of Liverpool; Bruch was
        himself a Protestant and not Jewish as is sometimes sup-
        posed.

1850   Xaver Scharwenka, German pianist, teacher, and composer,
        is born at Samter. With his brother, Philipp, he founded
        the Scharwenka Conservatory in Berlin.

1872   Alexander Scriabin, Russian composer, is born in Moscow.

1902   Mark Brunswick, American composer and educator, is born
        in New York City.

1903   Maurice Abravanel, conductor since 1947 of the Utah State
        Symphony Orchestra, is born in Saloniki, Greece.

1920   Earl Kim, American composer and educator, is born in
        Dinuba, California.

1924   Jacques Ibert's Escales (Ports of Call) for orchestra, is per-
        formed in Paris.

1926   Emile Paladilhe dies in Paris, aged eighty-one.

1933   Vladimir de Pachman dies in Rome, aged eighty-four.

1940   Alexander Kipnis makes his debut at the Metropolitan Opera,
        New York City.

1942   Emma Calvé dies at Millau, France, at eighty-three years.

1950   Francis Poulenc's Piano Concerto has its premiere in Boston
        with the composer as soloist.

1960   Galina Vishnevskaya makes her concert debut in New York
        City.

1961   Gordon Binkerd's Symphony no. 3 has its premiere in New
        York City.

1964   Mary Costa makes her Metropolitan Opera debut in Verdi's
        La Traviata.

        The American Society of Composers, Authors and Publishers
        (ASCAP) receives a congratulatory letter from President
        Lyndon Johnson in honor of its fiftieth anniversary.

1967   Elliott Carter's Piano Concerto is first performed at the
        Boston Symphony Concert.

        JANUARY 7

1727   Pierre-Montan Berton, French composer, is born at Maubert-
        Fontaines.

1857   Franz Liszt's Piano Concerto no. 2 in A has its premiere in
        Weimar, Germany, with Hans von Bronsart, soloist, and the
        composer conducting.

1895   Clara Haskil, Rumanian pianist, is born in Bucharest.

1898   Rimsky-Korsakov's opera Sadko receives its premiere in
        Moscow and becomes popular with Russian audiences.

1899   Francis Poulenc, French composer and one of "Les Six," is
        born in Paris.

1900   John Brownlee, Australian-American baritone and music
        administrator, is born in Geelong.

1904   Antiochos Evangelatos, Greek composer and conductor, is
        born in Lixori.

1907   Nicanor Zabaleta, Spanish harpist, is born in San Sebastian.

1917   Ulysses Kay, American composer, arranger, teacher, and
        publisher's consultant, is born in Tucson, Arizona.

1921   Ignaz Friedman makes his American debut in New York City.

1922   Jean-Pierre Rampal, French flute virtuoso, is born in
        Marseilles.

1933   Louis Gruenberg's opera Emperor Jones based on O'Neill's

drama and starring Lawrence Tibbett is first produced by
the Metropolitan Opera, in New York City.

1938   Morgan Powell, American composer, trombonist, and teacher,
is born in Graham, Texas.

1946   Adamo Didur dies in Katowice, Poland, aged seventy-one.

1952   Gail Kubik's Pulitzer Prize-winning <u>Symphonie-Concertante</u>
has its premiere in New York City.

1955   Marian Anderson makes her debut at the Metropolitan Opera
in New York City, singing Ulrica in Verdi's <u>Un Ballo in maschera.</u>

1964   Colin McPhee dies in Los Angeles at the age of sixty-two.

1967   Carl Schuricht dies in Corseaux-sur-Vevey, Switzerland, aged
eighty-six.

JANUARY 8

1567   Jacobus Vaet, Flemish composer of masses and motets, dies
in Vienna, aged thirty-eight.

1705   George Frideric Handel's first opera, <u>Almira</u>, with German
and Italian arias, has its premiere, in Hamburg.

1713   Arcangelo Corelli dies in Rome, aged fifty-nine.

1812   Sigismond Thalberg, Austrian pianist and composer, is born
in Geneva.

1830   Hans von Bülow, German pianist, writer, and conductor, is
born in Dresden. He was one of the first to conduct without a score ("Better to have the score in your head than
your head in the score."). His wife, Cosima Liszt, daughter
of Franz Liszt, left him for Richard Wagner, whose works
von Bülow had helped make famous.

1831   Franz Krommer dies in Vienna, aged seventy-one.

1892   Hans Kindler, Dutch-born American conductor and cellist,
is born in Rotterdam.

1896   Jaromir Weinberger, Czech-born émigré and nationalistic
composer who settled in Florida, is born in Prague.

1905   Giacinto Scelsi, Italian composer, is born in La Spezia.

1906   Artur Rubinstein makes his New York debut as soloist in the
piano concerto of Saint-Saëns.

1911   Florent Schmitt's orchestral work <u>La tragédie de Salomé</u> is premiered, in Paris.

1912   Rudolf Escher, Dutch composer, music educator, and author of monographs on Ravel and Debussy, is born in Amsterdam.

1914   Charles Mills, American composer, is born in Asheville, North Carolina.

1915   Karl Dönch, Austrian baritone, is born in Hagen, Germany.

1920   Maud Powell dies in Uniontown, Pennsylvania, at age fifty-one.

1923   Giorgio Tozzi, American bass, is born in Chicago.

1924   Benjamin Lees, American composer and teacher, is born in Harbin, China.

Antal Ribári, Hungarian composer and pianist, is born in Budapest.

Robert Starer, Austrian-born American composer, is born in Vienna. In 1963 he joined the faculty of Brooklyn College (New York).

1935   Elvis Presley, American rock 'n roll singer, is born in Tupelo, Mississippi.

1940   Roger Sessions's Violin Concerto has its premiere, in Chicago.

1960   Seymour Shifrin's <u>Three Pieces for Orchestra</u> is first performed by the Minneapolis Symphony Orchestra.

Joan Sutherland sings in <u>La Traviata</u> in Covent Garden, London.

1971   Dmitri Shostakovich's Symphony no. 15 receives its premiere, in Moscow, with Maxim Shostakovich, son of the composer, conducting.

1975   Richard Tucker dies while on tour, in Kalamazoo, Michigan, aged sixty-one.

1978   Vladimir Horowitz marks the fiftieth anniversary of his American debut by playing Rachmaninoff's Piano Concerto no. 3 with the New York Philharmonic, Eugene Ormandy conducting.

JANUARY 9

1839   John Knowles Paine, American organist and composer, is
        born in Portland, Maine.

1844   Julian Gayerré, Spanish operatic tenor and founder of a sing-
        ing school for indigent youths, is born in Roncal.

1886   Antonin Dvořák's Symphony no. 2 receives its American pre-
        miere by the New York Philharmonic, Theodore Thomas con-
        ducting.

1899   Ernestine Schumann-Heink makes her Metropolitan Opera
        debut singing Ortrud in Lohengrin of Wagner.

1900   Joseph Frederick Wagner, American composer and conductor,
        is born in Springfield, Massachusetts.

1902   Sir Rudolf Bing, operatic impressario, general manager of
        the Metropolitan Opera from 1950-1972, is born in Vienna.
        He became an English citizen and was knighted in 1971.

1914   Kenny Clarke, American jazz drummer, is born in Pittsburgh.

1916   James Pease, American bass-baritone, is born in Indianapolis.

1926   John "Bucky" Pizzarelli, American jazz guitarist, is born in
        Paterson, New Jersey.

1939   Wladamiro Ganzarolli, Italian baritone, is born in Venice.

1941   Joan Baez, American folksinger and pacifist, is born in
        Staten Island, New York.

1943   Ariel Bybee, American soprano, is born in Reno, Nevada.

1948   Walter Piston's Pulitzer Prize-winning Symphony no. 3 is
        first performed, in Boston.

1966   Noah Greenberg dies in New York City at age forty-six.

1976   William Bolcom's Seasons, for guitar, is given its premiere,
        in New York City.

1979   Avery Claflin dies in Greenwich, Connecticut, aged eighty.

JANUARY 10

1876   Charles Coussemaker dies in Bourbourg, France, at age
        seventy. He had collected a very large music library (listed
        in a Brussels catalog for auction).

1886   Anton Bruckner's <u>Te Deum</u> receives its first performance with orchestra in Vienna.

1895   Benjamin (Louis Paul) Godard dies in Cannes, France, aged forty-five.

        Meyer Davis, American bandleader, is born in Ellicott City, Maryland.

1897   Vincent d'Indy's symphonic variations, <u>Istar</u>, is premiered simultaneously by William Mengelberg in Amsterdam and Eugène Ysaÿe in Brussels.

1903   Jean Paul Morel, French conductor and teacher, is born in Abbeville.

1904   Mitrofan Petrovich Belaieff dies in St. Petersburg, aged sixty-seven.

1906   Nathan Rakhlin, Russian conductor, is born in Snovsk.

1907   Abram Stasevich, Russian conductor, is born in Simferopol.

1910   Jean Martinon, French conductor and composer, is born in Lyons.

1926   Walter Gieseking makes his American concert debut at Town Hall, New York City.

1928   Wallace Berry, American composer, author, and educator, is born in La Crosse, Wisconsin.

1929   Derek Hammond Stroud, English bass, formerly an optician, is born in London.

1931   Charles Ives's <u>Three Places in New England</u> receives its first performance, in New York City.

1933   Akira Miyoshi, Japanese composer, is born in Tokyo.

1934   Franz Schmidt's Symphony no. 4 has its premiere in Vienna.

1935   Sherrill Milnes, American baritone, is born in Downer's Grove, Illinois.

1941   Frank Bridge dies in Eastbourne, England, aged sixty-one.

1947   Ferruccio Tagliavini makes his Metropolitan Opera debut, New York City.

1953   Paul Badura-Skoda makes his concert debut in New York City.

1969   John Brownlee dies in New York City, aged sixty-nine.

1978   Henri Dutilleux's <u>Timbres, espace, mouvement</u> for orchestra
        is first performed, in Washington.

JANUARY 11

1763   Giovanni Platti dies in Würzburg, Germany, aged sixty-five.

1801   Domenico Cimarosa dies in Venice at age fifty-one.

1856   Christian Sinding, Norwegian composer and teacher (including
        a stint at the Eastman School of Music), is born in Kongs-
        berg.

1875   Reinhold Glière, Russian composer, teacher, and folksong
        collector, is born in Kiev.

1895   Laurens Hammond, engineer and founder of the electronic
        keyboard instrument company that bears his name, is born
        in Evanston, Illinois.

1901   Vassili Sergeievitch Kalinnikov dies in Yalta, Crimea, aged
        thirty-four.

1902   Maurice Duruflé, French organist and composer, is born in
        Louviers.

1904   Mozart's <u>The Magic Flute</u> receives its Metropolitan Opera
        premiere, starring Marcella Sembrich.

1909   Gunnar Berg, Danish composer who studied with Jeppesen
        and Honegger, is born in St. Gall, Switzerland.

1925   Aaron Copland's Symphony for Organ and Orchestra is given
        its premiere by the New York Symphony Society, Walter
        Damrosch conducting.

1928   Andrea Guiot, French soprano, is born in Garons-Garde.

1932   Egon Petri makes his American concert debut in New York
        City.

1934   Lotte Lehmann makes her Metropolitan Opera debut in New
        City, starring in <u>Die Walküre</u> of Wagner.

1935   Samuel Barlow's one-act opera <u>Mon ami Pierrot</u> is produced
        for the first time, in Paris.

        Marcella Sembrich dies in New York City at age seventy-six.

1940   Mark De Voto, American composer and editor, is born in Cambridge, Massachusetts.

        Sergei Prokofiev's ballet Romeo and Juliet is produced in Leningrad.

1954   Oscar Straus dies in Bad Ischl, Austria, at age eighty-three. He had dropped the final "s" from Strauss to separate from other musical Strausses.

1959   John Joubert's Piano Concerto has its premiere, in Manchester, England.

1968   Rodion Shchedrin's Chimes for orchestra, commissioned by the New York Philharmonic Orchestra, is first performed in New York City.

        Mariano Stabile dies in Milan at age seventy-nine, having retired from the stage in 1960.

1975   Max Lorenz dies in Salzburg, aged seventy-three.

        JANUARY 12

1674   Giacomo Carissimi dies in Rome, aged sixty-eight.

1715   Jacques Duphly, French composer of organ and clavecin music, is born in Rouen.

1723   Francesca Cuzzoni, celebrated Italian soprano, born ca. 1700 in Parma, makes her debut in Handel's opera Ottone, in London.

1836   Arabella Goddard, English pianist, is born near St. Malo, France.

1876   Ermanno Wolf-Ferrari, Italian opera composer, is born in Venice.

1894   Rossini's opera Semiramide receives its Metropolitan Opera premiere, starring Nellie Melba and Edouard de Reszke.

1908   Leopold Ludwig, Austrian conductor, is born in Witkowitz.

1917   Walter Hendl, American conductor and music administrator, is born in West New York, New Jersey.

1921   Leo Smit, American pianist and composer, is born in Philadelphia.

        Town Hall, with 1,500-seat capacity, opens in New York City.

1926   Morton Feldman, American avant-garde composer, is born in New York City.

1927   Salvatore Martirano, American composer and teacher, is
        born in Yonkers, New York.

1928   Vladimir Horowitz makes his American debut as soloist in
        Tchaikovsky's Piano Concerto no. 1 with the New York
        Philharmonic Orchestra, Sir Thomas Beecham conducting.
        It also marks Beecham's American debut.

1934   Ernest Bloch's Sacred Service is first performed, in Turin,
        Italy.

        William Metcalf, American baritone, is born in New Bedford,
        Massachusetts.

1937   Vincenzo Sardinero, Spanish baritone, is born in Barcelona.

1941   Anne Howells, English mezzo-soprano, is born in Southport.

1946   George Duke, American jazz musician, is born in San Raphael,
        California.

1958   Arthur Shepherd dies in Cleveland, Ohio, aged seventy-seven.

        JANUARY 13

1690   Gottfried Heinrich Stölzel, German composer, is born in
        Grünstadtl.

1838   Ferdinand Ries dies in Frankfurt, aged fifty-three.

1842   Heinrich Hofmann, German pianist, is born in Berlin.

1864   Stephen Foster dies penniless in Bellevue Hospital in New
        York City, aged thirty-seven.

1866   Vassili Sergeievitch Kalinnikov, Russian composer, is born
        in Voin.

1903   Charles Kullman, American tenor, is born in New Haven,
        Connecticut.

1904   Richard Addinsell, English theatrical and film composer, is
        born in London. Best known is his Warsaw Concerto from
        the film Suicide Squadron.

        Béla Bartók's symphonic poem Kossuth causes an uproar at
        its premiere, in Budapest, for caricaturing the German
        national hymn.

1936   Christiana Sorell, Austrian soprano, is born in Vienna.

1938   Rudolf Firkušný makes his American debut in Town Hall, New York City.

Ernest John Moeran's Symphony in G minor receives its premiere, in London.

1939   Leonard Warren makes his Metropolitan Opera debut, starring in Simon Boccanegra of Verdi.

1944   Igor Stravinsky's Circus Polka, commissioned by the Ringling Brothers Circus, has its first performance, in Boston.

1956   Tito Gobbi makes his American debut at the Metropolitan Opera, starring in Tosca of Puccini.

1971   Henri Tomasi dies in Paris, aged sixty-nine.

1974   Raoul Jobin dies in Quebec, aged sixty-seven.

1979   Marjorie Lawrence dies in Little Rock, Arkansas, aged sixty-nine. Her autobiography refers to the interruption of her career due to an attack of infantile paralysis and her successful recovery.

1980   André Kostelanetz dies on vacation in Port-au-Prince, Haiti, aged seventy-eight. He was known for summer concerts and his arrangements of light popular music.

JANUARY 14

1850   Jean De Reszke, Polish tenor, brother of singers Josephine and Edouard, is born in Warsaw. His mother was his first music teacher.

1875   Albert Schweitzer, Alsatian-born organist, medical missionary, and Bach authority, is born in Kaysersberg. He is the only musician to have received the Nobel Peace Prize (1947).

1888   Stephen Heller dies in Paris, aged seventy-four; he had lived most of his life there, a successful pianist and composer.

1889   Ilma di Murska commits suicide by poison at age fifty-two in Munich. An operatic soprano, she was born in Croatia in 1836.

1896   Jacobo Ficher, Russian-Argentine composer and founder of the Argentine Composers League, is born in Odessa.

1900   Giacomo Puccini's opera Tosca is conducted in its premiere by Leopoldo Mugnone in Rome's Teatro Constanzi.

1911   George Tremblay, Canadian-American composer, is born in Ottawa. He studied with Schoenberg in California.

1925   Grace Hoffman, American contralto, is born in Cleveland, Ohio.

1929   Louis Quilico, Canadian baritone, is born in Montreal.

1936   Thomas Briccetti, American composer, is born in Mt. Kisco, New York.

1940   Siegmund Nimsgern, German bass, is born in St. Wendel.

1949   Joaquín Turina dies in Madrid, aged sixty-six; he was a professor at Madrid's Conservatory of Music beginning in 1931.

1955   Heitor Villa-Lobos's Symphony no. 8 and his Harp Concerto are given their first performances in Philadelphia.

1960   Paul Creston's Violin Concerto no. 1 has its premiere in Detroit.

        William Flanagan's Concert Ode has its first hearing in Detroit.

1964   Quincy Porter's Symphony no. 2 receives its premiere in Louisville, Kentucky.

1965   Henri Dutilleux's Cinq métaboles is first performed in Cleveland.

        Jeannette MacDonald dies in Houston, Texas, aged fifty-seven.

1976   Lazar Berman, Soviet pianist, plays his first American concert at Miami University in Oxford, Ohio.

1978   Robert Heger, at age ninety-one, dies in Munich.

JANUARY 15

1775   Giovanni Battista Sammartini, Italian organist and composer and teacher of Christoph Gluck, dies in Milan, aged about seventy-four.

1866   Ernest M. Skinner, American organ builder, is born in Clarion, Pennsylvania. His company built the organ for the National Cathedral in Washington.

1890   Peter Ilyitch Tchaikovsky's ballet Sleeping Beauty is first staged in St. Petersburg.

1908   Luisa Tetrazzini makes her New York operatic debut singing
        in Verdi's <u>La Traviata</u> at the Manhattan Opera House. She
        remained with the Manhattan Opera until its closing in 1910.

1909   Gene Krupa, American jazz drummer and bandleader, is
        born in Chicago.

        Elie Siegmeister, American composer, teacher, writer, and
        conductor, is born in New York City.

1923   Gabriel Pierné's ballet <u>Cydalise et le chèvre-pied</u> has its
        premiere in Paris at the Opéra.

1925   Ruth Slenczynska, American pianist and teacher, is born in
        Sacramento, California.

1926   Enrico Toselli dies at age forty-two in Florence. His mar-
        riage in 1907 to the former Princess Luise of Saxony made
        headlines.

1927   Richard Kogel, German bass, is born in Munich.

1932   Enrique Raxach, Spanish-Dutch composer, is born in Bar-
        celona. He studied in Germany and Switzerland, finally
        settled in Holland in 1962.

1935   Malcolm Frager, American pianist and a Russian-language
        major, is born in St. Louis.

1941   Olivier Messiaen's <u>Quatuor pour la fin du temps,</u> for violin,
        clarinet, cello, and piano is performed in Görlitz German
        prison camp in World War II, the composer at the piano.
        He was a war prisoner for two years before returning to his
        organist post in Paris.

1958   Samuel Barber's opera <u>Vanessa</u> is given its premiere by the
        Metropolitan Opera in New York; the libretto is by Gian
        Carlo Menotti.

1976   Paul Chihara's <u>Missa Carminum,</u> for a cappella chorus, is
        first sung in Los Angeles.

JANUARY 16

1672   Francesco Mancini, Italian composer and organist, is born
        in Naples.

1728   Niccolò Piccinni, Italian opera composer, is born in Bari.
        He spent the latter part of his life in Paris, where his
        operas rivaled those of Gluck.

1739   George Frideric Handel's oratorio <u>Saul</u> is first sung in London.

1800   Luigi Cherubini's opera <u>Les deux journées</u> is given its pre-
        miere at the Théâtre Feydeau in Paris and is enthusiastically
        received.

1869   Alexander Borodin's Symphony no. 1 has its first performance,
        in St. Petersburg.

1872   Henri-Paul Busser, French composer, organist, and con-
        ductor, is born in Toulouse. He lived to almost 102 years
        old; his centenary was celebrated in Paris with concerts of
        his works.

1886   Amilcare Ponchielli dies in Milan, aged fifty-one. Through
        his pupils, Mascagni, Puccini, and Leoni, he influenced the
        course of Italian opera.

1891   Léo Delibes dies in Paris at the age of fifty-four. In 1881
        he was appointed professor of composition at the Conserva-
        toire.

1897   Katherine Goodson makes her piano debut at a Saturday Pop
        Concert in London.

1905   Ernesto Halffter, Spanish composer, is born in Madrid. A
        student of Manuel de Falla, he completed Falla's unfinished
        <u>Atlántida</u>.

1914   Roger Wagner, American choral conductor (Roger Wagner
        Chorale) is born in Le Puy, France.

1928   Pilar Lorengar, Spanish soprano, is born in Saragoza.

        Ezra Sims, American composer and music librarian at
        Harvard University, is born in Birmingham, Alabama.

1932   Jean Cox, American tenor, is born in Gadsden, Alabama.

1933   Frida Leider makes her Metropolitan Opera debut in New
        York, starring in Wagner's <u>Tristan und Isolde</u>.

1934   Marilyn Horne, American soprano, is born in Bradford,
        Pennsylvania.

        Richard Wernick, American composer and teacher, is born
        in Boston.

1957   Arturo Toscanini, aged eighty-nine, dies in New York, one
        of the greatest conductors of the time.

1969   Vernon Duke dies in Santa Monica, California, aged sixty-
        two.

1975   Thor Johnson, at age sixty-one, dies in Nashville, Tennessee, where he had been director of the Nashville Orchestra Association since 1967.

JANUARY 17

1676   Pier Francesco Cavalli dies in Venice, aged seventy-three. An organist, then maestro di cappella at San Marco in Venice, he composed not only church music but also many operas.

1713   John Stanley, blind English organist and composer, a pupil of Maurice Greene, is born in London.

1734   François-Joseph Gossec, Belgian composer, is born in Vergnies. He spent most of his long life in Paris, a creator and innovator in forms and sonorities.

1738   Jean François Dandrieu, French organist and composer, dies in Paris, aged about fifty-six.

1750   Tomaso Albinoni dies at age seventy-eight in Venice. His contemporary J.S. Bach admired and arranged his music.

1826   Juan Crisostomo Arriaga dies in Paris, aged nineteen, already known for his compositions.

1857   Wilhelm Kienzl, Austrian composer, is born in Waizenkirchen. He studied with Rheinberger and Liszt; lectured and wrote on music.

1869   Alexander Dargomizhsky dies in St. Petersburg, aged fifty-five. He was president of the Russian Music Society.

1877   Hans Jelmoli, Swiss pianist and composer, is born in Zurich.

1890   Yuri Fayer, Russian conductor, is born in Kiev.

1901   Pietro Mascagni's opera Le Maschere is simultaneously premiered in six cities.

1907   Henk Badings, Dutch composer, is born in Bandung, Indonesia.

1919   Ignace Jan Paderewski, concert pianist, becomes premier of Poland, participating in the Versailles peace conference later.

1927   Donald Erb, American composer and teacher, is born in Youngstown, Ohio.

1930   Robert Ceely, American composer and educator, is born in Torrington, Connecticut.

1934   Sydney Hodkinson, Canadian composer and teacher, is born
        in Winnipeg.

        Cedar Walton, American jazz pianist and composer, is born
        in Dallas.

1941   Harl McDonald's Suite from Childhood, for harp and orchestra,
        has its premiere in Philadelphia.

1943   Billy Harper, American jazz saxophonist and teacher, is born
        in Houston.

1960   Jon Vickers makes his debut at the Metropolitan Opera in
        New York.

1969   Grażyna Bacewicz dies at fifty-five in Warsaw, where she
        had been a professor.

        JANUARY 18

1835   César Cui, Russian composer and member of "The Five,"
        is born in Vilna. He was a fortifications expert for the
        army and son of a soldier in Napoleon's army who had stayed
        in Russia.

1841   Emmanuel Chabrier, French composer, is born in Ambert.

1871   Giovanni Bottesini's opera Ali Baba is produced in London.

1886   Joseph Tichatschek dies at age seventy-eight in Dresden.

1903   Berthold Goldschmidt, German composer, is born in Ham-
        burg.

1907   Katherine Goodson makes her American debut with the Boston
        Symphony Orchestra.

        Puccini's Manon Lescaut has its Metropolitan Opera premiere
        under the composer's direction and stars Caruso, Cavalieri,
        and Scotti.

1908   Frederick Delius's Brigg Fair--English Rhapsody is performed
        in Liverpool.

1919   Juan Orrego-Salas, Chilean composer and educator, is born
        in Santiago.

1927   Evelyn Lear, American soprano and wife of Thomas Stewart,
        is born in New York City.

1929 Abram Chasins is soloist in his first Piano Concerto in its premiere with the Philadelphia Orchestra, Ossip Gabrilowitsch conducting.

1937 Pierre Luboschutz and his wife, Genia Nemenoff, make their debut as duo-pianists in New York City.

1942 Jacques Ibert's Ouverture de fête is first performed in Paris.

1967 Jan Smeterlin dies in London, aged seventy-four, regarded highly for his interpretations of Chopin's music.

1968 Richard Rodney Bennett's Symphony no. 2 is given its first performance in New York City.

1977 Paul Nordoff dies at age sixty-seven in Herdecke, West Germany. He published two books on music therapy with handicapped children.

JANUARY 19

1576 Hans Sachs dies at age eighty-one in Nuremberg.

1674 Jean Baptiste Lully's opera Alceste receives its premiere, in Paris.

1765 Johann Joachim Agrell dies in Nuremberg at age sixty-three.

1810 Ferdinand David, German violinist and teacher, is born in Hamburg.

1833 Louis Joseph F. Herold dies at age forty-one in Thernes, France.

1853 Giuseppe Verdi's opera Il Trovatore is first produced at the Teatro Apollo, in Rome.

1873 Camille Saint-Saëns's Cello Concerto no. 1 has its premiere, in Paris.

1884 Jules Massenet's opera Manon is given its first performance at the Opéra Comique in Paris.

Albert Louis Wolff, French conductor, is born in Paris.

1898 Alexander Glazounov's ballet Raymonda receives its premiere, in St. Petersburg.

1903 Boris Blacher, German composer, is born in Newchwang, China.

1909   Hans Hotter, German bass-baritone known for Wagnerian
        roles, is born in Offenbach.

1922   Titta Ruffo makes his first appearance with the Metropolitan
        Opera in New York, starring in Rossini's Barber of Seville.

1924   Georges Auric's ballet Les Fâcheux, written for Diaghilev,
        is first staged in Monte Carlo.

1936   Elliott Schwartz, American composer, educator, and co-
        director of the Bowdoin Music Press, is born in Brooklyn.

1939   David Van Vactor conducts his award-winning Symphony no.
        1 in its premiere in New York City.

1948   Douglas Moore's Farm Journal, for chamber orchestra, is
        first performed in New York City.

1969   György Ligeti's Ten Pieces for Wind Quintet receives its
        premiere in Malmö, Sweden.

1970   Judith Blegen sings in The Magic Flute in her first Metro-
        politan Opera role in New York.

        Shulamit Ran's O, the Chimneys is first performed in New
        York City.

1972   Michael Rabin dies unexpectedly at age thirty-five in New
        York City.

        JANUARY 20

1586   Johann Hermann Schein, German composer, is born in
        Grünhain, the son of a pastor.   In 1616 he became cantor
        at Leipzig's Thomasschule.

1649   Marc' Antonio Cesti's opera Orontea opens in Venice; it is
        his first opera and proves a success.

1774   Florian Leopold Gassmann dies in Vienna, aged forty-four.
        A teacher as well as a composer, he counted Salieri among
        his pupils.

1821   Wilhelmine Schröder-Devrient first sings in opera at age
        sixteen, performing in Mozart's Magic Flute.

1833   Gertrud Elisabeth Mara dies in Reval, Russia, aged eighty-
        three.   She had been a singing teacher there for twenty years.

1855   Ernest Chausson, French composer, is born in Paris into a
        well-to-do family.

1876   Josef Hofmann, Polish piano virtuoso, is born in Pedgorze.
        Considered the outstanding performer of his day, he toured
        widely, eventually settling in the United States and becoming
        a citizen.

1891   Emmanuel Bay, Russian-American pianist known for his
        accompanying, is born in Simferopol, the son of a cantor.
        For many years he accompanied Jascha Heifetz on tours.

        Mischa Elman, Russian violinist, is born in Talnoy. He
        studied with Brodsky and Auer, becoming a great virtuoso
        and performing with major orchestras around the world.

1892   Alfredo Catalani's opera La Wally opens in Milan; it was his
        last and best work.

1894   Walter Piston, American composer and Harvard University
        professor, is born in Rockland, Maine.

1899   Alexander Tcherepnin, Russian-American composer and
        pianist, is born in St. Petersburg. His sons, Serge and
        Ivan, teach electronic-music development.

1913   Ethel Leginska makes her American debut in a piano recital
        in New York City.

1928   Antonio de Almeida, French conductor, is born at Neuilly-
        sur-Seine.

1933   Antonio Scotti makes his final appearance at the Metropolitan
        Opera after thirty-three years on the staff.

1935   Ugo Benelli, Italian tenor, is born in Genoa.

        Robert Casadesus is piano soloist in Mozart's Coronation
        Concerto in his American debut, performing with the New
        York Philharmonic.

1939   Charles Ives's Sonata no. 2, "Concord, Mass. 1840-1860,"
        which requires a strip of wood on the keyboard for tone-
        cluster effects, has its first complete performance in New
        York City, John Kirkpatrick playing it from memory.

1952   Arthur Farwell dies at seventy-nine in New York City. He
        was a champion of American music, promoting it through-
        out his life.

1961   Francis Poulenc's Gloria in G for soprano, chorus and
        orchestra, is first performed in Boston and becomes one
        of his most famous compositions.

1972   Jean Casadesus dies in an auto accident in Ontario, Canada,
        aged forty-four. The son of pianists Robert and Gaby

Casadesus, he had performed with them in his father's Concerto for Three Pianos.

JANUARY 21

1626   John Dowland, Irish-born lutenist and composer, dies at age sixty-three in London, where he had lived part of his life. He was regarded as the leading lutenist; his works were harmonically innovative. He was born in December of 1562 and had traveled widely.

1816   Luigi Cherubini's Requiem is first performed in Paris; he is considered a master of counterpoint, especially in sacred music.

1846   Albert Lavignac, French theorist and musicologist, is born in Paris.

1851   Albert Lortzing dies in Berlin, aged forty-nine; his last opera had been staged in Frankfurt the night before his death.

1874   Euphrosyne Parepa-Rosa dies at age thirty-seven in London; she first sang in opera at age sixteen.

1880   Nikolai Rimsky-Korsakov's opera May Night opens in St. Petersburg.

1904   Leoš Janáček's opera Jenufa has its premiere in Brno; it was later performed throughout Europe and America.

1906   Gunnar Johansen, Danish-American pianist and composer, is born in Copenhagen.

1916   Houston Bright, American composer and teacher, is born in Midland, Texas.

1918   Antonio Janigro, Italian cellist and conductor, is born in Milan.

1921   Hilde Rössl-Majdan, Austrian contralto, is born in Moosbierbaum.

1926   Franco Evangelisti, Italian avant-garde composer, is born in Rome.

1927   Albert Roussel's orchestral Suite in F is first performed in Boston.

1930   Dmitri Shostakovich's Symphony no. 3, "May First," receives its premiere, in Leningrad.

1938   Erich Leinsdorf makes his conducting debut at the Metro-
        politan Opera.

1941   Placido Domingo, Spanish-born and Mexican-raised tenor, is
        born in Madrid.

1947   Bohuslav Martinů's Toccata e due canzona, for small orches-
        tra, is given its premiere, in Basel.

1948   Ermanno Wolf-Ferrari dies at age seventy-two in Venice; his
        early operas are still widely performed.

1958   Ataulfo Argenta, director of the National Orchestra since
        1945, dies in Madrid, aged forty-four.

1959   Lamar Stringfield dies at age sixty-one in Asheville, North
        Carolina. He developed The University of North Carolina's
        Institute of Folk Music.

1961   John Becker dies the day before his seventy-fifth birthday in
        Wilmette, Illinois; he was an editor for New Music Quarterly.

1965   Gérard Souzay makes his Metropolitan Opera debut in New
        York City.

1968   Gustaf Allan Pettersson's Symphony no. 6 is first performed,
        in Stockholm.

1977   John Vincent dies at age seventy-four in Santa Monica, Cali-
        fornia. From 1946 to 1969 he taught at the University of
        California in Los Angeles.

        JANUARY 22

1575   Queen Elizabeth I of England grants a license to Thomas
        Tallis and William Byrd to print music for twenty-one years.

1727   Claude Balbastre, French organist and composer, is born at
        Dijon.

1775   Manuel del Popolo García, Spanish tenor, singing teacher,
        and conductor, is born in Seville. His son, Manuel, and
        daughters, Maria Malibran and Pauline Viardot-García, were
        famous singers.

1859   Johannes Brahms is soloist in his first Piano Concerto in its
        premiere in Hannover, with Joseph Joachim conducting.

1870   Charles Tournemire, French organist and composer, is born
        in Bordeaux. He studied with Franck and d'Indy and was
        organist at Ste. Clotilde.

1886   John Becker, American composer and educator, is born in Henderson, Kentucky. He taught at several Midwestern universities and served on the editorial board of New Music Quarterly.

1887   Gilbert and Sullivan's comic opera Ruddigore opens in London.

1897   Rosa Ponselle, American soprano, is born in Meriden, Connecticut.

1904   George Balanchine, Russian-American choreographer, is born in St. Petersburg.

1907   The Metropolitan Opera's premiere of Strauss's Salome produces such violent protests that it was removed from the repertory for many years.

1911   Suzanne Danco, Belgian soprano, is born in Brussels.

        Roberto García-Morillo, Argentine composer and music critic, is born in Buenos Aires.

1916   Henri Dutilleux, French composer, is born in Angers. In 1938 he won the Grand Prix de Rome and later was associated with Paris radio.

1920   William Warfield, American baritone, is born in Helena, Arkansas.

1921   André Hodeir, French music critic and writer on jazz, is born in Paris.

1923   Leslie Bassett, American composer, is born in Hanford, California. A University of Michigan faculty member, he has won many awards.

1924   James Louis "J. J." Johnson, American jazz trombonist and composer, is born in Indianapolis.

1926   Aurèle Nicolet, Swiss flutist and teacher, is born in Neuchâtel.

1929   Adolf Brodsky dies in Manchester, England, aged seventy-seven. Since 1895 he had taught, then directed, the Royal College of Music there.

        Petr Eben, Czech composer, is born in Zamberk. He has taught musicology at the University of Prague.

1936   Paul Hindemith's Trauermusik, for viola and strings, is written and performed for the memorial service for King George V in London.

1940   Eberhard Weber, German jazz bassist, is born in Stuttgart.

1943   Michael Urbaniak, Polish jazz musician who plays a five-
        string violin, is born in Warsaw.

1964   Marc Blitzstein dies from a brain injury suffered in a bar
        brawl in Martinique; he was fifty-eight.

JANUARY 23

1752   Muzio Clementi, Italian-born and English-educated pianist
        and composer, is born in Rome. His piano studies Gradus
        ad Parnassum (after Fux's treatise on counterpoint) still test
        pianistic abilities. Clementi stayed in London, becoming a
        piano manufacturer.

1789   Marco Bordogni, Italian tenor and voice teacher, is born in
        Gazzaniga.

1837   John Field dies of alcoholism at age fifty-four in Moscow.
        He had taught and concertized in Russia for many years; a
        pianist, he composed mostly for that instrument.

1858   Luigi Lablache dies in Naples, aged sixty-three. He had been
        singing master to Queen Victoria for a brief time.

1895   Edward MacDowell's Suite no. 2, "Indian," has its premiere
        in New York City.

1908   Serge Koussevitzky makes his conducting debut with the Berlin
        Philharmonic Orchestra.

        Edward MacDowell dies at age forty-seven in New York City
        after several years as a complete invalid.

1933   Joel Spiegelman, American composer, conductor, and harp-
        sichordist, is born in Buffalo, New York. He organized a
        chamber orchestra, comprised of Soviet Jewish émigrés who
        came here in the 1970's.

1935   Teresa Zylis-Fara, Polish soprano, is born in Wilno.

1936   Carlos Chávez's Sinfonia India is first performed on a radio
        broadcast.

1973   Edward "Kid" Ory dies in Honolulu, aged eighty-six, one of
        the New Orleans jazz greats.

1976   Paul Robeson dies in Philadelphia, aged seventy-seven. Not
        only a singer and actor, he was trained as a lawyer; real-

izing the inequities for minorities, became a political radical (he was himself a black).

JANUARY 24

1705   Carlo Farinelli (né Carlo Broschi), the most famous Italian castrato singer of his day, is born in Andria. He sang for King Philip V of Spain the same several arias nightly for many years to ease the monarch's melancholy.

1712   Frederick II (Frederick the Great), King of Prussia, German amateur flutist, music patron, and composer, is born in Berlin. A flute student of Quantz, he established a court orchestra and opera house. From 1740 to 1767 Carl Philipp Emanuel Bach was his chief harpsichordist, whose father, Johann Sebastian Bach, wrote his Musical Offering on a theme of Frederick II.

1776   Ernst Theodor Amadeus Hoffmann, German writer and composer, is born in Königsberg. Known principally for his writing, he influenced the Romantic school of literature enormously.

1813   The Royal Philharmonic Society of London is founded.

1829   William Mason, American pianist and teacher, is born in Boston. His father was Lowell Mason and his brother Henry, who later was a partner in the Mason & Hamlin piano-manufacturing firm.

1835   Vincenzo Bellini's last opera, I Puritani, is first staged at the Théâtre-Italien in Paris.

1851   Gaspare Spontini dies, aged seventy-six, in Ancona, Italy.

1875   Camille Saint-Saëns's symphonic poem Danse macabre is given its premiere, in Paris.

1883   Friedrich von Flotow dies in Darmstadt at age seventy.

1913   Norman Dello-Joio, American composer and organist, is born in New York City; he studied organ with his father and composition with Hindemith and Wagenaar.

1918   Gottfried von Einem, Austrian opera composer, is born in Bern, Switzerland.

1919   Leon Kirchner, American composer and Harvard University music professor, is born in Brooklyn, New York.

1922   Carl Nielsen's Symphony no. 5 is first performed, in Copen-
        hagen.

1924   Klaus George Roy, Austrian-born American musicologist,
        critic, and composer, is born in Vienna.

1925   John Ferrante, American countertenor, is born in Hartford,
        Connecticut.

1926   Otto Klemperer makes his American conducting debut as
        guest of the New York Symphonic Society Orchestra.

1933   John Carewe, English conductor, is born in Derby.

1935   Nicolae Bretan's opera Eroii de la Rovine is first staged, in
        Cluj, Rumania.

1937   Nicolae Bretan's opera Horia has its premiere, in Cluj,
        Rumania.

        Dmitri Mitropoulus makes his American conducting debut in
        Boston.

1952   Hilding Rosenberg's Symphony no. 6, "Sinfonia Semplice,"
        receives its premiere in Gävle, Sweden.

1960   Edwin Fischer dies in Zurich at age seventy-three.

1976   Jacob Gilboa's Beth Alpha Mosaic, for female voice, chamber
        ensemble and tape, is first performed, in Chicago.

        JANUARY 25

1866   Antonio Scotti, Italian baritone, is born in Naples; he became
        a Metropolitan Opera singer, remaining for thirty-three years.

1886   Wilhelm Furtwängler, German conductor, is born in Berlin,
        where he eventually led the Berlin Philharmonic. His clashes
        with Nazi authorities were resolved, but he was later accused
        of collaborating.

1902   Franz Schmidt's Symphony no. 1 is first performed in Vienna.

1909   Richard Strauss's opera Electra has its premiere in Dresden.
        Ernestine Schumann-Heink sang in it but thought the vocal
        lines "frightful".

1911   Julia Smith, American composer, teacher, and pianist, is
        born in Denton, Texas.

1913   Witold Lutoslawski, Polish composer, is born in Warsaw.
        A soldier in World War II, he became a German prisoner,
        returning to a career in music after the war.

        Alfred Nieman, English composer and pianist, is born in
        London.

1914   William Strickland, American conductor, is born in Defiance,
        Ohio. He founded and first directed the Nashville Symphony
        Orchestra (1946-51).

1917   Krystyna Szcepanska, Polish mezzo-soprano, is born in
        Nasielsk.

1929   Benny Golson, American jazz musician and composer
        (M*A*S*H* television series), is born in Philadelphia.

1936   Carole Bogard, American soprano, is born in Cincinnati.

1945   Richard Tucker first sings with the Metropolitan Opera,
        starring in Ponchielli's La Gioconda.

1954   Maria Stader makes her New York City debut in a song re-
        cital at Town Hall.

1967   Ettore Bastianini dies in Sirmione, Italy, aged forty-four;
        he was known for his singing in Verdi operas.

        JANUARY 26

1790   Wolfgang Amadeus Mozart's opera Cosi fan tutti receives its
        first performance at Vienna's Burgtheater.

1795   Johann Christoph Friedrich Bach dies in Bückeburg, Germany,
        aged sixty-two; he was the ninth son of Johann Sebastian
        Bach and a fine musician.

1852   Frederick Corder, English composer and composition teacher,
        is born in London; he founded the Society of British Com-
        posers in 1905.

1860   Wilhelmine Schröder-Devrient dies at age fifty-five in Coburg.
        Her baritone father was her first teacher in voice.

1905   Arnold Schoenberg conducts the premiere of his symphonic
        poem Pelleas und Melisande in Vienna.

1911   Richard Strauss's opera Der Rosenkavalier opens in Dresden's
        Königliches Opernhaus.

1922   Ralph Vaughan Williams's Symphony no. 3, "Pastoral," is
        first performed by the Royal Philharmonic Society, Sir
        Adrian Boult conducting.

1923   Giacomo Lauri-Volpi first appears with the Metropolitan
        Opera, singing in Verdi's Rigoletto.

1924   Warren Benson, American composer and teacher, is born in
        Detroit.

        Alexander Tcherepnin is soloist in the premiere of his Piano
        Concerto no. 2 in Paris.

1934   Roy Harris's Symphony no. 1 is first performed, in Boston.

1945   Jacqueline DuPré, English cellist and owner of the "Davidov"
        Stradivarius cello, is born in Oxford.

1947   Grace Moore dies in an air crash near Copenhagen, aged
        forty-eight.

1948   Ignaz Friedman dies at age sixty-five in Sydney, Australia,
        where he had settled a few years earlier after a career as
        concert pianist.

        John Avery Lomax dies in Greenville, Mississippi, aged
        eighty. With his son, Alan, he spent a lifetime researching
        American folksongs.

1950   Paul Schoeffler makes his American operatic debut with the
        Metropolitan Opera in New York.

1952   Ernst von Dohnanyi's Violin Concerto no. 2, scored for
        orchestra without violins, is first performed, in San An-
        tonio, Texas.

1957   Francis Poulenc's religious opera, Les Dialogues des
        Carmélites, opens at Milan's La Scala, Nino Sanzogno con-
        ducting.

1967   Frank Martin's Cello Concerto has its first performance, in
        Basel.

1974   Julius Patzak dies at age seventy-five in Rottach-Egern, Ger-
        many. He sang many years at the State Opera in Munich,
        then at the Vienna Opera.

1975   Toti Dal Monte, aged eighty-one, dies in Pieve di Soligo,
        Italy; after leaving opera, she taught singing.

1977   Bruce Hungerford dies in an auto accident in the Bronx, New
        York, aged fifty-four. Besides his career as pianist, he was
        also a photographer and archaeologist.

JANUARY 27

1731   Bartolommeo Cristofori, instrument maker to Ferdinando de'
Medici, dies in Florence at age seventy-five.

1756   Wolfgang Amadeus Mozart, Austrian composer and pianist,
is born in Salzburg, son of violinist and composer Leopold
Mozart.   The young Mozart demonstrated his supreme genius
at an early age--a true child prodigy.

1806   Juan Crisostomo Arriaga, Spanish composer, is born in
Rigoitia.   By the age of thirteen he wrote an opera and was
accepted at the Paris Conservatory.

1823   Edouard Lalo, French composer, is born in Lille.   The
performances of his violin works by Sarasate brought him
recognition.

1844   Ferenc Erkel's opera Hunyady László, considered the first
national Hungarian opera, opens in Budapest.

1885   Jerome Kern, American composer of musicals, is born in
New York City.

1886   Olin Downes, American music critic for the New York Times
from 1924 to 1955, is born in Evanston, Illinois.

1895   Emanuel Balaban, American conductor and Eastman School
of Music professor, is born in Brooklyn.

1901   Giuseppe Verdi dies at age eighty-seven in Milan and is regarded as the greatest figure in Italian opera.

1906   Josef Lhévinne makes his American debut in New York City
with the Russian Symphony Orchestra conducted by Vassily
Safonov.

Mozart's Don Giovanni is staged at the Metropolitan Opera
to honor the composer's sesquicentennial.

1913   Milton Adolphus, American composer, is born in New York
City.   Although not a professional musician, he has written
a great deal.

1915   Jack Brymer, English clarinetist, is born in South Shields.

1918   Skitch Cedric Henderson, American bandleader and pianist,
is born in Halstad, Minnesota.

Gian Francesco Malipiero's Pause del silenzio (first part)
receives its premiere in Rome.

1928   Jean-Michel Damase, French composer and pianist, is born in
Bordeaux.

1932   Lothar Klein, German-Canadian composer and teacher, is born in Hannover.

1937   John Ogdon, English pianist, is born in Manchester. In 1962 he won the Tchaikovsky Competition in Moscow.

1938   Constant Lambert's ballet, Horoscope, has its first performance, in London.

1944   Paul Creston's Saxophone Concerto has its premiere, in New York.

1946   Paul Kalisch dies at age ninety at St. Lorenz am Mondsee, Austria. He and his wife, Lilli Lehmann, both sang in Wagnerian operas.

1948   Jean-Philippe Collard, French pianist, is born in Mareuil-sur-Ay.

1949   Boris Asafiev dies in Moscow, aged sixty-four; his compositions were mostly for the stage, but he is noted as a Russian music historian.

1951   Cesare Siepi makes his American debut at the Metropolitan Opera.

1955   Sir Michael Tippett's opera The Midsummer Marriage opens in London's Covent Garden, John Pritchard conducting.

1956   Erich Kleiber dies in Zurich, aged sixty-five. In 1935 he left Germany for South America to protest the Nazi government, conducting there and later in the United States.

1961   Leontyne Price and Franco Corelli make their debuts at the Metropolitan Opera, starring in Verdi's Il Trovatore.

1972   Mahalia Jackson dies in Evergreen Park, Illinois, aged sixty. A gospel singer, she sang for conventions and political groups.

JANUARY 28

1791   Louis Joseph F. Herold, French opera composer, is born in Paris.

1794   Johann Gottlob Breitkopf dies in Leipzig, aged seventy-four.

1806   Etienne Méhul's opera Les Deux aveugles de Tolède is first staged in Paris.

1832   Franz Wüllner, German pianist, conductor, and composer, is born in Münster.

1841   Victor Nessler, Alsatian composer and conductor, is born in
        Baldenheim.

1866   Carl Emil Seashore, Swedish-born American psychologist who
        devised test and instruments for measuring musical abilities,
        is born in Mörlunda.

1875   Julián Carrillo, Mexican composer and violinist, is born in
        Ahualulco. He constructed instruments using fractional di-
        visions of tones and devised a notation for them.

1887   Artur Rubinstein, Polish-born American piano virtuoso, is
        born in Lodz.

1898   Vittorio Rieti, Italian-American composer, is born in Alex-
        andria, Egypt.

1903   Verdi's _Ernani_ receives its New York premiere at the Metro-
        politan Opera, starring Marcella Sembrich, Antonio Scotti,
        and Edouard de Reszke.

1916   Enrique Granados's opera _Goyescas_ (based on his piano
        pieces) is produced by the Metropolitan Opera in New York
        City.

1918   Amelita Galli-Curci makes her New York debut, singing in
        Meyerbeer's _Le Pardon de Ploermel_.

1930   Emmy Destinn dies in Budejovice, Czechoslovakia, aged
        fifty-one.

1931   Ezio Flagello, American bass-baritone, brother of Nicolas
        Flagello, is born in New York City.

1932   Verdi's _Simon Boccanegra_ receives its American premiere
        at New York's Metropolitan Opera, starring Lawrence Tibbett,
        Ezio Pinza, and Maria Müller.

1933   Spiro Malas, American bass, is born in Baltimore, Maryland.

1935   Mikhail Ippolitov-Ivanov, at age seventy-five, dies in Moscow.

1936   Robert Suderburg, American composer, conductor, and pianist,
        is born in Spencer, Iowa.

1941   Aaron Copland's _A Quiet City_, a suite from the film, is first
        performed, in New York City.

1944   Leonard Bernstein's Symphony no. 1, "Jeremiah," has its
        premiere with the Pittsburgh Symphony Orchestra, the com-
        poser conducting.

        John Tavener, English composer, is born in London; he
        studied composition with Lennox Berkeley.

1947   Reynaldo Hahn dies at age seventy-two in Paris. In 1945 he became Music Director of the Paris Opéra.

1960   Jacques de Menasce dies in Gstaad, Switzerland, aged fifty-four. In 1941 he came to New York, continuing his concert career in America and Europe.

1972   Scott Joplin's opera Treemonisha has its premiere in the version prepared by T. J. Anderson, in Atlanta, Georgia.

JANUARY 29

1715   Georg Christoph Wagenseil, Austrian court composer and teacher, is born in Vienna.

1728   John Christopher Pepusch's ballet-opera The Beggar's Opera is first produced, in London. The libretto is by John Gay.

1781   Mozart's opera Ideomeneo is first staged, in Munich.

1782   Daniel-François Auber, French opera composer, is born in Caen.

1801   Johannes Bernardus van Bree, Dutch composer and violinist, is born in Amsterdam.

1852   Sir Frederic Cowen, English composer, is born in Kingston, Jamaica. He was conductor of the London Philharmonic Orchestra for many years.

1862   Frederick Delius, English composer, is born in Bradford.

1866   Romain Rolland, French musicologist and author, is born in Clamecy.

1876   Havergal Brian, long-lived English composer, considered an eccentric, is born in Dresden, Staffordshire.

1898   Maria Müller, Austrian soprano, is born in Leitmeritz.

1924   Luigi Nono, Italian lawyer and avant-garde composer, member of the Italian Communist Party Central Committee, is born in Venice. He married Arnold Schoenberg's daughter, Nuria.

1936   Constant Lambert's masque for chorus and orchestra Summer's Last Will and Testament is performed, in London.

1940   Justino Diaz, American bass, is born in Puerto Rico.

1955   Ingolf Dahl's symphonic legend <u>The Tower of Saint Barbara</u>
        receives its premiere, in Louisville, Kentucky.

1962   Fritz Kreisler dies in New York City, aged eighty-six.

JANUARY 30

1697   Johann Joachim Quantz, German flutist, composer, and flute
        master for Frederick the Great, is born in Oberscheden.

1817   Carl Maria von Weber, called by the King of Saxony to the
        directorship of the German Opera Theater, makes his debut
        as conductor in Dresden.

1861   Charles Martin Loeffler, Alsatian-born American composer,
        is born in Mulhouse.

1862   Walter Damrosch, son of Leopold Damrosch, is born in
        Breslau, Germany, and brought to the United States as a
        child.   His NBC music-appreciation programs for children
        and his orchestral conducting made him nationally known.

1885   Wagner's opera <u>Die Walküre</u> is given its Metropolitan Opera
        premiere, Leopold Damrosch conducting.

1892   Charles Haubiel, American composer and teacher, is born
        in Delta, Ohio.

1911   Roy Eldridge, American jazz musician, is born in Pittsburgh.

1917   Joseph Bonnet makes his American debut as organ recitalist
        in New York City.

1921   Carl Nielsen's incidental music <u>The Mother</u> has its premiere,
        in Copenhagen.

1924   Helen Vanni, American mezzo-soprano, is born in Davenport,
        Iowa.

1957   Alfonso Letelier's suite for orchestra <u>Aculeo</u> has its premiere
        in Louisville, Kentucky.

1958   Sir William Walton's <u>Partita for Orchestra</u> receives its first
        performance, in Cleveland.

1963   Francis Poulenc dies in Paris at age sixty-four.

1970   William Schuman's canticle for orchestra <u>In Praise of Shahn</u>
        is given its premiere, in New York City.   It was written
        in memory of the American painter Ben Shahn.

JANUARY 31

1729   George Frideric Handel's opera <u>Admeto, re di Tessaglia</u>
        opens at London's Haymarket Theatre. During this season
        Handel applied for British citizenship.

1759   François Devienne, French musician who composed princi-
        pally for wind instruments, is born in Joinville.

1783   Caffarelli dies in Naples, aged seventy-two.

1797   Franz Schubert, famed Austrian composer (including more
        than 600 lieder), is born in Lichtenthal near Vienna.

1906   Benjamin Frankel, English composer whose works reflect
        his Communist beliefs, is born in London.

1915   Alan Lomax, American musicologist and folksong collector,
        son and assistant of John Avery Lomax, is born in Austin,
        Texas.

1916   Maria Barrientos makes her first appearance with the Metro-
        politan Opera in New York.

1921   Mario Lanza, American tenor who starred in the film <u>The
        Great Caruso</u>, is born in Philadelphia. His singing inspired
        the young Luciano Pavarotti.

1925   Vernon Duke's ballet <u>Zéphyr et Flore</u> is first staged in Paris.

1935   Mario Castelnuovo-Tedesco's Cello Concerto receives its
        premiere with the New York Philharmonic Orchestra, Gregor
        Piatigorsky as soloist.

1937   Philip Glass, American avant-garde composer, is born in
        Baltimore. After study with Nadia Boulanger he met Ravi
        Shankar and went to India to study Oriental modalities.

1952   Leon Kirchner's <u>Sinfonia</u> is first performed in New York City.

1953   Vittorio Giannini's opera <u>The Taming of the Shrew</u> (in con-
        cert form) is given its premiere by the Cincinnati Symphony
        Orchestra.

1955   Renata Tebaldi stars in Verdi's <u>Otello</u> in her Metropolitan
        Opera debut in New York.

1967   Giovanni Martinelli returns to the stage to sing in Puccini's
        <u>Turandot</u> after an absence of seventeen years.

FEBRUARY 1

1690   Francesco Maria Veracini, Italian violinist and composer, is born in Florence.

1701   Johan Joachim Agrell, Swedish composer and conductor, is born at Löth.

1827   Felix Mendelssohn's <u>Overture to a Midsummer Night's Dream</u> has its first public performance in Stettin, Karl Loewe conducting from manuscript.

1859   Victor Herbert, Irish-born American composer of light operas, cellist, and one of the founders of the American Society of Composers, Authors and Publishers (ASCAP), is born in Dublin.

1869   Julius Conus, Russian violinist and composer, is born in Moscow.

1875   Sir William Sterndale Bennett dies in London, aged fifty-eight.

1893   Giacomo Puccini's opera <u>Manon Lescaut</u> has its premiere, in Turin's Teatro Regio.

1896   Giacomo Puccini's opera <u>La Bohème</u> receives its premiere, in Turin's Teatro Regio, Arturo Toscanini conducting.

1922   Gerardo Rusconi, Italian composer, is born in Milan.

        Renata Tebaldi, Italian soprano, is born in Langhirano.

1927   Flaviano Labo, Italian tenor, is born in Borgonova.

1933   Sadao Watanabe, Japanese jazz saxophonist, is born in Tochigi.

1934   Robert Stern, American composer and educator, is born in Paterson, New Jersey.

1946   Carol Neblett, American soprano, is born in Modesto, California.

1953   Dmitri Kabalevsky conducts his Piano Concerto no. 3, "Youth,"
        in Moscow, Valdimir Ashkenazy, soloist.

1978   Vittorio Rieti's Concerto for String Quartet and Orchestra
        has its premiere performance in New York City.

FEBRUARY 2

1594   Giovanni Pierluigi da Palestrina, regarded as the greatest
        composer of the Catholic Church, dies in Rome, aged about
        seventy.

1669   Louis Marchand, French composer and organist who failed
        to show in competition with J. S. Bach, is born in Lyons.

1762   Girolamo Crescentini, Italian artificial soprano, is born in
        Urbania.

1785   Isabella Colbran, Spanish soprano and wife of Gioacchino
        Rossini, is born in Madrid.

1789   Armand-Louis Couperin is killed by a runaway horse in Paris;
        one of the four organists at Notre Dame, he was sixty-one.

1790   Domenico Donzelli, Italian tenor, is born in Bergamo.

1875   Fritz Kreisler, Austrian-American violin virtuoso and com-
        poser, is born in Vienna.

1900   Gustave Charpentier's opera Louise opens at the Opéra
        Comique in Paris. His mistress was also named Louise.

1901   Jascha Heifetz, Russian-American violin virtuoso, is born in
        Vilna.

        Gerhard Hüsch, German baritone, is born in Hannover.

1911   Jussi Bjoerling, Swedish tenor, is born in Stora Tuna.

1919   Lisa Della Casa, Swiss soprano, is born in Burgdorf.

1921   Nicolae Bretan's one-act opera Luceafarul has its premiere
        in Cluj, Rumania.

1924   Edward "Sonny" Stitt, American jazz saxophonist, is born in
        Boston.

1927   Stan Getz, American jazz bandleader and saxophonist, is
        born in Philadelphia.

1929   Waldemar Kmentt, Austrian tenor, is born in Vienna.

1934   John Charles Thomas, in his Metropolitan Opera debut, sings
        in Verdi's La Traviata.

1935   Kirsten Flagstad stars in Wagner's Die Walküre in her
        American debut at the Metropolitan Opera.

1940   Martina Arroyo, American operatic soprano, is born in New
        York City.

1969   Giovanni Martinelli, at age eighty-three, dies in New York,
        where he taught singing after his opera retirement.

1974   Jean Absil dies in Brussels at the age of eighty; from 1922
        to 1964 he directed music at the Academy of Etterbeek in
        Brussels.

1977   Ned Rorem's organ suite A Quaker Reader is first performed,
        in New York City.

FEBRUARY 3

1736   Johann Georg Albrechtsberger, Austrian music theorist, com-
        poser, and teacher of Beethoven, is born in Klosterneuburg.

1748   Joseph Fiala, Bohemian oboist and composer, is born in
        Lochovice.   He died in 1816 in Donaueschingen (date unknown).

1809   Felix Mendelssohn, German composer and grandson of philoso-
        pher Moses Mendelssohn, is born in Hamburg.   His Jewish
        family had converted to Christianity and added Bartholdy to
        their surname.

1814   Johann Anton Koželuch dies in Prague, aged seventy-five.

1817   Emile Prudent, French pianist, teacher, and composer, is
        born in Angoulême.   An orphan, he was adopted by a piano
        tuner.

1823   Gioacchino Rossini's opera Semiramide, after Voltaire's
        tragedy, is first staged, in Venice at Teatro la Fenice.

1844   Hector Berlioz's overture Le Carnaval romain receives its
        first performance, in Paris.

1868   Giulio Gatti-Casazza, director of the Metropolitan Opera in
        New York from 1908 to 1935, is born in Undine, Italy.

1904   Luigi Dallapiccola, Italian composer, is born in Pisino.

1910   Blas Galindo, Mexican composer and teacher, is born in San
        Gabriel, Jalisco.

1911   Jehan Alain, French composer, principally for piano or organ,
        is born in Paris.

1915   Richard Bales, American composer and conductor of the
        National Gallery Orchestra of Washington, is born in Alex-
        andria, Virginia.

1927   Claire Watson, American soprano, is born in New York City.

1933   John Handy, American jazz musician, is born in Dallas,
        Texas.

1939   Helga Dernesch, Austrian soprano, is born in Vienna.

1951   John Weinzweig organizes the Canadian League of Composers
        in Toronto and becomes its first president.

1956   Elie Siegmeister's Clarinet Concerto has its premiere in
        Oklahoma City, Oklahoma.

1957   Avery Claflin's La grande Bretèche, after Balzac's story, is
        aired on CBS radio.

1968   Tullio Serafin dies in Rome, aged eighty-nine.

1975   Robert Evett dies in Takoma Park, Maryland, aged fifty-two.

FEBRUARY 4

1740   Carl Mikael Bellman, Swedish composer, who also wrote the
        words to his songs, is born in Stockholm.

1774   Franz Tuma dies in Vienna, aged sixty-nine.

1781   Josef Mysliveczek dies in Rome, aged forty-three.

1846   Therese von Brunsvik writes in her diary: " ... Beethoven!
        It seems like a dream that he was the friend, the intimate of
        our house--a stupendous spirit! Why did not my sister J.,
        as the widow Deym, accept him as her husband? ... "

1893   Bernard Rogers, American composer and composition teacher,
        is born in New York City.

1912   Erich Leinsdorf, Austrian-born American conductor, is born
        in Vienna.

1924   Claudio Arrau makes his American debut as soloist with the Boston Symphony Orchestra.

1932   Ivan Davis, American piano virtuoso, is born in Electra, Texas.

1935   Martti Talvela, Finnish bass, is born in Hütola.

1936   Mary Pracht, American soprano, is born in Bellaire, Ohio.

1940   William Workman, American baritone, is born in Valdosta, Georgia.

1945   Alan Hovhaness's Lousadzak, "Coming of Light," for piano and strings, has its premiere, in Boston.

1949   Fritz Reiner makes his Metropolitan Opera debut, conducting Richard Strauss's Salome.

        Ljuba Welitsch makes her debut at the Metropolitan Opera, starring in Salome.

1974   Michel Andrico dies in Bucharest, aged seventy-nine.

FEBRUARY 5

1810   Ole Bornemann Bull, Norwegian violinist, is born in Bergen.

1852   Jenny Lind and her accompanist, Otto Goldschmidt, are married in Boston.

1886   Wagner's Rienzi receives its Metropolitan Opera premiere, Anton Seidl conducting.

1887   Giuseppe Verdi's opera Otello receives its premiere, in Milan.

1895   Mikhail Ippolitov-Ivanov conducts the premiere of his symphonic suite Caucasian Sketches in Moscow.

        Rosina Lhévinne makes her debut with the Moscow Symphony Orchestra.

1907   Ludwig Thuille dies at age forty-five in Munich.

1917   Otto Edelmann, Austrian bass-baritone, is born in Vienna.

1921   John Pritchard, English conductor, is born in London.

1939   Carl Orff's opera Der Mond, after a fairy tale of Grimm, is first staged, in Munich.

1952   John Vincent's Symphony in D is first performed, in Louisville, Kentucky.

1958   Sir Michael Tippett's Symphony no. 2 is first performed, in London.

1959   Leonie Rysanek makes her Metropolitan Opera debut, substituting on short notice for Maria Callas.

1962   Jacques Ibert dies at age seventy-one in Paris.

1963   Robert Kelly's Symphony no. 3, "Emancipation Symphony," is given its first hearing, in Washington.

1969   Thea Musgrave's Clarinet Concerto is given its premiere, in London.   The soloist plays while walking through the orchestra.

1970   Elliott Carter's <u>Concerto for Orchestra</u> is first performed by the New York Philharmonic Orchestra.

FEBRUARY 6

1496   Johannes Ockeghem, Flemish composer and teacher, dies in Tours, aged about seventy-six (old-style calendar).   He was a pupil of Dufay and teacher of Josquin Des Prez.

1813   Gioacchino Rossini's opera <u>Tancredi</u> opens in Venice at the Teatro La Fenice and is later translated into twelve languages.

1818   Charles Henry Litolff, English pianist, composer, and music publisher, is born in London.

1851   Robert Schumann conducts the premiere of his Symphony no. 3, "Rhenish," in Düsseldorf.

1881   Karl Weigl, Austrian composer who became an émigré to New York after the 1938 Nazi Anschluss, is born in Vienna.

1887   Richard Bonnelli (real name Bunn), American baritone, is born in Port Byron, New York.

1896   Julie Dorus-Gras dies in Paris, aged ninety.

1900   George Brunis, American jazz trombonist, is born in New Orleans.

1903   Claudio Arrau, Chilean pianist and supervisor of the Beethoven piano sonatas Urtext edition, is born in Chillán.

1909 Marcella Sembrich makes her last Metropolitan Opera appear-
      ance in New York.

1917 Arthur Gold, Canadian pianist and duo-pianist with Robert
      Fizdale, is born in Toronto.

1924 Nadia Reisenberg makes her American debut as piano recital-
      ist in New York's Aeolian Hall.

1926 Vladimir Petrov, Soviet tenor, is born in Moscow.

1929 Minnie Hauk dies at age seventy-seven in Triebschen, Swit-
      zerland.

1930 Albert Roussel's Petite Suite, for orchestra, is first performed
      in Paris.

1933 Henry Brant's Angels and Devils, for flute ensemble, has
      its premiere in New York City.

1937 Wieslaw Ochman, Polish tenor, is born in Warsaw.

1938 Ellsworth Milburn, American composer, is born in Greens-
      burg, Pennsylvania.

1944 Arnold Schoenberg's Piano Concerto is performed in New York
      City.

1954 Fernando Corena makes his Metropolitan Opera debut in New
      York.

1963 Werner Josten dies in New York City, aged seventy-seven.

1976 John La Montaine's Bicentennial opera, Be Glad, Then,
      America, is produced at University Park, Pennsylvania.

FEBRUARY 7

1779 William Boyce dies in Kensington, England, aged sixty-eight.

1792 Domenico Cimarosa's opera Il Matrimonio segreto opens in
      Vienna at the Burgtheater. Hurriedly composed for the Em-
      peror Leopold II, it is still in the repertoire.

1871 Heinrich Engelhard Steinway dies in New York City, aged
      seventy-three.

1873 Tchaikovsky's Symphony no. 2, "Little Russian," has its
      premiere in Moscow.

1875   Edouard Lalo's <u>Symphonie espagnole</u>, for violin and orchestra, is performed with Pablo de Sarasate as soloist, in Paris.

1878   Ossip Gabrilowitsch, Russian-born American pianist and conductor, is born in St. Petersburg. He married contralto Clara Clemens, daughter of Mark Twain.

1883   Eubie Blake, American jazz pianist and song composer, is born in Baltimore, the son of former slaves.

1889   Claudia Muzio, Italian soprano, is born in Pavia.

1892   Jan Smeterlin, Polish pianist, is born in Bielsko.

1897   Quincy Porter, American composer, teacher, and music administrator, is born in New Haven, Connecticut.

1908   George Whitefield Chadwick's <u>Symphonic Sketches</u> is performed in Boston.

1924   Marcel Grandjany makes his American debut in New York City.

1925   Marius Constant, Rumanian-born French composer and conductor, is born in Bucharest.

1928   Grace Moore makes her Metropolitan Opera debut, singing in <u>La Bohème.</u>

1931   Deems Taylor's opera <u>Peter Ibbetson</u> is produced by the Metropolitan Opera in New York City.

1933   Stuart Burrows, British tenor, is born in Pontypridd, Wales.

1938   David Van Vactor's <u>5 Bagatelles,</u> for strings, receives its premiere in Chicago.

1966   Ferruccio Busoni's Piano Concerto (with male chorus) has its New York premiere under George Szell conducting the Cleveland Orchestra.

1973   Eubie Blake is honored on his ninetieth birthday by the American Society of Composers, Authors and Publishers (ASCAP).

FEBRUARY 8

1709   Giuseppe Torelli dies in Bologna, aged fifty-one.

1741   André Grétry, French opera composer, is born in Liège, Belgium.

1810   Norbert Burgmüller, German composer, younger brother of
        Johann Friedrich Franz, is born in Düsseldorf.

1874   Modest Mussorgsky's opera Boris Godunov is first staged at
        the Imperial Opera House in St. Petersburg.

1904   Jean Sibelius's Violin Concerto has its premiere in Helsinki,
        Finland.

1906   Artur Balsam, Polish-born pianist, accompanist to violinists
        Menuhin and Francescatti, is born in Warsaw. After the
        1938 Nazi Anschluss he emigrated to America.

1907   Arnold Schoenberg's Chamber Symphony is introduced in
        Vienna.

1915   Newell Jenkins, American conductor and musicologist, is
        born in New Haven, Connecticut.

1925   Alvin Brehm, American composer, is born in New York
        City.

1934   Virgil Thomson's opera buffa Four Saints in Three Acts, to
        Gertrude Stein's libretto, is first produced, in Hartford,
        Connecticut.

1935   Tugomir Franc, Austrian bass, is born in Zagreb, Yugoslavia.

1938   Elly Ameling, Dutch soprano, is born in Rotterdam.

1940   Talib Rasul Hakim, American composer and educator, né
        Stephen A. Chambers, is born in Asheville, North Carolina.

1944   Lina Cavalieri is killed during an air raid in Florence, Italy,
        aged sixty-nine.

1946   Béla Bartók's Piano Concerto no. 3 receives its premiere
        posthumously, in Philadelphia with György Sándor as soloist.

1949   Franco Leoni dies in London, aged eighty-four.

1959   Elie Siegmeister's Symphony no. 3 is performed in Oklahoma
        City.

1963   Benjamin Lees's Violin Concerto has its first hearing, in
        Boston.

1964   Vincenzo Bellezza dies in Rome, aged seventy-five.

FEBRUARY 9

1812   Franz Anton Hoffmeister dies in Vienna, aged fifty-eight

1885   Alban Berg, Austrian composer using the twelve-tone tech-
        nique of Arnold Schoenberg, is born in Vienna.

1893   Giuseppe Verdi's opera Falstaff is first performed, in Milan's
        La Scala.

1909   Harald Genzmer, German composer, is born in Bremen.

1924   George Guest, English conductor and organist, is born in
        Bangor, Wales.

1928   Franz Crass, German bass-baritone, is born in Wipperfürth.

1940   Licia Albanese makes her Metropolitan Opera debut, singing
        in Madama Butterfly.

1941   Morton Gould's Spirituals for Orchestra receives its pre-
        miere in New York City.

1943   Ryland Davies, Welsh tenor, is born in Cwm, Ebbw Vale.

1951   Eddy Duchin dies at age forty-one in New York City.

        Ernest Hutcheson dies in New York City, aged seventy-nine.

1956   Karl Böhm makes his American conducting debut with the
        Chicago Symphony Orchestra.

1960   Ernst von Dohnányi dies in New York City, aged eighty-two.

1961   Felix Labunski's Symphonic Dialogues is first performed, in
        Cincinnati.

1974   Kiri Te Kanawa, New Zealand opera singer, makes her
        Metropolitan Opera debut in New York with three hours'
        notice as a substitute in Otello. Part Maori and part Irish,
        she is descended from the family of Sir Arthur Sullivan.

1976   Percy Faith dies at age sixty-seven in Los Angeles.

FEBRUARY 10

1744   George Frideric Handel's ode Semele is first performed in
        London.

1788   Johann Peter Pixis, German pianist, teacher, and composer,
        is born in Mannheim.

1843   Adelina Patti, daughter of Italian singers, is born in Madrid. She was one of the greatest coloratura sopranos of the century.

1870   Alessandro Bonci, Italian tenor, is born in Cesena.

1881   Jacques Offenbach's opera Tales of Hoffmann is produced posthumously in Paris.

1882   Nikolai Rimsky-Korsakov's opera The Snow Maiden has its first performance, in St. Petersburg.

1910   Maria Cebotari, Soviet soprano, is born in Kishinev, Besarabia.

1914   Larry Adler, American harmonica virtuoso, is born in Baltimore. Milhaud wrote a Suite for Harmonica and Orchestra for him.

1923   Cesare Siepi, Italian soccer player and bass-baritone, is born in Milan. He has sung at the Metropolitan and Vienna State Operas.

1927   Ernst Krenek's jazz opera Jonny spielt auf opens in Leipzig.

        Leontyne Price, American soprano who was inspired as a child by a concert given by Marian Anderson, is born in Laurel, Mississippi.

        Brian Priestman, English conductor, is born in Birmingham. From 1970 to 1978 he conducted the Denver Symphony, then leaving to direct the Miami Philharmonic.

1932   Cornelius Opthof, Dutch-Canadian baritone, is born in Rotterdam.

1940   Roberta Flack, American jazz singer and pianist, is born in Black Mountain, North Carolina.

1950   William Schuman's Violin Concerto is performed in its premiere by Isaac Stern in Boston.

        Armen Tigranian, aged seventy, dies in Tbilisi, where he had settled and taught since 1913.

1961   Walter Piston's Pulitzer Prize-winning Symphony no. 7 is first performed, in Philadelphia.

1966   Richard Rodney Bennett's Symphony no. 1 has its premiere, in London.

1976   Ulysses Kay's Southern Harmony is given its premiere by the North Carolina Symphony Orchestra.

FEBRUARY 11

1785   Wolfgang Amadeus Mozart is the soloist in the premiere of
        his Piano Concerto in D minor (K. 466) in Vienna. Having
        come directly to the concert hall from the copyists, he per-
        forms it without rehearsal.

1795   Carl Mikael Bellman dies in Stockholm a week after his fifty-
        fifth birthday.

1830   Hans Bronsart von Schellendorf, German composer and pianist,
        is born in Berlin. He studied with Kullak and Liszt.

1840   Gaetano Donizetti's opera La Fille du régiment opens at the
        Opéra-Comique in Paris. It is the first of his French operas.

1843   Giuseppe Verdi's opera I Lombardi is immediately successful
        in its premiere at La Scala, Milan.

1847   Thomas A. Edison, American inventor who created the first
        phonograph "speaking machine," is born in Milan, Ohio.

1883   The Adagio and Scherzo of Anton Bruckner's Symphony no.
        6 are first performed in Vienna.

1903   Anton Bruckner's Symphony no. 9 has its premiere in Vienna,
        with his Te Deum substituted for the Finale.

1907   Giacomo Puccini attends the American premiere of his opera
        Madama Butterfly, conducted by Arturo Toscanini at the Metro-
        politan Opera in New York.

1912   Rudolf Firkušný, Czech-born pianist and teacher at the
        Juilliard School of Music in New York, is born in Napajedla.

1915   Percy Grainger is acclaimed in his first American piano re-
        cital, given in New York City.

1926   Alexander Gibson, Scottish conductor, is born in Motherwell.

1930   Hilde Somer, Austrian-American pianist, is born in Vienna.
        At fourteen she began her study with Rudolf Serkin.

1938   Edith Mathis, Swiss soprano, is born in Lucerne.

1939   Franz Schmidt dies at seventy-two in Perchtoldsdorf, Austria.

1949   Giovanni Zenatello dies, aged seventy-two, in New York City,
        where he had taught singing; Lily Pons was a pupil.

1952   Hugo Weisgall's opera The Tenor is first staged in Baltimore.

1953   Carlos Chávez's Symphony no. 4, "Sinfonía romantica," has

its premiere in Louisville, Kentucky, with the composer conducting.

1971   Hans Werner Henze's <u>Compases para Preguntas ensimismadas</u>
is first performed in Basel.

1973   David Bedford's <u>The Sword of Orion,</u> for instrumental ensemble, receives its premiere in Buffalo, New York.

Morton Feldman's <u>Voices and Instruments II</u>, for vocal and
instrumental ensemble, is given its premiere in Buffalo, New
York.

FEBRUARY 12

1728   Agostino Steffani dies in Frankfurt, Germany, aged seventy-
three.   From 1688 to 1711 he was Kapellmeister at Hannover,
preceding Handel.

1760   Johann Ladislaus Dussek, Bohemian composer and pianist,
is born at Caslav.

Jean Philippe Rameau's ballet <u>Les Paladins</u> is staged in Paris.

1812   Ludwig van Beethoven's Piano Concerto no. 5, "Emperor,"
is performed in Vienna with Carl Czerny, soloist.   One
writer believed the new concerto "did not succeed."

1894   Hans von Bülow dies in Cairo, aged sixty-four.   Understanda-
bly bitter toward Richard Wagner, he still conducted his
works.

1896   Ambroise Thomas dies in Paris, aged eighty-four.   In 1871
he became director of the Paris Conservatoire.

1898   Roy Harris, American composer and teacher, is born in
Lincoln County, Oklahoma.

1902   Anny Konetzni, Austrian soprano, is born in Vienna.

1915   Emil Waldteufel, at age seventy-seven, dies in Paris, where
he had lived most of his life.

1917   Thomas Scherman, American conductor, is born in New York,
the son of Book-of-the-Month Club founder Harry Scherman.

1923   Mel Powell, American composer, band arranger, and music
administrator, is born in New York City.

Franco Zeffirelli, opera producer and designer, is born in
Florence, Italy.

1924   George Gershwin is soloist in his <u>Rhapsody in Blue</u>, for piano and jazz orchestra, in Aeolian Hall, New York, with Paul Whiteman conducting.

1932   Yevgeny Kibkalo, Soviet baritone, is born in the Soviet Union.

1959   George Antheil dies in New York, aged fifty-eight.

1973   Benjamin Frankel at age sixty-seven dies in London.

FEBRUARY 13

1700   Vittoria Tesi, Italian contralto, is born in Florence.

1725   George Frideric Handel's opera <u>Rodelinda</u> opens in London.

1741   Johann Joseph Fux, Austrian composer and theorist, Kapell-meister to the court since 1713, dies in Vienna, aged about eighty.

1746   Giovanni Giuseppe Cambini, Italian composer, is born in Leghorn.

1778   Fernando Sor, Spanish guitarist and composer, is born in Barcelona.

1851   Anna Essipoff, Russian pianist and teacher, is born in St. Petersburg. A pupil of Leschetizky, she later married him.

1867   Johann Strauss, Jr.'s <u>The Beautiful Blue Danube Waltz</u> is given its first performance in Vienna.

1870   Leopold Godowsky, Russian-American pianist and teacher, is born in Soshly, near Vilna.

1873   Feodor Chaliapin, extraordinary Russian bass, is born in Kazan.

1874   Johann Friedrich Franz Burgmüller dies at sixty-seven in Beaulieu, France.

1883   Richard Wagner, wintering in Venice, dies at sixty-nine.

1891   Alexander Kipnis, Russian bass, is born in Zhitomir, Ukraine.

1892   Joseph Massart, teacher of Sarasate and Wieniawski, dies in Paris, aged eighty.

1905   Leonard Ellinwood, American musicologist and music librarian, is born in Thomastown, Connecticut.

1908   Gerald Strang, Canadian-American composer, is born in
       Claresholm; he was an assistant to Arnold Schoenberg.

1914   The American Society of Composers, Authors and Publishers
       (ASCAP) is formally organized in New York under Victor
       Herbert's directorship.

1920   Eileen Farrell, American soprano, is born in Willimantic,
       Connecticut.

1926   Barney Childs, American composer, Rhodes scholar, and
       English professor, is born in Spokane, Washington.

1937   Bidú Sayão stars in _Manon_ in her Metropolitan Opera debut.

1943   William Schuman's _Prayer in Time of War_ has its premiere
       during World War II in Pittsburgh.

1952   Alfred Einstein dies in El Cerrito, California, aged seventy-
       one.   From 1918 to 1933 he edited the _Zeitschrift für
       Musikwissenschaft._

1953   Carl Orff's semioperatic _Il Trionfo d'Afrodite_ is first per-
       formed at Milan's La Scala.

1956   Ernest Toch's fairy tale _Peter Pan_ receives its premiere in
       Seattle.

1966   Pilar Lorengar makes her Metropolitan Opera debut in New
       York.

1968   Ildebrando Pizzetti dies at eighty-seven in Rome, where he
       had taught composition for many years.

1976   Lily Pons, celebrated soprano who toured World War II
       battlefields, dies in Dallas, Texas, aged seventy-seven.

1978   Roger Reynolds's _Fiery Winds_, for orchestra, is first per-
       formed in New York City.

       Andrés Segovia, a week before his eighty-fifth birthday, plays
       a concert celebrating the fiftieth anniversary of his American
       debut, in New York City.

       FEBRUARY 14

1590   Gioseffo Zarlino, Italian music theorist, teacher, and com-
       poser, dies in Venice, aged about seventy-two.   A Franciscan,
       he was maestro di cappella for his last twenty-five years.

1602   Pier Francesco Cavalli, early Italian opera composer, is
        born in Crema.

1727   George Frideric Handel becomes an English citizen.

1813   Alexander Dargomizhsky, Russian composer and pianist, is
        born in Tula district.

1829   Vincenzo Bellini's opera La Staniera receives its premiere,
        in Milan.

1857   Johannes Bernardus van Bree dies at age fifty-six in Amsterdam.

1882   Ignaz Friedman, Polish pianist, is born in Podgorze.

1917   Willian McCauley, Canadian composer for television and film
        documentaries, is born in Tofield, Alberta.

1920   Erik Satie's symphonic drama Socrate has its premiere, in
        Paris.

1921   Jeanne Demessieux, French organist known for improvisations,
        is born in Montpellier.

1923   Carl Fischer dies at age seventy-three in New York City.

1941   Bruno Walter makes his conducting debut at the Metropolitan
        Opera in Beethoven's Fidelio.

FEBRUARY 15

1571   Michael Praetorius, German organist, composer, and music
        historian, is born in Kreuzberg.

1621   Michael Praetorius dies on his fiftieth birthday in Wolfen-
        büttel, Germany.

1740   Ernst Eichner, German composer and bassoon player, is
        baptized in Arolsen. He dies in Pottsdam in 1777.

1797   Heinrich Engelhard Steinway, founder of the piano manufactur-
        ers bearing his name, is born in Wolfshagen, Germany; the
        family name was originally Steinweg.

1857   Mikhail Glinka dies at age fifty-two in Berlin.

1858   Marcella Sembrich, Polish soprano, is born in Wisniewczyk.

1868   Tchaikovsky's Symphony no. 1, "Winter Dreams," has its first
        performance, in Moscow.

1884   Alfred Piccaver, English tenor, is born in Long Sutton.

1885   Leopold Damrosch dies at age fifty-two in New York City.

1899   Georges Auric, French composer, member of "Les Six," is
        born in Lodève.

1907   Jean Langlais, blind French organist and composer, is born
        in La Fontenelle.

1918   Maria Bergmann, German pianist, is born in Höchst.

1923   Bruno Walter makes his American conducting debut with the
        New York Symphony Society.

1926   Raymond Wolansky, American bass, is born in Cleveland,
        Ohio.

1939   Nikolai Miaskovsky's Symphony no. 19, for band, has its
        first performance, in Moscow.

1940   The American Music Center, a library and information cen-
        ter, is founded in New York City.

1945   Paul Creston's Symphony no. 2 receives its premiere, in
        New York City.

1947   Erich Wolfgang Korngold's Violin Concerto is performed by
        the St. Louis Symphony Orchestra, Jascha Heifetz, soloist.

1953   Joseph Krips makes his American debut as conductor, with
        the Buffalo Philharmonic.

1958   David Diamond's orchestral suite World of Paul Klee is
        given its premiere, in Portland, Oregon.

1965   Nat "King" Cole dies in Santa Monica, California, aged forty-
        seven.

1974   Kurt Atterberg dies in Stockholm, aged eighty-six. A com-
        poser, he also wrote as a music critic for a Stockholm news-
        paper.

1975   Eugene Istomin, American pianist, marries Marta Casals,
        widow and former pupil of Pablo Casals.

1977   Max Loy dies in Nuremberg, Germany, at age sixty-three.
        Since 1971 he was music director of the Nuremberg Opera.

FEBRUARY 16

1829   François Joseph Gossec dies in Paris, aged ninety-five.

1847   Philipp Scharwenka, German composer and teacher, brother of Xaver, is born in Samter.

1855   Franz Liszt is the soloist in his Piano Concerto no. 1 in its first performance, in Weimar.

1866   David Mannes, American violinist and conductor, is born in New York City. He founded there the David Mannes School of Music.

1878   Selim Palmgren, Finnish composer and conductor, is born in Pori.

1886   Louis Köhler dies in Königsberg, Germany, aged sixty-five.

1892   Jules Massenet's opera Werther has its premiere, in Vienna.

1893   Jean Sibelius's tone poen En Saga is first performed, in Helsinki.

1896   Alexander Brailowsky, Russian pianist, is born in Kiev.

1907   Fernando Previtali, Italian conductor, is born in Adria.

        Alec Wilder, American composer, arranger, and author of American Popular Song (1972), is born in Rochester, New York.

1922   Sir Geraint Evans, Welsh baritone, is born in Pontypridd.

1934   William Tinker, American organist and harpsichordist, is born in St. Louis.

1936   Eliahu Inbal, Israeli conductor, is born in Jerusalem.

        Edgard Varèse's Density 21.5 for flute solo, named for Georges Barrère's platinum flute of specific gravity 21.5, is performed by Barrère in New York City.

1938   John Corigliano, American composer, son of violinist John Corigliano, is born in New York City.

1956   Leon Kirchner's Toccata, for strings, winds and percussion, receives its premiere, in San Francisco.

1957   Josef Hofmann, at age eighty-one, dies in Los Angeles.

1968   Healey Willan dies in Toronto, aged eighty-seven.

1975   Norman Treigle dies suddenly of a heart attack in New
        Orleans, aged forty-seven.

FEBRUARY 17

1653   Arcangelo Corelli, Italian composer and violinist, creator
        of the concerto grosso and considered the father of modern
        violin technique, is born in Fusignano.

1696   Ernst Gottlieb Baron, German lutenist and writer on lutes,
        is born at Breslau.

1732   Louis Marchand dies at age sixty-three in Paris.

1807   Etienne Méhul's opera Joseph is first produced, in Paris.

1820   Henri Vieuxtemps, Belgian violinist and composer, is born
        at Verviers.

1841   Ferdinando Carulli dies in Paris, aged seventy.

1859   Giuseppe Verdi's opera Un Ballo in maschera based on the
        assassination of Gustavus III of Sweden, is given its first
        performance, in Rome.   For political reasons the opera's
        locale was altered on several occasions.

1888   Vincenzo Bellezza, Italian conductor, is born in Bari.

1889   César Franck's Symphony in D minor is first heard, in Paris.

        Geoffrey Toye, English conductor and composer, is born in
        Winchester.

1901   Ethelbert Nevin dies in New Haven, Connecticut, aged thirty-
        eight.

1902   Marian Anderson, American contralto who became the first
        black member of the Metropolitan Opera and later a United
        Nations delegate, is born in Philadelphia.

1904   Giacomo Puccini's opera Madama Butterfly is poorly received
        at its premiere, at La Scala, Milan; Rosina Storchio has
        the title role.

1909   Marjorie Lawrence, Australian-born operatic soprano (with the
        Metropolitan Opera) and voice teacher, is born near Mel-
        bourne.

1913   René Leibowitz, Polish-French composer, conductor, and
        musicologist, is born in Warsaw.

1914   Ernst von Dohnányi's <u>Variations on a Nursery Song,</u> for
        piano and orchestra, is first performed in Berlin with the
        composer as soloist.

1925   Alwina Valleria dies in Nice, aged seventy-six.

1926   Friedrich Cerha, Austrian composer and conductor, is born
        in Vienna.

        Lee Hoiby, American composer, is born in Madison, Wiscon-
        sin.

        Lauritz Melchior stars in <u>Tannhäuser</u> in his Metropolitan
        Opera debut in New York City.

1927   John Ronsheim, American composer and teacher, is born in
        Cadiz, Ohio.

        Deems Taylor's opera <u>The King's Henchman,</u> commissioned
        by the Metropolitan Opera, is first staged there.

1937   John Brownlee makes his first appearance with the Metropoli-
        tan Opera, singing in <u>Rigoletto.</u>

1956   Juan Orrego Salas's Symphony no. 2 has its first hearing in
        Minneapolis.

1961   Elie Siegmeister's Flute Concerto is given its first perform-
        ance in Oklahoma City.

1962   Bruno Walter dies in Beverly Hills, California, aged eighty-
        five; he was regarded as a foremost conductor of Mahler's
        symphonies.

1977   Elliott Carter's <u>A Symphony of Three Orchestras</u> has its
        premiere in New York City.

        FEBRUARY 18

1743   George Frideric Handel's oratorio <u>Samson</u> is first performed
        at London's Covent Garden Theatre.

1806   Brigida Banti-Giogi, Italian soprano, dies in Bologna, aged
        about forty-six.

1839   Ludwig Berger dies in Berlin, aged sixty-one.

1850   Sir George Henschel, German-born conductor, singer and com-
        poser, is born in Breslau. He was the Boston Symphony Orches-
        tra's first conductor (1881-84) before he settled in England.

1864   Gustave Schirmer, American music publisher, is born in
        New York City, son of Gustav Schirmer, German publisher.

1893   Hector Berlioz's opera La Damnation de Faust, which was
        adapted for the stage by Raoul Gunsbourg, has its premiere
        in Monte Carlo and stars tenor Jean De Reszke. Berlioz
        had originally written it as an oratorio.

1919   Deems Taylor's chamber-orchestra suite Through the Look-
        ing Glass (later rescored for full orchestra) has its first
        performance in New York City.

1924   Joseph Victor Capoul dies at age eighty-four in France. In
        1897 he became manager of the Grand Opéra in Paris.

1926   Rita Gorr, Belgian mezzo-soprano, is born in Ghent.

1934   Aldo Ceccato, Italian conductor of the Detroit Symphony from
        1973 to 1977, is born in Milan.

1936   Willy Burkhard's oratorio Das Gesicht Jesajas (The Vision
        of Isaiah), considered his masterpeice, is performed in
        Basel.

1947   Gian Carlo Menotti's short humorous opera The Telephone
        is first staged by the New York Ballet Society.

1956   Gustave Charpentier dies in Paris, aged ninety-five. He is
        known for his one successful opera, Louise.

1967   Manuel Palau dies in Valencia, aged seventy-four.

1968   Gordon Crosse's Violin Concerto no. 1 is given its premiere,
        in London.

FEBRUARY 19

1605   Orazio Vecchi dies in Modena, Italy, aged fifty-four.

1736   George Frideric Handel's ode Alexander's Feast is first
        performed in Covent Garden, London.

1743   Luigi Boccherini, Italian cellist and composer (principally of
        chamber music), is born in Lucca.

1858   Tobias Matthay, English pianist and teacher, is born in
        London. He authored many publications about his art of
        piano playing, known as the Matthay System.

1880   Arthur Shepherd, American composer, conductor, teacher, and
        music critic, is born in Paris, Idaho.

1897 Willi Domgraf-Fassbänder, German baritone, is born in Aachen.

1912 Stan Kenton, American jazz bandleader, is born in Wichita, Kansas.

1913 Alvin Etler, American oboist and composer, is born in Battle Creek, Michigan.

1914 Riccardo Zandonai's opera Francesca da Rimini opens in Turin.

1922 Josef Matěj, Czech composer, is born in Brusperk.

1923 Donald Lybbert, American composer and teacher, is born in Cresco, Iowa.

1925 Jindřich Feld, Czech composer and teacher, is born in Prague.

1939 Vladimir Atlantov, Soviet tenor and member of the Bolshoi Theater, son of a professional singer, is born in Leningrad.

1944 Nicolai Medtner is soloist in his Concerto no. 3 for piano in its premiere, in London.

1954 Wallingford Riegger's Concerto for Piano and Woodwinds receives its premiere, in Washington.

1955 Ben Weber's Prelude and Passacaglia is given its first performance, in Louisville, Kentucky.

1967 Joseph Krips makes his conducting debut with the Metropolitan Opera in New York City.

1973 Joseph Szigeti dies in Lucerne, aged eighty.

1975 Luigi Dallapiccola dies in Florence, aged seventy-one.

FEBRUARY 20

1724 George Frideric Handel's opera Julius Caesar receives its premiere at King's Theatre, London.

1770 Ferdinando Carulli, Italian guitarist, teacher, and composer, is born in Naples. In 1825 he authored a guitar method book (Paris).

1791 Carl Czerny, Austrian pianist, teacher, and composer, who was Beethoven's pupil, is born in Vienna.

1816   Gioacchino Rossini conducts the premiere of his new opera, The Barber of Seville, in Rome's Teatro Argentina.

1874   Mary Garden, Scottish soprano, who was raised in the United States, is born in Aberdeen.

1881   Anton Bruckner's Symphony no. 4, "Romantic," is first performed, in Vienna.

1897   Vassili Kalinnikov's Symphony in G minor has its premiere, in Kiev.

1911   Alexander Kopylov dies near St. Petersburg, aged fifty-six.

        Robert McBride, American composer, whose music reflects Mexican and jazz elements, is born in Tucson, Arizona.

1926   Carol Smith, American-born Swiss contralto, is born in Oak Park, Illinois.

1929   Toshiro Mayuzumi, Japanese composer, is born in Yokohama.

1930   Pierre Gabaye, French composer, is born in Paris.

1937   Sergei Prokofiev's symphonic suite Lieutenant Kijé, from the film music, receives its premiere, in Paris, with the composer conducting.

1958   Isidor Philipp dies following a fall in the Paris Métro, aged ninety-four.

1961   Percy Grainger, aged seventy-eight, dies in White Plains, New York.

1962   Henri Lazerof's Viola Concerto is first performed, in Monaco (winning first prize at the International Competition in Monaco).

1963   Ferenc Fricsay dies of leukemia in Basel, aged forty-eight.

1969   Ernest Ansermet, aged eighty-five, dies in Geneva.

1970   Albert Wolff dies in Paris, aged eighty-six, conductor for many years at the Opéra-Comique. From 1919 to 1921 he conducted the French repertory at the Metropolitan Opera.

FEBRUARY 21

1801   Johann Wenzel Kalliwoda, Bohemian violinist, conductor, and composer, is born in Prague.

1836   Léo Delibes, French composer of operas and ballets, is
        born in St. -Germain-du-Val.

1844   Charles Marie Widor, French organist and composer, teacher
        of Albert Schweitzer, is born in Lyons. For more than
        sixty years he was organist at St. - Sulpice in Paris.

1856   Theodor Döhler, aged forty-one, dies in Florence.

1884   John Pyke Hullah dies in London, aged seventy-one.

1886   Modest Mussorgsky's opera <u>Khovanshchina</u> is completed by
        Rimsky-Korsakov and produced for the first time, in St.
        Petersburg.

1893   Andrés Segovia, Spanish guitar virtuoso, is born in Linares.

1909   Anatol Liadov's <u>Enchanted Lake</u> has its premiere in St.
        Petersburg.

1917   Francis Madeira, American conductor, pianist, and teacher,
        is born in Jenkintown, Pennsylvania. He organized the
        Rhode Island Philharmonic Orchestra in Providence in 1945.

1920   Darius Milhaud's ballet <u>Le Boeuf sur le toît</u> is produced in
        Paris.

1922   John McCollum, American tenor, is born in Coalinga,
        California.

1927   Walter Hartley, American composer and teacher, is born in
        Washington.

1929   Ottorino Respighi's symphonic poem <u>Feste romane</u> is first
        performed, by the New York Philharmonic Orchestra under
        the direction of Arturo Toscanini.

1930   Adolph Weiss's <u>American Life</u>, for large orchestra, receives
        its premiere, in New York City.

1956   Edwin Franko Goldman, aged seventy-eight, dies in New York
        City.

1961   Marilyn Horne and Joan Sutherland make their New York
        debuts at Town Hall in a concert performance of Bellini's
        <u>Beatrice di Tenda</u> under the auspices of the American Opera
        Society.

1971   Adolph Weiss dies in Van Nuys, California, aged seventy-nine.

FEBRUARY 22

1761   Erik Tulindberg, Finnish composer, is born in Lillkyro.

1810   Frédéric Chopin, Polish pianist and composer (principally for
        piano), is born in Zelazowa Wola.

1817   Niels Gade, Danish composer, is born in Copenhagen.

1836   Mitrofan Petrovich Belaieff, Russian music publisher, is
        born in St. Petersburg. In his honor Borodin, Glazunov,
        Liadov, and Rimsky-Korsakov cooperatively wrote a string
        quartet on notes "B-la-f".

1849   Alexander Ernst Fesca dies in Brunswick, Germany, aged
        twenty-eight.

1876   Giovanni Zenatello, Italian tenor and teacher (Lily Pons a
        pupil), is born in Verona.

1878   Franz Hünten dies in Koblenz, Germany, aged eighty-four.

1890   Benno Moiseiwitsch, Russian pianist, is born in Odessa.

1903   Robert Weede, American baritone, is born in Baltimore.

        Hugo Wolf dies in Vienna, aged forty-two.

1907   Maurice Ravel's Introduction et Allegro, for harp, flute,
        clarinet, and string quartet, is first performed in Paris.

1908   Irving Kolodin, American music critic and author, is born
        in New York City.

1926   Walter Gieseking makes his American debut at Aeolian Hall,
        New York City.

1931   Mario Ancona dies in Florence, aged seventy.

1932   Johanna Gadski dies following an auto accident in Berlin,
        at the age of fifty-nine.

1934   Thomas Paul, American bass, is born in Chicago.

1938   Dmitri Kabalevsky's opera Colas Breugnon has its premiere
        in Leningrad.

1941   Paul Creston's award-winning Symphony no. 1 is first per-
        formed, in New York City.

        Morton Gould's Latin American Symphonette is first heard,
        in Brooklyn, New York.

1945   Virgil Thomson conducts the first performance of his <u>Symphony on a Hymn Tune</u> in New York City.

1946   Ramón Vinay makes his Metropolitan Opera debut.

1947   Tom Scott's <u>Ballad of the Harp Weaver</u>, for narrator, harp, chorus, and string quartet, receives its premiere, in New York City.

1952   Boris Koutzen's daughter, Nadia, is soloist in the premiere of his Violin Concerto, in Philadelphia.

1962   Benjamin Lees's <u>Concerto for Orchestra, no. 1</u> is first performed in Rochester, New York.

FEBRUARY 23

1648/9 John Blow, English composer and organist at Westminster Abbey, is baptized at Newark-on-Trent.

1685   George Frideric Handel, German-born English composer, is born in Halle.   He Anglicized his name from Georg Friedrich Händel.

1704   Georg Muffat dies in Passau, Germany, aged fifty.

1749   Gertrud Elisabeth Mara, German soprano, is born in Kassel.

1835   Jacques François Halévy's opera <u>La Juive</u> is first produced, at the Paris Opéra.

1854   Franz Liszt conducts from manuscript the first performance of his symphonic poem <u>Les Préludes</u> in Weimar.   It is a benefit concert for widows of former Court Orchestra members.

1905   Herbert Fromm, German-born American composer, is born in Kitzingen.

        Elinor Remick Warren, American song composer and pianist, is born in Los Angeles.

1912   Rayner Brown, American composer, is born in Des Moines, Iowa.

1913   Arnold Schoenberg's <u>Guerre-Lieder</u>, for soli, mixed chorus, and orchestra, is first performed, in Vienna.

1916   Charles Tomlinson Griffes's <u>White Peacock</u>, for piano, is performed by Winifred Christie in New York City.

1918   Sophie Menter, German pianist and teacher who married cellist David Popper, dies in Munich.

1920   Hall Overton, American composer, pupil of Persichetti, and also a jazz pianist, is born in Bangor, Michigan.

1922   Ilse Hollweg, German soprano, is born in Solingen.

1924   Lejaren Hiller, American composer using computers in his works, is born in New York City. Formerly a chemistry professor at the University of Illinois, he returned there later to teach music.

1927   Régine Crespin, French soprano, is born in Marseilles.

1931   Nellie Melba dies in Sydney, Australia, aged seventy-one.

1934   Edward Elgar dies in Worcester, England, aged seventy-six.

1945   Russell Riepi, American composer, teacher, and pianist, is born in Illinois.

1954   Rosalind Elias makes her Metropolitan Opera debut in Die Walküre.

1956   Leon Kirchner is soloist in his Piano Concerto no. 1 in its premiere in New York City.

1962   Judith Raskin makes her Metropolitan Opera debut, starring in Mozart's Marriage of Figaro.

FEBRUARY 24

1607   Claudio Monteverdi's opera Orfeo is first staged, in Mantua.

1704   Marc-Antoine Charpentier, French composer who was opposed by Lully, dies in Paris, aged about seventy-eight.

1711   George Frideric Handel's opera Rinaldo, his first to be staged in London, receives its premiere and is well acclaimed.

1766   Samuel Wesley, English organist and composer, is born in Bristol.

1771   Johann Baptist Cramer, German pianist and teacher, known for his piano studies, is born in Mannheim.

1842   Arrigo Boito, Italian opera composer, librettist, and poet, is born in Padua.

1876   Edvard Grieg's incidental music to Ibsen's drama <u>Peer Gynt</u>
        is first performed with the drama at Christiania (Oslo).

1877   Rudolph Ganz, Swiss-American pianist and conductor, direc-
        tor of Chicago Musical College from 1929 to 1954, is born
        in Zurich.

1929   André Messager dies in Paris, aged seventy-five.

1934   Renata Scotto, Italian soprano, is born in Savona.

1939   Roy Harris's Symphony no. 3 has its premiere, in Boston.
        In 1976 it was the first American symphony played in China
        during the tour of the Philadelphia Orchestra under Ormandy's
        direction.

1956   Walter Piston's Symphony no. 5, commissioned by the
        Juilliard School of Music for its fiftieth anniversary, is first
        performed, in New York City.

1975   Marcel Grandjany dies in New York City, aged eighty-three.

        ## FEBRUARY 25

1643   Marco da Gagliano dies in Florence, aged sixty.

1682   Alessandro Stradella is murdered in a love triangle in Genoa,
        aged thirty-seven.   He is the hero of Flotow's opera <u>Ales-
        sandro Stradella</u>.

1727   Armand-Louis Couperin, French organist at St.-Gervais for
        forty years, is born in Paris.

1852   Thomas Moore dies in Devizes, England, at the age of seventy-
        two.

1888   Benjamin (Louis Paul) Godard's masterpiece, the opera
        <u>Jocelyn,</u> is produced in Brussels.

1890   Dame Myra Hess, English pianist, is born in London.   She
        was a pupil of Tobias Matthay.

1905   Serge Koussevitzky is soloist in the premiere of his Double-
        bass Concerto, in Moscow.

1906   Anton Arensky dies at the age of forty-four in a tuberculosis
        sanatorium in Terijoki, Finland.

1932   M. William Karlins, American composer and teacher, is
        born in New York City.

Carl Ruggles's <u>Sun-Treader</u> receives its premiere, in Paris.

1933   Richard Crooks makes his Metropolitan Opera debut, starring in <u>Manon</u> of Massenet.

1936   Alice Ehlers, harpsichordist, makes her American debut in Town Hall.

1937   Frances Steiner, American cellist and conductor, is born in Portland, Oregon.

1943   George Harrison, English rock singer, member of The Beatles, is born in Liverpool.

1956   Everett Helm's Piano Concerto no. 2 is given its premiere, in Louisville, Kentucky.

FEBRUARY 26

1752   George Frideric Handel's oratorio <u>Jephtha</u> has its premiere in Covent Garden Theatre, London.

1770   Anton Reicha, Bohemian-born French composer, is born in Prague.

Giuseppe Tartini dies in Padua, aged seventy-seven.

1822   Franz Strauss, German horn virtuoso and composer, the father of Richard Strauss, is born in Parkstein.

1832   Frédéric Chopin makes his Paris debut as a pianist.

1878   Emmy Destinn, Czech soprano, is born in Prague.

1879   Frank Bridge, English composer, conductor, and teacher (Benjamin Britten a pupil), is born in Brighton.

1914   Witold Rowicki, Polish conductor and composer, is born in Taganrog, Soviet Union.

1922   Camille Saint-Saëns's suite <u>Carnival of the Animals</u> is first performed, in Paris.   He never permitted its publication during his lifetime.

1924   Mark Bucci, American composer, is born in New York City.

Silvio Varviso, Swiss conductor, is born in Zurich.

1927   Donald Gramm, American bass, is born in Milwaukee, Wisconsin.

1930   Lazar Berman, Soviet pianist, is born in Leningrad.

1932   Ruth-Margaret Pütz, German soprano, is born in Krefeld.

1935   Georges Bizet's first symphony (discovered in 1933) is given its premiere, in Basel.

1936   Antonio Scotti dies in Naples, aged seventy.

1939   Clifford Curzon makes his American debut at Town Hall, New York City.

1943   Kent Kennan's <u>Night Soliloquy</u> is performed by the NBC Symphony under Toscanini's direction. Toscanini himself chose to perform this symphonic piece, for flute and orchestra.

1959   George Rochberg's Symphony no. 2 receives its premiere, in Cleveland, Ohio.

1964   Ernest Kanitz's opera-cantata <u>Visions at Midnight</u> is first performed, in Los Angeles.

1970   Ethel Leginska dies in Los Angeles, aged eighty-three.

FEBRUARY 27

1563   William Byrd is appointed organist at Lincoln Cathedral, England.

1814   Ludwig van Beethoven conducts his Symphony no. 8 in its premiere, in Vienna.

1839   Joseph Victor Capoul, French tenor and manager of the Grand Opéra in Paris, is born in Toulouse.

1846   Joaquín Valverde, Spanish composer of zarzuelas, is born in Badajoz.

1848   Sir Charles Hubert Hastings Parry, English composer, writer on music, and music administrator, is born in Bournemouth.

1856   Mattia Battistini, Italian baritone, is born in Rome.

1873   Enrico Caruso, Italian tenor, is born in Naples.

1887   Alexander Borodin dies suddenly while attending a fancy-dress ball in St. Petersburg at the age of fifty-three.

1888   Lotte Lehmann, German-born American soprano, is born in Perleberg.

1891   Issay Dobrowen, Russian conductor, is born in Nizhny-
        Novgorod.

        Georges Migot, French composer and artist, is born in Paris.

1909   Ben Webster, American jazz saxophonist, is born in Kansas
        City, Missouri.

1923   Viktor Kalabis, Czech composer, is born at Cerveny Kostelec.

1935   Mirella Freni, Italian soprano, is born in Modena.

        Alberto Remedios, English tenor, is born in Liverpool.

1936   Riccardo Cassinelli, Argentine tenor, is born in Buenos Aires.

1947   Peter Mennin's Symphony no. 3 has its premiere, in New
        York City.

1949   Elliott Carter's Woodwind Quintet and Cello Sonata are first
        performed, in New York City.

        FEBRUARY 28

1860   Mario Ancona, Italian baritone, is born in Leghorn.

1862   Charles Gounod's opera La Reine de Saba is first staged,
        in Paris.

1876   John Alden Carpenter, American composer and businessman,
        is born in Park Ridge, Illinois.

1877   Sergei Bortkiewicz, Russian pianist and composer, is born
        in Kharkov.

1882   Geraldine Farrar, American soprano, is born in Melrose,
        Massachusetts.

        The Royal College of Music is founded in London.

1896   Guiomar Novaes, Brazilian-born pianist (New York City resi-
        dent), is born in São João da Boã Vista.

1903   Ethel Newcomb makes her debut as soloist with the Vienna
        Philharmonic Orchestra.

1904   Vincent d'Indy's Symphony no. 2 is first performed at
        Paris.

1908   Pauline Lucca dies in Vienna, aged sixty-six.

1912   Carl Nielsen's Symphony no. 3, "Sinfonia espansiva," and his
        Violin Concerto receive their premieres, in Copenhagen.

1915   William Lichtenwanger, American music editor and music
        librarian (Library of Congress), is born in Asheville, North
        Carolina.

1917   George Malcolm, English harpsichordist and conductor, is
        born in London.

1921   Donald H. White, American composer and teacher, is born
        in Narberth, Pennsylvania.

1926   Seymour Shifrin, American composer and teacher, is born
        in Brooklyn, New York.

1928   Amy Fay dies in Watertown, Massachusetts, aged eighty-five.

1929   Ildebrando Pizzetti's Concerto dell'estate is given its pre-
        miere, in New York City.

        Joseph Rouleau, Canadian bass, is born in Matane, Quebec.

1934   Sylvia Geszty, Hungarian soprano, is born in Budapest.

1936   Roy Harris's Symphony no. 2 and his Prelude and Fugue for
        Strings are presented by the Boston Symphony Orchestra
        and the Philadelphia Symphony Orchestra, respectively.

1975   Karl Wilson Gehrkens dies in Elk Rapids, Michigan, aged
        ninety-three.

1976   Ralph Shapey's oratorio Praise, for bass-baritone, chorus,
        and orchestra, is first performed, in Chicago.

        Julia Smith's Piano Concerto has its premiere, in Dallas,
        Texas.

        FEBRUARY 29

1748   Jean-Philippe Rameau's ballet Zaïs is first performed in
        Paris.

1792   Gioacchino Rossini, Italian opera composer, is born in
        Pesaro.

1828   Daniel-François Auber's opera Masaniello (La Muette de
        Portici) is produced in Paris.

1836   Giacomo Meyerbeer's opera Les Huguenots has its premiere
        in Paris.

1904   Jimmy Dorsey, American clarinet and saxophone player,
        brother of trombonist Tommy Dorsey, is born in Shenandoah,
        Pennsylvania.

1920   Ivan Petrov, Soviet bass, is born in Irkutsk.

1924   Florent Schmitt's ballet Le Petit elfe ferme-l'oeil, after a
        fairy tale of Hans Christian Andersen, is given at the Opéra-
        Comique, Paris.

1948   Boris Blacher's opera Die Nachtschwalbe (The Night Swallow)
        arouses an outcry for its pornographic subject at its opening
        in Leipzig.

        David Diamond's Violin Concerto no. 2 receives its premiere
        in Vancouver, Canada.

1952   Carlos Chávez's Violin Concerto is given its first performance
        in Mexico City.

1968   Howard Hanson's Symphony no. 6 has its premiere in New
        York City.

1976   Carlisle Floyd's opera for the Bicentennial, Bilby's Doll, is
        first produced, in Houston, Texas.

MARCH 1

1643   Girolamo Frescobaldi, a major influence in the development of Baroque music, dies in Rome at age fifty-nine.

1777   Georg Christoph Wagenseil dies in Vienna, aged sixty-two.

1835   Ebenezer Prout, English music theorist, editor, and teacher, is born in Oundle.

1882   Theodor Kullak dies in Berlin, aged sixty-three.

1896   Dimitri Mitropoulos, Greek-American conductor and composer, is born in Athens.

1904   Glenn Miller, American trombonist and big-band leader, is born in Clarinda, Iowa.

1918   Emil Sjögren dies at age sixty-four in Stockholm.

1927   Lucine Amara, American soprano, is born in Hartford, Connecticut.

1930   Pierre Max Dubois, French composer, is born in Graulhet.

1942   Dmitri Shostakovich's Symphony no. 7, "Leningrad," is first performed in Kuibishev, the temporary Soviet capital during World War II.

1947   Moray Welsh, Scottish cellist, is born in Haddington.

1958   Ildebrando Pizzetti's opera Assassinio nella cattedrale, after T.S. Eliot's Murder in the Cathedral, receives its premiere in Milan's La Scala with Gianandrea Gavazzeni conducting.

1972   Victor Babin dies in Cleveland, Ohio, aged sixty-three.

Vladimir Golschmann dies in New York City at age seventy-eight.

1976   Jean Martinon dies in Paris at sixty-six.

MARCH 2

1695   Bernhard Christoph Breitkopf, founder of the book and music
        publishing firm in Leipzig, is born in Klausthal Harz.

1824   Bedřich Smetana, Bohemian composer, is born at Leitomischl.

1900   Kurt Weill, German composer of modern operas and musicals,
        is born in Dessau.   When the Nazis came into control, he
        emigrated to the United States.

1904   Emma Calvé sings her farewell Carmen at New York Metro-
        politan Opera.

1905   Marc Blitzstein, American composer, is born in Philadelphia.

1915   Anthony Lewis, English conductor and composer, is born in
        Bermuda.

1917   John Gardner, English composer, opera coach, and teacher,
        is born in Manchester.

1921   Robert Simpson, English composer and biographer of Carl
        Nielsen, is born in Leamington.

1922   Denis Stevens, English musicologist, conductor, and violinist,
        is born in High Wycombe.

1977   Benjamin Lees's Dialogue, for cello and piano, receives its
        premiere in New York City.

MARCH 3

1671   The Académie des Opéras is inaugurated in Paris.

1706   Johann Pachelbel dies at age fifty-two in Nuremberg, Germany.

1768   Nicola Antonio Porpora dies in Naples, aged eighty-one.

1802   Adolphe Nourrit, French tenor and son of an opera tenor, is
        born in Montpellier.

1824   Giovanni Battista Viotti dies in London at age forty-eight.

1842   Felix Mendelssohn conducts the first performance of his Sym-
        phony no. 3, "Scotch," in Leipzig's Gewandhaus.

1854   Giovanni Rubini dies at age fifty-nine in Romano, Italy.

1869   Sir Henry J. Wood, English conductor and composer, is born in London.

1870   Johannes Brahms's Alto Rhapsody is first sung by Pauline Viardot-García, for whom it was written.

1875   Georges Bizet's opera Carmen is given its premiere, at the Opéra-Comique in Paris.

1886   James Friskin, Scottish-born American composer and pianist, is born in Glasgow.

1891   Ruy Coelho, Portuguese composer, principally of operas, is born in Alcaçer do Sal.

1899   Richard Strauss's tone poem Ein Heldenleben, is first performed, in Frankfurt.

1909   Bruno Walter makes his English conducting debut with the Royal Philharmonic Society in London.

1918   Frank Wigglesworth, American composer and teacher, is born in Boston.

1922   Kazimierz Serocki, Polish composer and pianist, is born in Torun.

1932   Eugène d'Albert dies at sixty-seven in Riga.

1935   Feodor Chaliapin sings his farewell recital in New York City.

1940   Harl McDonald's humoresque Arkansas Traveler receives its premiere in Detroit.

1950   Halsey Stevens's Symphony no. 1 (revised version) is first performed, in Los Angeles.

1961   Paul Wittgenstein dies in Manhasset, New York, aged seventy-three.

1963   Gian Carlo Menotti's television opera Labyrinth, for which he wrote the libretto, is first televised.

1970   Marilyn Horne makes her Metropolitan Opera debut in New York City.

MARCH 4

1678   Antonio Vivaldi, Italian composer known as the "Red Priest," for his red hair, is born in Venice, son of Giovanni Battista Vivaldi, a violinist at the ducal chapel of San Marco.

1877   Peter Ilyitch Tchaikovsky's ballet Swan Lake is first staged, in Moscow. It was poorly produced and dropped from the repertory.

1878   Napoleone Moriani dies at age sixty-nine in Florence.

Peter Ilyitch Tchaikovsky's Fourth Symphony receives its premiere in Moscow, and it is dedicated to his patroness, Mme. Nadezhda von Meck.

1895   Bjarne Brustad, Norwegian composer and violist, is born in Oslo.

1905   Alexander Glazounov's Violin Concerto receives its first performance, in St. Petersburg with Leopold Auer, soloist.

1915   Carlos Surinach, Spanish-American composer and conductor, is born in Barcelona.

1921   Halim El-Dabh, Egyptian composer and teacher (Kent State University in Ohio), is born in Cairo. He has created his own drum notation system.

Daniel Gregory Mason's Prelude and Fugue, for piano and orchestra, is given its premiere in Chicago.

1925   Moritz Moszkowski dies in Paris, aged seventy.

1927   Julián Carrillo's Concertino for Fractional Tones is first performed by the Philadelphia Orchestra, Leopold Stokowski conducting.

1928   Samuel Adler, German-American composer, organist, and teacher, is born in Mannheim.

1929   Bernard Haitink, Dutch conductor, is born in Amsterdam.

José Maria Mestres-Quadreny, Spanish composer, is born in Manresa.

1934   Mario Davidowsky, Argentine composer, United States resident since 1958, is born in Buenos Aires.

1941   Edoardo Mascheroni dies at age eighty-eight in Ghirla, Italy.

1943   Henry C. Colles dies in London, aged sixty-three.

1960   Leonard Warren dies on stage in New York City during a performance of La Forza del destino. His age was forty-eight.

1965   György Ligeti's <u>Poème symphonique</u>, for 100 metronomes at
        differing speeds, is first performed, in Buffalo, New York.

1966   Jānis Mediņš dies at age seventy-five in Stockholm.

        MARCH 5

1778   Thomas Arne dies in London a week before his seventy-eighth
        birthday.

1853   Arthur Foote, American composer, teacher, and organist at
        Boston's First Unitarian Church (for thirty-two years), is
        born in Salem, Massachusetts.

1868   Arrigo Boito's opera <u>Mefistofele,</u> for which he wrote his own
        libretto, has its premiere in Milan at La Scala.

1887   Heitor Villa-Lobos, Brazilian composer and collector of over
        1,200 folksongs, is born in Rio de Janeiro.

1889   Edward MacDowell is soloist in the first performance of his
        Piano Concerto no. 2 in D minor, in New York City.

1918   Zara Dolukhanova, Soviet mezzo-soprano, recipient in 1966
        of the Lenin Prize, is born in Moscow.

1931   Barry Tuckwell, Australian-born French horn player, a resi-
        dent of England, is born in Melbourne.

1933   Gian Francesco Malipiero's Violin Concerto no. 1 receives
        its premiere, in Amsterdam.

1935   William Fischer, American composer and arranger, executive
        director of the Society of Black Composers, is born in Shelby,
        Mississippi.

1944   Walter Piston's Symphony no. 2 is first performed, in Wash-
        ington.

1947   Alfredo Casella dies in Rome at the age of sixty-three.

1948   Ezio Pinza makes his farewell Metropolitan Opera appearance
        in New York City, starring in <u>Don Giovanni.</u>

1950   Eugene Fodor, American violinist, prize-winner in 1974 in
        the International Tchaikovsky Violin Contest, is born in Tur-
        key Creek, Colorado.   He shared second prize--no first
        prize was awarded.

1953   Sergei Prokofiev dies in Moscow at the age of sixty-one. It is the
        same day as Josef Stalin's passing.

1956   Erich Itor Kahn dies in New York City, aged fifty.

1965   Walter Piston's Symphony no. 8 receives its premiere, in
        Boston.

1973   Paul Kletzki dies in Liverpool, England, at the age of seventy-
        two.

1974   Sol Hurok, aged eighty-five, dies in New York City.

MARCH 6

1715   Antonio Vivaldi plays the violin for Johann Uffenbach, a
        visiting German music lover, who commissions Vivaldi to
        write several concerti grossi.

1823   Marietta Alboni, Italian contralto who studied with Rossini,
        is born in Cesena; she was Jenny Lind's rival in fame with
        the public.

1831   Vincenzo Bellini's opera La Sonnambula has its premiere per-
        formance in Milan's Teatro Carcano.

1853   Giuseppe Verdi's opera La Traviata is first staged at the
        Teatro la Fenice in Venice.

1870   Oscar Straus, Austrian operetta composer who later became
        a French citizen, is born in Vienna. He dropped the final
        "s" of his name to distinguish himself from the other
        Strausses.

1872   Paul Juon, Russian composer who studied with Arensky, is
        born in Moscow.

1900   Friedrich Bechstein dies at age seventy-three in Berlin.

1914   Kiril Kondrashin, Soviet conductor, is born in Moscow.

1918   Robert Stewart, American composer and violinist, is born
        in Buffalo, New York.

1921   Julius Rudel, Austrian-American conductor and director of
        the New York City Opera Company, is born in Vienna.

1926   H. C. Robbins Landon, American musicologist who discovered
        the lost Haydn Mass in G (no. 13), is born in Boston.

        William Schmidt, American composer, is born in Chicago.

1927   Norman Treigle, American bass-baritone, is born in New
        Orleans.

1930   Lorin Maazel, American conductor, is born in Neuilly, France.

1932   John Philip Sousa dies in Reading, Pennsylvania, aged seventy-seven.

1933   Edgard Varèse's Ionisation, for forty percussion instruments, piano, and two sirens, is first performed, in New York City.

1934   Walter Piston's Concerto for Orchestra receives its premiere performance in Cambridge, Massachusetts.

1936   Rubin Goldmark dies in New York City at the age of sixty-three.

1937   Siegfried Vogel, German bass-baritone, is born in Chemnitz.

1944   Kiri Te Kanawa, New Zealand soprano, is born in Gisborne.

1966   Richard Hageman, at age eighty-three, dies in Beverly Hills, California.

1967   Nelson Eddy dies in Miami Beach, Florida, aged sixty-five.

        Zoltán Kodály, aged eighty-four, dies in Budapest.

1970   Jan Kapr's Omaggio alla tromba, for two trumpets, wind orchestra, piano, and timpani, receives its premiere, in Prague.

1971   Thurston Dart dies of cancer at age forty-nine, in London.

        MARCH 7

1574   John Wilbye, English madrigalist, is baptized at Diss in Norfolk.

1786   Franz Benda dies in Neuendorf, Germany, aged seventy-six.

1809   Johann Georg Albrechtsberger dies at age seventy-three in Vienna.

1838   Jenny Lind makes her operatic debut, starring in Weber's Der Freischütz at the Stockholm Opera.

1875   Maurice Ravel, French composer, is born in Ciboure.

1895   Juan José Castro, Argentine composer and conductor, is born in Avellaneda.

1897   Johannes Brahms attends his last concert and hears his Symphony no. 4 being conducted by Hans Richter.

1899   Vincent d'Indy's <u>Chansons et danses,</u> for seven wind instruments, receives its first performance, in Paris.

1917   Robert Erickson, American composer who has devised instruments for performing his works, is born in Marquette, Michigan.

1931   Mady Mesplé, French soprano, is born in Toulouse.

1934   Eugene Holmes, American baritone, is born in Brownsville, Texas.

1941   Camargo Guarnieri's <u>Dansa Brasileira</u> is given its premiere in São Paulo.

1947   Mark Brunswick's Symphony in B-flat has its first performance, in Minneapolis.

1950   Alexander Brott's Violin Concerto receives its premiere, in Montreal.

1953   Vincent Persichetti's <u>Pageant,</u> for band, receives its first performance, in Miami.

1965   Easley Blackwood's Symphony no. 3 has its premiere, in Chicago.

1971   Gian Carlo Menotti's opera <u>The Most Important Man</u> is performed by the New York City Opera Company. The opera, dealing with racial conflict, Menotti feels is one of his best, contrary to reviews.

1973   Josef Matěj's Cello Concerto is first performed, in Prague.

1979   Guiomar Novaes dies in her native Brazil at São Paulo at the age of eighty-three; she had been a concert pianist for more than seventy years.

        Klaus Egge dies in Oslo, aged seventy-two.

        MARCH 8

1714   Carl Philipp Emanuel Bach, German composer and the third son of Johann Sebastian Bach, is born in Weimar.

1839   Adolphe Nourrit, depressed, jumps from the roof of his lodgings in Naples, dying at the age of thirty-seven.

1849   Otto Nicolai's opera <u>Die lustigen Weiber von Windsor</u> (after Shakespeare's play) has its premiere, in Berlin.

1869   Hector Berlioz dies in Paris at the age of sixty-two.

1898   Richard Strauss's <u>Don Quixote</u>, for cello solo and orchestra,
        has its premiere performance, in Cologne.

1902   Jean Sibelius conducts his Symphony no. 2 in Helsinki in its
        first performance.

1903   Georges Enesco conducts his two <u>Rumanian Rhapsodies</u> in
        their premieres, in Bucharest.

1904   Nikos Skalkottas, Greek composer who studied with Schoenberg.
        is born on the island of Euboca.

1911   Alan Hovhaness, American composer whose music reflects
        his Armenian heritage, is born in Somerville, Massachusetts.

1934   Christian Wolff, French-born composer, is born in Nice.   In
        1962 he began teaching Latin and Greek at Harvard University.

1935   Liselotte Rebmann, German mezzo-soprano, is born in Stutt-
        gart.

1939   Horst Laubenthal, German tenor, is born in Eisfeld.

        Robert Tear, Welsh tenor, is born in Barry.

1945   Giovanni Martinelli makes his farewell appearance in Bellini's
        <u>Norma</u> at the Metropolitan Opera in New York City.

1957   Othmar Schoeck dies in Zurich, aged seventy.

        Iannis Xenakis's <u>Pithoprakta</u> has its premiere, in Munich.

1961   Sir Thomas Beecham, at the age of eighty-one, dies in Lon-
        don.

        MARCH 9

1715   Antonio Vivaldi brings ten concerti grossi to Johann Uffenbach,
        who had commissioned them only three days earlier.   Vivaldi
        states these were composed expressly for him.

1737   Josef Mysliveczek, Bohemian opera composer and friend of
        Mozart, is born in Ober-Sarka.

1748   George Frideric Handel's oratorio <u>Joshua</u> is first sung in
        London.

1804   Alphonse Leduc, French music publisher of Paris, is born
        in Nantes.

1831   Franz Liszt first hears Niccolò Paganini perform and then
        sketches the transcription of his Campanella Studies.

1842   Giuseppe Verdi's opera Nabucco is first staged, in Milan's
        La Scala.

1844   Giuseppe Verdi's opera Ernani is first produced, in Venice.

1861   Ferenc Erkel's opera Bánk-Bán is given its premiere, in
        Budapest.

1868   Ambroise Thomas's opera Hamlet receives its premiere, in
        Paris.

1873   Antonin Dvořák's cantata Hymnus, for chorus and orchestra,
        is first performed and attracts attention because of its patri-
        otic theme calling for self-determination.

1877   Peter Ilyitch Tchaikovsky's symphonic fantasy Francesca da
        Rimini, is first performed, in Moscow.

1910   Samuel Barber, American composer, nephew of singer Louise
        Homer, is born in West Chester, Pennsylvania.

1923   Nicola Zaccario, Greek bass, is born in Piraeus.

1927   John Beckwith, Canadian composer and former music critic
        for the Toronto Star, is born in Victoria, British Columbia.

1930   Ornette Coleman, American jazz saxophonist and composer,
        is born in Forth Worth, Texas.

        Thomas Schippers, American conductor who was with the
        Cincinnati Symphony Orchestra from 1970 to 1977, is born
        in Portage, Michigan.

1966   Thomas Stewart makes his Metropolitan Opera debut, starring
        in Verdi's Falstaff, in New York City.

1973   Paul Turok's Lyric Variations, for oboe and strings, is first
        performed, in Louisville, Kentucky.

MARCH 10

1785   Wolfgang Amadeus Mozart is the soloist in the premiere per-
        formance of his C major Concerto, in Vienna.

1808   Napoleone Moriani, Italian tenor, is born in Florence.

1832   Muzio Clementi dies in Evesham, England, at the age of eighty.

1837   (Giuseppe) Saverio Mercadante's opera <u>Il Giuramento</u> is first produced, in Milan. Considered his best work, it was long in the repertory.

1839   Dudley Buck, American church organist and composer of much sacred music, is born in Hartford, Connecticut.

1840   (Giuseppe) Saverio Mercadante's opera <u>La Vestale</u>, has its premiere performance in Naples.

1844   Pablo de Sarasate, Spanish violinist and composer, is born in Pamplona.

1870   Ignaz Moscheles dies in Leipzig, aged seventy-five.

1875   Karl Goldmark's opera <u>Die Königen von Saba</u> is given its first performance, in Vienna.

1877   Alexander Borodin's Symphony no. 2 is first heard, in St. Petersburg.

1884   Maria Barrientos, Spanish soprano, is born in Barcelona.

1888   César Franck's symphonic poem <u>Psyché</u> is given its premiere, in Paris.

1892   Arthur Honegger, French composer, one of the group known as "Les Six," is born in Le Havre.

1903   Bix Beiderbecke, American jazz cornet player and composer, is born in Davenport, Iowa.

1908   Owen Brannigan, English bass-baritone, is born in Annitsford.

1910   Carl Reinecke dies in Leipzig, aged eighty-five.

1915   Sir Charles Groves, English conductor, is born in London.

1921   Maurice Bevan, English bass, is born in London.

1932   Wallingford Riegger's <u>Dichotomy</u> for orchestra receives its premiere, in Berlin.

1971   Mabel Daniels dies in Boston at age ninety-two.

1977   E. Power Biggs dies in Boston, aged seventy.

MARCH 11

1772   Johann Adam von Reutter, Jr., dies in Vienna, aged sixty-three.

1791   (Franz) Joseph Haydn conducts from the piano the first of the London symphonies in the Hanover Square Rooms in London. It is so successful that the adagio is encored.

1829   Felix Mendelssohn initiates the Bach revival when he presents the <u>Passion According to St. Matthew</u> of Johann Sebastian Bach in Berlin.

1830   Vincenzo Bellini's opera <u>I Capuleti e i Montecchi</u> is first staged at Teatro la Fenice in Venice.

1851   Giuseppe Verdi's opera <u>Rigoletto</u> (after Hugo's <u>Le Roi s'amuse</u>), receives its premiere, in Venice at Teatro la Fenice.

1867   Giuseppe Verdi's opera <u>Don Carlos</u> has its first performance, in Paris.

1876   Carl Ruggles, American composer, is born in Marion, Massachusetts.

1879   Alexander Borodin's <u>Polovtsian Dances</u> (performed as an orchestral entity), from <u>Prince Igor,</u> receives its premiere, in St. Petersburg.

1897   Henry Cowell, American composer known for his piano "tone cluster" technique, is born in Menlo Park, California.

1903   Lawrence Welk, American conductor of popular music and television personality, is born in Strasburg, North Dakota.

1911   Howard Mitchell, American cellist and conductor, is born in Lyons, Nebraska. He conducted the National Symphony Orchestra in Washington from 1949 to 1970.

       Bassols Xavier Montsalvatge, Spanish composer, is born in Gerona.

1913   John Weinzweig, Canadian composer, is born in Toronto.

1915   Maurice Ravel's ballet (from the piano suite) <u>Ma Mère l'Oye</u> is given at the Paris Opéra in its premiere.

1917   Ottorino Respighi's symphonic poem <u>Fountains of Rome</u> is first performed, in Rome.

1926   Ilhan Kemaleddin Mimaroglu, Turkish-born American composer, principally of electronic music, and writer on music, is born in Istanbul.

1929   Colin McPhee's Concerto for Piano with Wind Octet has its premiere, in Boston.

1932   Ernestine Schumann-Heink makes her last Metropolitan Opera appearance at the age of seventy.

1956   Sergey Vassilenko dies in Moscow at the age of seventy-three.

1967   Geraldine Farrar dies in Ridgefield, Connecticut, aged eighty-five.

MARCH 12

1628   John Bull, English organist and composer, dies in Antwerp, aged sixty-six, on March 12 or 13. In 1617 he had gone to Antwerp to become the organist at Notre Dame Cathedral.

1710   Thomas Arne, English composer (including the song Rule, Britannia!, which became a national patriotic song), is born in London.

1832   Friedrich Kuhlau dies in Copenhagen, aged forty-five.

1857   Giuseppe Verdi's opera Simon Boccanegra has its premiere, in Venice.

1888   Hans Knappertsbusch, German conductor, is born at Elberfeld.

1914   Jan Kapr, Czech composer, is born in Prague.

1921   Ralph Shapey, American composer, teacher, and conductor, is born in Philadelphia.

1925   Helga Pilarczyk, German soprano whose specialty is the performance of modern music, is born in Schöningen.

1926   Rolv Yttrehus, American composer and teacher, is born in Duluth, Minnesota.

1936   Elizabeth Vaughan, Welsh soprano, is born in Llangyllin.

1937   Jenö Hubay dies in Vienna at the age of seventy-eight.

        Charles Marie Widor dies in Paris, aged ninety-three.

1941   Erkki Salmenhaara, Finnish composer, is born in Helsinki.

1943   Aaron Copland's Fanfare for the Common Man, for brass and percussion, receives its premiere in Cincinnati.

1951   Harold Bauer dies in Miami, Florida, at age seventy-seven.

1955   Charlie Parker dies in New York City, aged thirty-four.

1964   Sir Benjamin Britten conducts his Cello Concerto, written for

and performed by Mstislav Rostropovich in its premiere,
in Moscow.

1971   Luciano Berio's Memory for Electronic Piano and Electronic
Harpsichord is performed in New York City with Berio and
Peter Serkin at the respective keyboards.

1977   Matt Doran's one-act opera Marriage Counselor is first
staged in Los Angeles.

1979   Gerhard Stolze dies in Garmisch-Partenkirchen, Germany,
at age fifty-two.

MARCH 13

1700   Michel Blavet, French flutist and composer, is born in
Besançon.

1797   Luigi Cherubini's opera Médée receives its premiere, in
Paris.

1842   Luigi Cherubini dies in Paris, aged eighty-one.

1845   Felix Mendelssohn conducts his Violin Concerto in E minor
in its premiere, in Leipzig, with Ferdinand David, soloist.
Mendelssohn frequently consulted David during the writing of
this concerto.

1860   Hugo Wolf, Austrian song composer, is born in Windisch-
Graz.

1883   Enrico Toselli, Italian pianist and composer, is born in
Florence.

1889   Emma Eames makes her opera debut, starring in Gounod's
Roméo et Juliette at the Paris Opéra. The composer had
selected her to sing in his opera.

Enrico Tamberlik dies three days before his sixty-ninth
birthday, in Rome.

Felice Varesi, a leading Italian operatic baritone, dies in
Milan, aged about seventy-six.

1890   Fritz Busch, German conductor and brother of Adolf Busch,
is born in Siegen.

1894   Bruno Walter makes his conducting debut at the Cologne
Opera.

1911   José Ardévol, Spanish-born Cuban composer whose works
        exalt the Cuban revolution, is born in Barcelona.

1918   Lili Boulanger dies in Mézy, France, aged twenty-four; her
        sister was Nadia Boulanger, famed composition teacher.

1925   Jennifer Vyvyan, English soprano, is born in Broadstairs.

1933   Rosalind Elias, American mezzo-soprano, is born in Lowell,
        Massachusetts.

1958   Maria Müller dies in Bayreuth, Germany, at the age of sixty.

1964   Ernst Toch's "Jephta, Rhapsodic Poem," Symphony no. 5, has
        its premiere performance in Boston.

1976   Milton Babbitt's Concerti for Violin, Small Orchestra and
        Synthesized Tape has its first performance, in New York
        City.

MARCH 14

1681   Georg Philipp Telemann, German composer who was a con-
        temporary of Johann Sebastian Bach, is born in Magdeburg.

1804   Johann Strauss, Sr., Austrian composer and father of Josef
        and Johann, Jr., is born in Vienna.

1847   Giuseppe Verdi's opera Macbeth is first staged, in Florence.

1871   Olive Fremstad, Swedish-American soprano, is born in
        Stockholm and adopted by an American couple in Minnesota.

1885   Gilbert and Sullivan's comic opera Mikado has its premiere,
        in London.

1915   Alexander Brott, Canadian composer and conductor, is born
        in Montreal.

1926   François d'Assise Morel, Canadian composer, is born in Mont-
        real.

1929   Feodor Chaliapin stars in Boris Godunov for the last time
        at the Metropolitan Opera in New York City.

1932   Marius Rintzler, German bass, is born in Bucharest, Rumania.

1941   David Van Vactor's Overture to a Comedy, no. 2, is given
        its premiere performance in Indianapolis.

1952   Dai-Keong Lee's Symphony no. 2 has its premiere in San
        Francisco.

1955   Boris Blacher's Viola Concerto is first performed, in
        Cologne.

1963   Robert Simpson's Symphony no. 3 receives its premiere per-
        formance in Birmingham, England.

1975   Ulysses Kay's Quintet Concerto, for five brass soli and or-
        chestra, is given its first hearing, in New York City.

1976   Paul Creston's Hyas Illahee, for chorus and orchestra, has
        its first performance, in Shreveport, Louisiana.

        MARCH 15

1790   Nicola Vaccai, Italian opera composer and voice teacher, is
        born in Tolentino.

1807   Ludwig van Beethoven conducts the first performance of his
        Symphony no. 4 in Vienna at a concert given for his benefit.

1864   Johan Halvorsen, Norwegian violinist, composer, and con-
        ductor, is born in Drammen.   He married a niece of Edvard
        Grieg and was influenced by Grieg's music in his own works.

1885   César Franck's symphonic poem Les Djinns is performed in
        Paris.

1901   Colin McPhee, American composer and ethnomusicologist
        who is an authority on Balinese music, is born in Montreal.

1908   Kurt Baum, German tenor, is born in Cologne.

        Maurice Ravel's Rapsodie espagnole receives its premiere
        performance, in Paris.

1911   Alexander Scriabin performs the piano part in his Symphony
        no. 5 "Prometheus: Poem of Fire," which is conducted by
        Koussevitzky in Moscow in its premiere performance.   It is
        the composer's most ambitious work and was written for
        Koussevitzky.

1916   Harry James, American jazz trumpeter, is born in Albany,
        Georgia.

1926   Ben Johnston, American composer who uses nonstandard
        instrument tuning, is born in Macon, Georgia.

1927   Aaron Rosand, American violinist, is born in Hammond, Indiana.

1928   Nicolas Flagello, American composer and pianist (accompanist for various famous singers), is born in New York City.

1929   Antonietta Stella, Italian soprano, is born in Perugia.

1950   Gian Carlo Menotti's Pulitzer Prize-winning serious opera The Consul is first produced, in New York City.

MARCH 16

1736   Giovanni Battista Pergolesi dies at age twenty-six of consumption in Pozzuoli, Italy, and is buried in a common grave.

1750   George Frideric Handel's oratorio Theodora is first performed in London.

1756   Antonio Bernacchi dies in Bologna, aged seventy. Handel had engaged him to sing for his Italian Opera in London.

1820   Enrico Tamberlik, Italian tenor, is born in Rome. Verdi wrote a part for him in his opera La Forza del destino.

1833   Vincenzo Bellini's opera Beatrice di Tenda proves a distinct failure at its premiere in Teatro la Fenice, Venice.

1870   Peter Ilyitch Tchaikovsky's overture Romeo and Juliet is conducted in its premiere by Nicholas Rubinstein, in Moscow.

1894   Jules Massenet's opera Thaïs opens at the Paris Opéra and is a continuing favorite.

1903   Nikolai Lopatnikoff, Russian-American pianist, composer, and composition teacher, is born in Tallinn.

1920   John Addison, former teacher at the Royal College of Music, is born in Cobham, England. His music is principally for films and documentaries.

1925   Paolo Montarsolo, Italian baritone, is born in Portici.

1928   Christa Ludwig, German mezzo-soprano, is born in Berlin.

1929   Edwin London, American composer, conductor, and educator, is born in Philadelphia.

1935   Teresa Berganza, Spanish mezzo-soprano, is born in Madrid.

1942   Bohuslav Martinů's <u>Sinfonietta giocosa</u>, for piano and chamber orchestra, has its premiere in New York City.

1957   Irene Dalis makes her Metropolitan Opera debut singing in Verdi's <u>Don Carlos</u>.

1967   James Friskin, author of <u>The Principles of Pianoforte Practice</u>, dies at eighty-one in New York City.

1968   Mario Castelnuovo-Tedesco dies at seventy-two in Los Angeles.

1974   Iain Hamilton's opera <u>The Catiline Conspiracy</u>, for which he wrote the libretto (based on Ben Jonson), is staged for the first time, in Stirling, Scotland.

MARCH 17

1805   Manuel Patricio García, Spanish vocal teacher, is born in Madrid.

1830   Frédéric Chopin makes his concert debut in Warsaw as soloist in his Piano Concerto in F minor. It is the first hearing for this concerto, known as his Second although composed earlier than the E minor concerto (which was published first).

1839   Josef Rheinberger, German composer, organist, and teacher, is born in Vaduz, Liechtenstein.

1862   Jacques François Halévy dies in Nice, France, at the age of sixty-two.

1884   Joseph Bonnet, French organist and composer, is born in Bordeaux. He published an anthology of early French organ music.

1910   Joaquín Valverde dies in Madrid, aged sixty-four.

1911   Robert Goldsand, Austrian pianist, is born in Vienna.

1917   Nat "King" Cole, American jazz pianist and singer, is born in Montgomery, Alabama; he was the first black artist to have a radio sponsor.

1920   John La Montaine, American composer and teacher, holder of the Nixon Chair at Whittier College in California, is born in Oak Park, Illinois.

1930   Betty Lou Allen, American mezzo-soprano, is born in Campbell, Ohio.

1945   Nikolai Miaskovsky's Cello Concerto has its premiere, in
        Moscow.

1951   Victoria de Los Angeles makes her American opera debut singing
        in Gounod's Faust at the Metropolitan Opera in New York
        City.

        Paul Dessau's opera Das Verhör des Lukullus, written as
        propaganda against military dictatorship, is first staged, in
        Berlin. Following severe criticism, it was withdrawn.

1952   Juan José Castro's prize-winning opera Prosperina y el
        extranjero is given its premiere at La Scala, Milan.

1954   Quincy Porter's Pulitzer Prize-winning Concerto Concertante,
        for two pianos and orchestra, is first heard, in Louisville,
        Kentucky.

1967   Thomas Beversdorf's Two-Piano Concerto receives its pre-
        miere, in Bloomington, Indiana.

        Marvin David Levy's opera Mourning Becomes Elektra, to
        O'Neill's libretto, is first produced at the Metropolitan Opera
        in New York.

1968   Henri Pousseur's Votre Faust is given its American premiere
        in concert version in Buffalo, New York.

1979   Giacomo Lauri-Volpi dies at age eighty-six in Valencia,
        Spain.

        MARCH 18

1844   Nicolai Rimsky-Korsakov, Russian composer and one of the
        group known as "The Five," is born in Tikhvin.

1882   Gian Francesco Malipiero, Italian composer, teacher, and
        editor of the collected works of Monteverdi and Vivaldi, is
        born in Venice.

1884   Willem van Hoogstraten, Dutch conductor, is born in Utrecht.

1902   Arnold Schoenberg's Verklärte Nacht, for string sextet, has
        its first hearing, in Vienna.

1904   Anatol Liadov's symphonic tableau, Baba Yaga, receives its
        premiere performance in St. Petersburg.

1905   John Kirkpatrick, American pianist and teacher, is born in
        New York City. His performance of Ives's "Concord" Sonata

was a tour de force and helped bring recognition to Ives.

1927   Sergei Rachmaninoff is soloist in the premiere of his Piano Concerto no. 4 with the Philadelphia Orchestra, Leopold Stokowski conducting. It is also the premiere of his Russian Songs (3), for chorus and orchestra.

1929   John Macurdy, American bass, is born in Detroit.

1949   Peter Mennin's Symphony no. 4, "The Cycle," is performed in New York City in its premiere.

1953   Henri Dutilleux's Le Loup has its premiere, in Paris.

1955   Igor Markevitch makes his American conducting debut with the Boston Symphony Orchestra.

1970   Roger Sessions's Rhapsody for Orchestra is given its first performance, in Baltimore.

1973   Lauritz Melchior dies in Santa Monica, California, two days before his eighty-third birthday.

1976   Gordon Crosse's Epiphany Variations is first performed, in New York City.

MARCH 19

1671   The Académie de Musique is founded in Paris.

1859   Charles Gounod's opera Faust (after Goethe) is first staged at the Théâtre-Lyrique, in Paris.

1873   Max Reger, German composer, organist, and teacher, is born in Brand. He is the only composer whose last name reads the same backward as forward--a real palindrome.

1883   Mily Balakirev conducts his symphonic poem Tamara in St. Petersburg in its premiere performance.

1892   Peter Ilyitch Tchaikovsky's Nutcracker Suite from the ballet receives its premiere, in St. Petersburg.

1910   Sam Raphling, American composer, pianist, and teacher, is born in Fort Worth, Texas.

1915   Nancy Evans, English contralto, is born in Liverpool.

1929   Robert Muczynski, American composer, is born in Chicago.

1931   Alban Berg's opera <u>Wozzeck</u> arouses interest in its first
        American production in Philadelphia under Stokowski's
        direction. Its Berlin premiere had been violently criticized.

1938   Ludwig Wüllner dies at age seventy-nine in Berlin.

1944   Sir Michael Tippett's oratorio <u>A Child of Our Time</u> is given
        its premiere, in London.

1950   William Warfield makes his debut in a song recital in Town
        Hall, New York City.

1956   Jean Madeira sings her first major role at the Metropolitan
        Opera in Bizet's <u>Carmen</u>.

1957   Blas Galindo's Symphony no. 2 shares first prize at the
        Caracas Music Festival in Venezuela.

1972   George Perle's <u>Sonata quasi una fantasia</u>, for clarinet and
        piano, is first heard, in Buffalo, New York.

1976   Gustaf Allan Pettersson's song cycle <u>Vox Humana</u>, for soli,
        chorus, and strings, receives its premiere in Stockholm.

MARCH 20

1812   Johann Ladislaus Dussek dies in St.-Germain-en-Laye,
        France, aged fifty-two.

1887   Vincent d'Indy's <u>Symphony on a French Mountain Air</u>, for
        piano and orchestra, is first performed, in Paris at a
        Lamoureux Concert.

1890   Beniamino Gigli, Italian tenor, is born in Recanati.

        Lauritz Melchior, Danish-born American tenor, is born in
        Copenhagen.

1892   Grigori Stolyarov, Soviet conductor, is born in Odessa.

1914   George Butterworth's <u>The Banks of Green Willow</u>, based on
        folk themes, is first performed in London.

1915   Sviatoslav Richter, Soviet virtuoso pianist, is born in Zhito-
        mir.

1916   John Hollingsworth, English conductor, is born in Enfield.

1918   Bernd Alois Zimmermann, German composer and teacher,
        is born in Bleisheim.

1927   John Joubert, South African composer, is born in Capetown.

1928   The New York Symphony Society and the New York Philhar-
       monic Society unite to form the Philharmonic-Symphony
       Society Orchestra of New York.

1931   Antonio Tauriello, Argentine composer, is born in Buenos
       Aires.

1934   Yngvar Krogh, Norwegian baritone, is born in Oslo.

1952   Alexander Tcherepnin's Symphony no. 2 has its premiere in
       Chicago.

1955   Gordon Binkerd's Symphony no. 1 is given its premiere at
       the University of Illinois in Urbana.

1959   John Vincent's <u>Symphonic Poem After Descartes</u> is first per-
       formed, in Philadelphia.

1977   Victor Grauer's <u>Polyhyperchord</u> receives its premiere in
       Buffalo, New York.

MARCH 21

1685   Johann Sebastian Bach, German composer and organist and
       the most renowned of the musical Bach family, is born in
       Eisenach.   Married twice, he was the father of twenty chil-
       dren.   His works are regarded as the greatest of polyphonic
       music; his prolificacy in composition is echoed in the phrase
       "Nicht Bach aber Meer haben wir" (Not a brook but an ocean
       have we).

1750   Franz Christoph Neubauer, Czech violinist and composer, is
       born in Melnik.

1839   Modest Mussorgsky, Russian composer and member of the
       group known as "The Five," is born in Karevo.

       Franz Schubert's Symphony in C major, "The Great," is
       posthumously performed in Leipzig's Gewandhaus under the
       direction of Felix Mendelssohn.

1900   Paul Kletzki, Polish conductor, is born in Lodz.

1905   Hilde Konetzni, Austrian soprano and sister of Anny Konetzni,
       is born in Vienna.

1914   Paul Tortelier, French cellist and composer, author of a
       cello manual, is born in Paris.

1917   Anton Coppola, American opera conductor, is born in New York City.

1921   Arthur Grumiaux, Belgian violinist, is born in Villers-Perwin.

1927   Robert Goldsand makes his American debut in a piano recital at Carnegie Hall, New York City.

1934   Franz Schreker dies in Berlin, two days before his fifty-sixth birthday.

1935   Nigel Rogers, English tenor, is born in Wellington.

1936   Alexander Glazounov dies in Neuilly-sur-Seine, France, aged seventy.

1939   Delfina Ambroziak, Polish soprano, is born in Rowne.

1951   Willem Mengelberg dies in Chur, Switzerland, exiled from his native Holland for his wartime Nazi sympathies, at age seventy-nine.

1959   Cornell MacNeil stars in Verdi's Rigoletto in his debut at the Metropolitan Opera in New York City.

1971   William Mayer's Octagon, for piano and orchestra, is first performed, in New York City.

1973   Antoni Szalowski dies in Paris, aged sixty-five.

MARCH 22

1687   Jean Baptiste Lully dies in Paris at the age of fifty-four.

1842   Mykola Lysenko, Russian composer, is born in Grinki, Ukraine.

1891   Emanuel List, Austrian bass, is born in Vienna.

1912   Martha Mödl, German soprano and former bookkeeper, is born in Nuremberg.

1943   Joseph Schwanter, American composer and educator, is born in Chicago.

1963   William Kraft's Concerto Grosso receives its premiere, in San Diego, California.

1973   Alberto Ginastera's Piano Concerto no. 2 is first performed in Indianapolis, with Hilde Somer as soloist.

MARCH 23

1703   Antonio Vivaldi is received into the priesthood at age twenty-
        five.

1729   Johann Sebastian Bach's St. Matthew Passion is first performed,
        in Leipzig.

1748   Johann Gottfried Walther dies at age sixty-three in Weimar.

1777   Bernhard Breitkopf dies in Leipzig, aged eighty-two.

1792   (Franz) Joseph Haydn's Symphony in G major, "Surprise
        Symphony," has its premiere in London.   A loud drumbeat
        at the conclusion of the pianissimo theme in the Andante
        movement is the "surprise."

1826   Ludwig Minkus, Austrian composer of ballet music who spent
        his musical career in Russia, is born in Vienna.

1834   Julius Reubke, German composer and pianist, a pupil of
        Liszt, is born in Hausneindorf.

1877   Caroline Unger dies in Florence, aged seventy-three.

1878   Franz Schreker, Austrian composer, teacher, and music
        administrator at Berlin's Hochschule für Musik, is born in
        Monaco.

1881   Egon Petri, Dutch pianist and teacher, is born in Hannover,
        Germany.

        Nicolas Rubinstein dies in Moscow, aged forty-five.

1895   Dane Rudhyer, French-born American composer (mostly self-
        taught), an astrologer and student of theosophy, is born in
        Paris.

1906   Camille Erlanger's opera Aphrodite is first staged in the
        Opéra Comique, in Paris.

1908   Sergey Mikhailovitch Liapunov's Rhapsody on Ukrainian
        Themes for piano and orchestra has its premiere in Berlin
        with Ferruccio Busoni as soloist.

1910   Paul Reif, Czech-born American composer who received the
        Purple Heart in World War II, is born in Prague.

1912   Reinhold Glière's Symphony no. 3, "Ilya Murometz," is
        given its first hearing, in Moscow.

1917   Ernest Bloch conducts his Trois poèmes juifs at its premiere
        in Boston.

1918   Henry F. Gilbert's symphonic poem <u>Dance in Place Congo</u> is performed as a ballet at the Metropolitan Opera in New York City.

1923   Manuel de Falla's <u>Retablo de Maese Pedro</u> has its premiere (in concert form) in Madrid.

1933   Norman Bailey, English baritone, is born in Birmingham.

1935   Samuel Barber's <u>Music for a Scene from Shelley</u> is performed by the New York Philharmonic Orchestra in its premiere.

1939   Boris Tishchenko, Soviet composer, is born in Leningrad.

1946   Marc Blitzstein's <u>Airborne Symphony</u> has its first performance in New York City.

1962   Irving Fine's <u>Symphony 1962</u> is given its premiere by the Boston Symphony Orchestra.

MARCH 24

1654   Samuel Scheidt dies at age sixty-six in Halle, Germany.

1721   Johann Sebastian Bach completes the Brandenburg Concerto no. 6.

1740   John Antes, American-born Moravian missionary and amateur composer, is born in Frederickstownship, Pennsylvania. Three string trios, discovered in 1949, are the earliest American works in this genre.

1808   Maria Felicità Malibran, née García, is born in Paris. Daughter of tenor Manuel García, she became a renowned contralto.

1821   Mathilde Marchesi de Castrone, German vocal teacher, is born in Frankfurt.

1860   Joseph Joachim's Violin Concerto, "Hungarian," has its premiere in Hannover, Germany.

1882   Giuseppe (Gino) Marinuzzi, Italian conductor and composer, is born in Palermo.

1890   Francesco Tamagno makes his American debut starring in Verdi's <u>Otello</u> at the Metropolitan Opera in New York City.

1910   Jacques Chailley, French musicologist and conductor of the Paris Ancient Instrument Ensemble, is born in Paris.

1911   Enrique Jordá, Spanish conductor, is born in San Sebastian.

1914   Leland Procter, American composer and teacher, is born in
        Newton, Massachusetts. He is married to pianist Alice
        McElroy Procter.

1916   Enrique Granados, returning from New York during World
        War I, dies at sea when the ship was sunk by a German
        submarine.

1921   Déodat de Sévérac dies at age forty-eight in Céret, France.

1924   Jean Sibelius conducts his Symphony no. 7 at its premiere
        in Stockholm.

1928   Byron Janis, American pianist and former pupil of Horowitz,
        is born in McKeesport, Pennsylvania.

1932   Randall Thompson's Symphony no. 2 is first performed, in
        Rochester, New York.

1949   Andrzej Panufnik's Tragic Overture (recomposed as the
        original was burned in Warsaw's fires of World War II) re-
        ceives its premiere, in New York City.

1969   Per Nørgaard's Voyage into the Golden Screen, for chamber
        orchestra, has its first performance, in Copenhagen.

        MARCH 25

1699   Johann Adolph Hasse, German composer of Italian-style
        operas, is born in Bergedorf.

1784   François-Joseph Fétis, Belgian musicologist, music theorist,
        composer, and music biographer, is born in Mons. His
        eight-volume Biographie universelle des musiciens is a land-
        mark in musicology; he spent thirty years revising the liturgy
        and plainsong of the Roman Catholic Church.

1867   Arturo Toscanini, Italian conductor, is born in Parma;
        although long a resident in the United States, he retained
        his Italian citizenship.

1875   Gilbert and Sullivan's comic opera Trial by Jury is first
        staged in London.

1881   Béla Bartók, Hungarian composer and pianist, is born in
        Nagyszentmiklos. With Zoltán Kodály he made an extensive
        collection of folksongs.

1910   Mario Peragallo, Italian composer, is born in Rome.

1912   Magda Olivero, Italian soprano, is born in Saluzzo.

1918   Claude Debussy dies of cancer at age fifty-five, in Paris.

1924   Julia Perry, American composer, is born in Lexington, Kentucky.

1928   Mario Sereni, Italian baritone, is born in Perugia.

1935   Jack Behrens, American composer, is born in Lancaster, Pennsylvania.

1939   Heitor Villa-Lobos's _Bachianas Brasileiras, no. 5_, for soprano and eight cellos, has its premiere in Rio de Janeiro.

1942   Aretha Franklin, American "soul singer," is born in Memphis, Tennessee.

1946   Igor Stravinsky's _Ebony Concerto_, for clarinet and swing band, written for Woody Herman, has its premiere in Carnegie Hall in New York City.

1958   Robert Parris's Concerto, for five kettledrums and orchestra, is given its first performance in Washington.

1961   Ezra Laderman's children's opera _The Hunting of the Snark_ (after Lewis Carroll) is first produced in New York City.

1965   Jack Beeson's opera _Lizzie Borden_ has its premiere in New York City.

1973   Sir Noel Coward dies at Port Maria, Jamaica, aged seventy-three.

1979   Anton Heiller dies at age fifty-five in Vienna.

MARCH 26

1566   Antonio de Cabezón, blind Spanish organist and composer, dies in Madrid, aged about fifty-six. He has been called "the Spanish Bach."

1723   Johann Sebastian Bach's _St. John Passion_ has its first hearing on Good Friday services at St. Thomas-Kirche, in Leipzig.

1755   Karl Heinrich Graun's passion cantata _Tod Jesu_, is first sung in the Cathedral of Berlin.

1827   Ludwig van Beethoven dies in Vienna at age fifty-six.

1828   Franz Schubert gives a public concert of his own works in Vienna, and it proves an artistic and financial success.

1871   François-Joseph Fétis dies in Brussels, a day after he celebrated his eighty-seventh birthday.

1874   Oskar Nedbal, Czech composer and conductor, is born in Tabor. He was a pupil of Antonin Dvořák.

1884   Wilhelm Backhaus, German pianist and teacher, is born in Leipzig.

1886   Al Jolson (né Asa Yoelson), Russian-American entertainer and singer, is born in St. Petersburg. He starred in the first important sound movie, The Jazz Singer, in 1927.

1899   Viorica Ursuleac, Rumanian soprano, wife of conductor Clemens Kraus, is born in Cernauti.

1905   André Cluytens, Belgian conductor, is born in Antwerp.

1918   César Cui dies at age eighty-three in St. Petersburg.

1921   Arnold Van Mill, Dutch bass, is born in Schiedam.

1923   Clifton Williams, American conductor, composer, and teacher, is born in Traskwood, Arkansas.

1925   Pierre Boulez, French conductor and composer, is born in Montbrison.

        Claudio Spies, Chilean-born composer, a member of the Princeton University faculty, is born in Santiago.

1931   Carl Vollrath, American composer and teacher, is born in New York City.

1936   Erich Urbanner, Austrian composer, is born in Innsbruck.

1943   William Schuman's Pulitzer Prize-winning cantata A Free Song (after Walt Whitman) is first performed, in Boston.

1954   Seth Bingham's Connecticut Suite, for organ and strings, receives its premiere performance in Hartford, Connecticut.

1958   Witold Lutoslawski's Musique funèbre, for string orchestra (in memory of Béla Bartók), is first performed, in Katowice, Poland.

1960   Mark Bucci's Concerto for Kazoo (later named Concerto for a Singing Instrument), is performed by the New York

Philharmonic Orchestra with Anita Darian, kazoo.

Ralph Shapey's <u>Evocation,</u> for violin, piano, and percussion, receives its premiere, in New York City.

1976   Karel Husa's ballet <u>Monodrama</u> is first staged in Indianapolis, Indiana.

MARCH 27

1745   George Frideric Handel's oratorio <u>Balshazzar</u> is first per- formed, in London.

1757   Johann Wenzel Anton Stamitz dies in Mannheim at the age of thirty-nine.

1808   (Franz) Joseph Haydn's approaching seventy-sixth birthday is celebrated in Vienna with a performance of his <u>Creation.</u> It is his last public appearance; Beethoven and Salieri greet him.

1833   Genevieve Ward, American soprano, is born in New York City.

1851   Vincent d'Indy, French composer and writer on music, is born in Paris.

1892   Ferde Grofé, American composer, café pianist, and arranger (scoring Gershwin's <u>Rhapsody in Blue</u>), is born in New York City.

1914   Ralph Vaughan Williams's <u>London Symphony</u> in its original version receives its premiere at Queen's Hall, London, under the direction of Geoffrey Toye.

1917   Giacomo Puccini's opera <u>La Rondine</u> is first staged, in Monte Carlo.

1924   Sarah Vaughan, American jazz singer and television enter- tainer, is born in Newark, New Jersey.

1927   Mstislav Rostropovich, Soviet cellist, son and grandson of professional cellists and husband of singer Galina Vishnevskaya, is born in Baku.   In March of 1978 he and his wife sought asylum in the United States when stripped of their Soviet citizenship.

1928   Pauline Tinsley, English soprano, is born in Wigan.

1929   Werner Josten's <u>Concerto sacro I-II,</u> for piano and strings, receives its premiere performance in New York City.

1960   Toshiro Mayuzumi's <u>Mandala-Symphonie</u> is first performed, in Tokyo.

1975   Sir Arthur Bliss dies in London, aged eighty-three. In 1953 he succeeded Arnold Bax as Master of the Queen's Musick.

MARCH 28

1796   Friedrich Wilhelm Rust dies in Dessau, Germany, aged fifty-six.

1800   Antonio Tamburini, Italian baritone, is born in Faenza.

1804   Ivan Khandoshkin, Russian violinist and composer (a liberated serf) who was the first to use Russian folktunes in instrumental music, dies in St. Petersburg, aged about fifty-seven.

1842   The Vienna Court Orchestra plays its first concert as an ensemble. Its founder is the composer Otto Nicolai, Court Opera conductor.

1871   Willem Mengelberg, Dutch conductor, is born in Utrecht.

1880   Rosina Lhévinne, Russian-born pianist and teacher at Juilliard School of Music, wife of Josef Lhévinne, is born in Kiev.

1881   Modest Mussorgsky dies at age forty-two in St. Petersburg.

1890   Paul Whiteman, American bandleader of popular music, known as the "King of Jazz," is born in Denver, Colorado.

1896   Umberto Giordano's opera <u>Andrea Chénier</u> is first staged at La Scala, Milan; the libretto is by Luigi Illica.

1898   Anton Seidl dies of ptomaine poisoning in New York City, aged forty-seven.

1903   Rudolf Serkin, Austrian pianist, teacher, and music administrator, is born in Eger. He married the daughter of violinist Adolph Busch.

1910   Eduard Haken, Czech bass, is born in Shklin, Russia.

1919   Jacob Avshalomov, American composer and son of Aaron Avshalomov, is born in Tsingtao, China.

Paul Doktor, Austrian-born American violist and teacher, a former editor of viola music for G. Schirmer, Inc., is born in Vienna.

1930   Robert Ashley, American composer, co-director of Mills
        College Center for Contemporary Music, is born in Ann
        Arbor, Michigan.

1936   Elizabeth Bainbridge, English mezzo-soprano, is born in
        Britain.

1937   Karol Szymanowski dies in Lausanne, Switerland, aged fifty-
        four.

1943   Sergei Rachmaninoff dies in Beverly Hills, California, at the
        age of sixty-nine.   A few weeks earlier he became an Ameri-
        can citizen.

1951   Douglas Moore's Pulitzer Prize-winning opera Giants in the
        Earth is given its premiere in New York City.

1958   W. C. Handy dies in New York, aged eighty-four, remembered
        for his St. Louis Blues.

        George Rochberg's Symphony no. 1 is first performed, in
        Philadelphia.

1963   Alec Templeton dies at age fifty-three, in Greenwich,
        Connecticut.

1974   Jennifer Vyvyan dies in London, aged forty-nine.

1976   Peter Mennin's Voices, for voice, percussion, piano, harp,
        and harpsichord, receives its premiere, in New York City.

        MARCH 29

1795   Ludwig van Beethoven performs his Piano Concerto no. 2 in
        B-flat at a concert in the Burgtheater, Vienna, in his first
        public appearance.

1825   Johann Andreas Amon, German musician who for many years
        was the music director at Heilbronn, dies in Wallerstein,
        aged about sixty-two.

1871   Royal Albert Hall opens in London.

1879   Peter Ilyitch Tchaikovsky's opera Eugene Onegin (after Push-
        kin) has its premiere in Moscow.

1888   Charles-Henri Alkan, at age seventy-five, dies in Paris,
        crushed by a falling bookcase.

1901   Jean de Reszke makes his farewell appearance at the

Metropolitan Opera, starring in <u>Lohengrin</u>.

1902   Mario Rossi, Italian conductor, is born in Rome.

Sir William Walton, English composer, is born in Oldham.

1906   E. Power Biggs, English-born American organist, is born in Westcliff.

1912   Fritz Ollendorff, Swiss bass, is born in Darmstadt.

1918   Pearl Bailey, American jazz singer, is born in Newport News, Virginia.

1936   Lucretia Bori sings a farewell program at the Metropolitan Opera in New York City.

Richard Rodney Bennett, English composer (including film scores), is born in Broadstairs.

Lenore Kirschstein, German soprano, is born in Stetten.

1938   William Brown, American tenor, is born in Jackson, Mississippi.

1957   Jean Martinon makes his American conducting debut with the Boston Symphony Orchestra.

1967   Yuji Takahashi's <u>Prajna Paramita</u>, for soprano and instrumental ensemble, premieres in Buffalo, New York.

1977   Fritz Ollendorff dies on his sixty-fifth birthday in Zurich.

MARCH 30

1764   Pietro Locatelli dies in Amsterdam at age sixty-eight.

1779   Carl Friedrich Peters, founder of the German music publishing firm, is born in Leipzig.

1872   Frederick Austin, English baritone and composer, is born in London.

Sergey Vassilenko, Russian composer and conductor, is born in Moscow.

1920   Juilliard Musical Foundation is incorporated in New York City.

1924   Milko Kelemen, Croatian composer, teacher, and co-founder of the Zagreb Biennial Festival of New Music, is born in Podrawska Slatina, Yugoslavia.

1926   Werner Torkanowsky, German-American conductor, is born
        in Berlin. He conducted the New Orleans Philharmonic
        Symphony Orchestra from 1963 to 1977.

1927   Barry Morell, American tenor and former wool merchant,
        is born in New York City.

1932   Luigi Zaninelli, American composer, is born in Raritan,
        New Jersey.

1935   Karl Berger, German-American scholar and jazz musician,
        is born in Heidelberg. His doctoral dissertation is on music
        ideology.

        Gordon Mumma, American composer of electronic music,
        is born in Framingham, Massachusetts.

1936   Gianni Maffeo, Italian baritone, is born in Vigevano.

1951   Walter Piston's Symphony no. 4 has its first hearing, in
        Minneapolis.

1955   Harl McDonald dies in Princeton, New Jersey, at age fifty-
        five. His book New Methods of Measuring Sound was pub-
        lished in 1935.

1963   Alexander Gauk dies in Moscow, aged sixty-nine.

        MARCH 31

1703   Johann Christoph Bach dies in Eisenach, Germany, aged
        sixty.

1732   (Franz) Joseph Haydn, Austrian composer who inscribed all
        his scores with "Laus Deo" or "Soli Deo Gloria," is born
        in Rohrau. Known affectionately as "Papa Haydn" and
        "Father of the Symphony," he was also Beethoven's teacher
        for a brief period.

1841   Robert Schumann's Symphony no. 1, "Spring," is first per-
        formed, in Leipzig.

1872   Sergei Pavlovich Diaghilev, Russian impressario, founder of
        the Ballet Russe, is born in Gruzino, Novgorod district.
        He commissioned Stravinsky and many others to write ballets.

1873   Domenico Donzelli, Italian tenor, dies in Bologna, aged about
        eighty-three.

1880   Henryk Wieniawski dies at age forty-four in Moscow.

1893   Clemens Heinrich Krauss, Austrian conductor, is born in Vienna. He was the librettist for Richard Strauss's opera <u>Capriccio;</u> he was married to the singer Viorica Ursuleac.

1901   Antonin Dvořák's opera <u>Rusalka</u> is first staged, in Prague.

       Sir John Stainer dies in Verona, Italy, aged sixty.

1911   Elisabeth Grümmer, German soprano, is born in Diedenhofen, Alsace.

1913   Anton Webern's <u>Six Pieces for Orchestra</u> is first performed in Vienna.

1924   Frederick Guthrie, American bass, is born in Pocatello, Idaho.

1932   Carlos Chávez's ballet <u>Horsepower</u> is staged in Philadelphia.

1940   John Stewart, American tenor, former college teacher, is born in Cleveland, Ohio.

1947   Ulysses Kay's <u>Short Overture</u> receives its premiere, in New York City.

1964   Ulysses Kay's <u>Umbrian Scene</u> has its first hearing, in New Orleans.

1968   Elly Ney dies at eighty-five in Tutzing, Germany.

1973   Kurt Thomas dies at Bad Oeynhausen, West Germany, aged sixty-eight.

       Richard Trythall's <u>Second Round,</u> for harpsichord and tape, is first performed in Buffalo, New York, with the composer at the harpsichord.

APRIL 1

1732   (Franz) Joseph Haydn's birthdate is listed in the parish register in Rohrau, Austria, although he listed it as March 31 in a short biography years later. Haydn is said to have explained that his brother Michael preferred the March date.

1747   George Frideric Handel's oratorio _Judas Maccabaeus_ is first performed, in London.

1865   Giuditta Pasta dies at her Lake Como villa in Italy, aged sixty-seven.

1866   Ferruccio Busoni, Italian pianist, composer, and teacher, is born in Empoli.

1869   Alexander Dreyshock, considered Liszt's rival in pianistic technical dexterity, dies at age fifty in Venice.

1873   Sergei Rachmaninoff, Russian piano virtuoso and composer, is born on his family's estate near Oneg. He became an American citizen shortly before he died.

1901   Boris Koutzen, Russian-American violinist, teacher, and composer, is born in Uman.

1907   Walter Kaufmann, Czech-American conductor and composer, is born in Karlsbad.

1909   Eddy Duchin, American popular pianist and orchestra leader, is born in Cambridge, Massachusetts.

1913   Manuel de Falla's opera _La Vida breve_ is first staged, in Nice.

1917   Scott Joplin, titled "King of Ragtime," dies insane in a New York City hospital, aged forty-eight.

       Dinu Lipatti, Rumanian pianist and composer, is born in Bucharest.

108

1921   William Bergsma, American composer and teacher, is born
        in Oakland, California.

1926   Charles Bressler, American tenor, is born in Kingston,
        Pennsylvania.

1927   Boris Koutzen's <u>Solitude</u>, for orchestra, receives its pre-
        miere, in Philadelphia, marking the composer's twenty-sixth
        birthday.

1937   Gian Carlo Menotti's one-act opera buffa <u>Amelia Goes to the
        Ball</u> is first given by the Academy of Music in Philadelphia.
        Menotti, who wrote the libretto, is considered one of the
        foremost composer-librettists of the present day.

1952   Kirsten Flagstad makes her final appearance at the Metro-
        politan Opera, starring in an English translation of Gluck's
        <u>Alceste.</u>

1954   Aaron Copland's opera <u>The Tender Land</u> is given its pre-
        miere, in New York City.

1976   David Diamond's Violin Concerto no. 3, is first performed,
        in New York City.

        Artur Rubinstein is awarded the United States Medal of
        Freedom by President Ford. It is the highest honor given
        a civilian.

        APRIL 2

1800   Ludwig van Beethoven's Symphony no. 1 and Piano Concerto
        no. 1 are given their first performances at a concert in
        Vienna, with Paul Wranitzky conducting and the composer as
        soloist. Critics complained that the symphony began with a
        discord.

1851   Adolf Brodsky, Russian-born violinist, is born in Taganrog.
        It was to him that Tchaikovsky dedicated his violin concerto
        after Auer refused to play it. Most of his professional life
        was spent in England.

1861   Ernest Van Dyck, Belgian tenor, is born in Antwerp.

1905   Kurt Herbert Adler, Austrian-American opera conductor, is
        born in Vienna. After Hitler's Anschluss he emigrated and
        led the San Francisco Opera Company for more than twenty-
        five years.

1913   Lauritz Melchior makes his opera debut as a baritone at

Copenhagen's Royal Opera. He became a celebrated tenor.

1924   Murray Dickie, Scottish tenor, is born in Bishopstown.

1928   Fritz Uhl, Austrian tenor, is born in Vienna.

Alain Vanzo, French tenor, is born in Monaco.

1951   Simon Barere dies while performing a piano concert in Carnegie Hall, New York, at the age of fifty-four.

1958   Toshiro Mayuzumi's Nirvana-Symphonie is given its premiere in Tokyo.

1961   Wallingford Riegger dies in New York City after he was thrown to the sidewalk in an accident. He was seventy-five years old.

1973   Jascha Horenstein dies in London, aged seventy-four. His interpretations of Mahler were highly respected.

APRIL 3

1834   The Neue Zeitschrift für Musik first appears, with Robert Schumann a contributing editor.

1843   The Leipzig Conservatory opens officially under the directorship of Felix Mendelssohn.

1850   Jan Václav Tomášek dies in Prague at age seventy-five, a most noted teacher.

1868   Franz Berwald, aged seventy-one, dies in Stockholm.

1869   Edvard Grieg is soloist in the premiere of his Piano Concerto, performed in Copenhagen.

1895   Mario Castelnuovo-Tedesco, Italian-American composer, is born in Florence.

1897   Johannes Brahms dies in Vienna at age sixty-three, of cancer.

1901   Richard D'Oyly Carte dies in London, aged fifty-six, after introducing many improvements in theatrical management.

1905   Lili Kraus, Hungarian-English pianist, is born in Budapest. During World War II she was imprisoned by the Japanese in Southeast Asia, where she had been on concert tour.

1910   Frances Alda, soprano, is married to Giulio Gatti-Casazza, manager of the Metropolitan Opera.

1913   George Barati, Hungarian-American conductor, composer and
        cellist, is born in Györ.

1918   Sixten Ehrling, Swedish pianist and conductor, is born in
        Malmö. In 1978 he became principal guest conductor of
        Denver Symphony Orchestra.

1925   Jean de Reszke dies in Nice, aged seventy-five.

1928   Kersten Meyer, Swedish contralto, is born in Stockholm.

1940   Anja Silja, German soprano, is born in Berlin.

1950   Kurt Weill dies in New York City, at the age of fifty.

1959   David Van Vactor's Symphony no. 2 has its premiere, in
        Pittsburgh.

1966   Richard Rodney Bennett's Variations for Orchestra receives
        its American premiere in New York City by the London
        Symphony Orchestra.

1971   Pinchas Zukerman, Israeli violinist, makes his debut in
        New York City.

1972   Ferde Grofé dies in Santa Monica, California, at the age of
        eighty.

        APRIL 4

1739   George Frideric Handel's oratorio Israel in Egypt is given
        its first performance, in London. It is the second of three
        oratorios written this year.

1803   Ludwig van Beethoven's oratorio Christus am Ölberg has its
        premiere at the Theater an der Wien, Vienna.

1843   Hans Richter, German conductor associated with Wagner, is
        born in Raab, Hungary.

1859   Giacomo Meyerbeer's opera Le Pardon de Ploërmel is first
        staged, at the Opéra-Comique, Paris.

1875   Pierre Monteux, French conductor who conducted the pre-
        mieres of many modern ballet scores, is born in Paris.

1882   Mary Howe, American composer, is born in Richmond,
        Virginia.

1897   Ernest Chausson's Poème, for violin and orchestra, is first performed by Eugène Ysaÿe, soloist with the Concerts Colonne, Paris.

1898   Joe Venuti, Italian-American jazz violinist, is born in Lecco.

1905   Eugene Bozza, French composer and conductor, is born in Nice.

1931   George Whitefield Chadwick dies in Boston, aged seventy-six.

1935   Bernard Rogers's <u>Once Upon a Time</u>, "Five Fairy Tales," receives its first hearing, in Rochester, New York.

1937   Laura Zinnini, Italian contralto, is born in Trieste.

1954   Arturo Toscanini conducts his last concert from Carnegie Hall in New York, ten days after his eighty-seventh birthday.

1965   Lothar Klein's <u>Epitaphs,</u> in memory of Hemingway, Camus, and President Kennedy, and his <u>Trio Concertante</u> are given their premieres in New Orleans.

1968   William Kraft's <u>Contextures: Riots--Decade '60</u> is first performed, in Los Angeles.

1969   Samuel Adler's <u>From out of Bondage,</u> a Biblical cantata, is given its first hearing, at Temple Sinai in Brookline, Massachusetts.

1972   Stefan Wolpe, aged sixty-nine, dies in New York City. He came to the United States after Hitler's Anschluss.

1975   George Rochberg's Violin Concerto receives its premiere with the Pittsburgh Symphony Orchestra, Isaac Stern, soloist.

1977   Eugene Zador dies in Hollywood, California, aged eighty-two.

APRIL 5

1752   Sébastian Erard, French piano and harp manufacturer, is born in Strasbourg.

1784   Ludwig Spohr, German violinist, composer, and conductor, is born in Brunswick.

1803   Ludwig van Beethoven is soloist in his Piano Concerto no. 3 in its premiere at an all-Beethoven concert in Vienna's Theater an der Wien. Also on the program is the premiere of his Symphony no. 2.

1869   Albert Roussel, French composer whose music reflects his
        travels in Indochina, is born in Tourcoing.

1874   Johann Strauss, Jr.'s operetta Die Fledermaus is first
        staged, in Vienna.

1908   Herbert von Karajan, Austrian conductor, is born in Salzburg.

1911   Goddard Lieberson, English-American composer and music-
        company executive, is born in Hanley.   As president of
        Columbia Records he promoted long-playing discs.

1925   Kieth Engen, American bass, is born in Frazee, Minnesota.

1928   Heitor Villa-Lobos's Dansas Africanas receives its premiere,
        in Paris.

1930   Mary Costa, American soprano, is born in Knoxville, Tennes-
        see.

1946   Charles Ives's Symphony no. 3, awarded the Pulitzer Prize,
        is first performed, in New York City.

        Vincent Youmans dies in Denver, aged forty-seven, of tuber-
        culosis.

1967   Mischa Elman dies in New York City, aged seventy-six, his
        name a synonym for violin virtuosity.

1973   Herbert Graf dies in Geneva, Switzerland, aged sixty-nine.
        He had spent more than twenty-five years in the United States
        in directing operas.

1976   Meyer Davis dies in New York City, aged eighty-one.

APRIL 6

1660   Johann Kuhnau, German organist, theorist, and music scholar,
        is born in Geising.   He preceded Bach as cantor at the
        Thomaskirche in Leipzig.

1708   Johann Adam von Reutter, Jr., Austrian composer and court
        choirmaster (the young Joseph Haydn was in his choir), is
        born in Vienna.

1757   Alessandro Rolla, Italian violinist, composer, and teacher,
        is born in Pavia.   Paganini was one of his students.

1815   Robert Volkmann, German composer who was popular in his
        day, is born in Lommatzsch.

1885   Carlos Salzedo, French-American harpist, composer, and
        teacher, is born in Arcachon.

1887   Nicolae Bretan, Rumanian opera singer and composer of
        operas and lieder, is born in Nasaud.

1900   Andrés Sás, French-Peruvian composer, teacher, and col-
        lector of Peruvian folksongs, is born in Paris.

1921   Andrew W. Imbrie, American composer and teacher, is born
        in New York City.

1922   Arabella Goddard dies in Boulogne, France, aged eighty-six.

1929   Edison Denisov, Soviet composer who was named by his
        engineer father for Thomas Edison, is born in Tomsk.

        André Previn, German-born American pianist, conductor of
        the London Symphony Orchestra, and film-score composer,
        is born in Berlin.

1931   Joan Carlyle, English soprano, is born in Wirral.

1935   Stanley Kolk, American tenor, is born in Fremont, Michigan.

1967   Miklós Rózsa's Piano Concerto is performed by Leonard
        Pennario, soloist with the Los Angeles Philharmonic, in its
        premiere there.

1971   Igor Stravinsky dies in New York City, aged eighty-eight.
        He is buried in the Russian corner of the cemetery island
        of San Michele, near Venice.

        APRIL 7

1726   Charles Burney, English music historian who traveled
        throughout Europe as a music journalist, is born in Shrews-
        bury.

1783   Ignaz Holzbauer dies in Mannheim, Germany, at age seventy-
        one.

1794   Giovanni-Battista Rubini, Italian tenor, is born in Romano.

1805   Ludwig van Beethovan conducts the first public performance
        of his Symphony no. 3, "Eroica," in Vienna's Theater an
        der Wien.

1899   Robert Casadesus, French pianist and composer, is born in
        Paris into a notable family of musicians.

1908   Percy Faith, American conductor and arranger of popular
        music, is born in Toronto, Canada.

1915   Billie Holiday, American jazz singer, is born in Baltimore.

1920   Ravi Shankar, Indian sitar virtuoso and composer of several
        film scores, is born in Benares.

1923   Reynaldo Hahn's light opera Ciboulette is first produced, in
        Paris at the Théâtre des Variétés.

1931   Donald Harris, American composer and teacher, is born in
        St. Paul, Minnesota.

1932   Grayston Burgess, English conductor and countertenor, is
        born in Cheriton.

1978   Ernest Kanitz dies in Menlo Park, California, two days before
        his eighty-fourth birthday.   After the 1938 Anschluss in
        Austria he emigrated to the United States and taught music
        theory in several American colleges.

        APRIL 8

1533   Claudio Merulo, Italian composer and organ virtuoso, is
        born in Correggio.   He was organist at San Marco, Venice;
        later, court organist at Parma.

1692   Giuseppe Tartini, Italian violin virtuoso, composer, and
        theorist, is born in Pirano.   His Devil's Trill Sonata was
        discovered posthumously and reputedly came to him in a
        dream.

1773   Giuseppini Grassini, Italian contralto who was persuaded by
        Napoleon to come to Paris, is born in Varese.

1848   Gaetano Donizetti dies at age fifty, in Bergamo.

1858   Anton Diabelli dies in Vienna, aged seventy-six.

1876   Amilcare Ponchielli's opera La Gioconda (which includes the
        popular Dance of the Hours) receives its premiere, in Milan.

1889   Sir Adrian Boult, English conductor, is born in Chester.

1894   Anton Bruckner's Symphony no. 5 is first performed, in
        Graz, Austria.

1902   Josef Krips, Austrian conductor, is born in Vienna.

1904   John Henry Antill, Australian composer, conductor, and ethnomusicologist, is born in Sydney. While working for the railway, he designed a steam whistle that could produce a major ninth chord.

1906   Raoul Jobin, Canadian tenor, is born in Quebec.

1920   Charles Tomlinson Griffes dies at age thirty-five in New York City.

1923   Franco Corelli, Italian tenor who aided his singing by imitating great voices on the phonograph, is born in Ancona.

1927   Edgard Varèse's Arcana, for orchestra, is first performed in Philadelphia, Leopold Stokowski conducting.

1929   Walter Berry, Austrian baritone, former engineering student and husband of singer Christa Ludwig, is born in Vienna.

1930   John Reardon, American baritone, is born in San Francisco.

1931   Abram Chasins's Three Chinese Pieces (orchestral version) is performed by the New York Philharmonic Orchestra and is the first American work conducted by Arturo Toscanini.

1937   Arthur Foote dies in Boston, aged eighty-four.

1938   Joseph "King" Oliver dies in Savannah, Georgia, at age fifty-two. The Smithsonian has reissued his group's 1923 early jazz recordings.

        Vern Sutton, American tenor, is born in Oklahoma City.

1970   Martin Bresnick's computer composition PCOMP is first heard, in Vienna.

1975   Beverly Sills makes her Metropolitan Opera debut starring in Rossini's Siege of Corinth.

        APRIL 9

1717   Georg Matthias Monn, Austrian composer and organist, is born in Lower Austria.

1794   Theobald Böhm, German flutist who improved flute construction on an acoustical basis, is born in Munich.

1841   Joseph Fischer, German-born American music publisher, is born in Silberhausen.

1846   Sir Francesco Paolo Tosti, Italian voice teacher and song
        composer, is born in Ortona. He taught the British royal
        family and was knighted in 1908.

1888 ⋅ Sol Hurok, Russian-American impressario, is born in Pogar.
        He fled to New York City from Jewish persecution, becoming
        a manager for Russian artists and ballets.

1894   Ernest Kanitz, Austrian-American composer, is born in
        Vienna.

1898   Julius Patzak, Austrian tenor, is born in Vienna.

        Paul Robeson, American bass-baritone, actor, lawyer, All-
        American football player, Phi Beta Kappa, and civil-rights
        activist, is born in Princeton, New Jersey.

1906   Antal Dorati, Hungarian-American conductor and composer,
        is born in Budapest.

1916   Manuel de Falla's Nights in the Gardens of Spain, for piano
        and orchestra, has its premiere in Madrid.

1919   Noah Greenberg, American conductor, musicologist, and
        founder of New York Pro Musica Antiqua, is born in New
        York City.

1926   Edgard Varèse's Amériques is first performed, in Philadel-
        phia; Leopold Stokowski defies popular taste in his conducting
        the Philadelphia Orchestra in this dissonant work.

1933   Sigfrid Karg-Elert dies in Leipzig, aged fifty-five.

1935   Aulis Sallinen, Finnish composer, conductor, and teacher, is
        born in Salmi.

1937   Robert Elmore's tone poem Vally Forge is first performed
        by the Philadelphia Orchestra, Leopold Stokowski conducting.

1939   Marian Anderson sings to 75,000 people at her Lincoln Me-
        morial Concert, sponsored by First Lady Eleanor Roosevelt
        and others to protest the racial discrimination shown when
        Anderson was denied the use of Washington's Constitution Hall,
        owned and administered by the Daughters of the American
        Revolution.

1948   Samuel Barber's Knoxville: Summer of 1915, for voice and
        orchestra, receives its first hearing, in Boston, with Eleanor
        Steber, soloist.

1955   Ramiro Cortés's award-winning Sinfonia Sacra is first per-
        formed by the New York Philharmonic Orchestra.

1959   Benjamin Lees's _Prologue, Capriccio and Epilogue_ is given
        its premiere, in Portland, Oregon.

1960   Arthur Benjamin dies at age sixty-six in London.

1963   Benno Moiseiwitsch, known for his performances of Romantic
        piano music, dies in London, aged seventy-three.

        APRIL 10

1864   Eugène d'Albert, Scottish-born German pianist (a student of
        Liszt) and composer, is born in Glasgow. In one of his six
        marriages he was briefly husband of famed pianist Teresa
        Carreño, and in another, of singer Hermine Finck.

1868   Johannes Brahms conducts his _German Requiem_ for the first
        time in its entirety on Good Friday in Bremen Cathredal.

1892   Victor de Sabata, Italian opera conductor and composer, is
        born at Trieste.

1900   Mary Garden successfully completes the performance of
        Louise in Paris when the leading soprano became ill. It
        marks her continuing in the role.

1903   Herbert Graf, Austrian opera stage director, is born in
        Vienna.

1913   Italo Montemezzi's opera _L'Amore dei tre re_ is first staged
        in La Scala, Milan; Tullio Serafin conducting.

1919   Gabriel Fauré's stage music _Masques et bergamasques_ is
        given its premiere, in Monte Carlo.

1927   Luiga Alva, Peruvian operatic tenor, is born in Lima.

1935   Jorge Mester, Mexican-American conductor (Aspen Music
        Festival), is born in Mexico City.

        Ralph Vaughan Williams's Symphony no. 4 has its premiere,
        in London.

1938   Denny Zeitlin, American jazz keyboard performer and com-
        poser who is a professional San Francisco psychiatrist, is
        born in Chicago.

1952   Frederick Austin dies in London, aged eighty.

1965   Paul Reif's _Philador's Defense--A Musical Chess Game_, for
        chamber orchestra, is first performed, in New York City.

1971   Ezra Laderman's cantata <u>And David Wept</u> is aired on CBS
        television in its premiere, in New York City.

APRIL 11

1682   Jean Joseph Mouret, French composer, is born in Avignon.
        One of his fanfares for trumpet became the theme for Public
        Television's "Masterpiece Theater."

1884   Vincent d'Indy's <u>La Mort de Wallenstein</u> (third part of a
        symphonic trilogy), is performed, in Paris.

1888   The Concertgebouw is inaugurated in Amsterdam.

1891   Antonin Dvořák's <u>Dumky Trio</u> is first performed in Prague;
        the composer at the piano.

1908   Karel Ančerl, Czech conductor (and, for a short time di-
        rector of the Toronto Symphony), a survivor of Auschwitz
        concentration camp, is born in Tučapy.

1916   Alberto Ginastera, Argentine composer and teacher, is born
        in Buenos Aires.

1919   The New Symphony Orchestra, organized by Edgard Varèse
        for performing modern music, presents its first program
        in New York City.

1926   Gervase De Peyer, English clarinetist, is born in London.

1938   Kurt Moll, German bass, is born in Buir.

1941   Arnold Schoenberg becomes an American citizen and changes
        his name from Schönberg.

1959   Eric Blom dies in London, aged seventy.

1965   David Amram's Passover opera <u>The Final Ingredient</u> is pro-
        duced on television in New York City.

1967   Alan Hovhaness's <u>Holy City,</u> for orchestra, is first heard,
        in Portland, Maine.

APRIL 12

1684   Nicola Amati dies in Cremona, Italy, at age eighty-seven;
        he is the most illustrious of the violin-making family.

1710   Caffarelli (real name Gaetano Majorano), Italian artificial
       soprano, is born in Bitonto. The Largo from Handel's
       Serse was written for him.

1716   Felice de' Giardini, Italian violinist and composer, is born
       in Turin.

1722   Pietro Nardini, Italian violinist (a pupil of Tartini) and com-
       poser, is born in Leghorn.

1760   Ernst Gottlieb Baron dies in Berlin, aged sixty-four.

1801   Joseph Lanner, Austrian violinist and composer, credited,
       along with Johann Strauss, Sr., in creating the Viennese
       waltz, is born in Vienna.

1814   Charles Burney, whose History of Music appeared in four
       volumes, dies in Chelsea, England, at age eighty-eight.

1826   Carl Maria von Weber conducts his opera Oberon in its pre-
       miere in London's Covent Garden.

1844   Franz Kullak, German pianist and composer, son of Theodor
       Kullak, is born in Berlin.

1873   Giorgio Polacco, Italian conductor, is born in Venice.

1898   Lily Pons, French-American soprano and movie star, is
       born in Draguignan.

1907   Imogen Holst, English musician and biographer of her father,
       Gustav Holst, is born in Richmond.

1909   Lionel Hampton, American jazz vibraphonist, drummer,
       bandleader, and pianist, is born in Louisville, Kentucky.

1919   István Anhalt, Hungarian-Canadian composer and teacher, is
       born in Budapest.

1920   Robert Fizdale, American pianist, duo-pianist with Arthur
       Gold, is born in Chicago.

1928   Jean-François Paillard, French conductor and musicologist,
       is born in Vitry-le-François.

1931   Miguel Aguilar-Ahumada, Chilean composer and pianist, is
       born in Huara.

       Martin Boykan, American pianist, composer, and teacher,
       is born in New York City.

1932   Henri Lazarof, Bulgarian-American composer and teacher,
       is born in Sofia.

1933   Montserrat Caballé, Spanish soprano, is born in Barcelona.

Mario Castelnuovo-Tedesco's Violin Concerto no. 2, "The
Prophets," is performed by Jascha Heifetz (who commissioned
the work) as soloist with the New York Philharmonic Orchestra, Arturo Toscanini conducting.

1938   Feodor Chaliapin dies at sixty-five in Paris.

1956   John Joubert's Symphony no. 1 is first heard, in Hull, England.

1957   Wallingford Riegger's Symphony no. 4 is given its premiere,
at the University of Illinois, Urbana.

APRIL 13

1742   George Frideric Handel's oratorio <u>Messiah</u> is first performed,
in Dublin. The custom of standing during the Hallelujah
Chorus began with the first London performance, when the
audience rose, carried away by its grandeur.

1799   Ludwig Rellstab, German music critic and editor of a music
periodical, is born in Berlin.

1810   Félicien-César David, French composer, is born in Cadenet.

1816   Sir William Sterndale Bennett, English composer, conductor,
and pianist, is born in Sheffield.

1826   Franz Danzi dies in Schwetzingen, Germany, aged sixty-two.

1886   Ethel Leginska (real name Liggins), English pianist and composer, is born in Hull.

1896   The American Guild of Organists is founded in New York
City.

1911   Nino Sanzogno, Italian conductor and composer, is born in
Venice.

1930   Howard Mayer Brown, American musicologist and teacher,
is born in Los Angeles. He is editor of a series of books
on Italian operas.

1938   Frederic Rzewski, American composer and pianist, is born
in Westfield, Massachusetts. He has accompanied cellist
Charlotte Moorman.

1941   Margaret Price, British soprano, is born in Tredegar, Wales.

1943   Randall Thompson's <u>A Testament of Freedom</u>, for men's
        voices and orchestra, is first performed, at the University
        of Virginia.

1944   Cécile Chaminade dies in Monte Carlo at the age of eighty-
        six.

1952   Morton Gould conducts his Symphony no. 4, for band, in its
        premiere at West Point, New York.

1957   Gordon Binkerd's Symphony no. 2 receives its first hearing
        at the University of Illinois, Urbana.

        Ellis Kohs's Symphony no. 2, with chorus, is first performed,
        at the University of Illinois, Urbana.

1958   Van Cliburn wins the Tchaikowsky Competition in Moscow,
        the first American to score this triumph.

1959   Eduard van Beinum dies in Amsterdam, aged fifty-eight.

1961   Luigi Nono's <u>Intolleranza 1960,</u> a protest against social
        inequalities, at its premiere in Venice proves politically con-
        troversial.

1976   Walter Ross's <u>Jefferson Symphony,</u> for chorus and orchestra,
        is given its first performance in Charlottesville, Virginia.

        APRIL 14

1759   George Frideric Handel dies in London, aged seventy-four.
        He is buried in Westminster Abbey.

1843   Joseph Lanner dies in Oberdobling, Austria, aged forty-two.

1857   Edgar Stillman Kelley, American composer and teacher, is
        born in Sparta, Wisconsin.   He was a music critic and
        writer on music.

1883   Léo Delibes's opera <u>Lakmé</u> is first staged, in Paris at the
        Opéra-Comique.   He composed the title role for Marie Van
        Zandt of Brooklyn.

1900   Salvatore Baccaloni, Italian bass, is born in Rome.

1906   Hunter Johnson, American composer, is born in Benson,
        North Carolina.

1919   Karel Berman, Czech baritone, is born in Jindrechův.

1933   Morton Subotnick, American composer employing multimedia
        in his works, is born in Los Angeles.

1958   Katherine Goodson dies in London, aged eighty-five.

1967   Krzysztof Penderecki's oratorio Dies Irae, for soli, chorus,
        and orchestra, is first performed, in Krakow.

1972   Paul Chihara's Grass, a concerto for double bass and orches-
        tra, has its premiere, at Oberlin College, Ohio.

        Roger Sessions's Concertino for Chamber Orchestra, is given
        its premiere in Chicago.

1975   Jean Paul Morel dies in New York City, aged seventy-two.

1977   Leon Kirchner's opera Lily (after Saul Bellow's novel Hender-
        son, the Rain King) is first staged in New York City.

        APRIL 15

1688   Johann Friedrich Fasch, German composer and court Kapell-
        meister, a contemporary of J. S. Bach, is born in Buttelstadt.

1738   George Frideric Handel's only comic opera, Serse, has its
        premiere at the Haymarket Theatre in London.

1894/5 Bessie Smith, American blues singer, is born in Chattanooga,
        Tennessee (possibly 1898 birth year). She is known as
        "Empress of the Blues."

1904   Frances Alda makes her opera debut in Massenet's Manon
        at the Opéra-Comique in Paris.

1911   Yuri Arbatsky, Russian music scholar, is born in Moscow.
        He was a consultant with the Newberry Library in Chicago.

1915   Manuel de Falla's ballet El Amor brujo is first staged, in
        Madrid.

1924   Neville Marriner, English conductor and violinist, is born in
        Lincoln. Founder of the Los Angeles Chamber Orchestra, he
        was earlier founder-conductor of the Academy of St. Martin-
        in-the-Fields in London.

1925   Juan Oncina, Spanish tenor, is born in Barcelona.

1926   Douglas Moore's opera Pageant of P. T. Barnum is first per-
        formed, in Cleveland, Ohio.

1927   Frederick Shepherd Converse's orchestral fantasy <u>Flivver Ten
       Million,</u> noting the ten millionth Ford car produced, has its
       premiere, in Boston.

1929   Renato Cioni, Italian tenor, is born in Portaferraio.

1931   Aaron Copland's prize-winning <u>A Dance Symphony</u> is first
       played by the Philadelphia Orchestra, Leopold Stokowski
       conducting.

1936   Hector Quintanar, Mexican composer and conductor, is born
       in Mexico City.

1976   William Schuman's <u>Concerto on Old English Rounds,</u> for viola,
       women's chorus, and orchestra, receives its first performance
       in New York City.

APRIL 16

1735   George Frideric Handel's opera <u>Alcina</u> is first staged at
       Covent Garden Theatre, London.

1849   Giacomo Meyerbeer's opera <u>Le Prophète</u> has its premiere
       at the Paris Opéra and stars Pauline Viardot-García.

1858   Johann Baptist Cramer dies in London at eighty-seven.

1882   Seth Bingham, American organist, composer, and teacher,
       is born in Bloomfield, New Jersey.

1887   Alice Ehlers, Austrian harpsichordist, is born in Vienna.

1893   Federico Mompou, Spanish composer, principally for piano,
       is born in Barcelona.

1897   Milton J. Cross, American radio announcer for the Metro-
       politan Opera broadcasts for many years, is born in New
       York City.

1924   Henry Mancini, American award-winning composer for films
       and television series, is born in Cleveland, Ohio.

1926   Marie Collier, Australian soprano, is born in Ballarat.

1942   Samuel Barber's <u>Essay no. 2,</u> for orchestra, has its pre-
       miere, in New York City.

1945   Leo Sowerby's Pulitzer Prize-winning <u>Canticle of the Sun,</u> for
       chorus and orchestra, is first performed, in New York City.

1956   Vincent Persichetti's Symphony no. 6, for band, receives its premiere, in St. Louis.

1973   István Kertész dies by drowning as he was swimming in the Mediterranean off the Israeli coast.   He was forty-three.

APRIL 17

1683   Johann David Heinichen, German composer and theorist, is born in Krüssuln.

1741   Johann Gottlieb Naumann, German composer, is born in Blasewitz.

1774   Jan Václav Tomásek, Czech organist, composer and teacher, is born at Skutsch.

1837   Louis-Gilbert Duprez makes his opera debut in Rossini's William Tell in Paris at the Opéra.

1882   Artur Schnabel, Austrian pianist and teacher, a pupil of Leschetizky, is born in Lipnik.

1897   Harald Saeverud, Norwegian composer, is born in Bergen.

1900   Willy Burkhard, Swiss composer, is born in Evillard sur Bienne.

1903   Gregor Piatigorsky, Russian-born American cellist and collaborator in a trio with Jascha Heifetz and Leonard Pennario, is born in Ekaterinoslav.

1914   Janine Micheau, French soprano, is born in Toulouse.

1923   Gianni Raimondi, Italian tenor, is born in Bologna.

1932   Graziella Sciutti, Italian soprano, is born in Turin.

1942   Alfred Hertz dies in San Francisco, aged sixty-nine.

1971   Pierre Luboschutz dies in Rockport, Maine, aged seventy-nine.

1973   Emanuel Balaban dies in New York City, aged seventy-eight.

1974   Herbert Elwell dies in Cleveland, Ohio, at age seventy-five.

APRIL 18

1605   Giacomo Carissimi, Italian composer who contributed to the development of the sacred oratorio, is baptized in Marino.

1777   Ludwig Berger, German piano teacher and composer (Felix Mendelssohn a pupil), is born in Berlin.

1800   Ludwig van Beethoven accompanies Wenzel Punto, horn player, in Beethoven's Sonata for Piano and Horn in its first hearing, in Vienna.

1819   Franz von Suppé, Austrian light-opera composer, is born in Spalato, Dalmatia.

1873   Jean-Jules Aimable Roger-Ducasse, French composer, is born in Bordeaux.

1882   Leopold Stokowski, English-born American conductor, whose introduction of contemporary works and orchestral transcriptions of Bach's organ works in orchestral programs stirred controversy, is born in London.

1888   Frida Leider, German opera soprano, is born in Berlin.

1898   Ernest Chausson's Symphony receives its premiere performance, in Paris.

1907   Miklós Rózsa, Hungarian-born American composer (including film scores) and teacher, is born in Budapest.

1913   Kent Kennan, American composer, teacher, and author of music textbooks, is born in Milwaukee.

1932   Nadezda Kniplova, Czech soprano, is born in Ostrava.

1934   George Shirley, American tenor, is born in Indianapolis.

1936   Ottorino Respighi dies in Rome, aged fifty-six.

1944   Leonard Bernstein's ballet Fancy Free is performed by the Ballet Theater at its premiere at the Metropolitan Opera.

1958   Easley Blackwood's prize-winning Symphony no. 1 receives its first hearing, in Boston.

        Quincy Porter's symphonic suite New England Episodes receives its premiere, in Washington.

1966   Joseph Maddy dies in Traverse City, Michigan, at age seventy-four. It is near the National Music Camp. which he founded in Interlochen.

1973   Willie "The Lion" Smith dies in New York City, aged seventy-five.

APRIL 19

1774   Christoph Willibald Gluck's opera Iphigénie en Aulide, adapted from Racine, is first staged at the Paris Opéra with the Dauphine Marie Antoinette attending.

1805   Charles Coussemaker, French musicologist, editor of the complete works of Adam de la Halle, and jurist, is born in Bailleul.

1876   Samuel Sebastian Wesley dies in Gloucester, England, at age sixty-five.

1882   Karl Wilson Gehrkens, American music educator, is born at Kelley's Island, Ohio; he was professor of school music at Oberlin Conservatory.

1892   Germaine Tailleferre, the only woman in the French group of composers known as "Les Six," is born in Pau-St.-Maur.

1916   William Presser, American composer and teacher, is born in Saginaw, Michigan.

1919   Barbara Marchisio dies at Mira, Italy, at age eighty-five.

1921   Will Ogdon, American composer and teacher, is born in Redlands, California.

1924   Hertha Topper, Austrian contralto, is born in Graz.

1936   Alban Berg's Violin Concerto (subtitled "Requiem for Manon" and dedicated to "the memory of an angel," the eighteen-year-old deceased Manon Gropius, granddaughter of Gustav Mahler), is given its premiere, in Barcelona with Louis Krasner, soloist.

1947   Murray Perahia, American pianist, is born in New York City.

1959   Ned Rorem's Symphony no. 3 is first performed, in New York City.

1974   Felix Labunski's Primavera has its premiere, in Cincinnati.

APRIL 20

1643   Christoph Demantius dies in Freiberg, Germany, aged seventy-five.

1814   Theodor Döhler, Italian pianist and composer, is born in Naples. He was a piano student of Czerny.

1869   Karl Loewe dies in Kiel, Germany, aged seventy-two.

1879   Henry Cope Colles, English music scholar, is born in Bridgnorth.

1881   Nikolai Miaskovsky, Russian composer (a pupil of Rimsky-Korsakov) and teacher, is born in Novogeorgievsk.

1934   Claude Calès, French baritone, is born in Villeneuve.

1954   Jean-Michel Damase makes his American debut in New York City as pianist-composer.

1978   Aurelio de la Vega's Adios, written for Zubin Mehta's farewell to the Los Angeles Philharmonic Orchestra, is first heard there, Mehta conducting.

APRIL 21

1889   Efrem Zimbalist, Russian-American violinist (a pupil of Leopold Auer), teacher, and head of the Curtis Institute, is born at Rostov-on-the-Don.

1899   Randall Thompson, American composer, music administrator, and Harvard University professor, is born in New York City.

1907   Antoni Szalowski, Polish composer, is born in Warsaw.

1911   Leonard Warren, American baritone, is born in New York City.

1916   Eldon Rathburn, Canadian composer and staff composer for the National Film Board of Canada, is born in Queenstown, New Brunswick.

1918   Sergei Prokofiev conducts his Classical Symphony in its premiere, in St. Petersburg.

1920   Bruno Maderna, Italian-born German conductor and composer, is born in Venice.

1923   Arthur Custer, American composer and teacher who served
        with the United States Information Agency in Madrid (1960-
        62), is born in Manchester, Connecticut.

1924   Vincent Youmans's musical No, No, Nanette opens in Detroit.

1925   Harold Blackburn, Scottish bass, is born in Hamilton.

1933   Easley Blackwood, American composer and pianist, is born
        in Indianapolis.

1939   Alan Rawsthorne's Symphonic Studies receives its first per-
        formance in Warsaw at the International Society for Contempo-
        rary Music Festival.

1951   Olive Fremstad dies at age eighty at Irvington-on-Hudson,
        New York. She served as the model for Willa Cather's
        heroine of The Song of the Lark.

1958   Manuel Infante dies in Paris, aged seventy-four.

1961   James Melton dies in New York City at age fifty-seven.

1973   Sir Arthur Bliss's Variations, for orchestra, receives its
        premiere in London, Leopold Stokowski conducting.

        APRIL 22

1658   Giuseppe Torelli, Italian violinist and composer, is born in
        Verona.

1723   Johann Sebastian Bach is elected cantor of St. Thomas Church
        in Leipzig.

1858   Dame Ethel Smyth, English composer and woman suffragist,
        is born in Rectory.

1892   Edouard Lalo dies in Paris at sixty-nine.

1912   Paul Dukas's ballet La Péri is first staged, in Paris.

        Kathleen Ferrier, English contralto, is born in Higher Walton.

        Miguel Querol Gavaldá, Spanish musicologist, is born in
        Ulldecona.

1916   Yehudi Menuhin, violin virtuoso, is born in New York City.

1922   Geraldine Farrar makes her last Metropolitan Opera appearance,
        singing in Leoncavallo's Zaza.

Charles Mingus, American jazz bassist and composer, is born in Nogales, Arizona.

1925   André Caplet dies in Paris at forty-six.

1932   Michael Colgrass, American composer and percussionist, is born in Chicago. His _Déjà vu_, concerto for four percussionists and orchestra, won the 1978 Pulitzer Prize.

James Melton makes his concert debut in New York City.

1935   Fiorenza Cossotto, Italian contralto, is born in Crescentino.

1944   Harry Partch's 8 Hitchhiker Inscriptions from a Highway Railing is first performed, in New York's Carnegie Chamber Hall.

Joshua Rifkin, American pianist, conductor, composer, and musicologist, is born in New York City.

1958   Andrew Imbrie's Violin Concerto premieres in San Francisco.

1961   Alberto Ginastera's Piano Concerto no. 1 is given its first performance, in Washington.

1962   Solomon Pimsleur dies in New York City, aged sixty-one.

1969   Peter Maxwell Davies's Eight Songs for a Mad King (George III), for voice and instruments, premieres, in London.

APRIL 23

1627   Heinrich Schütz's opera _Dafne_ is produced at Hartenfels Castle for the wedding of Princess Sophia of Saxony. Although the music is lost, it marks the beginning of German opera.

1691   Jean Henri d'Anglebert, French composer and clavecin player, dies in Paris, aged about sixty-three.

1857   Ruggiero Leoncavallo, Italian opera composer, is born in Naples.

1872   Arthur Farwell, American composer and teacher, founder of the Wa-Wan Press for publishing American music, is born in St. Paul, Minnesota.

1882   Albert Coates, English conductor, is born in St. Petersburg, Russia.

1891   Sergei Prokofiev, Soviet composer whose style of composition occasioned severe criticism from Soviet officials, is born in Sontsovka.

1900 Henri Barraud, French composer and former director of Radiodiffusion Télévision Française, is born in Bordeaux.

1904 George Whitefield Chadwick's concert overture Euterpe is performed by the Boston Symphony Orchestra.

1910 Alfred Casella conducts his rhapsody Italia, based on folk themes, in its premiere, in Paris.

1914 Olive Fremstad makes her final appearance at the Metropolitan Opera in New York City.

1919 Bülent Arel, Turkish-born composer, radio sound engineer and teacher of electronic music in the United States, is born in Istanbul.

1922 Edgard Varèse's Offrandes, for voice and small orchestra, is given its premiere in New York City, Carlos Salzedo conducting.

1924 Arthur Frackenpohl, American composer and teacher, is born in Irvington, New Jersey.

1927 Russell Smith, American composer (including film and television scores), is born in Tuscaloosa, Alabama.

1939 Charles Haubiel's Miniatures, for string orchestra, is first performed, in New York City.

1941 Judith Blegen, American soprano, is born in Missoula, Montana.

1948 André Jolivet's Concerto for Ondes Martenot and Orchestra is first performed, in Vienna.

1952 Elisabeth Schumann dies in New York City, aged sixty-six.

1958 Robert Kurka's opera The Good Soldier Schweik (from Jaroslav Hasek) is first staged posthumously in New York City Center.

APRIL 24

1706 Giovanni Battista Martini, Italian composer and teacher, a Franciscan priest who collected a large music library, is born in Bologna.

1721 Johann Philipp Kirnberger, German music theorist and teacher and a violinist to Frederick the Great, is born in Saalfeld.

1801   (Franz) Joseph Haydn's oratorio <u>The Seasons</u> (German text by Gottfried van Swieten after James Thomson) is first performed, in Vienna.

1846   Girolamo Crescentini dies in Naples, aged eighty-four.

1897   György Kósa, Hungarian composer, pianist, and teacher, is born in Budapest.

1913   Violet Archer, Canadian composer and pianist, teacher of composition at the University of Alberta, is born in Montreal.

1919   Camille Erlanger dies in Paris, aged fifty-five.

1941   John Williams, concert guitarist, is born in Australia.

1944   Norma Burrows, Irish soprano, is born in Bangor.

1945   Hubert Bath dies in Harefield, England, at sixty-one.

1948   Manuel Ponce dies in Mexico City, aged sixty-five.

1952   Salvatore Martirano's chamber opera <u>The Magic Stones</u> is first staged, at Oberlin College, Ohio.

1977   Alexander Semmler dies in Kingston, New York, aged seventy-six.

APRIL 25

1841   Pauline Lucca, Austrian soprano, is born in Vienna.

1881   Gilbert and Sullivan's operetta <u>Patience</u> is first staged, in London.

1906   John Knowles Paine dies in Cambridge, Massachusetts, aged sixty-seven.

1918   Ella Fitzgerald, American jazz singer, is born in Newport News, Virginia.

        Astrid Varnay, Swedish-American soprano, is born in Stockholm.

1922   John Bavicchi, American composer, conductor, and teacher, is born in Boston.

1926   Giacomo Puccini's last opera, <u>Turandot</u> (the last scene completed by Franco Alfano), is produced posthumously at La Scala in Milan.

1927   Robert Boudreau, American conductor and trumpeter, is
       born in Bellingham, Massachusetts. He organized the Ameri-
       can Wind Symphony Orchestra in Pittsburgh to perform con-
       temporary music.

       Siegfried Palm, German cellist, is born in Barmen.

1929   Albert Roussel's Psalm 80, for tenor, chorus, and orchestra,
       has its premiere, in Paris.

1951   Jerzy Fitelberg dies in New York City, aged forty-seven.

1959   David Mannes dies in New York at age ninety-three. Three
       years earlier, on his ninetieth birthday, a celebration was
       held at the Metropolitan Museum in his honor.

1976   Alexander Brailowsky dies in New York City, aged eighty.

1979   Leopold Ludwig dies in Lüneberg, aged seventy-one.

       APRIL 26

1812   Friedrich von Flotow, German opera composer, is born in
       Teutendorf.

1899   Jan Sibelius's Symphony no. 1 receives its premiere, in
       Helsinki.

1900   Joseph Fuchs, American violinist and concertmaster of the
       Cleveland Symphony Orchestra (1926-40), is born in New
       York City.

1925   Wilma Lipp, Austrian soprano, is born in Vienna.

1935   Victor Ewald dies in Leningrad, aged seventy-four.

1951   John Alden Carpenter dies in Chicago at age seventy-five.

1959   John Cage's Fontana Mix, which uses ten transparent sheets
       superimposed variously, is first performed, in New York
       City.

1965   Aaron Avshalomov dies in New York City, aged seventy.

       Charles Ives's Symphony no. 4 is performed posthumously
       in its entirety for the first time, in New York City. Three
       conductors take part: Leopold Stokowski, José Serebrier,
       and David Katz, leading the American Symphony Orchestra
       and members of the Schola Cantorum.

1967   James Pease dies in New York City, aged fifty-one.

        APRIL 27

1867   Charles Gounod's opera <u>Roméo et Juliette</u> opens in Paris at
        the Théâtre-Lyrique, starring Marie Miolan-Carvalho.

1871   Sigismond Thalberg dies in Posillipo, Italy, at age fifty-nine.

1894   Nicolas Slonimsky, Russian-American musicologist and music
        lexicographer, is born in St. Petersburg.

1915   Alexander Scriabin dies in Moscow, aged forty-three.

1927   Jaromir Weinberger's opera <u>Schwanda, the Bagpiper</u> has its
        premiere at the Czech Opera in Prague.

1928   Igor Stravinsky's ballet <u>Apollo</u> (<u>Apollon musagète</u>) receives
        its first performance, in Washington.

1931   Igor Oistrakh, Soviet violinist, son of David Oistrakh, is
        born in Odessa.

1937   Igor Stravinsky conducts his ballet <u>Jeu de cartes</u> at its initial
        performance by the American Ballet at the Metropolitan Opera
        House in New York City.

1942   Emil von Sauer dies in Vienna, aged seventy-nine.

1944   Douglas Moore's <u>In Memoriam</u> is given its premiere, in
        Rochester, New York.

        Gardner Read's tone poem <u>Night Flight</u> has its first hearing,
        in Rochester, New York.

1952   Alexei Haieff's award-winning Piano Concerto is first per-
        formed in New York City with Leo Smit, soloist; Leopold
        Stokowski conducting.

1954   Torsten Ralf dies in Stockholm at fifty-three.

1971   Lowell Cross's <u>Lunar Laser Beam</u> is supposedly broadcast
        via Leningrad, the moon, and Los Angeles in honor of Nico-
        las Slonimsky's seventy-seventh birthday.

1977   Henry Brant's <u>Long Life,</u> for a cappella chorus, is first
        sung for Nicolas Slonimsky's birthday.

APRIL 28

1865   Giacomo Meyerbeer's final opera, L'Africaine, receives its
        premiere posthumously at the Opéra in Paris.

1871   Louise Homer, American operatic contralto, aunt of composer
        Samuel Barber, is born in Pittsburgh.

1873   Harold Bauer, English-born concert pianist who began his
        musical career as a concert violinist, is born in Kingston-
        on-Thames.

1892   John Jacob Niles, American folksinger and collector of south-
        ern Appalachian folksongs, is born in Louisville, Kentucky.

1920   Nan Merriman, American contralto, is born in Pittsburgh.

1938   David Diamond's Elegy in Memory of Maurice Ravel, for
        brass, harp and percussion, is first performed, in Rochester,
        New York.

1940   Luisa Tettrazzini dies in Milan, aged sixty-eight.

1942   Giulia Barrera, American contralto, is born in Brooklyn.

1957   Glenn Gould makes his European debut, performing with the
        Berlin Philharmonic, Herbert von Karajan conducting.

1962   Arthur Custer's Sinfonia de Madrid receives its premiere in
        Madrid.

1964   Donald Keats's Elegiac Symphony is given its premiere, in
        Kansas City, Missouri.

1966   Douglas Moore's opera Carrie Nation, about the famed
        temperance worker, is first staged, in Lawrence, Kansas.

APRIL 29

1798   (Franz) Joseph Haydn's oratorio The Creation is first per-
        formed at Schwarzenberg Palace, Vienna, in a private read-
        ing for the Austrian aristocracy. The first public performance
        takes place on March 19, 1799 (Haydn's nameday).

1800   Johann Christian Fischer, German oboist and composer, dies
        in London, aged about sixty-seven.

1879   Sir Thomas Beecham, English conductor, is born in St.
        Helens.

1885   Wallingford Riegger, American composer and conductor, is born in Albany, Georgia.

1895   Sir Malcolm Sargent, English conductor, is born in Ashford.

1899   Duke Ellington (né Edward Kennedy Ellington), American jazz pianist, composer, and bandleader, is born in Washington.

1902   Theodore Chanler, American composer, is born in Newport, Rhode Island.

1906   Victor Herbert conducts a benefit concert at the Hippodrome in New York City for San Francisco earthquake victims.

1920   Harold Shapero, American composer, is born in Lynn, Massachusetts.

1922   "Toots" Thielemans, Belgian jazz guitarist, harmonica player, and composer of television's Sesame Street theme music, is born in Brussels.

1929   Václav Kučera, Czech composer whose works mirror his political bent, is born in Prague.

        Peter Sculthorpe, Australian composer whose works contain influences of Indonesian and Australian aborigines, is born in Launceston.

1930   Claus Ogerman, German jazz musician, is born in Ratibor.

1936   Zubin Mehta, Indian-born conductor, appointed in 1961 to the Los Angeles Philharmonic Orchestra and to the New York Philharmonic Orchestra in 1978, is born in Bombay.

1938   Kenneth Riegel, American tenor, is born in Womelsdorf, Pennsylvania.

1969   Duke Ellington receives the Presidential Medal of Freedom on his seventieth birthday at the White House.

        Julius Katchen dies in Paris, aged forty-two.

1972   Manfred Gurlitt dies in Tokyo, aged eighty-one.

APRIL 30

1870   Franz Lehár, Hungarian composer of operettas, is born in Komorn.

1892   Norbert Sprongl, Austrian composer, is born in Obermarkersdorf.

1902   Claude Debussy's only opera, <u>Pélleas et Mélisande</u>, is first
        staged at the Opéra-Comique in Paris, starring Mary Garden
        as Mélisande.

1916   Robert Shaw, American choral and orchestral conductor,
        founder of the Robert Shaw Chorale, is born in Red Bluff,
        Iowa.

1927   Henri Sauguet's ballet <u>La Chatte</u> has its premiere, in Monte
        Carlo.

1960   Giorgio Polacco dies in New York City, aged eighty-seven.

1972   Vinko Globokar's <u>Discours II,</u> for trombone and tape, has
        its premiere in Buffalo, New York.

MAY 1

1582   Marco da Gagliano, Italian opera composer, is born in Gagliano.

1602   William Lawes, English composer, is baptized at Salisbury.
       In 1645 he is killed by a stray shot in the seige of Chester.

1761   (Franz) Joseph Haydn enters the service of Prince Esterházy
       as Kapellmeister, in Eisenstadt, Austria.   It begins an as-
       sociation lasting some thirty years.

1786   Wolfgang Amadeus Mozart's opera buffa The Marriage of
       Figaro is first staged in the Burgtheater, Vienna.

1872   Hugo Alfvén, Swedish composer, violinist, and choral con-
       ductor, is born in Stockholm.

1886   César Franck's Symphonic Variations, for piano and orchestra,
       receives its premiere, in Paris.

1899   Jón Leifs, Icelandic composer, conductor, and music director
       of Icelandic Radio, is born in Sólheimar.

1895   Leo Sowerby, American organist, composer, and teacher, is
       born in Grand Rapids, Michigan.

1903   Luigi Arditi dies at Hove, England, aged eighty.

1904   Antonin Dvořák dies in Prague at age sixty-two.   A national
       day of mourning is declared for his funeral (May 4).

1909   Sergei Rachmaninoff conducts his symphonic poem Isle of the
       Dead at its premiere, in Moscow.

1913   Walter Susskind, Czech-born American pianist and conductor,
       is born in Prague.   In 1978 he was guest conductor of the
       Cincinnati Symphony Orchestra.

1924   Earl George, American pianist and composer, is born in
       Milwaukee.

1937   Bo Nilsson, Swedish composer, largely self-taught, is born
        in Skellefteaa.

1942   William Bergsma's ballet Señor Commandante has its first
        hearing, in Rochester, New York.

1964   Pierre Boulez makes his conducting debut in New York City.

1971   Thomas Beversdorf's Vision of Christ, a mystery play, is
        first performed, at Bucknell University, Lewisburg, Pennsyl-
        vania.

        Dave Brubeck's oratorio Truth Has Fallen has its premiere
        at the opening of the Center for Arts, Midland, Michigan.

1978   Aram Khachaturian dies in Moscow, aged seventy-four.

1980   John Jacob Niles dies at his home near Lexington, Kentucky,
        at the age of eighty-eight. He accompanied his singing on
        a dulcimer.

MAY 2

1627   Lodovico da Viadana, Italian composer and chapel master at
        Mantua Cathedral, a Franciscan monk, dies at Gualtieri, aged
        about sixty-seven.

1660   Allesandro Scarlatti, Italian opera composer, is born at
        Palermo. He is regarded as founder of the Neapolitan School
        of music of the eighteenth century. Domenico Scarlatti is
        his son.

1843   Karl Ziehrer, Austrian operetta composer and bandleader, is
        born in Vienna.

1864   Giacomo Meyerbeer dies in Paris, aged seventy-two. He
        was in charge of the rehearsals for his last opera, L'Africaine,
        at the time of his death.

1903   Oivin Fjelstad, violinist and conductor, is born in Norway.

1905   Alan Rawsthorne, English composer and teacher, is born in
        Haslingden.

1915   Jan Hanuš, Czech composer, is born in Prague. He has
        assisted in preparing the complete critical edition of Dvořák's
        collected works.

1920   Jacob Gilboa, Czech-born Israeli composer, is born in Košice.

1935   Jacques Ibert's <u>Concertino da Camera,</u> for saxophone and chamber orchestra, receives its first performance, in Paris.

1936   Sergei Prokofiev's symphonic fairy tale <u>Peter and the Wolf</u> has its premiere at a children's concert, in Moscow.

Michael Rabin, American violinist, is born in New York City into a musical family.

1948   Jeannine Altmeyer, American soprano, is born in Pasadena, California.

1951   Ulysses Kay's <u>Sinfonia in E</u> is given its first hearing, in Rochester, New York.

1955   Dietrich Fischer-Dieskau makes his American debut in a song recital in New York City.

1965   William Bolcom's <u>Oracle,</u> for orchestra, receives its premiere, in Seattle.

MAY 3

1704   Heinrich von Biber dies in Salzburg at age fifty-nine.   He was influential in founding the German school of violin playing.

1729   Florian Leopold Gassmann, Austrian composer, is born in Brüx.

1794   (Franz) Joseph Haydn's "Clock Symphony" has its premiere at London's Haymarket Theatre.   The second movement's rhythmic tick-tock provides its nickname; it is one of the Salomon Symphonies.

1831   Louis Joseph F. Herold's opera <u>Zampa</u> is first staged at the Opéra-Comique, Paris.

1844   Richard D'Oyly Carte, English impressario (owner of the Savoy Theatre) associated with the Gilbert and Sullivan comic operas, is born in London.

1856   Adolphe-Charles Adam dies in Paris, aged fifty-two.   Known as a creator of French comic operas, he is now remembered for his song <u>Cantique de Noël.</u>

Max Alvary, German tenor, is born in Düsseldorf.

1867   Fanny Persiani dies at Neuilly-sur-Seine, aged fifty-four.

1886   Marcel Dupré, French organist and composer, known for his improvisations, is born in Rouen.

1893   Horatio Parker's oratorio <u>Hora Novissima</u> receives its premiere in New York City.

1912   Virgil Fox, American organist, is born in Princeton, Illinois.

1914   Robert W. Ottman, American music theorist and professor, is born in Fulton, New York. His theory textbooks are widely used.

1917   Ernest Bloch conducts his <u>Israel Symphony</u> and <u>Schelomo,</u> a rhapsody for cello and orchestra, in their premieres, in New York City with Hans Kindler, cello soloist.

1918   Léopold Simoneau, Canadian tenor, is born in Quebec City.

1919   Pete Seeger, American folksinger and songbook compiler, is born in New York City. He is son of ethnomusicologist Charles Seeger and nephew of poet Alan Seeger.

1920   John Lewis, American jazz pianist and composer, is born in LaGrange, Illinois. He formed and led the Modern Jazz Quartet with Milt Jackson, Percy Heath, and Kenny Clarke in 1952.

1929   Francis Poulenc's <u>Concert champêtre</u>, for harpsichord and chamber orchestra, is first heard in Paris with Wanda Landowska (who commissioned the work) as soloist.

1934   Burrill Phillips's <u>Selections from McGuffey's Reader</u> receives its premiere, in Rochester, New York.

       Bernard Rogers's <u>Three Japanese Dances</u> is first performed, in Rochester, New York.

1952   Ralph Vaughan Williams's <u>Romance,</u> for harmonica and orchestra, has its first hearing, in New York City.

1955   Juan Orrego-Salas's <u>Serenata Concertante</u> is first performed, in Louisville, Kentucky.

1967   Evelyn Lear makes her New York debut in a song recital at Philharmonic Hall.

MAY 4

1604   Claudio Merulo dies in Parma, Italy, aged seventy-one; the last eighteen years of his life were spent as court organist there.

1655   Bartolommeo Cristofori, Italian harpsichord maker, credited
        with inventing the piano, is born in Padua.

1855   Camille Pleyel dies in Paris, aged sixty-six, after more than
        thirty years in the piano-manufacturing firm founded by his
        father.

1860   Emil Nikolaus von Reznicek, Austrian composer, conductor,
        and music professor, is born in Vienna.

1890   Raul Rosenfeld, American music critic, is born in New York
        City.

1891   Frederick Jacobi, American composer who often used American
        Indian themes, is born in San Francisco.

1905   Mátyás Seiber, Hungarian-English composer, is born in Buda-
        pest.

1920   Ralph Vaughan Williams's Symphony no. 2, "A London Sym-
        phony" (revised version), is conducted in its premiere by
        Albert Coates in Queens Hall, London.

1921   John Van Kesteren, Dutch tenor and former electrical engi-
        neer, is born in The Hague.

1928   Maynard Ferguson, Canadian-American jazz trumpeter and
        bandleader, is born in Verdun, Quebec.

1930   Roberta Peters, American soprano, is born in New York City.

1931   Gennady Rozhdestvensky, Soviet conductor, is born in Moscow.

1953   Thomas Tertius Noble dies in Rockport, Massachusetts, the
        day before his eighty-sixth birthday.

1955   Georges Enesco dies in Paris at age seventy-three following
        a stroke the preceding July. In his honor his native Rumanian
        village was renamed Enescu.

        MAY 5

1726   George Frideric Handel's opera <u>Alessandro</u> is first staged,
        at London's King's Theatre.

1819   Stanislaw Moniuszko, Polish composer and church organist
        (in Vilna), is born in Ubiel, Minsk province of Russia.

1867   Thomas Tertius Noble, English-American organist and com-
        poser (principally religious works), is born in Bath.

1869   Hans Pfitzner, German composer, is born in Moscow of
        German parents.

1891   Carnegie Hall first opens in New York City with a week of
        concerts; Peter Ilyitch Tchaikovsky is guest conductor of four
        of the programs.

1900   Hans Schmidt-Isserstedt, German conductor, is born in Ber-
        lin.

1906   Maria Caniglia, Italian soprano, is born in Naples.

1907   Yoritsuné Matsudaira, Japanese composer, is born in Tokyo.

1908   Kurt Böhme, German bass, is born in Dresden.

1913   Grazyna Bacewicz, Polish composer and violinist, is born
        in Lodz.

1917   Claude Debussy in his last public appearance provides the
        piano accompaniment in his Violin Sonata in its premiere
        performance, Gaston Poulet, violinist.

1924   Alexandre Tansman's Danse de la soucière is first performed,
        in Brussels.

1941   Sir Benjamin Britten's first opera, Paul Bunyan, is first
        sung in New York City at Columbia University; the text is
        by W. H. Auden.

1946   Douglas Moore's Symphony in A receives its premiere, in
        Paris.

1953   Frank LaForge dies while playing the piano at a dinner given
        by the Musicians Club in New York City. He is seventy-three.

1971   Halim El-Dabh's Opera Flies, commemorating the May 4,
        1970, Kent State University shootings, has its premiere, in
        Washington.

1977   George Crumb's Star Child is first performed by the New
        York Philharmonic Orchestra and requires four conductors,
        orchestra, soprano solo, children's chorus, percussion en-
        semble, and carillon of bell ringers; Pierre Boulez is general
        director.

MAY 6

1714   Anton Raaff, German singer, a friend of Mozart, is born in
        Gelsdorf.

1796   Ludwig van Beethoven is lauded by August von Schall in a
        letter he sends from Dresden to the Elector Maximilian Franz:
        "Beethoven was here for about eight days. Everyone who
        heard him play on the clavier was delighted.... His Electoral
        Highness ... presented him with a gold snuff box."

1814   Heinrich Wilhelm Ernst, Czech violinist and composer, is
        born in Brünn.

1871   Leopold Damrosch makes his American debut in New York
        City as conductor of the Männergesangverein Arion, a Ger-
        man men's choir.

1892   Ernest Guiraud dies in Paris at fifty-four.

1898   Jascha Horenstein, Russian conductor, is born in Kiev.

1915   George Perle, American composer and writer on music theory,
        is born in Bayonne, New Jersey.

1932   Konrad Ragossnig, Austrian lutenist and guitarist, is born
        in Klagenfurt.

1936   Hans Jelmoli dies in Zurich, aged fifty-nine.

1944   Carl Engel dies in New York City, aged sixty.

1947   Louise Homer dies in Winter Park, Florida, at the age of
        seventy-six.

        MAY 7

1667   Johann Jakob Froberger dies in Héricourt, France, aged
        fifty. He was serving the Duchess Sybille of Württemberg
        in his last years.

1704   Karl Heinrich Graun, German composer of Italian-style
        operas, brother of Johann Gottlieb Graun, is born in Wahren-
        brück.

1747   Johann Sebastian Bach, with his son Wilhelm Friedemann,
        visits King Frederick II of Prussia, the visit resulting in his
        Musikalische Opfer ("Musical Offering").

1793   Pietro Nardini dies in Florence, aged seventy-one.

1800   Niccolò Piccinni dies in Paris, aged seventy-two.

1824   Ludwig van Beethoven's Symphony no. 9, "Choral," is first
        performed, in Vienna's Kärntnerthor Theater, Michael Umlauf

conducting. Deaf for many years, Beethoven was still turning pages after the end of the performance, so a chorus member turned him to the audience to receive the applause.

1825　Antonio Salieri dies in Vienna at the age of seventy-four.

1833　Johannes Brahms, German composer, a friend of Robert and Clara Schumann, is born in Hamburg.

1836　Norbert Burgmüller dies in Aachen, Germany, at age twenty-six, mourned by musicians as another Schubert.

Euphrosyne Parepa-Rosa, English soprano, is born in Edinburgh.

1840　Peter Ilyitch Tchaikovsky, Russian composer, is born in Votkinsk. Unconsciously nationalistic, he was a symbol of Western romanticism in the Russian setting.

1850　Anton Seidl, Hungarian conductor who assisted Richard Wagner in preparing the Ring tetralogy, is born in Budapest.

1888　Edouard Lalo's opera Le Roi d'Ys opens at the Opéra-Comique in Paris.

1901　Marcel Poot, Belgian composer, teacher, and administrator at Brussels Conservatory, is born in Vilvorde.

1927　Elisabeth Söderström, Swedish soprano, is born in Stockholm.

1931　Helge Brilioth, Swedish tenor, is born in Lund.

1936　Cornelius Cardew, avant-garde English composer who assisted Karlheinz Stockhausen (1958-60), is born in Gloucester.

1942　Felix Weingartner dies in Winterthur, Switzerland, aged seventy-eight.

1945　Frank Martin's oratorio In Terra Pax, for soli, double chorus, and orchestra, written for Radio Geneva for the end of World War II in Europe, is immediately broadcast.

1947　Virgil Thomson's opera The Mother of Us All, on the life of American suffragist Susan B. Anthony (to Gertrude Stein's libretto), is first staged, in New York City.

1965　Robert Evett's Symphony no. 2, "Billy Ascends," receives its first hearing, in Washington.

1970　Carlos Estrada dies in Montevideo, aged sixty.

1977　Gunnar Berg's Filandre, for flute, clarinet, and violin, is first performed, in Buffalo, New York.

MAY 8

1745   Karl Stamitz, German composer, son of Johann Wenzel Anton
        Stamitz, is baptized in Mannheim.

1829   Mauro Giuliani dies in Naples, aged forty-seven. Beethoven
        had written some guitar music for his performances.

        Louis Moreau Gottschalk, American pianist and composer
        (principally for piano), is born in New Orleans.

1846   Oscar Hammerstein, playwright and opera impressario, is
        born in Stettin, Germany.

1906   David Van Vactor, American composer, flutist, conductor,
        and teacher, is born in Plymouth, Indiana.

1924   Arthur Honegger's symphonic movement Pacific 231 (named
        for a locomotive) has its premiere in Paris, Koussevitzky
        conducting.

1928   William Sydeman, American composer, is born in New York
        City.

1930   Heather Harper, British soprano, is born in Belfast.

1932   Carlo Cossutta, Italian tenor, is born in Trieste.

1938   Igor Stravinsky's Concerto Dumbarton Oaks, for sixteen wind
        instruments, is first performed, in Washington.

1944   Dame Ethel Smyth dies in Woking, England, aged eighty-six.

1945   Keith Jarrett, American pianist and composer, is born in
        Allentown, Pennsylvania.

1946   Gian Carlo Menotti's opera The Medium, for which he wrote
        the libretto, is first staged, in New York City at Columbia
        University. It shared a double bill with his opera The Tele-
        phone in 1955 on a European tour under the State Department's
        auspices.

1960   Hugo Alfvén dies in Falun, Sweden, aged eighty-eight.

1970   Gunther Schuller's children's opera The Fisherman and His
        Wife, after Grimm's fairy tale, has its premiere in Boston.

MAY 9

1707   Dietrich Buxtehude, German organist and composer, dies in

Lübeck, aged about seventy.   In 1705 Johann Sebastian Bach
traveled on foot from Arnstadt to Lübeck (200 miles) to hear
Buxtehude play.

1740   Giovanni Paisiello, Italian opera composer, is born in Taranto.

1775   Vittoria Tesi dies in Vienna, aged seventy-five.

1791   Francis Hopkinson dies in Philadelphia at age fifty-three.
A book of his songs he dedicated to George Washington.

1799   Claude Balbastre, aged seventy-two, dies in Paris, where he
had been organist at Notre Dame.

1812   Gioacchino Rossini's opera La Scala di seta is first staged,
in Venice.

1814   Adolph von Henselt, German pianist, teacher, and composer
who spent forty years teaching in Russia, is born at Schwa-
bach.

1855   Julius Röntgen, German-Dutch composer, is born in Leipzig.

1868   Anton Bruckner conducts his Symphony no. 1 in its premiere,
in Linz, Austria.

1905   Ernst Pauer dies in Jugenheim, Germany, aged seventy-eight.
From 1866 to 1896 he was pianist to the Austrian court; his
son, Max Pauer, was his pupil.

1914   Carlo Maria Giulini, Italian conductor, is born in Barletta.
He studied under Arturo Toscanini; in 1978 he became director of the Los Angeles Philharmonic Orchestra.

1939   Bruce Mather, Canadian composer, pianist, and teacher, is
born in Toronto.

1950   Norman Dello Joio's opera The Triumph of Saint Joan is
first produced at Sarah Lawrence College, Bronxville, New
York.

1954   Thomas Beversdorf's Symphony no. 3, for winds and percussion, receives its premiere, in Bloomington, Indiana.

1957   Ezio Pinza dies in Stamford, Connecticut, at age sixty-four.

1965   Vladimir Horowitz returns to the concert stage in New York
City after a twelve-year absence amid tremendous acclaim.

1974   Paul Reif's The Curse of Mauvais-Air is given its first hearing, in New York City.

1976   Valentino Bucchi dies in Rome, aged fifty-nine.   Since 1969 he had been musical consultant for Radio Italiano.

1977   Harold Spivacke dies in Washington, aged seventy-two. For
thirty-five years he headed the music division of the Library
of Congress.

1979   Ben Weber dies in New York City, aged sixty-two.

MAY 10

1697   Jean Marie Leclair, French violinist, regarded as one of the
eighteenth century's finest violin composers, is born in Lyons.

1780   Angelica Catalani, Italian soprano, is born in Sinigaglia.

1855   Anatol Liadov, Russian composer and teacher, from a family
of professional musicians, is born in St. Petersburg.

1869   Wilhelm Bernhard Molique dies in Cannstadt, Germany, aged
sixty-six.   Famed as a violinist, he spent seventeen years
in London, settling there after a political crisis in Germany.

1876   Richard Wagner's Grosser Festmarsch, commissioned for
the Philadelphia Centennial Exposition, is performed there
for the opening.

1885   Ferdinand Hiller dies in Cologne, aged seventy-three.   He
was influenced by Mendelssohn, but very critical of Richard
Wagner.

1898   Herbert Elwell, American composer and music critic for
thirty-two years with the Cleveland Plain Dealer, is born in
Minneapolis.

1904   Hugo Alfvén's orchestral rhapsody Midsommarvaka (Midsummer Vigil) has its premiere, in Stockholm.

1914   Richard Lewis, English tenor, is born in Manchester.

Lillian Nordica dies in Batavia, Java, while on tour.   She
was fifty-six.

1916   Milton Babbitt, American composer and music theorist, who
has taught music theory and mathematics at Princeton University, is born in Philadelphia.

1919   Peter Maag, Swiss conductor, is born in St. Gallen.

1933   Selma Kurz dies in Vienna, aged fifty-eight.

1938   Philip Winsor, American composer and teacher, is born in
        Morris, Illinois.

1957   Dmitri Shostakovich's Piano Concerto no. 2 is performed in
        its premiere by his son, Maxim Shostakovich, in Moscow.

1973   Owen Brannigan dies in Newcastle, England, aged sixty-five.

1975   Karel Husa's Steadfast Tin Soldier, for narrator and orches-
        tra, receives its premiere performance in Boulder, Colorado.

MAY 11

1791   Jan Hugo Voříšek, Bohemian composer and pianist, is born
        in Wamberg. He was a friend of Schubert and of Beethoven.

1849   Otto Nicolai dies in Berlin, aged thirty-eight, two months
        after suffering a stroke.

1865   Ilma di Murska, Croatian soprano, makes her operatic debut
        in London, starring in Lucia di Lammermoor.

1869   Francisco Lacerda, Portuguese folksong collector, conductor,
        and composer, is born in the Azores.

1882   Joseph Marx, Austrian composer and teacher, is born in
        Graz. He spent three years in Turkey as an adviser for
        music education.

1884   Alma Gluck, American soprano whose second husband was
        Efrem Zimbalist, is born in Bucharest, Rumania.

1885   Joseph "King" Oliver, American jazz cornetist and bandleader,
        is born on a plantation in Louisiana. His nephew is com-
        poser Ulysses Kay.

1888   Irving Berlin, Russian-American composer of popular music,
        is born in Temun. He is perhaps best remembered for his
        song White Christmas.

1895   William Grant Still, known as the "Dean of Afro-American
        Composers," is born in Woodville, Mississippi.

1902   Bidú Sayão, Brazilian soprano, is born in Niteroi.

1913   Salvador Camarata, American conductor and composer, is
        born in Glen Ridge, New Jersey.

1916   Max Reger dies in Leipzig, at age forty-three, of a heart
        attack.

1938   Harvey Sollberger, American composer, flutist, and conductor, is born in Cedar Rapids, Iowa.

1941   Henry Cowell's <u>Tales of the Countryside</u>, for piano and orchestra, is first performed in Atlantic City, New Jersey.

1947   Ture Rangström dies in Stockholm, aged sixty-two.

1954   Mátyás Seiber's Concertino for Clarinet and Strings receives its premiere, in London.

1955   Sir Arthur Bliss's Violin Concerto premieres in London.

1966   Andrew Imbrie's Symphony no. 1 is given its premiere by the San Francisco Symphony Orchestra.

1970   Johnny (John Cornelius) Hodges dies in New York City, aged sixty-two.

1976   Rudolf Kempe dies in Zurich, aged sixty-five.

MAY 12

1739   Jan Křtitel Vaňhal, Austrian composer, is born in Nechanicz.

1754   Franz Anton Hoffmeister, German composer and publisher, is born in Rottenburg.

1755   Giovanni Battista Viotti, Italian violinist and composer, court musician to Queen Marie Antoinette of France, is born in Fontanetto.

1832   Gaetano Donizetti's opera <u>L'Elisir d'amore</u> premieres in Milan.

1842   Jules Massenet, French opera composer and teacher, is born in Montaud.

1845   Gabriel Fauré, French composer, organist, and teacher, is born in Pamiers. He studied with Saint-Saëns; his own pupils included Ravel, Enesco, Roger-Ducasse, Florent Schmitt, and Nadia Boulanger.

1871   Daniel-François Auber dies in Paris, aged eighty-nine.

1884   Bedřich Smetana dies insane in Prague, aged sixty.

1888   Mariano Stabile, Italian baritone, is born in Palermo.

1903   Sir Lennox Berkeley, English composer, knighted in 1974, is born at Boar's Hill.

1915   Joseph Wood, American composer and composition teacher
        (at Oberlin College, Ohio), is born in Pittsburgh.

1916   Ellis B. Kohs, American composer and teacher, is born in
        Chicago.

        Ruth Watanabe, American musicologist, music librarian at
        Eastman School of Music in Rochester, New York, is born
        in Los Angeles.

1917   Béla Bartók's one-act ballet The Wooden Prince is first
        staged, in Budapest.

1926   Dmitri Shostakovich's Symphony no. 1 has its premiere, in
        Leningrad.

1931   Eugène Ysaÿe dies in Brussels, aged seventy-two.   Months
        earlier his foot had been amputated for diabetes.

1936   Dmitri Kabalevsky's Piano Concerto no. 2 is first performed,
        in Moscow.

1938   Arthur Honegger's cantata Jeanne d'Arc au bûcher receives
        its premiere, in Basel.

1941   Anthony Newman, organist, harpsichordist, and teacher, is
        born in Los Angeles.

1943   Reinhold Glière's Concerto for Coloratura Soprano and Orches-
        tra is given its first performance, in Moscow.

1944   Alberto Ginastera's Overture to the Creole Faust has its
        premiere in Santiago, Chile.

1945   Max Pauer dies in Jugenheim, Germany, aged seventy-eight.
        From 1908 to 1934 he directed Mannheim's Hochschule für
        Musik.

1951   Marcel Tournier dies in Paris at the age of seventy-one.

        MAY 13

1726   Francesco Antonio Pistocchi dies in Bolgona, aged about
        sixty-seven.   A priest, he founded the famous School of Sing-
        ing there.

1833   Felix Mendelssohn conducts his Symphony no. 4, "Italian,"
        in its premiere, in London.

1842   Sir Arthur Sullivan, English composer of comic operas who collaborated with librettist William S. Gilbert, is born in London.

1863   Emile Prudent dies at age forty-six in Paris.

1900   Herman Levi dies in Munich, aged sixty.

1912   Gil (Gilmore) Evans, Canadian jazz pianist, bandleader, and arranger, is born in Toronto.

1913   William Schwann, American organist and publisher, since 1949, of recorded music catalogs, is born in Salem, Illinois.

1916   Clara Louise Kellogg dies in New Hartford, Connecticut, aged seventy-three.

1935   Dominic Cossa, American bass-baritone, is born in Jessup, Pennsylvania.

1938   Ludovic Spiess, Rumanian tenor, is born in Cluj.

1953   Hermann Jadlowker, at age seventy-five, dies in Tel Aviv, Israel, where, after a career in opera, he had settled to teach.

MAY 14

1780   Pierre-Montan Berton dies in Paris at the age of fifty-three.

1832   Felix Mendelssohn conducts his Hebrides Overture, "Fingal's Cave," in its first performance, in London.

1847   Fanny Mendelssohn Hensel dies in Berlin, aged forty-one. Her death was a severe shock to her brother, Felix Mendelssohn.

1861   Adelina Patti, at age eighteen, makes her operatic debut in Covent Garden, London, singing in Bellini's La Sonnambula.

1869   Sigismund Stojowski, Polish-American pianist and teacher (at New York's Institute of Musical Art and Juilliard Summer School), is born in Strzelce.

1884   Samuel Samosud, Russian opera conductor, is born in Odessa.

1885   Otto Klemperer, German conductor who fled Germany in 1933, is born in Breslau.

1914   Richard Strauss's ballet Josephslegende is first staged, in Paris.

1917   Lou Harrison, American composer and conductor, is born
        in Portland, Oregon. For his vocal works he has written
        texts in Esperanto.

1925   Patrice Munsel, American soprano, is born in Spokane,
        Washington.

1930   Ara Berberian, American bass, is born in Detroit.

1938   Jan Peerce makes his operatic debut in Philadelphia, singing
        in Rigoletto.

1940   Peter Wimberger, Austrian bass, is born in Vienna.

1942   Aaron Copland's Lincoln Portrait, for speaker and orchestra,
        is given its premiere in Cincinnati, André Kostelanetz (who
        commissioned the work) conducting.

1960   Lucretia Bori dies in New York, aged seventy-two.

1965   Jacqueline DuPré makes her American debut in Carnegie Hall,
        New York City, playing the Cello Concerto of Elgar.

1967   Edison Denisov's Crescendo e diminuendo, for harpsichord
        and strings (in part with graphic notation), is first performed
        at the Zagreb Festival, Yugoslavia.

        Ezra Laderman's opera oratorio Galileo Galilei has its pre-
        miere on television in New York City.

1978   Alexander Kipnis dies in Westport, Connecticut, aged eighty-
        seven. His son is harpsichordist Igor Kipnis.

1979   Thomas Scherman dies at age sixty-two. He had assisted
        Otto Klemperer in conducting.

        MAY 15

1567   Claudio Monteverdi, Italian madrigalist who is also regarded
        as the father of modern opera, is baptized in Cremona.
        Spared by the plague, he took holy orders in 1632.

1808   Michael William Balfe, Irish composer of operas, is born
        in Dublin.

1813   Stephen Heller, Hungarian pianist and composer (principally
        for piano), is born in Budapest. From a Jewish family, he
        converted to Christianity.

1858   The new (present) Covent Garden building opens the season
        with Meyerbeer's opera Les Huguenots, in London.

1898   Eduard Reményi dies during a performance in San Francisco,
        aged sixty-seven.

1907   Josef Alexander, American composer, teacher of piano and
        composition, is born in Boston.

1908   Lars-Erik Larsson, Swedish composer and conductor, music
        director at Uppsala University, is born in Åkarp.

1912   Arthur Berger, American composer, teacher, and newspaper
        music critic, is born in New York City.

1920   Igor Stravinsky's ballet Pulcinella has its premiere performed
        by the Ballet Russe, in Paris.

1923   John Lanchberry, English conductor and composer, is born
        in London.

1925   Emmanuel Ghent, American composer and practicing psy-
        chiatrist in New York City, is born in Montreal.

1926   Clermont Pépin, Canadian composer and music administra-
        tor, is born in St. Georges-de-Beauce.

1941   Richard Wilson, American composer and faculty member at
        Vassar College, is born in Cleveland, Ohio.

1944   John Wilbraham, English trumpeter, is born in Bournemouth.

1952   Italo Montemezzi dies in Vigasio, Italy, aged seventy-six.

1958   John Cage's Concert, for piano and orchestra, is given its
        premiere, in New York City.

1978   Neville Marriner's appointment as music director of the
        Minnesota Symphony Orchestra in Minneapolis for the 1979-
        80 season is announced.

        MAY 16

1792   Teatro la Fenice opens in Venice, with Gasparo Pacchiarotti
        singing in his last public appearance.

1856   Alexander Dargomizhsky's opera Russalka (the libretto by the
        composer after Pushkin) is first produced, in St. Petersburg.

1892   Richard Tauber, Austrian-English tenor who enjoyed singing in light operas (especially Lehar's and Mozart's), is born in Linz.

1893   Paul Amadeus Pisk, Austrian-American musicologist, pianist, and composer, is born in Vienna.

1902   Jan Kiepura, Polish-American tenor, is born in Sosnowiec.

1912   Felix Prohaska, Austrian conductor, son of composer Carl Prohaska, is born in Vienna.   From 1961 to 1969 he directed the Hochschule für Musik in Hannover.

1919   Walter Liberace, American pianist and television entertainer, is born in West Allis, Wisconsin.

1927   Paul Angerer, Austrian conductor and composer, is born in Vienna.

1929   Lilli Lehmann dies in Berlin, aged seventy.   In addition to her opera career, she was also a teacher, numbering Geraldine Farrar and Olive Fremstad among her students.

1931   Donald Martino, American composer and professor of composition, is born in Plainfield, New Jersey.

1938   American Composers Alliance is founded in New York City.

1948   Quincy Porter's Viola Concerto is first performed at the Columbia University Festival in New York City.

        Wallingford Riegger's Symphony no. 3 receives its premiere, in New York City.

1954   Clemens Krauss dies in Mexico City while on tour.   He was sixty-one.

1966   Ralph Shapey's Rituals has its premiere performance, in Chicago.

1971   Irwin Bazelon's Concerto for 14 Players has its first hearing, in New York City.

1972   Jacob Druckman's Pulitzer Prize-winning Windows, for orchestra, is given its premiere, in Chicago, by the Chicago Symphony Orchestra.

1977   Eduard van Remoortel dies in Paris, aged fifty.

1978   William Steinberg dies in New York City, at age seventy-eight.

MAY 17

1779   Christoph Willibald Gluck's finest opera, Iphigénie en Tauride, opens at the Paris Opéra.

1866   Erik Satie, eccentric French composer, son of a music publisher, is born in Honfleur.

1890   Pietro Mascagni's most successful opera, Cavalleria Rusticana, is first staged, in Rome's Costanzi Theater.

1900   Nicolai Berezowsky, Russian-American composer and violinist, is born in St. Petersburg.

1901   Max Lorenz, German tenor, is born in Düsseldorf.

1902   Fausto Cleva, Italian-American conductor, is born in Trieste. He was chorusmaster and later conductor with the Metropolitan Opera in New York City.

        John Vincent, American composer and educator, is born in Birmingham, Alabama.

1904   Maurice Ravel's song cycle Shéhérazade, for solo voice and orchestra, has its premiere performance, in Paris.

1906   Zinka Milanov, Yugoslav soprano, is born in Zagreb.

1918   Birgit Nilsson, Swedish soprano, is born in Karup.

1921   Dennis Brain, English French-horn virtuoso, is born in London.

1923   Peter Mennin, American composer and president of the Juilliard School of Music in New York City, is born in Erie, Pennsylvania.

1924   Gabriel Bacquier, French baritone, is born in Beziers.

1935   Paul Dukas dies in Paris, aged sixty-nine. Shortly before his death he destroyed some manuscripts of uncompleted compositions.

1939   Sergei Prokofiev's cantata Alexander Nevsky is first performed in Moscow.

1941   David H. Cope, American composer and cellist, is born in San Francisco.

1944   Paul Crossley, English concert pianist, is born in Dewsbury.

1948   Olga Samaroff dies in New York City, aged sixty-five.

1969   Leonard Bernstein conducts the New York Philharmonic in his last concert as director. He resigned in order to have more time for composing.

W. C. Handy is honored in the issuance of a commemorative stamp in Memphis, Tennessee, where his song Memphis Blues originated.

MAY 18

1616   Johann Jakob Froberger, German organist and composer who is credited with originating the keyboard suite, is born in Stuttgart.

1733   Georg Böhm dies in Lüneburg, Germany, aged seventy-one.

1830   Karl Goldmark, Hungarian composer who lived most of his life in Vienna, is born in Keszthely.

1832   Bonifazio Asioli dies in Correggio, Italy, aged sixty-two. His book on composition was published posthumously.

1887   Emmanuel Chabrier's comic opera Le Roi malgré lui is given its premiere, in Paris at the Opéra-Comique.

1892   Ezio Pinza, Italian operatic bass and star of the musical South Pacific, is born in Rome.

1897   Paul Dukas's Sorcerer's Apprentice is first performed under the composer's direction, in Paris at a concert of the Société Nationale.

1901   Henri Sauguet, French composer, is born at Bordeaux.

1907   Clifford Curzon, English pianist, a pupil of Artur Schnabel, is born in London.

1909   Isaac Albéniz dies at Cambo-les-Bains shortly before his forty-ninth birthday.

1910   Pauline Viardot-García dies in Paris, aged eighty-eight. She possessed the holograph of Mozart's Don Giovanni and left it to the Library of the Paris Conservatory.

1911   Gustav Mahler dies of pneumonia in Vienna, aged fifty.

1913   Perry Como, American popular singer and television star, is born in Canonsburg, Pennsylvania.

1914   Boris Christoff, Bulgarian bass, is born in Plovdiv.

1917   Erik Satie's ballet Parade is first staged by Diaghilev's Ballet Russe, in Paris.

1929   Roger Matton, Canadian composer and professor of composition at Laval University in Quebec City, is born in Granby,
Quebec.

1939   Douglas Moore's opera The Devil and Daniel Webster has its
premiere performance in New York City.

1940   Luigi Dallapiccola's one-act opera Volo di Notte is first
staged, in Florence.

1941   Milka Ternina dies in Zagreb, aged seventy-seven.   She had
been a distinguished Wagnerian singer.

1950   Lukas Foss's opera The Jumping Frog of Calaveras County
(after Mark Twain) is first performed, in Bloomington,
Indiana.

1966   William Bergsma's Violin Concerto has its premiere, in
Tacoma, Washington.

1971   Sergio Cervetti's Plexus, for small orchestra, receives its
first performance, in Washington.

1975   Leroy Anderson dies in Woodbury, Connecticut, aged sixty-
six.   During World War II he acted as a translator in Scandinavian languages for the United States Army.

1978   Henry Cowell's Quartet Romantic has its first complete performance at Alice Tully Hall in New York City.

MAY 19

1786   John Stanley dies in London, aged seventy-three.   He was an
esteemed friend of Handel.

1842   Gaetano Donizetti's opera Linda di Chamounix is given its
premiere in Vienna.

1859   Nellie Melba (née Mitchell), Australian soprano who coined her
last name from the city of Melbourne, is born in nearby
Burnley.

1876   Rosina Storchio, Italian soprano, is born in Venice.

1886   Camille Saint-Saëns's Symphony no. 3, for organ, two pianos,
and orchestra, "Organ Symphony," has its premiere, in
London.

1926   Paul Cooper, American composer and teacher, is born in
Victoria, Illinois.

1928   Henry F. Gilbert dies in Cambridge, Massachusetts, aged fifty-nine.

1933   The National Association for American Composers and Conductors is founded by Dr. Henry Hadley.

1935   Charles Martin Loeffler dies in Medfield, Massachusetts, at age seventy-four.

1954   Charles Ives dies in New York City at age seventy-nine.   An Ives Archive is now at Yale University.

1963   Margarete Matzenauer dies in Van Nuys, California, aged eighty-one.

1967   Per Nørgaard's Iris, for orchestra, is given its first hearing, in Copenhagen.

1969   Coleman Hawkins dies in New York City at age sixty-four. Thirty years earlier he had made his most influential recording, Body and Soul.

1970   Ellis B. Kohs's opera Amerika (abridged concert version) receives its premiere, in Los Angeles.

1971   Bernard Wagenaar dies in York, Maine, at seventy-six.

MAY 20

1896   Clara Wieck Schumann, widow of Robert Schumann and authoritative interpreter of his works, dies in Frankfurt, aged seventy-six.

1903   Jerzy Fitelberg, Polish composer, is born in Warsaw, the son of conductor Gregor Fitelberg, with whom he began his music studies.

1909   Erich Kunz, Austrian bass-baritone, is born in Vienna.

1925   Chester Ludgin, American baritone, is born in New York City.

1943   Tison Street, American composer, is born in Boston.   A graduate of Harvard University, he has won many awards.

1950   William Bergsma's Symphony no. 1 is aired on CBS in its premiere.

1971   Robert Evett's The Windhover, a concerto for bassoon and orchestra, is first performed, in Washington.

1974   Andrzej Panufniks's <u>Sinfonia Concertante</u>, for flute, harp, and strings, is first heard, in London.

1977   Alan Hovhaness's <u>Rubaiyat,</u> for narrator, accordion, and orchestra, is given its premiere, in New York City.

MAY 21

1812   Joseph Woelfl dies in obscurity, aged thirty-eight, in London.

1844   Amy Fay, American pianist, is born in Bayou Goula, Louisiana. A pupil of Liszt, she is best remembered for her book <u>Music Study in Germany,</u> which had more than twenty printings.

1892   Ruggiero Leoncavallo's opera <u>Pagliacci</u> is first staged, in Milan's Teatro dal Verme, Arturo Toscanini conducting.

1895   Franz von Suppé dies in Vienna, aged seventy-six.

1904   "Fats" (Thomas) Waller, American jazz pianist and composer, is born in New York City. His song <u>Ain't Misbehavin'</u> is also the title of the 1978 musical revue that was a tribute to him.

1907   Konstantin Ivanov, Russian conductor, is born in Yefremov.

1913   Gina Bachauer, Greek pianist, is born in Athens.

1924   Robert Parris, American composer and teacher, is born in Philadelphia.

1926   Forbes Robinson, English bass, is born in Macclesfield.

1928   Karl Christian Kohn, German bass, is born in Losheim-Saar.

1929   Georges Auric's ballet <u>Les Enchantements d'Alcine</u> receives its first performance, in Paris.

1933   Maurice André, French trumpet virtuoso, is born in Alès.

1939   Heinz Holliger, Swiss oboe virtuoso and composer, is born in Langenthal.

1962   Karlheinz Stockhausen's <u>Momente,</u> for soprano, four choruses, thirteen instruments, and percussion, has its premiere, in Cologne.

1971   Niccolò Castiglioni's <u>Sinfonia in Do,</u> for chorus and orchestra, is given its first performance, in Rome.

1975   William Bergsma's In Space, for soprano and instruments, has its premiere, in Seattle.

MAY 22

1813   Gioacchino Rossini's opera Italiana in Algeri is first produced, in Venice.

Richard Wagner, German opera composer, is born in Leipzig.

1820   Alexander Ernst Fesca, German pianist and composer, is born in Karlsruhe.

1836   Felix Mendelssohn's oratorio St. Paul is first performed at the Lower Rhine Festival in Düsseldorf, the composer conducting.

1872   Richard Wagner, celebrating his fifty-ninth birthday, is in Bayreuth for the laying of the cornerstone of the Festspielhaus. The theater is built according to Wagner's original plans.

1874   Giuseppe Verdi's Requiem Mass, "Manzoni Requiem," is conducted by him in its premiere in Milan Cathedral. It marks the first anniversary of the passing of Alessandro Manzoni.

1911   Claude Debussy's music for d'Annunzio's mystery play, Le Martyre de St. Sébastien, for soli, chorus, and orchestra, receives its first performance at the Théâtre du Châtelet, Paris.

1916   Gordon Binkerd, American composer and educator, is born in Lynch, Nebraska.

1925   James King, American tenor, is born in Dodge City, Kansas.

1933   John Browning, American pianist, is born in Denver.

1949   Hans Pfitzner dies in Salzburg at the age of eighty.

1965   Malcolm Williamson's children's opera The Happy Prince (after Oscar Wilde) has its first production, in Farnham, England.

1977   Hampton Hawes dies in Los Angeles at forty-eight.

MAY 23

1759   Wilhelm Friedrich Ernst Bach, German musician, Kapell-
        meister to the Queen of Prussia, and grandson of Johann
        Sebastian Bach, is born in Bückeburg.

1794   Ignaz Moscheles, German-Bohemian pianist and composer,
        a friend and teacher of Felix Mendelssohn, is born in Prague.

1814   Ludwig van Beethoven's opera Fidelio is staged successfully
        in Vienna's Kärntnertortheater after the third and final re-
        vision.

1826   W. A. Mozart's opera Don Giovanni has its American premiere
        at New York's Park Theater. Four of the famed García
        family of singers participate.

1901   Edmund Rubbra, English composer and teacher, is born in
        Northampton.

1912   Jean Françaix, French composer, is born in Le Mans.

1923   Alicia de Larrocha, Spanish pianist and interpreter of Spanish
        music, is born in Barcelona.

        François Lesure, French music librarian and musicologist,
        is born in Paris. Since 1970 he has been chief curator of
        the Bibliothèque Nationale.

1932   Ilva Ligabue, Italian soprano, is born at Reggio Emilia.

1971   Roger Sessions's cantata When Lilacs Last in the Dooryard
        Bloom'd, for soli, chorus, and orchestra, is first sung in
        Berkeley, California.

MAY 24

1781   Louis-François Dauprat, French composer and French-horn
        performer, is born in Paris.

1810   Ludwig van Beethoven's music to Goethe's Egmont is first
        performed at the Hofburg Theater, Vienna. Beethoven sup-
        plies the overture, four entr'actes, and songs for the play.

1888   Nellie Melba makes her London debut at Covent Garden in
        Donizetti's Lucia di Lammermoor.

1905   Sascha Gorodnitzki, Russian-American pianist, is born in
        Kiev. A graduate of the Juilliard School, he began teaching
        there in 1932.

1908   Krešimir Fribec, Croatian composer (principally vocal music), is born in Daruvar.

1911   Sir Edward Elgar's Symphony no. 2 has its premiere, in London.

1918   Béla Bartók's one-act opera The Castle of Duke Bluebeard is first staged, in Budapest.

1936   Harold Budd, American composer who earned his way in college as a jazz performer, is born in Los Angeles.

        Claudia Muzio dies in Rome, aged forty-seven.   From 1922 to 1933 she sang with the Chicago Opera.

1941   Bob Dylan (né Robert Zimmerman), American folksinger, is born in Duluth, Minnesota.

1968   Bernard Rogers dies in Rochester, New York, at the age of seventy-five.   He taught composition there at the Eastman School of Music beginning in 1929.

1970   Andrzej Panufnik's Universal Prayer, for soli, chorus, harps, and organ, is conducted in its premiere by Leopold Stokowski in St. John the Divine Cathedral, New York City.

1974   Duke Ellington dies in New York City at the age of seventy-five.   During his lifetime he received many honors, including a degree from Columbia University and the Presidential Medal of Freedom; he toured under the auspices of the State Department.

MAY 25

1863   Camille Erlanger, French composer, is born in Paris.

1870   Léo Delibes's ballet Coppélia is first staged, in Paris.

1878   Gilbert and Sullivan's comic opera H. M. S. Pinafore opens in London, beginning 700 consecutive performances.

1898   Mischa Levitzki, Russian-American pianist, is born in Kremenchug.

1904   Kurt Thomas, German choral conductor and author of a manual on choral conducting, is born in Tönning. The Choral Conductor, an English translation of his manual, was published in 1971.

1910   Scipio Colombo, Italian baritone, is born in Vincenza.

1917   Edouard de Reszke dies in Garnek, Poland, aged sixty-three.

1925   Aldo Clementi, Italian composer, is born in Catania.

1926   Miles Davis, American jazz trumpeter and bandleader, is born in Alton, Illinois.

1929   Beverly Sills (née Belle Silverman), American soprano, is born in Brooklyn, New York.

1934   Gustav Holst dies in London, aged fifty-nine. His daughter, Imogen, wrote a biography of her famous father.

1942   Emanuel Feuermann dies in New York City, aged thirty-nine.

1953   Marc Blitzstein's musical satire <u>The Harpies</u>, commissioned by the League of Composers, is first performed at the Manhattan School of Music in New York.

1961   Mario Castelnuovo-Tedesco's prize-winning opera <u>Il Mercante di Venezia</u> (Italian libretto by the composer after Shakespeare's <u>Merchant of Venice</u>) has its premiere at Maggio Musicale in Florence.

1978   Gilbert and Sullivan's comic opera <u>H. M. S. Pinafore</u> celebrates its centenary with a gala performance in San Francisco.

MAY 26

1893   Sir Eugene Goossens, English conductor and composer, is born in London.

1898   Ernst Bacon, American composer, conductor, songwriter, and poet, is born in Chicago.

1914   Igor Stravinsky's opera <u>Le Rossignol</u>, after Hans Christian Andersen's tale, is first performed at the Paris Opéra by Diaghilev's company, Pierre Monteux conducting.

1921   Inga Borkh, German-Swiss soprano, is born in Mannheim.

1924   Victor Herbert dies in New York City, aged sixty-five. He had been in the United States since his marriage in 1886.

1926   Georges Auric's ballet <u>La Pastorale</u>, written for Diaghilev, is first staged, in Paris. It is one of several ballets he wrote for the Russian impressario's Ballet Russe.

1933   Jimmie Rodgers, the "Singing Brakeman," dies in New York City, aged thirty-five.

1935   Susann McDonald, American harpist and teacher at the Juilli-
        ard School, is born in Rock Island, Illinois. She is known
        especially for performing contemporary music.

1938   William Bolcom, American pianist, composer, and educator,
        is born in Seattle.

        Teresa Stratas (née Anastasia Strataki), Canadian soprano,
        is born in Toronto.

1953   Karlheinz Stockhausen's Kontra-Punkte, for ten instruments,
        receives its premiere, in Cologne.

1967   George Crumb's Echoes of Time and the River: Four Pro-
        cessionals for Orchestra, which won the 1968 Pulitzer Prize,
        is first performed, in Chicago.

1971   Mark Brunswick dies in London, aged sixty-nine.

1978   Edwin London's Poebells, for two singers, narrator, and
        bells to accompany Edgar Allan Poe's poem The Bells, has
        its English premiere, at York University.

        MAY 27

1797   Anton Raaff dies in Munich at the age of eighty-three. Mo-
        zart wrote the role of Idomeneo for him in the opera of that
        name.

1799   Jacques François Halévy, French opera composer and teacher,
        is born in Paris.

1822   Joachim Raff, Swiss-born German composer and music ad-
        ministrator, is born in Lachen.

1840   Niccolò Paganini dies in Nice, aged fifty-seven.

1888   Louis Durey, music critic and composer, the oldest member
        of the French group known as "Les Six," is born in Paris.
        A Communist, he wrote for the party newspaper, L'Humanité.

1899   Maurice Ravel makes his conducting debut with the Société
        Nationale in a performance from manuscript of his Shéhéra-
        zade. The work was never published.

1906   Gustav Mahler conducts his Symphony no. 6 at its premiere
        in Essen, Germany.

1907   Mikhail Tavrizian, Soviet conductor of the Armenian State
        Theater and Ballet Orchestra, is born in Baku.

1928   Thea Musgrave, Scottish composer and teacher who frequently
        conducts the premieres of her major compositions, is born
        in Edinburgh. In her "space music" the instrumentalists
        often move around the orchestra or concert hall.

1929   Donald Keats, American composer, is born in New York City.

1938   Elizabeth Harwood, English soprano, is born in Kettering.

1947   Bohuslav Martinů's Symphony no. 5 is first performed, in
        Prague.

1962   Egon Petri dies at age eighty-one in Berkeley, California,
        ending a long career of concertizing and teaching.

1973   Ilona Kabos dies in London, aged seventy.

1976   Norman Dello Joio's Colonial Variants, for orchestra, has
        its premiere, in Philadelphia.

        MAY 28

1608   Claudio Monteverdi's opera Arianna, written for a ducal wed-
        ding, is performed before 6,000 guests in Mantua.

1779   Thomas Moore, Irish ballad singer, composer, and poet, is
        born in Dublin.

1787   Leopold Mozart dies in Salzburg, aged sixty-seven. He de-
        voted his life to fostering his son's musicianship; Wolfgang
        Amadeus outlived his father by only four years.

1805   Luigi Boccherini dies in Madrid, aged sixty-two. A prolific
        composer, his style was so similar to that of Haydn's that
        a saying originated: "Boccherini is the wife of Haydn."

1836   Anton Reicha dies in Paris, aged sixty-six. Among his pupils
        were Liszt and Gounod.

1841   Giovanni Sgambati, Italian pianist and composer, is born in
        Rome.

1890   Victor Nessler dies in Strasbourg, aged forty-nine.

1900   Sir George Grove dies in London, aged seventy-nine.

1903   Walter Goehr, German-English conductor, arranger, and com-
        poser, is born in Berlin.

1912   Tom (Thomas Jefferson) Scott, American composer and folk-
        singer, is born in Campbellsburg, Kentucky.

1916   Albert Lavignac dies in Paris, aged seventy.

1923   György Ligeti, Hungarian avant-garde composer and teacher,
        is born in Dicsöszentmartin.

        Jiří Válek, Czech composer and teacher, is born in Prague.

1925   Dietrich Fischer-Dieskau, German baritone, conductor, and
        author of books on music, is born in Berlin.   In World War
        II he was an English prisoner.

1931   Peter Westergaard, American composer and music-department
        chairman at Princeton University, is born in Champaign,
        Illinois.

1935   Richard Van Allen, English bass (a former science teacher),
        is born in Nottingham.

1938   Paul Hindemith's opera Mathis der Maler has its premiere
        performance, in Zurich.

1943   Dennis Riley, American composer and teacher, is born in
        Los Angeles.

        Elena Suliotis, Greek-Italian soprano, is born in Athens.

1973   Hans Schmidt-Isserstedt dies in Hamburg, aged seventy-three.

        MAY 29

1838   Pauline Anna Milder-Hauptmann dies in Berlin, aged fifty-two.
        Joseph Haydn is reported to have commented on her powerful
        voice: "Dear child, you have a voice like a house."

1860   Isaac Albéniz, Spanish composer and pianist (a child prodigy
        who ran away from home at thirteen), is born in Camprodón.

1892   Mario Chamlee (né Archer Cholmondeley), American tenor,
        is born in Los Angeles.

1897   Erich Wolfgang Korngold, Austrian-American composer and
        conductor, is born in Brno.

1905   Fela Sowande, Nigerian composer who was trained in London,
        is born in Oyo.

1910   Mily Balakirev dies in St. Petersburg, aged seventy-three;
        he was one of "The Five."

1911   Sir William S. Gilbert dies, at age seventy-four, of a heart attack after rescuing a drowning woman at Harrow Weald, England.

1913   Igor Stravinsky's ballet <u>Le Sacre du printemps</u> is performed by the Ballet Russe in its premiere in Paris, Pierre Monteux conducting.

1915   Igor Buketoff, American conductor, is born in Hartford, Connecticut.

Karl Münchinger, German conductor, is born in Stuttgart.

1922   Iannis Xenakis, Rumanian-Greek composer of electronic music, a former architecture student and assistant to Corbusier (1948-60), is born in Braila.

1935   Josef Suk dies at Benešov, Czechoslovakia, aged sixty-one.

1951   Joseph Bohuslav Foerster dies at Nový Vestec, Czechoslovakia, aged ninety-one.

1963   New York Philharmonic Promenade Concerts are inaugurated.

1977   Goddard Lieberson dies in New York City at the age of sixty-six. The recording of modern works by Columbia Records was due to his liberal policy.

MAY 30

1866   Bedřich Smetana's opera <u>The Bartered Bride</u> is first staged at the Czech Theatre in Prague. It proved tremendously popular.

1883   Riccardo Zandonai, Italian opera composer, is born in Sacco.

1893   Rosa Raisa, soprano, is born in Bialystok, Poland.

1908   Beveridge Webster, American pianist, is born in Pittsburgh.

1909   Benny (Benjamin David) Goodman, American clarinetist and jazz-band leader, is born in Chicago. He was called the "King of Swing."

1912   Alfred Deller, English countertenor, conductor, and founder of the Deller Consort to perform old English music, is born in Margate.

1919   George London (whose family name was Burnstein), Canadian-American bass-baritone, is born in Montreal.

1923   Camille Paul Chevillard dies at Seine-et-Oise, France, aged
        sixty-three.

1926   Eduard van Remoortel, Belgian conductor, is born in Brussels.

1927   Igor Stravinsky's opera-oratorio Oedipus Rex (after Sophocles)
        is first performed, in Paris.

1928   Gustav Leonhardt, Dutch organ and harpsichord recitalist
        and teacher, is born in 'sGraveland.

1932   Pauline Oliveros, American composer employing mixed media
        in her works, is born in Houston.

1938   Walter Piston's only ballet, The Incredible Flutist, is first
        performed, in Boston.

1954   André Jolivet's Symphony no. 1 has its premiere at Haifa,
        at the International Society for Contemporary Music Festival.

1962   Benjamin Britten's War Requiem, for soli, chorus, and orches-
        tra, is first performed in the rebuilt Coventry Cathedral,
        England.

1967   Billy Strayhorn dies in New York City, aged fifty-one. He
        had been a part of Duke Ellington's band as lyricist and ar-
        ranger.

1971   Marcel Dupré dies in Meudon, France, aged eighty-five. He
        had once given a series of recitals, playing Bach's complete
        organ works from memory.

1977   Paul Desmond dies in New York City, aged fifty-two. He
        had been a member of the Dave Brubeck Quartet.

        MAY 31

1656   Marin Marais, French viola-da-gambist and composer, a
        father of nineteen children, is born in Paris.

1809   (Franz) Joseph Haydn dies in Vienna, aged seventy-seven.
        Although he had long been in failing health, his end was
        hastened by the shock of bombardment of Vienna by the
        French.

1866   Vladimir Rebikov, Russian composer, is born in Krasnoyarsk.

1883   Frances Alda, New Zealand-American soprano, is born in Christ-
        church.

1901   Alfredo Antonini, Italian conductor, is born.

1905   Franz Strauss dies in Munich, aged eighty-three; he was the
        father of Richard Strauss.

1924   Vittorio Rieti's <u>Concertino for Five Wind Instruments and
        Orchestra</u> receives its premiere at the Prague Festival.

1931   Shirley Verrett, American mezzo-soprano, is born in New
        Orleans.

1938   Peter Yarrow, song composer and member of the American
        folksinging trio Peter, Paul and Mary, is born in New York
        City.

1953   Audrey Mildmay dies in London, aged fifty-two.

1955   Raoul Gunsbourg dies at age ninety-five in Monte Carlo,
        where he had directed the Monte Carlo Opera.

1961   Krzysztof Penderecki's <u>Threnody in Memory of the Victims
        of Hiroshima</u>, for strings, is first performed on Warsaw
        Radio.

1971   Max Trapp dies in Berlin, aged eighty-three.

JUNE 1

1639   Melchior Franck, German composer, dies in Coburg, aged about sixty. Since 1602 he had been Kapellmeister there.

1653   Georg Muffat, Alsatian organist and composer, is baptized at Megève. In 1690 he became Kapellmeister at Passau.

1723   Johann Sebastian Bach is formally inducted as cantor at the Thomasschule in Leipzig, a post he held until his death in 1750.

1804   Mikhail Glinka, Russian composer known as the "father of Russian music" for fostering the use of Russian folk-style music in polished idioms, is born at Novospasskoye.

1826   Friedrich Karl Bechstein, German piano manufacturer, is born in Gotha.

1881   Margarete Matzenauer, Hungarian singer who began as a contralto and later sang soprano, is born into a musical family at Temesvar.

1889   Sigrid Onégin, Swedish contralto, is born in Stockholm.

1892   Samuel Barlow, American composer, is born in New York City.

1899   Werner Janssen, American composer and conductor, is born in New York City.

1925   Ernest Bloch conducts the premiere of his Concerto Grosso no. 1, for strings and piano, in Cleveland, Ohio.

1929   Yehudi Wyner, Canadian-American composer, teacher and pianist, son of composer Lazar Weiner, is born in Calgary.

1941   Edo de Waart, Dutch conductor, named principal conductor and music director of the San Francisco Symphony Orchestra in 1977, is born in Amsterdam.

1946   Leo Slezak dies at Egern-am Tegernsee, Germany, aged
        seventy-two. He spent many years on the concert stage and
        in opera; his son, film actor Walter Slezak, published his
        father's letters in 1966.

JUNE 2

1834   Teresa Stolz, Bohemian soprano, is born at Kosteletz.

1857   Sir Edward Elgar, English composer and church organist, is
        born in Broadheath. He succeeded his father as church or-
        ganist at St. George's Roman Catholic Church in Worcester.

1863   Felix Weingartner, German conductor, is born in Zara, Dal-
        matia. He was also a music editor and writer on musical
        subjects.

1915   Robert Palmer, American composer associated with Cornell
        University since 1943, is born in Syracuse, New York.

1937   Alban Berg's unfinished opera, Lulu, consisting of two acts
        and part of a third, is first performed in Zurich.

        Louis Vierne dies in Paris while playing the organ at Notre
        Dame Cathedral, at the age of sixty-six.

1953   Alberto Ginastera's Variaciones Concertantes receives its
        premiere, in Buenos Aires.

        Sir William Walton's Coronation Te Deum, written for the
        coronation of Queen Elizabeth II, is first performed, in
        London.

JUNE 3

1832   Charles Lecocq, French operetta composer, is born in Paris.

1844   Emile Paladilhe, French composer, is born in Montpellier.

1851   Theodore Baker, American musicologist and music lexico-
        grapher, author of Baker's Biographical Dictionary of Mu-
        sicians and literary editor for G. Schirmer, Inc., music pub-
        lishers, is born in New York City.

1858   Julius Reubke dies in Pillnitz, Germany, aged twenty-four.
        He was a favorite pupil of Liszt; his death is widely mourned.

1875   Georges Bizet dies at Bougival, France, at age thirty-six--
        three months after the premiere of his opera Carmen.

1887   Roland Hayes, American tenor, son of former slaves, is
        born in Curryville, Georgia.

1896   Camille Saint-Saëns's Piano Concerto no. 5 is performed in
        its premiere in Paris by the composer.

1899   Johann Strauss, Jr., dies in Vienna, aged seventy-three.
        He had written almost 500 compositions of dance music as
        well as operettas.

1904   Jan Peerce, American tenor, former dance-band violinist
        and cantor, is born in New York City.

1931   Mabel Daniels's Deep Forest, for small orchestra, is given
        its premiere, in New York City.

1934   The American Musicological Society is formally incorporated
        in New York City, with Otto Kinkeldey as its first president.

1939   David Stock, American composer and conductor, is born in
        Pittsburgh.

1967   André Cluytens dies in Neuilly, France, at the age of sixty-
        two, having spent much of his life as an opera conductor.

1975   Frida Leider dies in Berlin, aged eighty-seven; in 1959 she
        published her autobiography in Berlin (English version in
        New York, 1966).

JUNE 4

1770   James Hewitt, English-American pianist, composer, and
        music publisher, is born in Dartmoor.

1872   Stanislaw Moniuszko, a professor at Warsaw Conservatory,
        dies, aged fifty-three. His opera Halka is considered the
        first truly national Polish opera.

1903   Eugen Mravinsky, Russian conductor, is born in St. Peters-
        burg.

1905   José Echaniz, Cuban pianist and member of the Eastman
        School of Music faculty for many years, is born in Havana.

        Albert Löschhorn dies in Berlin, aged eighty-five.

1907   Agathe Backer-Grøndahl dies at Ormöen, Norway, aged fifty-nine.   She studied with Hans von Bülow and Franz Liszt.

1909   Paul Nordoff, American composer, teacher, music therapist, and writer on music therapy, is born in Philadelphia.

1910   Anton Dermota, Yugoslav tenor, is born in Kropa.

1914   Jan Sibelius conducts the premiere of his symphonic poem <u>Oceanides</u> at the Norfolk Festival in Connecticut.   It is dedicated to Mr. and Mrs. Carl Stoeckel, who commissioned the work and on whose estate the festival takes place.

1917   Robert Merrill, American baritone, is born in Brooklyn.

1919   Manfred Jungwirth, Austrian bass, is born at St. Pölten.

1920   Fedora Barbieri, Italian contralto, is born in Trieste.

1922   Irwin Bazelon, American composer, is born at Evanston, Illinois.

1926   Ivo Zidek, Czech tenor, is born at Kravare.

1932   Oliver Nelson, American composer, conductor, and arranger, is born in St. Louis.   He had played with Count Basie and Duke Ellington.

1935   Colette Boky, Canadian soprano, is born in Montreal.

1940   Katherine Pring, English mezzo-soprano, is born in Brighton.

1951   Serge Koussevitzky dies at age seventy-six in Boston, where he had conducted the Boston Symphony Orchestra for twenty-five years.

JUNE 5

1625   Orlando Gibbons dies of a stroke in Canterbury, England, aged forty-one.   He was known especially for his church music.

1722   Johann Kuhnau dies in Leipzig, aged sixty-two.

1816   Giovanni Paisiello dies at age seventy-six in Naples.   He was a composer of more than 100 operas, only a few of which are ever revived.

1826   Carl Maria von Weber dies of tuberculosis in London, aged thirty-nine.

1879   Marcel Tournier, French harpist and composer, is born in
        Paris.

1885   Sir Julius Benedict dies at age eighty in London, where he
        had settled fifty years earlier.

1909   Alfred Uhl, Austrian composer and teacher, is born in Vienna.
        He was badly wounded in World War II, serving with the
        Austrian Army.

1919   Akeo Watanabe, Japanese conductor, founder and conductor
        of the Nippon Philharmonic Orchestra, is born in Tokyo.

1923   Daniel Pinkham, American organist, composer, and faculty
        member at New England Conservatory of Music, is born in
        Lynn, Massachusetts.

1937   Anne Pashley, British soprano, a former Olympic athlete
        at Melbourne, is born at Skegness.

1944   Riccardo Zandonai dies in Pesaro, Italy, aged sixty-one.

1971   James Levine makes his conducting debut with the Metro-
        politan Opera, conducting Puccini's Tosca. In 1973 he be-
        comes its principal conductor and three years later, its
        musical director.

JUNE 6

1807   Marietta Brambilla, Italian contralto and teacher, is born
        into a family of musicians at Cassano d'Adda.

        Adrien-François Servais, Belgian cellist and composer, is
        born at Hal.

1840   Sir John Stainer, English organist and composer, is born in
        London. His cantata The Crucifixion has been widely per-
        formed.

1869   Siegfried Wagner, conductor son of Richard and Cosima Liszt
        Wagner, is born in Triebschen, Switzerland. It was for him
        that his father wrote the Siegfried Idyll.

1881   Henri Vieuxtemps dies in Mustapha, Algiers, aged sixty-one.
        He had gone there to rest following a stroke.

1887   Adrian Schaposhnikov, Russian composer, is born in St.
        Petersburg.

1903   Aram Khachaturian, Soviet Armenian composer and conductor,
        is born in Tiflis.

1905   Arthur Mendel, American music scholar, educator, and critic, is born in Boston.

1915   Vincent Persichetti, American composer and music administrator, is born in Philadelphia.

1921   Darius Milhaud's ballet L'Homme et son désir is first staged, in Paris.

1922   Iain Hamilton, Scottish composer, is born in Glasgow.   He left an engineering profession to begin music study at age twenty-five.

1934   Philippe Entremont, French pianist, is born in Rheims.

1939   Giacomo Aragall, Spanish tenor, is born in Barcelona.

1940   Phillip Rhodes, American composer and teacher, is born in Forest City, North Carolina.

1942   Paul Esswood, English countertenor, is born in West Bridgeford.

1952   Pavel Kogan, Soviet violinist, son of violinist Leonid Kogan, is born in Moscow.

1953   György Ránki's opera King Pomade's New Clothes receives its premiere, in Budapest.

1976   Elisabeth Rethberg dies in Yorktown Heights, New York, aged eighty-one.

JUNE 7

1825   Maria Malibran at the age of seventeen makes her operatic debut in London.   She studied with her father, Manuel García.

1845   Leopold Auer, Hungarian violinist, is born in Veszprém. Among his students were Elman, Heifetz, and Zimbalist.

1873   Sir Landon Ronald, English conductor, is born in London.

1897   George Szell, Hungarian-American conductor of the Cleveland Orchestra for twenty-four years, is born in Budapest.

1908   Boris Goldovsky, Russian-American pianist and conductor, is born in Moscow.   From 1942 to 1962 he directed the opera workshop at Berkshire Music Center, Tanglewood, Massachusetts.

1911   Franz Reizenstein, German-English pianist and composer who
        fled to England with the rise of anti-Semitism, is born in
        Nuremberg.

1931   Peter Pindar Stearns, American composer, organist, and
        teacher, is born in New York City.

1932   Emil Paur dies at age seventy-six in Mistek, Bohemia.   From
        1893 to 1910 he led the Boston Symphony, then the New York
        and Pittsburgh orchestras.

1941   Jaime Laredo, American-trained Bolivian violinist, is born
        in Cochabamba.

1945   Sir Benjamin Britten's opera <u>Peter Grimes</u> is first staged
        in London, reopening the Sadler's Wells Theatre after World
        War II.

1951   Henri Dutilleux's Symphony receives its premiere, in Paris.

1954   Luigi Dallapiccola's <u>Piccola musica notturna</u> is first per-
        formed, in Hannover.

JUNE 8

1612   Hans Leo Hassler dies in Frankfurt of tuberculosis, aged
        forty-seven.   He found time from his organ duties to manu-
        facture and install musical clocks.

1671   Tomaso Albinoni, Italian violinist and composer of instru-
        mental and operatic works, is born in Venice.

1796   Felice de' Giardini dies in Moscow, aged eighty, becoming
        ill shortly after his arrival in Russia.

1810   Robert Schumann, German composer and conductor, is born
        in Zwickau.   He was one of the leaders of German Romanti-
        cism.

1814   Friedrich Heinrich Himmel dies in Berlin, aged forty-eight.

1868   Alberto Jonás, Spanish-American pianist and teacher, is born
        in Madrid.

1884   Henry Clay Work dies in Hartford, Connecticut, aged fifty-
        one.   A printer by trade, he is remembered for his songs;
        his Civil War song, <u>Marching Through Georgia,</u> and <u>Grand-
        father's Clock</u> are well known.

1906   Reginald Kell,   English-born clarinet virtuoso, is born in

York; after 1948 he resided in New York City.

1911   Bruno Bartolozzi, Italian musician who began his career as
        a concert violinist and later turned to composition, is born
        in Florence.

1912   Maurice Ravel's ballet Daphnis et Chloé is first staged, in
        Paris.

1926   Nellie Melba, at sixty-five, makes a farewell appearance at
        Covent Garden, singing before George V and Queen Mary.

1937   Carl Orff's scenic cantata on thirteenth-century poems,
        Carmina Burana, is first performed, in Frankfurt.

1940   Frederick Shepherd Converse dies in Westwood, Massachusetts
        aged sixty-nine.

1941   Harold Shapero's Nine Minute Overture, awarded the Prix de
        Rome, has its premiere performance in New York City.

1949   Emanuel Ax, Polish-American pianist, is born in Lvov.   In
        1973 he placed first in the Artur Rubinstein International
        Competition in Tel Aviv.

1953   Sir Benjamin Britten's Gloriana, written in honor of the new
        Queen's coronation six days earlier, is first performed at
        London's Covent Garden.

1974   Henry Brant's An American Requiem has its premiere, in Mt.
        Lebanon, Pennsylvania.

        JUNE 9

1361   Philippe de Vitry, French churchman and writer on music,
        dies at Meaux, aged sixty-nine.

1527   Heinrich Finck, German composer and Kapellmeister who
        served three Polish kings, dies in Vienna, aged about eighty-
        two.

1791   Johann Peter Müller, German composer, is born in Kessel-
        stadt.

1810   Otto Nicolai, German opera composer, is born in Königsberg.

1832   Manuel del Popolo García dies in Paris, aged fifty-seven.
        Among his best pupils were his two daughters, singers Maria
        Malibran and Pauline Viardot-García.

1865   Carl Nielsen, Danish composer, is born in Nørre-Lyndelse.
        He is credited with initiating the modern Danish school of
        composition.

1877   Titta Ruffo (né Ruffo Titta), Italian baritone, is born in Pisa.
        He transposed his name for professional reasons.

1891   Cole Porter, American musical-comedy composer, is born in
        Peru, Indiana.

1900   Fred Waring, American choral conductor and inventor of the
        Waring electric blender, is born in Tyrone, Pennsylvania.

1902   Gustav Mahler conducts his Symphony no. 3, "Ein Sommer-
        morgentraum," in its premiere, at Krefeld.

1904   London Symphony Orchestra gives its first concert under the
        direction of Hans Richter.

1912   Ingolf Dahl, German-American composer, conductor, and
        pianist, is born in Hamburg.   In 1945 he became a member
        of the faculty at the University of Southern California.

1928   Richard Cumming, American composer, conductor, and
        pianist, is born in Shanghai, China.

1938   Charles Wuorinen, American composer, pianist, and teacher,
        is born in New York City.

1940   Aaron Copland's Our Town, orchestral suite from the film,
        receives its premiere on CBS radio.

1948   Nathaniel Rosen, American cellist who won the gold medal
        in Moscow's 1978 Tchaikovsky Competition, is born in Los
        Angeles.

1949   Maria Cebotari dies in Vienna, aged thirty-nine.

1952   Adolph Busch dies in Guilford, Vermont, aged sixty.   He had
        organized the Busch Quartet and the Busch Trio.

1964   Louis Gruenberg dies in Los Angeles, aged seventy-nine.
        He was one of the organizers of the League of Composers.

1966   Sir Benjamin Britten's church parable The Burning Fiery
        Furnace is given its first performance, at Aldeburgh, Eng-
        land.

JUNE 10

1761   Niccolò Piccinni's comic opera La Buona figliuola maritata
       is first staged, in Bologna.

1849   Friedrich W. Michael Kalkbrenner, German pianist and com-
       poser, dies in Deuil, France, aged sixty-three.

1865   Richard Wagner's opera Tristan und Isolde is first performed
       in Munich under the direction of Hans von Bülow.

1899   Ernest Chausson dies in a bicycle accident near Limay,
       France, aged forty-four.

1904   Frederick Loewe, Austrian-American composer of musical
       comedies and popular sings, is born in Vienna.

1909   Edwin Gerschefski, American composer and teacher, is born
       in Meriden, Connecticut.

1911   Ralph Kirkpatrick, American harpsichordist and musicologist,
       is born in Leominster, Massachusetts.

1913   John Edmunds, American composer (principally of songs) and
       musicologist, is born in San Francisco.

       Thor Johnson, American conductor, is born in Wisconsin
       Rapids, Wisconsin.

1918   Arrigo Boito dies in Milan, aged seventy-six. He wrote the
       libretti for his own operas and also for two of Verdi's operas:
       Otello and Falstaff.

1921   Igor Stravinsky's Symphonies of Wind Instruments, in memory
       of Debussy, receives its premiere, in London.

1934   Frederick Delius, blind and a complete invalid his last twelve
       years, dies at Grez-sur-Loing, France, at age seventy-two.

1939   Sir Arthur Bliss's Piano Concerto, commissioned for British
       Week at the New York World's Fair, is first performed there
       with Sir Adrian Boult conducting; Solomon, soloist.

1941   Francis Poulenc's Concerto for Organ, Strings and Timpani
       is first performed, in Paris.

1954   Sir Noel Coward's musical comedy After the Ball, after
       Wilde's Lady Windermere's Fan, is first staged, in London.

JUNE 11

1704   (José Antonio) Carlos de Seixas, Portuguese organist and composer, is born in Coimbra.

1864   Richard Strauss, German composer and conductor, son of Franz Strauss, horn player, is born in Munich.

1898   Vassily Nebolsin, Russian conductor of the Bolshoi Symphony, is born in Kharkov.

1913   Ildebrando Pizzetti's incidental music to <u>La Pisanella</u> has its premiere, in Paris.

      Risë Stevens, American mezzo-soprano, is born in New York City.

1921   Arthur Honegger's cantata <u>Le Roi David</u> is first performed, in Mézières.

1924   Théodore Dubois dies in Paris, aged eighty-six.

1926   Carlisle Floyd, American drama composer and teacher, is born in Latta, South Carolina.

1932   Rolf Kühne, German baritone, is born in Aschersleben.

1934   Agustin Anievas, American pianist, is born in New York City.

1937   Benjamin Luxon, English baritone, is born in Camborne.

1942   Geoffrey Toye dies in London at the age of fifty-three.

1955   Alexandra Pakhmutova's Trumpet Concerto is given its premiere, in Moscow.

1960   Karlheinz Stockhausen's <u>Kontakte,</u> for electronic instruments, piano, and percussion, is first performed, in Cologne.

1970   Alan Hovhaness's <u>And God Created Great Whales,</u> for humpbackwhale solo (on tape) and orchestra, has its premiere in New York City, André Kostelanetz, who commissioned the work, conducting.

JUNE 12

1849   Angelica Catalani dies in Paris, aged sixty-nine.

1851   Pol Plançon, versatile opera bass, is born in Fumay, France.

1858   William Horsley dies in London, aged eighty-three. He wrote several theory books on music and was also a founder of the Philharmonic Society of London (1813).

1879   Mark Hambourg, Russian pianist, is born at Bugutchar. His first teacher was his father.

1885   Werner Josten, German-American composer, conductor, and faculty member at Smith College (1923-49), is born at Elberfeld.

1892   John Donald Robb, American composer and conductor as well as a lawyer, is born in Minneapolis.

1897   Alexandre Tansman, Polish-born French composer, pianist, and biographer of Igor Stravinsky, is born in Lodz.

1903   Sigma Alpha Iota, national music organization, is founded at Ann Arbor, Michigan.

1914   Maurice Ohana, French composer and pianist, is born in Casablanca.

1917   Teresa Carreño dies in New York City, aged sixty-three. She was reburied in her native Caracas in 1938.

       Hans Pfitzner's opera Palestrina, for which he wrote the libretto, is first produced, in Munich.

1932   Mimi Coertse, South African soprano, is born in Durban.

1957   Jimmy Dorsey dies in New York City, aged fifty-three. With his brother Tommy he was the subject of a film, The Fabulous Dorseys (1947).

1962   John Ireland dies in Washington, England, aged eighty-two. A number of British composers were his pupils.

       Toshiro Mayuzumi's symphonic poem Samsara receives its premiere in Tokyo.

1966   Hermann Scherchen dies in Florence, Italy, aged seventy-four. During World War I he was interned in Russia, later resuming his conducting career.

1967   Ezra Laderman's Magic Prison, for two narrators and orchestra, receives its first performance, in New York City.

JUNE 13

1757   Christian Ludwig Dieter, German composer and court musician, is born in Ludwigsburg. He died in Stuttgart some time in 1822.

1852   Robert Schumann's Manfred Overture is first performed at the Court Theater in Weimar, Germany.

1855   Giuseppe Verdi's opera I Vespri Siciliani is staged in Paris in its premiere at the Opéra. The first of Verdi's two French operas, it is poorly received.

1869   Eduard Poldini, Hungarian composer, is born in Budapest. His piano composition Doll Dance is internationally known.

1885   Elisabeth Schumann, German-American soprano, is born in Merseburg.

1899   Carlos Chávez, Mexican composer and conductor, is born in Calzada de Tacuba. He organized the Orquesta Sinfónica de Mexico in 1928 and conducted it until 1949.

1904   Oliviero De Fabritiis, Italian conductor, is born in Rome.

1911   Igor Stravinsky's ballet Petrouchka is first staged by the Ballet Russe, in Paris.

1927   Attila Zoller, Hungarian-American jazz guitarist, is born in Visegrad. He holds a patent for a bi-directional pick-up device for guitar and electric bass.

1929   Alan Civil, horn player and composer, is born in Northampton, England.

1935   Horst Hoffmann, Polish-German tenor, is born in Oppen.

1938   Gwynne Howell, British baritone, is born in Gorseinon, Wales.

1945   Darius Milhaud's Suite française is first performed by the Goldman Band, in New York City.

1951   Francis Poulenc's Stabat Mater, for a cappella chorus, is given its first performance at the Strasbourg Festival, France.

1952   Emma Eames dies in New York City, aged eighty-six.

1954   Ralph Vaughan Williams's Concerto for Bass Tuba receives its first performance, in London.

1960   Pierre Boulez's Pli selon pli, for voice and orchestra, has its premiere, in Cologne.

1962 Sir Eugene Goossens dies in London, aged sixty-nine. He had conducted orchestras in Europe, the United States, and Australia.

1964 Sir Benjamin Britten's church parable <u>Curlew River</u> is performed for the first time at Aldeburgh, England.

1973 Alvin Etler dies in Northampton, Massachusetts, aged sixty. He had been teaching at Smith College since 1949.

1976 Géza Anda dies in Zurich, aged fifty-four. He had conducted annual summer classes in piano music there.

JUNE 14

1594 Orlandus (Roland de) Lassus, Flemish-born composer and contrapuntist whose works number over 2,000, dies in Munich, aged about sixty-two.

1730 Antonio Sacchini, Italian opera composer, a favorite of the French court, is born in Florence.

1744 André Campra dies at Versailles, aged eighty-three. His opera-ballets were popular in the interim between Lully and Rameau.

1763 (Johann) Simon Mayr, prolific German opera composer, teacher of Donizetti, is born in Mendorf.

1789 Johann Wilhelm Hertel dies in Schwerin, Germany, aged sixty-one.

1835 Nicolas Rubinstein, Russian pianist and teacher, a brother of Anton Rubinstein, is born in Moscow.

1884 John McCormack, Irish-American tenor, is born in Athlone.

1909 Burl Ives, American folksinger and balladeer who accompanies himself on the guitar, is born in Jasper County, Illinois.

1910 Rudolf Kempe, German conductor, is born at Niederpoyritz.

1911 Johan (Severin) Svendsen dies in Copenhagen, aged seventy.

1918 Carter Harman, American music critic, recording-firm executive (CRI), and composer, is born in Brooklyn.

1921 Ralph Vaughan Williams's <u>The Lark Ascending,</u> romance for violin and orchestra, has its premiere, in London.

1927   Reinhold Glière's opera <u>The Red Poppy</u> is first staged, in Moscow.

1934   Nicolas Roussakis, Greek clarinetist, composer, and teacher, is born in Athens.

1942   Sir Benjamin Britten's <u>A Ceremony of Carols</u>, for treble voices and harp, receives its premiere, at Aldeburgh, England.

1944   Georges Barrère dies at Kingston, New York, aged sixty-seven. He founded the Barrère Little Symphony in 1914.

1949   Sir Benjamin Britten's <u>The Little Sweep,</u> for young people, has its premiere performance, at Aldeburgh, England.

1960   Vladimir Nikolaievitch Kriukov dies at Staraya Rusa, Soviet Union, at the age of fifty-seven.

1974   Knud Jeppesen dies at Aarhus, Denmark, aged eighty-one. He is acknowledged to be an outstanding musicologist.

JUNE 15

1763   Franz Danzi, German composer, cellist, and teacher of Carl Maria von Weber, is born in Mannheim.

1772   Louis-Claude Daquin dies in Paris, aged seventy-seven. From 1727 until his death he was organist at St. Paul in Paris.

1843   Edvard Grieg, Norwegian composer, is born in Bergen. He espoused a new Scandinavian idiom in his music.

1861   Ernestine Schumann-Heink, German-American contralto, is born in Lieben.

1864   Guy Ropartz, French composer and conductor, is born at Guingamp.

1872   Johanna Gadski, German soprano, is born at Anclam.

1893   Ferenc Erkel dies in Budapest, aged eighty-two. His songs became very popular.

1894   Robert Russell Bennett, American composer, arranger, and orchestrator of musical comedies, is born in Kansas City.

1900   Otto Luening, American composer, teacher, and co-founder of the Columbia-Princeton Electronic Music Center, is born in Milwaukee.

1902   Max Rudolf, German-American conductor, is born in Frank-
        furt.   He joined the staff of the Metropolitan Opera in New
        York and since 1970 conducted the opera class at Curtis
        Institute of Music in Philadelphia.

1921   Erroll Garner, American jazz pianist and composer, is born
        in Pittsburgh.

1924   Erik Satie's ballet Mercure is first staged, in Paris.

1938   Jean-Claude Eloy, French composer, is born at Mont-Saint-
        Aignan.

1962   Alfred Cortot dies in Lausanne, aged eighty-four, bringing
        to a close many decades of piano concerts and lectures on
        piano interpretation.

1967   Jacqueline DuPré, English cellist, marries painist-conductor
        Daniel Barenboim.   Since 1972 she has suffered from multi-
        ple sclerosis and no longer plays publicly.

        JUNE 16

1804   Johann Adam Hiller dies in Leipzig at the age of seventy-five.
        From 1789 to 1801 he was cantor and music director of the
        Thomasschule there.

1813   Otto Jahn, German musicologist, is born in Kiel.   His biogra-
        phy of Mozart is the first musical biography written according
        to the comparative critical method and becomes a model for
        others.

1853   Emil Sjögren, Swedish composer (especially of songs) and
        organist, is born in Stockholm.

1909   Willi Boskovsky, Austrian violinist and conductor, is born
        in Vienna.

1929   James K. Randall, American composer and faculty member
        at Princeton University, is born in Cleveland, Ohio.

1930   John Modenos, Cypriot-American baritone and Greek Orthodox
        choral conductor, is born in Cyprus.

1931   Lucia Dlugoszewski, American composer, pianist, and in-
        ventor of several percussion instruments, is born in Detroit.

1937   Marc Blitzstein's one-act opera The Cradle Will Rock, re-
        ceives its premiere in New York City, the composer at the
        piano.

1943   Sigrid Onégin dies in Magliaso, Switzerland, aged fifty-four.

JUNE 17

1818   Charles Gounod, French composer, organist, and conductor, is born in Paris.

1848   Victor Maurel, French baritone, is born in Marseilles.

1854   Henriette Sontag dies of cholera while on tour in Mexico City, aged forty-eight.

1868   Alphonse Leduc dies in Paris, aged sixty-four; his music-publishing business is carried on by his son Alphonse II.

1882   Igor Stravinsky, Russian-American composer, is born in Oranienbaum. His father was Feodor Stravinsky, bass singer at the St. Petersburg Opera.

1891   Pierre Luboschutz, Russian-American pianist and teacher, is born in Odessa. He and his wife, Genia Nemenoff, formed a duo-piano team. From 1962 to 1968 they headed the piano department at Michigan State University.

1900   Hermann Reutter, German composer, is born in Stuttgart. He taught composition from 1932 to 1966 at the Hochschule for Musik in Stuttgart.

1903   Victor Herbert's operetta Babes in Toyland is first staged, in Chicago.

1908   Webster Aitken, American pianist who is an exponent of Schubert's piano works, is born in Los Angeles.

John Verrall, American composer who taught at the University of Washington for twenty-five years, is born in Britt, Iowa.

1925   Georges Auric's ballet Les Matelots is given its first performance, in Paris.

1930   Ernst Toch's Geographical Fugue, for speaking chorus, is first performed at the Berlin Festival of New Music.

1931   Mignon Dunn, American mezzo-soprano, is born in Memphis, Tennessee.

1947   Francis Madeira, conductor, marries Jean Browning, opera singer.

JUNE 18

1677 Antonio Maria Bononcini, Italian opera composer, is born in Modena.

1757 Ignaz Pleyel, Austrian pianist, composer, and piano manufacturer, is born in Ruppertsthal.

1821 Carl Maria von Weber conducts the premiere of his opera Der Freischütz at the new Berlin Opera Theater.

1872 Katherine Goodson, English pianist who studied with Leschetizky, is born in Watford.

1891 Antonin Dvořák receives an honorary Doctor of Music at Cambridge University and conducts his G major Symphony and Stabat Mater.

1892 Edward Steuermann, Polish-American pianist, educator, and composer, is born in Sambor.

1907 Jeannette MacDonald, American soprano, is born; with Nelson Eddy she sang in musicals and films.

1913 Max Loy, German conductor and composer, is born in Nuremberg.

1927 Robert Ilosfalvy, Hungarian tenor, is born at Hodmezövasarhely.

1942 Paul McCartney, English rock 'n roll singer and member of The Beatles, is born in Liverpool.

1955 Pierre Boulez's cantata Le Marteau sans maître, receives its premiere, at Baden-Baden.

Willy Burkhard dies in Zurich at fifty-five; he had been a teacher at the Zurich Conservatory since 1942.

1958 Sir Benjamin Britten's one-act opera Noye's Fludde is first staged, at Aldeburgh, England.

1962 Volkmar Andreae dies in Zurich, aged eighty-two. He was a renowned conductor of choral works.

Manuel de Falla's opera Atlántida (completed by Ernesto Halffter) is produced posthumously, at La Scala in Milan.

1964 Alexander Melik-Pashayev dies at age fifty-eight in Moscow, where he had been principal conductor of the Bolshoi Theater from 1953 to 1962.

1967 Easley Blackwood's Violin Concerto has its premiere, in Bath, England.

1973   Fritz Mahler dies in Winston-Salem, North Carolina, aged
        seventy-one.

JUNE 19

1717   Johann Wenzel Anton Stamitz, Bohemian composer and vio-
        linist, is born in Deutsch-Brod.   He expanded the orchestra
        at Mannheim and developed the classical sonata form; he is
        considered the most important figure in the Mannheim group
        of composers.

1747   Alessandro Marcello dies in Padua, aged seventy-seven, hav-
        ing outlived his famous younger brother, Benedetto Marcello.

1854   Alfredo Catalani, Italian composition teacher and opera com-
        poser, is born in Lucca.

1898   Paul Müller-Zürich, Swiss conductor and composer, is born
        in Zurich.

1899   Sir Edward Elgar's Enigma Variations receives its premiere
        in London with Hans Richter conducting.

1902   Guy Lombardo, Canadian-American leader of the Royal Ca-
        nadians dance orchestra, is born in London, Ontario.

1924   Anneliese Rothenberger, German soprano, is born in Mann-
        heim.

1926   George Antheil's orchestral suite Ballet mécanique, which
        includes airplane propellers, is first performed, in Paris.

1972   Helge Roswänge dies in Munich, aged seventy-four.

JUNE 20

1756   Joseph Martin Kraus, German-Swedish composer and con-
        ductor, is born in Miltenberg.

1819   Jacques Offenbach, composer of French light operas, the son
        of a cantor, is born in Cologne.

1899   Helen Traubel, American soprano, is born in St. Louis,
        Missouri.

1901   Sir Edward Elgar's Cockaigne Overture receives its premiere,
        in Queen's Hall, London.

1931   Arne Nordheim, Norwegian composer and music critic, is born in Larvik.

1937   Stafford Dean, English bass, is born in Surrey.

1940   Jehan Alain is killed in action in World War II near Saumur, France, aged twenty-nine.

1946   André Watts, American pianist, is born in a United States Army camp at Nuremberg, Germany, to a Hungarian mother and an American soldier.

1947   Sir Benjamin Britten conducts his opera Albert Herring in its premiere at Glyndebourne, England.

1969   Krzysztof Penderecki's opera The Devils of Loudon is first staged, in Hamburg.

JUNE 21

1732   Johann Christoph Friedrich Bach, German composer, ninth son of Johann Sebastian Bach and known as the "Bückeburg Bach," is born in Leipzig.

1804   Karl Friedrich Curschmann, German composer (principally of lieder), is born in Berlin.

1862   Henry Holden Huss, American composer and pianist, is born in Newark, New Jersey. He is a descendant of Leonhard Huss, brother of martyred John Huss.

1868   Richard Wagner's opera Die Meistersinger von Nürnberg is conducted in its premiere by Hans von Bülow, in Munich.

1890   Richard Strauss conducts from manuscript the premiere of his orchestral tone poem Tod und Verklärung, in Eisenach, Germany.

1891   Hermann Scherchen, German conductor and music editor, is born in Berlin. He was known as a champion of new music.

1892   Hilding Rosenberg, Swedish composer and teacher, is born in Bosjökloster.

1893   Alois Hába, Czech composer, experimenter with the use of quarter-tones, is born in Vizovice.

1898   Avery Claflin, American composer whose choral work Lament for April 15 uses Internal Revenue forms as text, is born in Keene, New Hampshire.

Gabriel Fauré's incidental music for <u>Pelléas et Mélisande</u> (after Maeterlinck), is first performed, in London.

1908   Nikolai Rimsky-Korsakov dies in Liubensk, Russia, aged sixty-four.   The altercations with authorities about changing Pushkin's lines in his last opera, <u>Le Coq d'or</u>, were not resolved at the time of his death, of angina.

1913   Kurt List, Austrian-American composer and music critic, is born in Vienna.

1928   Judith Raskin, American soprano, is born in New York City.

1932   Lalo Schifrin, Argentine-American composer, arranger, and jazz-band leader, is born in Buenos Aires.   His theme for the television series <u>Mission: Impossible</u> won two Grammy awards.

1936   John Wakefield (né John Darling), English tenor, is born in Wakefield.

1967   Emanuel List dies in Vienna, aged seventy-six, famed for his Wagnerian roles in opera.

1972   Seth Bingham dies in New York City, aged ninety.   He had been an organ professor at Columbia University for many years.

JUNE 22

1763   Etienne Méhul, French opera composer, is born in Givet.

1830   Theodor Leschetizky, Polish pianist, teacher, and composer, a pupil of Czerny, is born at Lancut.   His pupils included Paderewski, Schnabel, and Gabrilowitsch.

1852   Albert Carré, French opera impressario, is born in Strasbourg.   From 1898 to 1912 he directed the Opéra-Comique, Paris.

1859   Frank Damrosch, German-American choral conductor, son of Leopold Damrosch, is born in Breslau.

1900   Jennie Tourel, Russian-American mezzo-soprano, is born in St. Petersburg.

1910   Sir Peter Pears, English tenor and co-founder with Benjamin Britten of the Aldeburgh Festival, is born in Franham.

1939   William Bergsma's ballet <u>Paul Bunyan</u> is first staged, in San Francisco.

1969   Alun Hoddinott's <u>Investiture Dances,</u> commissioned for the
        Prince of Wales's investiture, receives its premiere, in
        London.

1974   Darius Milhaud dies in Geneva, aged eighty-one. During
        World War II he taught at Mills College in Oakland, Califor-
        nia. In some of his works he introduced jazz elements,
        foreshadowing Gershwin.

        JUNE 23

1685   Antonio Bernacchi, Italian male soprano, is baptized in
        Bologna. After 1736 he opened a singing school in Bologna,
        having retired から opera.

1824   Carl Reinecke, German pianist and composer, conductor of
        Gewandhaus Concerts in Leipig from 1860 to 1895, is born
        in Altona.

1837   Ernest Guiraud, American-French composer, is born in New
        Orleans.

1892   Mieczyslaw Horszowski, Polish pianist, is born in Lwow.
        A pupil of Leschetizky, he played joint recitals with Casals.

1894   Marietta Alboni dies in Ville d'Avray, France, aged seventy-
        one.

1922   Francis Thorne, American composer and jazz pianist, is
        born in Bay Shore, New York. His grandfather was Gustave
        Kobbé, author of the <u>Complete Opera Book</u>.

1924   Cecil James Sharp dies in London, aged sixty-four, ending a
        varied career as lawyer in Australia, organist, and folksong
        collector in Europe and America.

1926   Anton Webern's <u>Five Orchestral Pieces</u> creates a sensation
        in its first performance, at Zurich Festival of the International
        Society for Contemporary Music.

1929   Henri Pousseur, Belgian composer who studied with Pierre
        Boulez, is born in Malmédy. He founded and directed the
        Studio de Musique Electronique, later absorbed by Centre de
        Recherches Musicales in Liège.

1943   James Levine, American pianist and conductor, is born in
        Cincinnati. From 1965 to 1970 he was assistant conductor
        of the Cleveland Orchestra, the youngest musician in such a
        position.

1956   Reinhold Glière, former teacher of Prokofiev and Miaskovsky,
        dies at age eighty-one in Moscow.

JUNE 24

1693   Pavel Vejvanovsky, Bohemian trumpeter and composer, dies
        in Kremsier, aged about fifty-three.

1882   Joachim Raff dies in Frankfurt, Germany, aged sixty. Among
        his pupils was the American composer Edward MacDowell.

1901   Harry Partch, American composer who devised a forty-three-
        tone scale and various musical instruments, is born in Oak-
        land, California.

1908   Hugo Distler, German church organist and composer, is born
        in Nuremberg.

1909   Milton Katims, American conductor and violist, is born in
        New York City.

1913   Heinrich Hollreiser, German conductor, is born in Munich.

1916   Ruth Shaw Wylie, American composer, is born in Cincinnati.

1921   The American Conservatory of Music at Fontainebleau, France,
        is inaugurated.

1922   Roy Travis, American composer, is born in New York City.

1935   Terry Riley, American avant-garde composer, is born in
        Colfax, California.

1937   Sir Eugene Goossens's opera Don Juan de Mañara is first
        staged, in London's Covent Garden.

1938   Lowell Cross, American composer, musicologist, and ex-
        ponent of electronic music, is born in Kingsville, Texas.

1970   Sir Arthur Bliss's Cello Concerto is first performed at Alde-
        burgh Festival, England, with Mstislav Rostropovich, soloist.

1976   Samuel Dushkin dies in New York City, aged eighty-four. He
        had worked with Stravinsky, helping him solve technical prob-
        lems in writing for the violin.

JUNE 25

1767   Georg Philipp Telemann dies in Hamburg, aged eighty-six,
the most notable of early German dramatic composers. In
his time he was better known than J. S. Bach.

1799   Ludwig van Beethoven writes the dedication of his Op. 18,
no. 1 to Carl Amenda, " ... accept this quartet as a small
token of our friendship. "

1822   Ernst Theodor Amadeus Hoffman dies in Berlin, aged forty-
six.   A proficient musician, he is best known for his writings.

1840   Felix Mendelssohn's Symphony no. 2, "Lobgesang" (a sym-
phony-cantata), is first performed in St. Thomas Church,
Leipzig.

1860   Gustave Charpentier, French opera composer, is born at
Dieuze.   He owes his fame to his most successful opera,
Louise.

1886   Arturo Toscanini makes his conducting debut in Rio de
Janeiro in performing Verdi's opera Aïda, substituting on
short notice.

1897   Hans Barth, German-American composer and pianist who
wrote for a quarter-tone portable piano, is born in Leipzig.

1910   Igor Stravinsky's ballet The Firebird is performed by the
Ballet Russe in Paris in its premiere.

1915   Rafael Joseffy dies in New York City, aged sixty-two, a
teacher of many American concert pianists.

1928   William Joseph Russo, American composer and arranger, is
born in Chicago.   He was a jazz trombonist with Stan Kenton's band.

1945   Jane Marsh, American soprano, is born in San Francisco.

JUNE 26

1770   Wolfgang Amadeus Mozart receives the Order of the Golden
Spur from the Pope in Rome; a title he never used (in German: Ritter).

1870   Richard Wagner's opera Die Walküre is first staged at the
Court Opera, in Munich.   The libretto is by the composer.

1885   Frieda Hempel, German soprano, is born in Leipzig.

1894   Michel Michelet (né Levin), Russian-American composer
        (including many film scores), is born in Kiev.

1900   Richard Crooks, American tenor, is born in Trenton, New
        Jersey.

1902   Hughes Cuénod, Swiss tenor, is born in Corseaux-sur-Vevey.

1912   Gustav Mahler's Symphony no. 9 is posthumously performed
        in Vienna, Bruno Walter conducting its premiere.

1914   Wolfgang Windgassen, French-born German tenor and opera
        director, is born at Annemasse.

1916   Giuseppe Taddei, Italian baritone, is born in Genoa.

1928   Jacob Druckman, American composer and faculty member at
        Yale University, is born in Philadelphia.

1933   Claudio Abbado, Italian conductor, is born in Milan.

JUNE 27

1789   Friedrich Silcher, German song composer and folksong col-
        lector, is born in Schnaith.

1812   John Pyke Hullah, English organist and composer, is born in
        Worcester.

1819   Albert Löschhorn, German composer and pianist, is born in
        Berlin.   He published a series of piano studies that are still
        used.

1884   Claude Debussy's cantata L'Enfant prodige is first performed,
        in Paris, and wins for the composer the Prix de Rome.

1898   Tibor Harsányi, Hungarian composer, is born in Magyarkan-
        izsa.

1922   George Walker, American composer and teacher of piano and
        music theory, is born in Washington.

1932   Anna Moffo, American soprano, wife of Robert Sarnoff (for-
        mer chairman of the board of RCA Records), is born in
        Wayne, Pennsylvania.

        Hugh Wood, English composer and music educator, is born
        in Parbold.

1968   Gunther Schuller's Concerto for Double Bass has its premiere,
        in New York City.

1970   Frank Martin's Piano Concerto no. 2 receives its first per-
        formance, in The Hague.

JUNE 28

1712   Jean-Jacques Rousseau, Swiss-born French philosopher, music
        critic, opera composer, and contributor to Diderot's Ency-
        clopédie, is born in Geneva. Rousseau's Dictionnaire de musique
        appeared in 1768 in Paris.

1745   Antoine Forqueray, French viola-da-gambist, composer, and
        royal chamber musician to Louis XIV, dies at Nantes, aged
        seventy-four.

1831   Joseph Joachim, Austrian virtuoso violinist, teacher, con-
        ductor, and composer, is born at Kittsee. In 1869 he organ-
        ized the Joachim Quartet.

1871   Luisa Tetrazzini, Italian soprano, is born in Florence.

1872   Carlotta Marchisio dies, aged thirty-seven, in Turin.

1874   Oley Speaks, American song composer and singer, a director
        of the American Society of Composers, Authors and Publishers
        (ASCAP) from 1924 to 1943, is born in Canal Winchester,
        Ohio.

1876   August Wilhelm Ambros dies in Vienna, aged fifty-nine,
        before completing the fourth volume of his Geschichte der
        Musik.

1902   Richard Rodgers, American composer of musical comedies,
        is born at Hammels Station, New York. First with lyricist
        Lorenz Hart and later with Oscar Hammerstein II, he pro-
        duced Pulitzer Prize-winning musicals (excerpts in Rodgers
        and Hart Songbook).

1957   Eduard Poldini dies at Corseaux, Switzerland, aged eighty-
        eight.

1966   Iannis Xenakis's Akrata, for sixteen wind instruments, is
        first performed, at Oxford, England.

1979   Paul Dessau dies in East Berlin, aged eighty-four.

1980   José Iturbi dies, at age eighty-four, in Hollywood, California.
        He had continued an active concert schedule until three months
        before his heart attack.

JUNE 29

1830   Ludwig van Beethoven's <u>Missa Solemnis</u> is performed in its entirety for the first time, at Warnsdorf.

1889   Nikolai Rimsky-Korsakov conducts an all-Russian program at the Paris World Exhibition, but attendance is not large.

1901   Nelson Eddy, American baritone and co-star with Jeanette MacDonald in film musicals, is born in Providence, Rhode Island.

1908   Leroy Anderson, American composer of light popular music and conductor, is born in Cambridge, Massachusetts.

1910   Frank Loesser, American composer of popular songs and musicals, brother of pianist Arthur Loesser, is born in New York City.

1911   Bernard Herrmann, American conductor and composer (including film scores), is born in New York City.

1914   Rafael Kubelík, Czech-Swiss conductor and composer, a son of Jan Kubelík, is born in Býchory.

1920   Juan Blanco, Cuban composer, is born in Havana.

1923   Wen-chung Chou, Chinese-American composer and composition teacher at Columbia University, is born in Cheefoo.

1924   Ezra Laderman, American composer, is born in New York City. His film score for <u>The Eleanor Roosevelt Story</u> won an Oscar.

1925   Hale Smith, American composer and publisher's consultant, is born in Cleveland. In 1970 he joined the music faculty of the University of Connecticut.

1941   Ignace Jan Paderewski dies at age eighty in New York City. At President Roosevelt's order he was buried in Arlington National Cemetery in Virginia.

JUNE 30

1722   Georg Benda, Czech-German composer, member of a large musical gamily, is baptized at Alt-Benatek, Bohemia.

1792   Francesco Antonio Rosetti, Bohemian composer, dies at Schwerin, Germany, aged about forty-two.

1845   Italo Campanini, Italian tenor who was wounded in Garibaldi's army in the Italian struggle for unification, is born in Parma.

1879   Teresa Stolz makes her farewell appearance in Verdi's Re-quiem, performed at La Scala, Milan.

JULY 1

1784   Wilhelm Friedemann Bach, eldest son of J. S. Bach, dies in Berlin, aged seventy-three.

1801   Ludwig van Beethoven writes his friend Carl Amenda: " ... you should know that my most precious gift, my hearing, has much deteriorated ... "

1897   The Music Division of the Library of Congress is founded, in Washington.

1906   Manuel Patricio García dies in London, at the age of 101. A singing teacher, he invented the laryngoscope, for which he received an honorary doctorate from Königsberg University.

1908   Peter Anders, German tenor, is born in Essen.

1925   Erik Satie dies in Paris, aged fifty-nine. He was the first there to use jazz in ballet.

1926   Hans Werner Henze, German composer and outspoken Communist, is born in Gütersloh.

1927   Béla Bartók is soloist in the premiere of his Piano Concerto no. 1, in Frankfurt.

1950   Emile Jaques-Dalcroze dies in Geneva, six days before his eighty-fifth birthday.

1964   Pierre Monteux dies in Hancock, Maine, aged eighty-nine.

1971   Wolf Trap Farm Park for Performing Arts is officially opened, in Vienna, Virginia.

1973   Laurens Hammond dies in Cornwall, Connecticut, aged seventy-eight.

1974   Edwin John Stringham dies at Chapel Hill, North Carolina, at the age of eighty-three. For more than twenty-six years he had taught in various colleges.

JULY 2

1636   Daniel Speer, German composer, teacher, and town piper who was imprisoned for eighteen months for criticizing the civil authorities, is born in Breslau.

1648   Arp Schnitger, German organ builder, is born in Golzwarden. His son assisted in the installation of several of the big church organs throughout northern Germany and Holland.

1714   Christoph Willibald Gluck, German opera composer and harpsichord and voice teacher of French queen Marie Antoinette, is born in Erasbach.

1723   Antonio Vivaldi agrees to guarantee two monthly concerts at the Pieta School for girls and will receive a sequin (a gold coin) for each concert. Each concert is to have several rehearsals.

1778   Jean-Jacques Rousseau dies in Ermenonville, France, aged sixty-six. His caustic music criticisms caused members of the Paris Opéra to burn him in effigy and exclude him from the theater.

1836   Ludwig Schnorr, German tenor who created the role of Tristan in Wagner's opera, is born in Munich.

1900   Jean Sibelius's symphonic poem <u>Finlandia</u> receives its premiere by the Helsinki Philharmonic Orchestra.

1906   Robert L. Sanders, American composer, organist, and teacher, is born in Chicago.

1911   Felix Mottl dies in Munich, aged fifty-four.

1914   Frederick Fennell, American conductor, is born in Cleveland, Ohio. He founded the Eastman Wind Ensemble at Eastman School of Music in Rochester, New York.

1935   Gilbert Kalish, American concert pianist, is born in Brooklyn.

1936   Olga Szönyi, Hungarian soprano, is born in Budapest.

1941   Dinu Ghezzo, Rumanian composer and teacher, is born in Tusla. Since 1966 he has resided in the United States.

1944   Christian Du Plessis, South African baritone, is born in Vryheid.

JULY 3

1848   Theodore Presser, American music publisher and co-founder
        of the Music Teachers National Association is born in Pitts-
        burgh.

1852   Rafael Joseffy, Hungarian-American pianist and teacher, is
        born in Hunfalu. He edited an authoritative edition of Chopin's
        works.

1854   Leoš Janáček, Czech composer, conductor, and teacher, is
        born in Hukvaldy.

1878   George M. Cohan, American popular-song composer, is born
        in Providence, Rhode Island. He was called the "Father of
        American musical comedy."

1879   Philippe Gaubert, French conductor, flutist, and composer, is
        born in Cahors.

1880   Carl Schuricht, German conductor, is born in Danzig.

1901   Ruth Crawford Seeger, American composer and folksong col-
        lector, is born in East Liverpool, Ohio.

1907   Gene (Romeo E. Gutsche) Gutchë, German-American composer,
        is born in Berlin.

1920   John Lessard, American composer, is born in San Francisco.

1922   David Ward, Scottish bass and a former naval officer, is born
        in Dumbarton.

1923   Jean Eichelberger Ivey, American composer and pianist, is
        born in Washington.

1926   Meyer Kupfermann, American composer, is born in New York
        City.

1939   Brigitte Fassbaender, German mezzo-soprano, is born in
        Berlin.

1945   Oscar Thompson dies in New York City, aged fifty-seven.
        His large one-volume Cyclopedia of Music and Musicians
        (1939) has had ten editions.

1957   Richard Mohaupt dies in Reichenau, Austria, aged fifty-two.
        In 1933 he fled Germany because his wife was Jewish, and
        for a time settled in New York City.

1959   Ethel Newcomb dies at Whitney Point, New York, aged eighty-
        three.

1964   Robert Ward's Pulitzer Prize-winning opera <u>The Lady from Colorado</u> is first staged, in Central City, Colorado.

1966   Deems Taylor dies in New York City, aged eighty. From 1942 to 1948 he was president of American Society for Composers, Authors and Publishers (ASCAP).

1973   Karel Ančerl dies in Toronto, aged sixty-five. In 1970 he had come to Canada to conduct the Toronto Symphony Orchestra.

1978   George M. Cohan's centennial is honored with the issuance of a new United States postage stamp.

JULY 4

1603   Philippe de Monte, Belgian contrapuntist, dies in Prague, aged about eighty-two. His last thirty-five years were spent in the service of Emperor Maximilian II in Vienna. In 1975 his complete works in a new edition began publication under R. B. Lenaerts's direction.

1623   William Byrd, English composer and organist, dies at Stondon, aged about eighty. Organist at the Chapel Royal under Queen Elizabeth, he is regarded as one of the greatest musicians of his time.

1694   Louis-Claude Daquin, French organist and composer, is born in Paris. In competition with Rameau, he won the appointment as organist at St. Paul.

1826   Stephen Foster, American song composer, is born in Lawrenceville (now part of Pittsburgh), Pennsylvania.

1887   Ferdinand Grossmann, Austrian conductor, is born in Tulln.

1900   Louis "Satchmo" Armstrong, American jazz trumpeter, is born in New Orleans.

1903   Flor Peeters, Belgian organist and composer, is born in Thielen.

1907   Howard Taubman, American music critic for the <u>New York Times,</u> is born in New York City. He has also written books on music.

1909   Alec Templeton, blind Welsh-American pianist and composer, is born in Cardiff. His humorous radio programs parodied great composers.

1911   Franco Ferrara, Italian conductor, is born in Palermo. Conductor Edo de Waart was one of his students.

1913   Leon Lishner, American bass, is born in New York City.

1925   Cathy Berberian, American mezzo-soprano, is born in Attleboro, Massachusetts.

1948   Clamma Dale, American soprano, is born in Chester, Pennsylvania. She placed first in the fiftieth annual Walter W. Naumburg voice competition.

1964   Leontyne Price, American soprano, receives the U.S. Medal of Freedom in Washington.

1978   Arthur Fiedler conducts his fiftieth Independence Day Concert in Boston.

        Flor Peeters's seventy-fifth birthday is celebrated in New York City's Riverside Church by an all-Peeters carillon recital.

JULY 5

1877   Wanda Landowska, Polish-born harpsichordist and authority on ancient music, is born in Warsaw. When the Nazis approached her home in Paris in 1940, she fled to Switzerland, leaving her extensive library and collection of instruments behind; eventually she came to the United States to settle.

1879   Volkmar Andreae, Swiss conductor, is born in Berne. From 1902 to 1949 he conducted the Zurich Municipal Chorus and directed the Zurich Conservatory.

1880   Jan Kubelík, Czech violinist, father of conductor Rafael Kubelík, is born near Prague.

1895   Gordon Jacob, English composer and faculty member for forty years at the Royal College of Music, is born in London.

1897   Paul Ben Haim (né Paul Frankenburger), German-Israeli composer and conductor, is born in Munich. In 1933 he fled Nazi persecution and changed his name, settling in Israel.

1918   George Rochberg, American composer, music editor, and teacher, is born in Paterson, New Jersey.

1924   Janos Starker, Hungarian-American cellist, is born in Budapest.

1926   Kenneth Gaburo, American composer and teacher, is born in
        Somerville, New Jersey.

1934   Tom Krause, Finnish baritone, is born in Helsinki.

1950   Peter Racine Fricker's prize-winning Symphony no. 1 receives
        its premiere at the Cheltenham Festival, England.

1953   Titta Ruffo dies in Florence, aged seventy-six.

1969   Wilhelm Backhaus dies at Villach, Austria, aged eighty-five.
        He made his last American concert tour at the age of seventy-
        two.

        JULY 6

1702   Nicolas-Antoine Lebègue, French court organist and composer
        of keyboard music, dies in Paris, aged about seventy-one.

1739   Friedrich Wilhelm Rust, German violinist and composer, is
        born in Wörlitz.

1864   Alberto Nepomuceno, Brazilian composer and director of the
        Instituto Nacional de Música in Rio de Janeiro, 1902-16, is
        born in Fortaleza.

1865   Emile Jaques-Dalcroze, Austrian-Swiss composer, creator of
        a system of rhythmic movements, is born in Vienna.   This
        system, "eurhythmics," contributed to the development of
        modern ballet.

1898   Hanns Eisler, German composer who was Hollywood assistant
        to Charlie Chaplin, is born in Leipzig.   Later he published
        the book Composing for the Films (1947).

1917   Dorothy Kirsten, American soprano, is born in Montclair,
        New Jersey.   For thirty years she sang at the Metropolitan
        Opera.

1918   Eugene List, American concert pianist, is born in Philadelphia.

1919   Ernst Haefliger, Swiss tenor, is born in Davos.

1927   Charles Whittenberg, American composer and teacher, is born
        in St. Louis.

1928   Peter Glossop, English baritone (a former bank clerk), is born
        in Sheffield.

1937   Vladimir Ashkenazy, Soviet pianist who studied with Lev Oborin,
        is born in Gorki.

1963   Leslie Bassett's Pulitzer Prize-winning <u>Variations for Orches-</u>
<u>tra</u> has its first performance, in Rome.

1971   Louis "Satchmo" Armstrong dies in Corona, New York, two
days after his seventy-first birthday.

1973   Otto Klemperer dies in Zurich at age eighty-eight; he had re-
covered completely from a brain-tumor operation in 1939.

JULY 7

1713   George Frideric Handel's <u>Utrecht Te Deum</u> is given its first
performance, in London.

1860   Gustav Mahler, Austrian composer and conductor, is born in
Kalischt, Bohemia.

1889   Giovanni Bottesini dies in Parma, Italy, aged sixty-seven.
In his last year he was made director of Parma Conservatory.

1911   Lowndes Maury, American composer, pianist, teacher, and
Hollywood arranger, is born in Butte, Montana.

Gian Carlo Menotti, Italian opera composer and librettist, is
born in Cadegliano.   He has taught at Curtis Institute in Philadelphia and has promoted the cause of American music.

1927   Jean Casadesus, French pianist, is born in Paris.   He is the
son of Robert and Gaby Casadesus, concert pianists.

1930   Ivan Sardi, Italian bass, is born in Budapest.

1935   Vinko Globokar, French composer (a pupil of Luciano Berio),
is born in Anderny.   Since 1965 he has taught trombone at
Cologne's Musikhochschule.

1937   Elena Obratzsova, Soviet mezzo-soprano, is born in Leningrad.

1940   Ringo Starr (né Richard Starkey), English drummer member
of The Beatles, is born in Liverpool.

1946   Richard Mohaupt's <u>Stadtpfeifermusik</u> is first performed at the
London Festival of the International Society for Contemporary
Music.

1956   Douglas Moore's folk opera <u>Ballad of Baby Doe</u>, based on a historical event, is staged in Central City, Colorado, where the
original incident took place.

1959   Ernest Newman dies at Tadworth, England, aged ninety,

continuing to the end to write his regular column in the
Sunday Times.

1968   William Joseph Russo's Three Pieces for Blues Band and
Orchestra has its first hearing, at Chicago's Ravinia Festival.

Leo Sowerby dies in Port Clinton, Ohio, aged seventy-three.
From 1925 to 1962 he taught composition at the American
Conservatory in Chicago.

1969   Gladys Swarthout dies in Florence, aged sixty-eight.   She
sang at the Metropolitan Opera for sixteen years.

1978   Paul Reif dies in New York City at the age of sixty-eight.

JULY 8

1726   Antonio Maria Bononcini dies in Modena, aged forty-nine.
His work included nineteen operas.

1791   (Franz) Joseph Haydn's Symphony no. 92, "Oxford," is first
performed in the Sheldonian Theatre when he is awarded
Doctor of Music by Oxford University.

1805   Luigi Ricci, Italian opera composer, is born in Naples.

1839   Fernando Sor dies in Paris, aged sixty-one.   His writing included pieces for guitar as well as a method.

1882   Percy Grainger, Australian pianist and composer, is born in
Melbourne.

1896   Richard Kountz, American composer and a department manager for M. Witmark music publishers (1927-39), is born in
Pittsburgh.

1900   George Antheil, experimental American composer who also
wrote film scores, is born in Trenton, New Jersey.   At one
time he dabbled in writing a column for the lovelorn.

1902   Hans Theodore David, German-American musicologist who was
known as an authority on J. S. Bach, is born in Speyer.

1912   Christel Goltz, German soprano, is born in Dortmund.

1914   Billy (William Clarence) Eckstine, American jazz singer and
bandleader, is born in Pittsburgh.

1931   Yuri Mazurok, Soviet baritone, a former engineer, is born
in Krasnik.

1938   Ernest Gerold Schramm, German bass, is born in Steinheim.

1940   The Berkshire Music Center opens at Tanglewood, Massachusetts, with Serge Koussevitzky as director and Aaron Copland,
assistant director.

1941   Philippe Gaubert dies in Paris, aged sixty-two.

1943   Sir Lennox Berkeley's Symphony no. 1 has its premiere, in London.

1946   Robert Pollock, American composer, is born in New York
City.

1968   Sir Lennox Berkeley's Magnificat, for chorus and orchestra,
receives its first performance, in London.

JULY 9

1697   Giovanni Platti, Italian composer who went to the court at
Würzburg in 1724, is born in Padua.

1747   Giovanni Bononcini dies in Vienna, aged forty-nine. Son of
Giovanni Maria Bononcini, he is best known of the family in
composition.

1842   Clara Louise Kellogg, American soprano, is born in Sumter-
ville, South Carolina.

1879   Ottorino Respighi, Italian composer, violinist, and conductor,
is born in Bologna. He was influenced by his study with
Rimsky-Korsakov in St. Petersburg.

1882   Richard Hageman, Dutch-American pianist, composer, and
conductor, is born in Leeuwarden.

1899   Ania Dorfmann, Russian-American pianist, is born in Odessa.

1904   Robert Whitney, American conductor of the Louisville Orchestra from 1937 to 1967, is born in Newcastle-on-Tyne, England. During his conductorship many new works were commissioned through Rockefeller Foundation grants.

1906   Elisabeth Luytens, English composer, is born in London.

1915   David Diamond, American composer, is born in Rochester,
New York.

1918   Herbert Brün, German-Israeli composer, is born in Berlin.
He has taught composition in the United States.

1921   Marianne Brandt dies in Vienna, aged seventy-eight.   After
        her operatic career she settled in Vienna to teach.

1924   Leonard Pennario, American pianist, is born in Buffalo, New
        York.

1929   Eberhard Wachter, Austrian baritone, is born in Vienna.

1933   Eraszébet Komlóssy, Hungarian contralto, is born in Salgotar-
        jan.

1936   David Zinman, American conductor, is born in New York City.
        In 1977 he became music director and conductor of the Ro-
        chester (N.Y.) Philharmonic Orchestra.

1938   Paul Chihara, American composer interned in Idaho in a
        World War II Nisei camp, is born in Seattle.

1960   Wlodzimierz Kotónski's Etude concrète, a single stroke of
        cymbals electronically metamorphosed, is first performed, in
        Darmstadt, Germany.

1969   Sir Lennox Berkeley's Symphony no. 3, in one movement, re-
        ceives its premiere in Cheltenham, England.

        JULY 10

1690   Domenico Gabrieli, Italian composer and cellist, dies in
        Bologna, aged about forty; he was one of the first to write
        for cello solo.

1825   Ludwig Fischer dies in Berlin, aged seventy-nine.   Mozart
        wrote an opera part for him in the Abduction from the
        Seraglio.

1835   Henryk Wieniawski, Polish violin virtuoso and composer, is
        born in Lublin.

1895   Carl Orff, German composer and innovative music educator
        of children, is born in Munich.

1904   Ebe Stignani, Italian mezzo-soprano, is born in Naples.

1913   Ljuba Welitsch, Bulgarian soprano, is born in Borisovo.

1919   Hugo Riemann dies in Leipzig, aged sixty-nine.   He was an
        important factor in the founding of the science of musicology.

1930   Josephine Veasey, English mezzo-soprano, is born in London.

1932   Gerd Nienstedt, German bass, is born in Hannover.

1933   Jan De Gaetani, American mezzo-soprano, is born in Mas-
        sillon, Ohio. Since 1973 she has taught at the Eastman
        School of Music.

1940   Helen Donath, American soprano, is born in Corpus Christi,
        Texas.

        Sir Donald Francis Tovey dies at Edinburgh, a week before
        his sixty-fifth birthday.

1941   Ferdinand "Jelly Roll" Morton dies in Los Angeles, aged
        fifty-five. Besides his ragtime and jazz background, he was
        also a professional gambler, making and losing great sums
        of money.

1947   Arlo Guthrie, American folksinger, son of balladeer Woody
        Guthrie, is born in Brooklyn. He is best known for his
        ballad Alice's Restaurant, also the name of a movie in which
        he starred.

1951   Luigi Nono's Polifonica, Monodia, Ritmica, for flute, clarinet,
        bass clarinet, saxophone, horn, piano, and percussion, is
        first performed, in Darmstadt.

1972   Jean Madeira dies in Providence, Rhode Island, aged fifty-
        three.

1979   Arthur Fiedler dies in Boston, aged eighty-four. He had con-
        ducted the Boston Pops Orchestra since 1930.

        JULY 11

1786   Karl Ditters von Dittersdorf's opera Doktor und Apotheker is
        first staged, in Vienna.

1807   Joseph Tichatschek, Bohemian tenor who was often praised by
        Richard Wagner, is born in Ober-Weckelsdorf.

1843   Anna Mehlig, German pianist, a pupil of Liszt, is born in
        Stuttgart.

1890   Edwin John Stringham, American music educator and com-
        poser, is born in Kenosha, Wisconsin.

1916   Howard Brubeck, American composer and teacher, brother of
        David Brubeck, is born in Concord, California.

1923   Ludmila Dvořáková, Czech soprano, is born near Prague.

1925   Mattiwilda Dobbs, American soprano, is born in Atlanta,
        Georgia.

Nicolai Gedda, Swedish tenor, is born in Stockholm.

1929   Hermann Prey, German baritone, is born in Berlin.

1937   George Gershwin dies of a brain tumor in Beverly Hills, California, aged thirty-eight.

1972   Gordon Crosse's Ariadne, for solo oboe and twelve players, is given its premiere at the Cheltenham Festival, England.

JULY 12

1675   Evaristo Felice dall' Abaco, Italian composer and cellist, is born in Verona.

1742   Evaristo Felice dall' Abaco dies in Munich on his sixty-seventh birthday.

1773   Johann Joachim Quantz dies in Potsdam, aged seventy-six. He had served Frederick the Great here since 1740 as chamber musician and court composer.

1861   Anton Arensky, Russian composer, is born in Novgorod.   He was choral conductor at the Imperial Chapel in St. Petersburg; earlier he had taught harmony at Moscow Conservatory.

1885   George Butterworth, English composer, is born in London. His life is cut short by World War I.

1895   Kirsten Flagstad, Norwegian soprano known for Wagnerian roles, is born in Hamar.

Oscar Hammerstein II, American lyricist grandson of Oscar Hammerstein, is born in New York City.   He collaborated with Jerome Kern, Richard Rodgers, and others in producing musical comedies.

1908   Johan Franco, Dutch-American composer, is born in Zaandam.

1934   Van Cliburn, American concert pianist, the first American to win the Tchaikovsky Prize in Moscow (1958), is born in Shreveport, Louisiana.   His first teacher was his mother.

1942   Richard Stoltzman, American clarinetist, is born in Omaha, Nebraska.

1946   Sir Benjamin Britten's chamber opera The Rape of Lucretia, to Ronald Duncan's libretto, is first staged at Glyndebourne, England.

1953   Joseph Jongen dies in Sart-lez-Spa, Belgium, aged seventy-
        nine. He continued to compose to the end of his life.

1972   Peter Maxwell Davies's opera _Taverner_ is first staged, in
        London's Covent Garden.

JULY 13

1829   Felix Mendelssohn's Concerto for Two Pianos and Orchestra
        is first performed in London at a benefit concert for Silesian
        flood victims; Ignaz Moscheles and the composer are soloists.

1924   Carlo Bergonzi, Italian tenor, is born in Parma.

1928   Donal Michalsky, American composer and composition teacher,
        is born in Pasadena, California.

1932   Per Nørgaard, Danish composer and teacher, is born in Gen-
        tofte.

1937   The first Festival of Pan-American Chamber Music opens in
        Mexico City.

1941   Leroy Southers, American composer and oboist, is born in
        Minot, North Dakota.

1951   Arnold Schoenberg dies in Los Angeles on Friday the thirteenth.
        Obsessed by the number thirteen (his age was 76; 7 + 6 = 13),
        he lay fearfully in bed all day, dying just before midnight.

JULY 14

1621   Jakob Stainer, Austrian violin maker, is born in Absam. He
        served in the court of Archduke Ferdinand Carl, but in 1669
        he was imprisoned for Lutheran leanings, and died insane in
        1683 in Absam.

1854   Alexander Kopylob, a minor Russian composer, is born in St.
        Petersburg.

1901   Gerald Finzi, English composer, is born in London.

1905   Nadia Reisenberg, Russian-American pianist, is born in Vilno.

1908   William Mason dies in New York City, aged seventy-nine. He
        wrote several textbooks on piano technique as well as piano
        works.

JULY

212

1912   Woody Guthrie (né Woodrow Wilson Guthrie), American folk-
       singer whose songs championed the poor, is born in Okemah,
       Oklahoma.   His son is Arlo Guthrie, also a folksinger.

1927   Patricia Kern, British soprano, is born in Swansea, Wales.

1930   Eric Stokes, American composer, is born in Haddon Heights,
       New Jersey.

1965   Leonard Bernstein conducts the New York Philharmonic Orches-
       tra in the premiere of his Chichester Psalms, for chorus and
       orchestra.   The Dean of Chichester in England had commis-
       sioned the work.

1972   Claus Ogerman's symphonic jazz ballet Some Times has its
       first performance, at Lincoln Center, New York City.

       JULY 15

1729   Johann David Heinichen dies at Dresden, aged forty-six.   In
       addition to his composing, he was also a lawyer, but his
       greatest work was a book on music theory.

1789   Jacques Duphly dies in Paris, aged seventy-four.

1857   Carl Czerny dies at age sixty-six, in Vienna.   He was a dedi-
       cated piano teacher and composer; his work has lately been
       regarded more highly.   Modern composers, including Stravin-
       sky, have expressed their admiration for Czerny.

1872   Alfred Hertz, German-American conductor, is born in Frank-
       furt.

1897   Paul Schoeffler, German bass, is born in Dresden.

1907   Gustave Schirmer, at age forty-three, dies in Boston, where
       he had organized the Boston Music Company.   He was also
       a joint partner in the New York firm founded by his father.

1914   Efrem Zimbalist, violinist, marries singer Alma Gluck in
       London.

1921   Jack Beeson, American composer, is born in Muncie, Indiana.

1930   Leopold Auer dies at Loschwitz, near Dresden, aged eighty-
       five.   Tchaikovsky had originally dedicated his violin concerto
       to Auer, but changed it to Brodsky when Auer suggested re-
       visions.

1933   Julian Bream, English guitarist and lutenist, is born in London.

1934   Harrison Birtwistle, English composer, is born in Accrington.
        In 1975 he joined the music faculty at the State University of
        New York, Buffalo.

1939   William Hellermann, American composer, is born in Milwau-
        kee.

1959   Ernest Bloch dies in Portland, Oregon, aged seventy-eight.
        He had taught composition to many American musicians.

1960   Lawrence Tibbett dies in New York City, aged sixty-three.
        Ten years earlier he had retired from the Metropolitan Opera.

        JULY 16

1858   Eugène Ysaÿe, Belgian violinist, conductor, and composer, is
        born in Liège.   From 1918 to 1922 he conducted the Cincinnati
        Orchestra.

1863   Fannie Bloomfield Zeisler, Austrian-American concert pianist,
        is born in Bielitz.

1868   Louis-François Dauprat dies in Paris, aged eighty-seven.

1901   Fritz Mahler, Austrian-American conductor, a nephew of
        Gustav Mahler, is born in Vienna.

1902   Heinrich Hofmann dies at Gross-Tabarz, Germany, aged sixty.
        A prolific composer, his music is no longer heard.

1904   Goffredo Petrassi, Italian composer and teacher of composition,
        is born in Zagarolo.

1917   Philipp Scharwenka dies in Bad Nauheim, Germany, aged
        seventy.   The Conservatory that he helped found had a repu-
        tation for its excellent teaching.

1927   Serge Baudo, French conductor of the Orchestre de Paris
        since 1967, is born in Marseilles.

1928   Anna Mehlig dies in Berlin, aged eighty-five.

1948   Pinchas Zukerman, Israeli violinist, is born in Tel Aviv.

1954   Lucien Muratore dies in Paris, aged seventy-seven.   He
        served as mayor of the town of Biot, France, after his
        operatic career.

1979   Alfred Deller dies in Bologna, aged sixty-seven.   His Con-
        sort revived interest in English madrigals.

JULY 17

1717   George Frideric Handel's <u>Water Music</u> is performed on a barge at an aquatic fête on the Thames River for King George I.

1830   Eduard Reményi, Hungarian violinist, is born in Miskolc; he was court violinist to Queen Victoria for a time.

1831   Therese Tietjens, German soprano, who sang principally in London, is born in Hamburg.

1836   Peter Jurgenson, Russian music publisher and friend and correspondent of Tchaikovsky, is born in Reval.   The firm, later managed by his son, was nationalized after the Revolution.

1839   Friedrich Gernsheim, German composer and conductor, is born in Worms.

1871   Carl Tausig, aged twenty-nine, dies of typhoid fever in Leipzig.

1875   Sir Donald Francis Tovey, English music scholar, editor, and composer, is born in Eton.

1877   Hermann Jadlowker, Latvian tenor and teacher, is born in Riga.

1913   Everett Helm, American composer and musicologist, is born in Minneapolis.

1916   Eleanor Steber, American soprano, is born in Wheeling, West Virginia.

1932   Niccolò Castiglioni, Italian-American pianist and composer, is born in Milan.   He has taught at various universities in the United States.

1935   Peter Schickele, American composer and arranger, a teacher at the Juilliard School in New York, is born in Ames, Iowa. He invented a composer, "P. D. Q. Bach," and wrote musical travesties in a pseudo-Baroque style.

1937   Gabriel Pierné dies at Ploujean, France, aged seventy-three.

1959   Billie Holiday dies at age forty-four in New York City.   She had started singing in Harlem nightclubs when she was fifteen.

1965   Edwin Hughes dies in New York City, aged eighty.   From 1920 to 1926 he edited piano music for G. Schirmer, Inc., including an edition of Bach's <u>Well-Tempered Clavier</u>.

1967   John Coltrane dies in Huntington, New York, aged forty.   He
        had played in many of the principal jazz bands.

1977   Witold Malcuzynski dies in Palma, Majorca, aged sixty-two.
        He was especially known as an interpreter of Chopin.

JULY 18

1670   Giovanni Bononcini, Italian opera composer, is born in Modena.
        In 1731 he was accused of plagiarism in London, and he left
        for Paris.

1821   Pauline Viardot-García, mezzo-soprano and daughter of Manuel
        del Populo García, is born in Paris.   A well-trained mu-
        sician, she also studied piano with Liszt and music theory
        with Reicha.

1849   Hugo Riemann, German musicologist, is born in Grossmehlra.
        His Musik-Lexikon is one of the standard works in music
        reference.

1872   Julius Fučik, Czech composer of band music, is born in
        Prague.

1873   Ferdinand David dies near Klosters, Switzerland, aged sixty-
        three.   He was a good friend of Mendelssohn, assisting him
        in the technical problems for violin performance of Mendels-
        sohn's Violin Concerto.

1894   Bernard Wagenaar, Dutch-American composer, is born in
        Arnhem.   In 1927 he joined the faculty of the Juilliard School
        in New York, where he taught composition.

1904   Harold Spivacke, American musicologist and music librarian,
        is born in New York City.   From 1937 to 1972 he was chief
        of the Music Division of the Library of Congress.

1923   Héctor Tosar, Uruguayan composer and teacher, is born in
        Montevideo.

1926   Verne Reynolds, American composer, horn teacher, and per-
        former, is born in Lyons, Kansas.

1930   Willard Straight, American composer and pianist, is born in
        Fort Wayne, Indiana.

1933   R. Murray Schafer, Canadian composer associated with the
        Canadian Broadcasting Corporation (CBC), is born in Sarnia,
        Ontario.

1934   Francisco Lacerda dies in Lisbon, aged sixty-five. He had organized the Orquestra Filarmonica in Lisbon.

        Roger Reynolds, American composer who also holds an engineering degree, is born in Detroit. His multimedia works are in graphic notation.

1972   Andrzej Panufnik's Concerto for Violin and String Orchestra is given its premiere, in London.

1976   Karlheinz Stockhausen's multimedia work Sirius is first performed at the Smithsonian Institute, Washington.

        JULY 19

1730   Jean-Baptiste Loeillet, known in England as John Loeillet, dies in London, aged forty-nine.

1811   Joseph Massart, Belgian violinist and teacher, is born in Liège. From 1843 to 1890 he was violin professor at the Paris Conservatoire.

1896   Paul Boepple, Swiss choral conductor and teacher, is born in Basel. After 1926 he lived in the United States.

1905   Louis Kentner, Hungarian pianist, is born in Karwin. Since 1935 he has lived in England and has published articles on Liszt.

1906   Klaus Egge, Norwegian composer who signs his scores with his name in notes: E-G-G-E, is born in Gransherad.

1913   Peggy Stuart Coolidge, American composer and pianist, is born in Swampscott, Massachusetts.

1920   Robert Mann, American violinist, composer, and conductor, is born in Portland, Oregon. A faculty member at the Juilliard School of Music, he founded the Juilliard String Quartet in 1948.

1954   Jean-Jules Aimable Roger-Ducasse dies in Le-Taillan-Medoc, France, aged eighty-one.

1976   Richard Wernick's 1977 Pulitzer Prize-winning Visions of Terror and Wonder, for mezzo-soprano and orchestra, is first performed at the Aspen Music Festival in Colorado.

JULY 20

1752   John Christopher Pepusch, German-English opera composer,
        dies in London, aged about eighty-five. He is remembered
        best for his original music and some arranged numbers in
        The Beggar's Opera.

1871   Ernest Hutcheson, Australian pianist and teacher, is born in
        Melbourne. He became head of the Juilliard School in New
        York City in 1937, having been the dean since 1924.

1872   Déodat de Sévérac, French composer, is born in Saint-Felix-
        de Caraman.

1914   Hermann Uhde, German baritone, is born in Bremen.

1924   Arnold Schoenberg's Serenade for clarinet, bass clarinet,
        mandolin, guitar, violin, viola, and cello, receives its pre-
        miere in Donaueschingen, Germany. The fourth movement
        has a sonnet by Petrarch for baritone.

1927   Michael Gielen, German conductor, is born in Dresden. He
        conducted the Royal Opera in Stockholm; in 1969 he became
        principal conductor of the Orchestre National de Belgique in
        Brussels.

1958   Iannis Xenakis's Achorripsis, for twenty-one instruments, is
        given its premiere, in Brussels.

JULY 21

1838   Johannes Nepomuk Maelzel dies on board ship in the harbor
        of La Guiara, Venezuela, while en route to the United States.
        He is sixty-five.

1864   Mary Anne Paton, Scottish soprano, dies in England, aged
        about sixty-one. An opera star in London, she married tenor
        Joseph Wood.

1865   Ludwig Schnorr dies in Dresden at the age of twenty-nine after
        a heart attack.

1870   Josef Strauss dies in Vienna, aged forty-two.

1883   Carl Engel, American musicologist and writer on music, is
        born in Paris. From 1922 to 1934 he headed the Music Divi-
        sion of the Library of Congress; he was also editor of Musi-
        cal Quarterly, and president of G. Schirmer, Inc., music-
        publishing company.

1920   Isaac Stern, Russian-American violin virtuoso, is born at
        Kremenetz. He has shown a wide range of interest in cul-
        tural affairs and in the cause of human rights.

1946   Paul Rosenfeld dies in New York City, aged fifty-six. An
        outstanding music critic, he championed modern American
        music.

1965   Cecil Effinger's opera Cyrano de Bergerac is first produced,
        at the University of Colorado at Boulder.

1978   James Galway, flute virtuoso, makes his New York concert
        debut. He had played first flute under Herbert von Karajan,
        whom he considered the "emperor of all conductors."

        JULY 22

1822   Luigi Arditi, Italian composer and conductor, is born in
        Crescentino.

1826   Julius Stockhausen, German baritone and teacher, is born in
        Paris.

1844   Richard Wagner's Eine Faust-Overtüre receives its premiere
        in Dresden.

1895   Hans Rosbaud, Austrian conductor, is born in Graz.

1902   Vladimir Nikolaievitch Kriukov, Soviet composer, is born in
        Moscow.

1913   Licia Albanese, Italian-American soprano, is born in Bari.

1914   Cecil Effinger, American composer, is born in Colorado
        Springs. From 1936 to 1977 he taught music at the Univer-
        sity of Colorado; he also invented a music typewriter, the
        "Musicwriter."

1919   Manuel de Falla's ballet The Three-Cornered Hat is first
        staged, in London.

1930   Carlos Chávez's ballet The Four Suns is first produced in
        Mexico City.

        JULY 23

1757   Domenico Scarlatti dies in Madrid, aged seventy-one. He had spent nearly thirty years at the Spanish court; his fame rests on his harpsichord compositions, which number over 600.

1796   Franz Berwald, Swedish composer and director of music at the University of Uppsala, is born in Stockholm.

1856   Arthur Bird, American composer and European music correspondent for American periodicals, is born in Belmont, Massachusetts.

1905   Erich Itor Kahn, German-American pianist, chamber-music accompanist, and composer, is born in Rimbach.

1916   Ben Weber, American composer who began studying in medicine, is born in St. Louis. He is one of the first American composers to use Schoenberg's twelve-tone procedures.

1921   Jerome Rosen, American composer, clarinetist, and teacher, is born in Boston.

1928   Leon Fleisher, American pianist and conductor, is born in San Francisco. When his right hand could no longer play, he began his conducting career.

1937   Richard Kness, American tenor, is born in Rockford, Illinois.

1961   Grace Bumbry triumphs as the first black American to sing in _Tannhäuser_ at the Bayreuth Festival in Germany.

JULY 24

1719   Arp Schnitger dies at Neuenfelde, Germany, at age seventy-one.

1739   Benedetto Marcello dies in Brescia, Italy, aged fifty-two. His greatest work is the settings of Giustiniani's paraphrases of the first fifty psalms.

1755   Francesco Antonio Uttini's opera _Il Re pastore_ is first produced, in Stockholm.

1803   Adolphe-Charles Adam, French comic-opera and ballet composer who was influenced by Boieldieu, is born in Paris.

1861   Maurice Renaud, French operatic baritone, is born in Bordeaux.

1880   Ernest Bloch, Swiss-American composer whose music reflects his Jewish heritage, is born in Geneva. He headed the Cleveland Institute of Music (1920-25) and the San Francisco Conservatory (1925-30).

1906   Pierre Fournier, French concert cellist, is born in Paris.

1918   Ruggiero Ricci, American violin virtuoso, is born in San Francisco.

1921   Giuseppe Di Stefano, Italian tenor, is born in Catania.

1922   Leo Kraft, American composer, is born in New York City, where he has taught at Queens College since 1947.

1937   Julie Rivé-King dies in Indianapolis, at the age of eighty-two.

1945   Rosina Storchio dies at age sixty-nine in Milan.

1947   Peter Serkin, American pianist, son and pupil of pianist Rudolf Serkin, is born in New York City.

1971   Alan Rawsthorne dies in Cambridge, England, aged sixty-six.

JULY 25

1654   Agostino Steffani, Italian opera composer, an ordained priest and political diplomat, is born in Castelfranco.

1867   Marcel Journet, French bass, is born in Grasse.

1883   Alfredo Casella, Italian composer, conductor, pianist, and writer on music, is born in Turin.

1900   Zoltán Fekete, Hungarian conductor and arranger, is born in Budapest.

1906   Johnny (John Cornelius) Hodges, American jazz alto saxophonist who played principally with the Duke Ellington Band, is born in Cambridge, Massachusetts.

1909   Gianandrea Gavazzeni, Italian conductor, composer, and writer on music, is born in Bergamo. He was conductor at La Scala, Milan, from 1965 to 1972.

1930   Maureen Forrester, Canadian contralto, is born in Montreal.

1934   Don Ellis, American jazz trumpeter, composer, and arranger, is born in Los Angeles.

1939   Richard Trythall, American composer and pianist, is born in Knoxville, Tennessee.

1943   Nan Merriman, mezzo-soprano, makes her debut as soloist with the NBC Symphony Orchestra, Arturo Toscanini conducting.

1956   Antonio Lauro is soloist in his Guitar Concerto in its pre-
        miere in Caracas.

1967   Andrés Sás dies in Lima, Peru, aged sixty-seven. With his
        wife he established the Sás-Rosay Academy of Music in Lima.

1969   Douglas Moore dies in Greenport, New York, at age seventy-
        five. From 1926 to 1962 he taught at Columbia University.

1970   Henri Dutilleux's Tout un monde lointain, for cello and orches-
        tra, is given its premiere in Aix-en-Provence, France.

1971   Leroy Robertson dies in Salt Lake City, aged seventy-four.

1976   Philip Glass's music drama Einstein on the Beach is first
        produced at the Festival at Avignon, France.

JULY 26

1782   John Field, Irish pianist and composer, a pupil of Clementi
        and originator of the keyboard nocturne, is born in Dublin.

1856   George Bernard Shaw, Irish music critic (under the pseudonym
        "Corno di Bassetto") and dramatist, is born in Dublin. His
        play Pygmalion was the basis for Frederick Loewe's musical,
        My Fair Lady.

1866   Francesco Cilèa, Italian opera composer, is born in Palmi.

1874   Serge Koussevitzky, Russian-American conductor and double-
        bass player, is born in Vishny-Volochok. In order to study
        music in Moscow, he was baptized, since Jews were forbidden
        to live there. From 1924 to 1949 he conducted the Boston
        Symphony Orchestra; in 1940 he founded the Berkshire Music
        Center at Tanglewood, Massachusetts.

1876   Ernest Schelling, American conductor, composer, and pianist,
        is born in Belvidere, New Jersey.

1882   Richard Wagner's opera Parsifal is first staged, in Munich,
        Hermann Levi conducting.

1924   Louis Bellson, American jazz drummer-- the "world's great-
        est," said Duke Ellington--and author of drum method books,
        is born in Rock Falls, Illinois. In 1952 he married jazz
        singer Pearl Bailey.

1928   Tadeusz Baird, Polish composer who was imprisoned in a
        German camp in World War II, is born in Grodzisk Mazowie-
        cki.

1929   Alexis Weissenberg, Bulgarian pianist, is born in Sofia.

JULY 27

1781   Mauro Giuliani, Italian guitarist and composer, is born in
Barletta.   He devised a guitar with a shorter fingerboard.

1783   Johann Philipp Kirnberger dies in Berlin, aged sixty-two.
He had studied with J. S. Bach and was known for his writings
in music theory.

1848   Vladimir de Pachmann, Russian pianist, is born in Odessa.
His stage antics were calculated to gain attention.

1867   Enrique Granados, Spanish composer, is born in Lérida.   His
series of piano pieces titled Goyescas were inspired by the
paintings and etchings of Goya.

1877   Ernst von Dohnányi, Hungarian pianist and composer, is born
in Poszony.   His first teacher was his father.

1883   Albert Franz Doppler dies in Baden, Austria, aged sixty-one.

1899   Harl McDonald, American composer, pianist, and business
manager of the Philadelphia Orchestra, is born near Boulder,
Colorado.

1912   Igor Markevitch, Soviet conductor and composer, is born in
Kiev.   Much of his career has been spent in Western Europe.

1915   Mario Del Monaco, Italian tenor, is born in Florence.

1918   Leonard Rose, American cellist, is born in Washington.   He
has played in various major orchestras and taught at the Curtis
Institute in Philadelphia.   A recitalist, he has also edited
cello music.

1924   Ferruccio Busoni dies in Berlin at the age of fifty-eight, ending a long career as a concert pianist and teacher.

1961   Theodore Chanler dies in Boston, aged fifty-nine.   His compositions were principally in smaller forms.

1962   Leonardo de Lorenzo dies in Santa Barabara, California, aged
eighty-six.   A flute teacher at the Eastman School of Music,
he also published several books of flute studies.

1971   Bernhard Paumgartner dies in Salzburg, aged eighty-three.
From 1917 to 1938 he directed the Mozarteum in Salzburg.

JULY 28

1741   Antonio Vivaldi is buried in Vienna in a cemetery for indigents.
       It was not until 1938 that the documentation was established
       that it was indeed in Vienna and not Venice, as had been as-
       sumed; he was sixty-three.

1750   Johann Sebastian Bach dies in Leipzig following a stroke; he
       was sixty-five.   A few days before his death he dictated the
       chorale prelude Vor deinen Thron tret' ich hiermit, his last
       composition.

1811   Giulia Grisi, Italian operatic soprano, is born in Milan.

1823   Ludwig Spohr's opera Jessonda is first staged, in Kassel.

1838   Bernhard Henrik Crusell dies in Stockholm, aged sixty-two.

1850   The Bach Gesellschaft is founded in Leipzig, marking the
       centenary of Bach's death.   The founders included the pub-
       lishers Härtel, and their purpose was to publish a complete
       edition of Bach's works.

1906   Gottlob Frick, German bass, is born in Ölbrunn.

1914   Carmen Dragon, American conductor of light popular music,
       is born in Antioch, California.

1941   Riccardo Muti, Italian conductor, is born in Naples.

1969   Frank Loesser dies at age fifty-nine in New York City.   Dur-
       ing World War II he wrote several army songs (Praise the
       Lord and Pass the Ammunition, Roger Young, etc.).

1972   Helen Traubel dies in Santa Monica, California, aged seventy-
       three.   In 1953 she resigned from the Metropolitan Opera
       when the management objected to her singing in New York
       City nightclubs.

JULY 29

1846   Sophie Mentor, German pianist and teacher, is born in Munich.

1856   Robert Schumann, at age forty-six, dies at an insane asylum
       in Endenich, Germany, where he had been confined for over
       two years.

1883   Manuel Infante, Spanish composer, is born in Osuna.   His
       piano compositions are mostly on Spanish themes.

1884   Boris Asafiev, Russian composer and music historian, is born
        in St. Petersburg. In 1948 he received the Stalin Prize for
        his biography of Glinka.

1887   Sigmund Romberg, Hungarian-American operetta composer, is
        born in Nagy-Kaniza.

1899   Ludwig Weber, Austrian bass, is born in Vienna.

        Karl Ziehrer's operetta Die Landstreicher is first staged, in
        Vienna.

1925   Mikis Theodorakis, Greek composer (including the film score
        for Zorba the Greek), is born in Chios.   For three years he
        was a political prisoner.

1930   Harold Enns, American bass-baritone, is born in Fresno,
        California.

1935   Peter Schreier, German tenor, is born at Meissen.

1936   Richard Van Vrooman, American tenor, is born in Kansas
        City.

1942   Bernd Weikl, German baritone, is born in Vienna.

1962   Gene Gutchë's Symphony no. 5, for strings, has its premiere,
        at Chautauqua, New York.

1970   Sir John Barbirolli dies in London, aged seventy.   His oboe
        concerto was dedicated to his wife, an oboist.

        JULY 30

1899   Gerald Moore, English pianist and accompanist, is born in
        Watford.

1921   Grant Johannesen, American concert pianist and music ad-
        ministrator, is born in Salt Lake City.   In 1963 he married
        cellist Zara Nelsova; they live in Cleveland, Ohio where he
        heads the Cleveland Institute of Music.

1924   Christopher Shaw, English composer and pianist, is born in
        London.

1931   Moshe Atzmon, Hungarian conductor, is born in Budapest.
        In 1972 he was named conductor of the Symphony Orchestra
        in Basel.

1968   Jón Leifs dies in Reykjavik, Iceland, aged sixty-nine.   In some of his works he employed Icelandic melodies and rhythms.

1970   George Szell dies in Cleveland, aged seventy-three. In his conducting he was known as a strict disciplinarian, bringing the Cleveland Orchestra to a very high degree of excellence.

1974   Lev Knipper dies in Moscow, aged seventy-five. He had made a study of Soviet folksongs and folk music.

JULY 31

1856   Marco Bordogni dies in Paris, aged sixty-seven.

1886   Franz Liszt dies at Bayreuth, aged seventy-four, ending a life reflecting the romantic spirit of the times. A prolific composer, he also made many transcriptions and arrangements and included free improvisations in his recitals.

1901   Alexander Schreiner, German-American organist, is born in Nuremberg. For many years he broadcast recitals from the Mormon Tabernacle in Salt Lake City.

1919   Norman Del Mar, English conductor, is born in London. He has published several monographs on composers and conducting.

1929   Don Garrard, Canadian bass, is born in Vancouver.

1930   Pedro Lavirgen, Spanish tenor, is born in Bujalance.

AUGUST 1

1740   Thomas Arne's masque <u>Alfred,</u> the finale of which contains <u>Rule, Britannia</u>, is first produced, at Cliveden, England.

1827   James Hewitt dies in Boston, aged fifty-seven. His musical battle-pieces catered to the fad of the times.

1831   Antonio Cotogni, Italian baritone and teacher, is born in Rome.

1899   William Steinberg, German-American conductor, is born in Cologne. From 1952 to 1976 he directed the Pittsburgh Symphony Orchestra.

1913   Jerome Moross, American ballet and ballet-opera composer, is born in Brooklyn.

1919   Oscar Hammerstein dies in New York City, aged seventy-three. He had built opera houses in New York, Philadelphia, and London.

1926   Theo Adam, German bass known for his Wagnerian roles, is born in Dresden.

Karl Kohn, Austrian-American pianist, composer, and teacher, is born in Vienna. He emigrated after the Nazi Anschluss.

1956   Howard Brubeck's <u>Four Dialogues</u>, for jazz combo and orchestra, has its premiere, in San Diego, California.

1973   Gian Francesco Malipiero dies in Treviso, Italy, aged ninety-one. From a musical family, he had received worldwide honors.

AUGUST 2

1891   Sir Arthur Bliss, English composer who was Musical Director of the BBC during World War II, is born in London.

1914   Roman Ryterband, Polish-American composer and pianist, is
        born in Lodz.

1920   Hans Hopf, German tenor, is born in Nuremberg.

1921   Enrico Caruso dies in Naples, aged forty-eight.   A year
        earlier he had received $15,000 in Mexico City for a single
        performance.

1922   John Boda, American composer, is born in Boyceville, Wis-
        consin.

1923   The International Society for Contemporary Music holds its
        first festival in Salzburg.

1927   Raymond Leppard, English conductor and harpsichord recital-
        ist, is born in London.

1931   John Shirley-Quirk, English baritone and former science
        teacher, is born in Liverpool.

1932   Marvin David Levy, American composer, is born in Passaic,
        New Jersey.

1935   John MacIvor Perkins, American composer, head of the Mu-
        sic Department of Washington University in St. Louis, is
        born in St. Louis.

1937   Gundula Janowitz, Austrian soprano, is born in Berlin.

1944   Joseph Bonnet dies at Ste. Luce-sur-Mer, Quebec, aged
        sixty.   Since 1940 he had taught at the Quebec Conservatory.

1945   Pietro Mascagni dies in Rome, aged eighty-one, forsaken by
        his friends in later years for his support of Fascism.

        Emil Nikolaus von Reznicek dies at eighty-five in Berlin.

1972   Rudolph Ganz dies in Chicago, aged ninety-five, teaching
        almost to the end.

1978   Carlos Chávez dies in Mexico City, aged seventy-nine, a
        champion of modern Mexican composers.

        AUGUST 3

1668   Dietrich Buxtehude marries the daughter of Franz Tunder,
        retiring organist at St. Mary Church in Lübeck, the marriage

a condition necessary to succeed Tunder. This notorious requirement later deterred Handel (and probably J.S. Bach) from applying for the position.

1778   The inauguration of the Teatro alla Scala in Milan is celebrated with the premiere of Antonio Salieri's opera Europa ricono-sciuta.

1784   Giovanni Battista Martini dies in Bologna, aged seventy-eight. Among his pupils were Mozart, Gluck, and Grétry.

1795   The Paris Conservatory is founded.

1829   Gioacchino Rossini's opera William Tell is first performed, in Paris.

1884   Louis Gruenberg, American composer and pianist, is born near Brest-Litovsk and brought to the United States as an infant.

1902   August Klughardt dies in Dessau, Germany, aged forty-four.

1917   Antonio Lauro, Venezuelan guitarist and composer, is born in Cuidad Bolivar.

1947   Maria Callas makes her international operatic debut in Verona, Italy, starring in La Gioconda. Also in the cast is Richard Tucker, making his Italian debut.

1957   Pablo Casals, at age eighty, marries his cello student Marta Montañez.

AUGUST 4

1782   Wolfgang Amadeus Mozart and Constanze Weber are married.

1875   Italo Montemezzi, Italian opera composer, is born in Vigasio.

1905   Boris Alexandrov, Soviet conductor of Soviet Army ensembles, is born in Bologoye.

1910   William Schuman, American composer and conductor, is born in New York City. From 1945 to 1962 he was president of the Juilliard School of Music; then president of Lincoln Center to 1969.

1920   Vladimir Rebikov dies at Yalta, aged fifty-four. In some of his works he abandoned cohesive form and experimented with whole-tone scales.

1927   Jess Thomas, American tenor, is born in Hot Springs, South
        Dakota.

1929   Gabriela Tucci, Italian soprano, is born in Rome.

1930   Siegfried Wagner, son of Richard and Cosima Wagner, dies
        at Bayreuth, Germany, aged sixty-one.

1931   Gregg Smith, American conductor and composer, is born in
        Chicago.

1932   Ugo Trama, Italian bass, is born in Naples.

1935   Victor Braun, Canadian baritone, is born in Windsor, Ontario.

1937   David Bedford, English composer and teacher, is born in London.

1940   Darius Milhaud's Cortège funèbre, for orchestra, is given its
        premiere, in New York City.

1942   Alberto Franchetti dies in Viareggio, aged eighty-one.

1972   Charles Wuorinen's Violin Concerto, for amplified violin and
        orchestra, has its first performance, at Tanglewood, Mas-
        sachusetts.

        AUGUST 5

1623   Marc' Antonio Cesti, Italian composer of operas and religious
        works, is born in Arezzo. He took religious orders, but was
        later released from them.

1811   Ambroise Thomas, French opera composer, is born in Metz.

1831   Sébastien Erard dies at his chateau near Paris, aged seventy-
        nine. He invented the repetition action for piano; his firm
        still leads in French manufacturing of pianos and harps.

1848   Nicola Vaccai dies in Pesaro, Italy, aged fifty-eight.

1890   Hans Gál, Austrian composer who fled to Edinburgh after the
        Nazi Anschluss, is born in Brunn. From 1945 to 1965 he
        lectured on music at the University in Edinburgh.

        Erich Kleiber, Austrian conductor who led the premiere of
        Berg's Wozzeck, is born in Vienna.

1893   Gustav Schirmer dies in Eisenach, Germany, aged sixty-three,
        a member of the distinguished family of music publishers.

1916   George Butterworth is killed in action World War I, near
        Pozières, France, aged thirty-one.

1926   Betsy Jolas, French composer, of American parents, is born
        in Paris.

1930   Erich Penzel, German horn player and teacher, is born in
        Leipzig.

1934   Michael Brozen, American composer, is born in New York
        City.

AUGUST 6

1883   Francesco Santoliquido, Italian composer and poet, author of
        short stories in English, is born in Naples.

1891   Charles Henry Litolff dies in Colombes, France, aged seventy-
        three. He was one of the early publishers of classical music
        in cheap editions.

1902   Margarete Klose, German contralto, is born in Berlin.

1904   Eduard Hanslick dies near Vienna, aged seventy-eight. From
        1861 to 1895 he was a professor at Vienna University.

1909   Karl Ulrich Schnabel, German pianist and composer, the son
        of pianist Artur Schnabel, is born in Berlin.

1929   Sandra Warfield, American mezzo-soprano, the wife of tenor
        James McCracken, is born in Kansas City.

1931   Bix Beiderbecke, American jazz musician, dies in New York
        City of alcoholism, aged twenty-eight.

1971   Fausto Cleva dies while conducting in Athens, aged sixty-nine.

1976   Gregor Piatigorsky dies at age seventy-three in Los Angeles,
        ending a long career as a concert cellist.

AUGUST 7

1815   Karl Johann Formes, German bass, is born in Mülheim.

1868   Sir Granville Bantock, English composer, conductor, and pro-
        fessor at Birmingham University (1907-34), is born in London.

1893   Alfredo Catalani dies in Milan, aged thirty-nine, dying of
        tuberculosis.

1913   David Popper dies in Baden, Austria, at the age of sixty-
        nine; he taught cello at the Budapest Conservatory for the
        last seventeen years.

1919   Kim Borg, Finnish bass, is born in Helsinki.

1921   Karel Husa, Czech-American composer who joined Cornell
        University's faculty, is born in Prague.

1925   Julián Orbón, Spanish-born composer and critic, a pupil of
        his father, is born in Aviles. He fled Spain, then Cuba,
        after their respective revoultions, settling finally in New
        York City.

1963   Salvador Bacarisse dies in Paris, where he had lived after
        the Spanish Civil War, aged sixty-four.

1970   Ingolf Dahl dies in Berne, Switzerland, aged fifty-eight. He
        had lived and taught in the United States since 1935.

1977   Howard Hanson's Symphony no. 7, for chorus and orchestra,
        titled "A Sea Symphony" (after Walt Whitman), is first per-
        formed for the fiftieth anniversary of the National Music
        Camp at Interlochen, Michigan.

        AUGUST 8

1754   Luigi Marchesi, Italian male soprano, is born in Milan.

1759   Karl Heinrich Graun dies in Berlin, aged fifty-five; his sacred
        works have outlasted his operas, particularly the oratorio
        Der Tod Jesu.

1857   Cécile Chaminade, French composer and pianist, is born in
        Paris.   Her piano works, written in a salon style, were
        popular and included her well-known Scarf Dance.

1882   Olga Samaroff (née Hickenlooper), American pianist and
        teacher, is born in San Antonio, Texas.   She was married
        for a time to Leopold Stokowski.

1886   Pietro Yon, Italian-American organist and composer, is born
        in Settimo Vittone.   From 1926 until his death he was or-
        ganist at St. Patrick's Cathedral in New York City.

1891   Adolph Busch, German-Swiss violinist and organizer of the
        Busch Quartet and Busch Trio, is born in Siegen.   The Trio

included pianist Rudolph Serkin, his son-in-law.

1905   André Jolivet, French composer, conductor, and composition professor at the Paris Conservatoire, is born in Paris.

1924   Thomas Beversdorf, American composer, trombonist, and composition teacher, is born in Yoakum, Texas.

1939   William Hibbard, American composer and educator, is born in Newton, Massachusetts.

1940   Alessandro Bonci dies in Viserba, Italy, aged seventy, having taught voice after his retirement from opera.

1946   Maria Barrientos dies in Ciboure, France, aged sixty-two.

1950   Nikolai Miaskovsky dies at age sixty-nine in Moscow. Since 1921 he had been professor of composition at Moscow Conservatory.

1966   Ulysses Kay's symphonic essay Markings, in memory of Dag Hammarskjöld, is first performed, in Rochester, Michigan.

1967   Jaromir Weinberger dies of a drug overdose in St. Petersburg, Florida.

1975   Julian Edwin "Cannonball" Adderley dies on tour in Gary, Indiana, aged forty-six.

AUGUST 9

1686   Benedetto Marcello, Italian composer and politician, brother of Alessandro Marcello, is born in Venice.

1862   Hector Berlioz conducts the premiere of his opera Beatrice et Benedict, for which he wrote the libretto (after Shakespeare's Much Ado About Nothing), in Baden-Baden.

1874   Reynaldo Hahn, Venezuelan-French composer, conductor, and music critic, is born in Caracas. He studied composition with Massenet, and his music reflects that influence.

1875   Albert W. Ketèlbey, English composer of semiclassical music (In a Persian Garden, In a Monastery Garden, and others) and music editor at Chappell's Music Publishing Company, is born in Aston.

1902   Zino Francescatti, French-American violinist, is born in Marseilles. His father had studied with Paganini.

Solomon (né Solomon Cutner), English pianist, is born in London.

1914   Ferenc Fricasy, Hungarian conductor, is born in Budapest.

1919   Ruggiero Leoncavallo dies in Montecatini, Italy, aged sixty-two. The holograph score of his opera Pagliacci is in the Library of Congress.

1955   Marion Bauer dies in South Hadley, Massachusetts, aged sixty-seven. Most of her work was in small forms.

1956   Birgit Nilsson makes her American debut at the Hollywood Bowl.

1963   Sir Lennox Berkeley's Four Ronsard Sonnets, for tenor and orchestra, is first performed, in London.

1966   Placido Domingo makes his American debut in Cavalleria Rusticana at the Metropolitan Opera in New York City.

Gösta Nystroem dies near Göteborg, aged seventy-five. He returned to Sweden in 1932 after living and studying abroad.

1975   Dmitri Shostakovich dies in Moscow, aged sixty-eight. His music had been attacked by Soviet officials many times over the years as decadent; but it was announced at his death that he was "a remarkable example ... contributing to musical culture." The publication of his collected works (42 volumes) will be completed in 1984.

AUGUST 10

1806   Michael Haydn, brother of Joseph Haydn, dies in Salzburg, aged sixty-eight.

1865   Alexander Glazounov, Russian composer who studied with Rimsky-Korsakov, is born in St. Petersburg. His teaching of composition and orchestration there influenced a generation of composers.

1893   Douglas Moore, American composer, teacher, and author of books on music, is born in Cutchogue, New York.

1909   Brian Easdale, English composer, is born in Manchester.

1914   Witold Malcuzynski, Polish pianist, is born in Warsaw.

1921   Agnes Giebel, Dutch soprano, is born in Heerlen.

1926   Marie-Claire Alain, French organist, is born in St. Germain-en-Laye.

1931   Renate Holm, German soprano, is born in Berlin.

1932   Alexander Goehr, German-English composer, son of Walter Goehr, is born in Berlin.

1970   Bernd Alois Zimmermann, with failing eyesight at age fifty-two, commits suicide in Königsdorf, Germany, after completing his morbid Requiem für einen jungen Dichter.

1972   Scott Huston's Symphony no. 4, for string orchestra, receives its premiere, in Cincinnati.

AUGUST 11

1862   Carrie Jacobs Bond, American romantic song composer (I Love You Truly, A Perfect Day, and others), is born in Janesville, Wisconsin.

1868   Halfdan Kjerulf dies in Grefsen, Norway, aged fifty-two. The Norwegian character of his songs had an influence on Grieg.

1922   International Society for Contemporary Music is founded.

1927   Alexander Yurlov, Soviet conductor of the Moscow Philharmonic Orchestra, is born in Leningrad.

1929   Alun Hoddinott, Welsh composer and teacher at the University College of South Wales, is born in Bargood.

1949   Karl Weigl dies in New York City at the age of sixty-eight. He had emigrated in 1938 after Hitler's Anschluss.

1951   Ebbe Hamerik drowns, aged fifty-two, in the Kattegat off the Danish coast.

AUGUST 12

1612   Giovanni Gabrieli, innovative Italian composer, organist, and teacher, dies in Venice, aged about fifty-five. Foremost in the Venetian school of musicians, he was the nephew and pupil of Andrea Gabrieli.

1633   Jacopo Peri dies in Florence, aged seventy-one, having served as maestro at various courts in Italy.

1644   Heinrich von Biber, Bohemian court violinist and composer,
        is born in Wartenberg

1845   Ludwig van Beethoven's monument is erected in Bonn, Ger-
        many.

1875   Ettore Panizza, Argentine conductor and composer, is born
        in Buenos Aires.

1911   Edward Downes, American music critic, writer, and lecturer
        on music, and son of Olin Downes, is born in Boston.

1914   Pol Plançon dies in Paris, aged sixty-three, having retired
        in 1906 from the Metropolitan Opera after thirteen years.

1928   Leoš Janáček dies in Ostrava, Czechoslovakia, aged seventy-
        four.   He believed in the artistic importance of folksongs and
        collected them in his native Moravia.

1938   Huguette Tourangeau, Canadian mezzo-soprano, is born in
        Montreal.

1961   Tom (Thomas Jefferson) Scott, dies in New York City, aged
        forty-nine.

AUGUST 13

1820   Sir George Grove, English musicologist known for his Diction-
        ary of Music and Musicians, is born in London.

1841   Bernhard Romberg dies in Hamburg, Germany, aged seventy-
        three.   In 1796 he and his cousin played a concert in Vienna
        with Beethoven.

1865   Emma Eames, American soprano, is born in Shanghai, China.

1876   Bayreuth's Festspielhaus is formally opened with a perform-
        ance of Richard Wagner's Ring des Nibelungen.

1879   John Ireland, English composer, organist, and teacher at the
        Royal College of Music (Benjamin Britten a pupil), is born
        in Inglewood.

1912   Jules Massenet dies in Paris, aged seventy.   His Meditation
        (from Thaïs) is regularly performed; Rimsky-Korsakov re-
        membered him as "a crafty fox."

1921   Louis Frémaux, French conductor, is born in Aire-sur-Lys.

1926   Valentina Levko, Soviet contralto, is born in Moscow.

1930   Margarethe Bence, American contralto, is born in Kingston, New York.

1939   Felicia Weathers, American soprano, is born in St. Louis.

1940   Gertrude Jahn, Austrian mezzo-soprano, is born in Zagreb, Yugoslavia.

1942   Sheila Armstrong, English soprano, is born in Ashington.

        Jerome Kessler, American cellist and conductor who is also a lawyer, is born in Ithaca, New York.

1948   Norman Dello Joio's ballet <u>Wilderness Stair</u> is first staged in New London, Connecticut, by Martha Graham.

1955   Florence Easton dies in New York, aged seventy. From 1917 to 1929 she was a member of the Metropolitan Opera staff.

AUGUST 14

1704   Johann Sebastian Bach takes the post of organist in Arnstadt.

1727   William Croft dies in Bath, England, at the age of forty-eight; he is buried in Westminster Abbey.

1810   Samuel Sebastian Wesley, English organist and composer of the Church of England, is born in London, the son of Samuel Wesley.

1913   Ferruccio Tagliavini, Italian tenor, is born in Reggio.

1923   William Flanagan, American composer and newspaper music critic, is born in Detroit.

        John Pozdro, American composer and teacher, is born in Chicago.

1924   Georges Prêtre, French conductor, is born in Waziers.

1937   Brian Fennelly, American composer and theorist, is born in Kingston, New York.

1938   Sir Landon Ronald dies in London, aged sixty-five.

1953   Friedrich Schorr, a specialist in Wagnerian opera roles, dies in Farmington, Connecticut, at the age of sixty-four.

1972   Oscar Levant dies at sixty-five in Beverly Hills, California.

1978   Joe (Giuseppe) Venuti dies in Seattle of cancer, aged eighty; he was the first to introduce violin into jazz combos.

AUGUST 15

1728   Marin Marais dies in Paris at the age of seventy-two. A virtuoso viola-da-gambist, he established a new method of fingering that influenced the technique of performance.

1772   Johannes Nepomuk Maelzel, German inventor of the metronome, is born in Regensburg. The initial of his last name is added to the tempo indication in music: M. M. 84 means Maelzel's metronome, 84 beats to the minute.

1858   Emma Calvé, French soprano, is born in Decazeville.

1872   Rubin Goldmark, American composer and teacher, is born in New York City; he was a nephew of Karl Goldmark.

1875   Samuel Coleridge-Taylor, English composer, is born in London.   He taught violin at the Royal Academy of Music and conducted the London Handel Society (1904-12).

1884   Edwin Hughes, American pianist, is born in Washington.

1887   Marion Bauer, American composer, composition teacher, and writer on music, is born in Walla Walla, Washington.

1890   Jacques Ibert, French composer and director of the Academy of Rome, 1937-55, is born in Paris.

1892   Knud Jeppesen, Danish musicologist, editor of Acta Musicologica, and composer, is born in Copenhagen.

1893   Alexander Gauk, Soviet conductor of the Leningrad Philharmonic Orchestra, is born in Odessa.

1907   Joseph Joachim dies in Berlin, aged seventy-six, regarded as one of the greatest of violin virtuosos.

1909   Hugo Winterhalter, American conductor and arranger of light popular music, is born in Wilkes-Barre, Pennsylvania.

1922   Lukas Foss, German-American pianist, composer, and conductor, is born in Berlin.

1924   Elsie Morison, Australian soprano, is born in Ballarat.

1925   Aldo Ciccolini, Italian pianist, is born in Naples.

1926   Julius Katchen, American pianist, is born in Long Branch, New Jersey.

1933   Richard Fredericks, American baritone, is born in Los Angeles.

Rita Hunter, English soprano, is born in Wallasey.

1951   Artur Schnabel dies in Morschach, Switzerland, aged sixty-nine. He was known for his piano interpretations of Beethoven.

1963   John Powell dies in Charlottesville, Virginia, aged eighty.

1966   Jan Kiepura dies in Rye, New York, aged sixty-four.

AUGUST 16

1799   Vincenzo Manfredini dies in St. Petersburg, aged sixty-one. He had taught Paul I of Russia during an earlier stay.

1863   Gabriel Pierné, French composer, conductor, and organist, is born at Metz.

1876   Richard Wagner's opera Siegfried is first staged at Bayreuth, Germany; Hans Richter conducting.

1892   Sophie Braslau, American contralto, is born in New York City.

1901   Olav Kielland, Norwegian conductor and composer, is born in Trondheim. In 1952 he organized Iceland's first symphony orchestra.

1916   Moura Lympany, English pianist, is born in Saltash.

1917   Roque Cordero, Panamanian composer, is born in Panama.

1929   Bill Evans, American jazz pianist and composer, is born in Plainfield, New Jersey.

1943   Carroll Glenn, violinist, marries pianist Eugene List.

1959   Wanda Landowska dies in Lakeville, Connecticut, aged eighty-two. She was one of the greatest performers on the modern harpsichord, and made many recordings of Baroque music.

1977   Elvis Presley dies in Memphis, Tennessee, aged forty-two, of drug abuse.

AUGUST 17

1686   Nicola Antonio Porpora, Italian composer (principally of operas) and singing teacher, is born in Naples.

1786   Frederick II (Frederick the Great), King of Prussia, dies in Potsdam, aged seventy-four. His flute sonatas and concertos were published in 1889.

1876   Richard Wagner's opera Götterdämmerung is first produced, in Bayreuth, Germany.

1880   Ole Bornemann Bull dies in Lysö, Norway, aged seventy. His attempts to establish Norwegian national music met with failure.

1901   Henri Tomasi, French composer, is born in Marseilles.

1903   Abram Chasins, American pianist and composer, is born in New York City. From 1946 to 1965 he was musical director of radio station WQXR there.

        Georges Sébastian, Hungarian conductor, is born in Budapest.

1912   Armen Tigranian's opera Anush is given its premiere in Alexandropol.

1928   T. J. (Thomas Jefferson) Anderson, American composer who orchestrated Scott Joplin's opera Treemonisha for its production in Atlanta, is born in Coatesville, Pennsylvania.

1936   Nikolai Ghiuselev, Bulgarian bass, is born in Pavlikeni.

1945   Giuseppe Gino Marinuzzi dies in Milan, aged sixty-three.

1958   Florent Schmitt dies in Neuilly-sur-Seine, France, aged eighty-seven, continuing to compose until his death. Two months earlier he attended the premiere of his symphony.

1961   Carlos Salzedo dies in Waterville, Maine, aged seventy-six. He had developed a "Salzedo Model" harp able to produce novel sonorities.

1974   Krzysztof Penderecki's Magnificat, for bass solo, choruses, and orchestra, receives its premiere, in Salzburg, Austria.

AUGUST 18

1745   Ludwig Fischer, German bass singer, is born in Mainz.

1750   Antonio Salieri, Italian opera composer and Beethoven's teacher, is born in Legnago. He was accused of trying to poison his rival, Mozart. Pushkin wrote a drama based on this rumor, which Rimsky-Korsakov set to music.

1785   Friedrich Wieck, German pianist and teacher, the father of Clara Schumann, is born in Pretzsch.

1849   Benjamin (Louis Paul) Godard, French composer, is born in Paris.

1857   Hans von Bülow marries Cosima, daughter of Franz Liszt.

1873   Leo Slezak, Austrian tenor, father of film actor Walter Slezak, is born in Mährisch-Schönberg.

1907   Howard Swanson, American composer whose songs have been sung by Marian Anderson, is born in Atlanta, Georgia.

1910   Herman Berlinski, German-American composer, is born in Leipzig. In World War II he joined the French Foreign Legion.

1914   Anna Essipoff dies at age sixty-three in St. Petersburg.

1922   Genevieve Ward dies in London, aged eighty-nine.

1933   Jules Bastin, Belgian bass, is born in Pont.

1946   John Henry Antill's suite from the ballet _Corroboree_ is given its premiere by the Sydney Symphony Orchestra, Sir Eugene Goossens conducting.

AUGUST 19

1858   Ludwig Wüllner, German singer, son of Franz Wüllner, is born in Münster.

1881   Georges Enesco, Rumanian composer and violinist whose first lessons were from a Rumanian gypsy, is born in Liveni-Virnaz.

1886   Robert Heger, German opera conductor and composer of instrumental works, is born in Strasbourg.

1905   Jacques de Menasce, Austrian pianist and composer, is born in Bad Ischl.

1929   Sergei Diaghilev dies in Venice, aged fifty-seven; he is considered the true originator of modern dance.

1943   Ernest John Moeran's Rhapsody, for piano and orchestra, is
first performed, in London.

1944   Lyn Vernon, Canadian mezzo-soprano, is born in Vancouver.

Sir Henry J. Wood dies in Hitchin, England, aged seventy-
five.

1952   Alberto Ginastera's ballet Estancia has its premiere, in
Buenos Aires.

1957   Leonard Bernstein's music drama West Side Story is given its
first performance, in Washington.

1961   Peggy Glanville-Hicks's opera Nausicaa is first staged, in
Athens, Greece.

AUGUST 20

1561   Jacopo Peri, innovative Italian composer credited with the
first music drama (opera) in monodic style, is born in Rome.

1813   Jan Křtitel Vaňhal dies in Vienna, aged seventy-four.   His
name in German is Johann Baptist Wanhal.

1843   Christine Nilsson, Swedish soprano, is born in Sjöabol.

1882   Peter Ilyitch Tchaikovsky's 1812 Overture has its premiere
on an all-Tchaikovsky program at the Art and Industrial Exhibition, in Moscow.

1888   Eric Blom, Swiss-English music scholar and editor of the
1954 edition of Grove's Dictionary of Music and Musicians, is
born in Berne.   He contributed many of the articles in the
nine-volume work.

1907   Anatole Fistoulari, Russian conductor, son of Gregory Fistoulari (opera conductor), is born in Kiev.   He settled in
England after World War II.

1927   Fanny Bloomfield Zeisler dies in Chicago, aged sixty-four.
Regarded as one of the best women pianists, she had lived
in Chicago since the age of five.

1947   Terry King, American cellist and conductor, is born in Los
Angeles.

AUGUST 21

1698   Giuseppe Antonio Guarneri, most famous of the Guarneri vio-
        lin makers, is born in Cremona. On his labels he inscribed
        IHS and so was known as Giuseppe del Gesu.

1893   Lili Boulanger, French composer and sister of composition
        teacher Nadia Boulanger, is born in Paris.

1898   Hugh Ross, English choral conductor and organist, is born
        in Langport.

1904   Count (William) Basie, American jazz-band leader, pianist,
        and composer, is born in Red Bank, New Jersey.

1926   Ben-Zion Orgad, German-Israeli composer, is born in Gel-
        senkirchen.

1932   Frederick Corder dies in London, aged eighty, having taught
        composition to many outstanding British musicians.

1933   Janet Baker, English mezzo-soprano, is born in York.   In
        1970 she received the Order of Commander of the British
        Empire.

1940   Paul Juon dies in Vevey, Switzerland, aged sixty-eight.

1951   Constant Lambert dies two days before his forty-sixth birth-
        day in London.

AUGUST 22

1741   George Frideric Handel begins work on his oratorio <u>Messiah</u>,
        and completes it three weeks later.

1827   Josef Strauss, Austrian waltz composer, brother of Johann
        Strauss, Jr., is born in Vienna.

1862   Claude Debussy, French composer, regarded as the creator
        of musical "impressionism," is born in St.-Germain-en-Laye.
        He briefly tutored the children of Mme. Nadezhda von Meck,
        the patroness of Tchaikovsky.

1868   Maude Powell, American violinist, is born in Peru, Indiana.

1909   Vitya Vronsky, Russian-American pianist, is born in Evpa-
        toria.   She married pianist Victor Babin.

1916   Robert Kenneth Rohe, American composer, conductor, and
        bassist, is born in New York City.

1922   Raphäel Arié, Bulgarian-Italian bass, is born in Sofia.

        Sofia Scalchi dies in Rome, aged seventy-one.

1928   Karlheinz Stockhausen, innovative German composer, is born
        in Modrath.   Considered a pioneer of "time-space" music,
        he began teaching composition in 1971 in Cologne's Musikhoch-
        schule.

1937   Robert Hale, American baritone, is born in San Antonio,
        Texas.

1955   Olin Downes dies in New York City, aged sixty-nine.

1968   Harrison Birtwistle's chamber opera Punch and Judy is first
        staged at the Edinburgh Festival, Scotland.

1970   Richard Donovan dies in Middletown, Connecticut, aged seventy-
        eight.   From 1936 to 1951 he conducted the New Haven Sym-
        phony Orchestra.

1976   Gina Bachauer dies in Athens, aged sixty-three, dying of a
        heart attack on the day she was to perform with the National
        Symphony Orchestra of Washington at the Athens Festival.

        AUGUST 23

1735   Jean-Philippe Rameau's opera-ballet Les Indes galantes re-
        ceives its premiere, in Paris.

1784   Giovanni Paisiello's opera Il Re Teodoro in Venezia is first
        staged, in Vienna.

1854   Moritz Moszkowski, German pianist and composer, is born in
        Breslau.

1900   Ernst Krenek, Austrian-American composer, conductor, teacher,
        and writer on music, is born in Vienna.   He was married
        briefly to Anna Mahler, daughter of composer Gustav Mahler.

1902   Teresa Stolz dies in Milan, aged sixty-eight.

1903   William Primrose, Scottish violist and founder of the Prim-
        rose Quartet, is born in Glasgow.

1905   Constant Lambert, English composer, conductor (principally
        of ballets), and music critic, is born in London.

1923   Wolfgang Sawallisch, German conductor of opera, is born in
        Munich.

1925   Wlodzimierz Kotónski, Polish avant-garde composer, is born
        in Warsaw.

1926   Herbert Beattie, American bass, is born in Chicago.

1930   George Green, American composer and violinist, is born
        in Mt. Kisco, New York.

1934   The Berkshire Symphonic Festival is founded by Dr. Henry
        Hadley in Stockbridge, Massachusetts.

1935   Loren Rush, American composer, is born in Fullerton,
        California.

1937   Albert Roussel dies in Royan, France, at the age of sixty-
        eight. Among his pupils were Eric Satie and Edgard Varèse.

1960   Oscar Hammerstein II dies in Doylestown, Pennsylvania, aged
        sixty-five. His greatest success as a lyricist was Show Boat,
        by Jerome Kern.

1962   Irving Fine dies in Natick, Massachusetts, aged forty-seven,
        a member of Brandeis University faculty.

1964   Igor Stravinsky's cantata to Hebrew texts, Abraham and Isaac,
        for baritone and orchestra, is given its premiere, in Jerusa-
        lem.

1971   Neville Marriner makes his American conducting debut with
        the New York Chamber Orchestra at Lincoln Center's Phil-
        harmonic Hall in New York City.

AUGUST 24

1669   Alessandro Marcello, Italian composer and scholar, brother
        of Benedetto Marcello, is born in Venice.

1837   Théodore Dubois, French organist who succeeded Saint-Säens
        at the Madeleine, and composer, is born at Rosnay.

1839   Eduard Napravnik, Bohemian-Russian conductor and composer,
        is born in Byst.

1841   Karl Friedrich Curschmann dies at Langfuhr, Germany, aged
        thirty-seven.

1846   Franz von Suppé's operetta Poet and Peasant is first produced,
        in Vienna.

1856   Felix Mottl, Austrian conductor, is born in Unter-St. Veit.

1910   Bernhard Heiden, German-American composer, a pupil of Hindemith and faculty member at Indiana University, is born in Frankfurt.

1924   Louis Teicher, popular duo-pianist with Arthur Ferrante, is born in Wilkes-Barre, Pennsylvania.

AUGUST 25

1742   (José Antonio) Carlos de Seixas dies in Lisbon, aged thirty-eight. His compositions were principally for keyboard instruments.

1774   Niccolò Jommelli dies in Naples, aged fifty-nine; he was called "the Italian Gluck."

1783   Wolfgang Amadeus Mozart's Mass in C is first performed in Salzburg.

1818   Elizabeth Billington, English operatic soprano, dies near Venice, aged about fifty-three. Her mother studied with Johann Christian Bach.

1870   Richard Wagner marries Cosima von Bülow, daughter of Franz Liszt and former wife of conductor Hans von Bülow.

1902   Stefan Wolpe, German-American composer, is born in Berlin.

1914   Alexei Haieff, Russian-American composer, is born in Blagoveshchensk, Siberia.

1915   Gré Brouwenstjn, Dutch soprano, is born in Den Helder.

        Walter Trampler, German-American violist and teacher, is born in Munich.

1918   Leonard Bernstein, versatile American composer, pianist, and conductor, is born in Lawrence, Massachusetts.

1937   Nancy Tatum, American soprano and former secretary, is born in Memphis, Tennessee.

1940   José Van Dam, Belgian bass, is born in Brussels.

1979   Stan Kenton dies in Hollywood, California, at the age of sixty-seven, following a stroke. After the big-band era ended, he continued to experiment with various jazz forms.

AUGUST 26

1846   Felix Mendelssohn's oratorio Elijah is given its premiere, in
       Birmingham, England.

1860   Friedrich Silcher dies in Tübingen, Germany, aged seventy-
       one. He began teaching at the University of Tübingen in 1817.

1894   Arthur Loesser, American pianist and music critic, brother
       of Frank Loesser, is born in New York City.

1915   Humphrey Searle, English composer and teacher whose works
       reflect his study with Webern, is born in Oxford.

1920   Frederick Prausnitz, German conductor, is born in Cologne.

1925   Gustavo Becerra (also Becerra Schmidt), Chilean composer,
       is born in Temuco.

1948   Oscar Lorenzo Fernandez dies in Rio de Janeiro, aged fifty.
       His music derives from Brazilian folksong.

1950   Giuseppe De Luca dies in New York City, aged seventy-three.
       He was known for his mastery of bel canto.

1957   Andrzej Panufnik's Rhapsody, for orchestra, has its first
       performance, in London.

1958   Ralph Vaughan Williams dies in London, aged eighty-five, just
       after completing his Symphony no. 9.

1960   Mark Hambourg dies in Cambridge, England, aged eighty-one.

1971   Francesco Santoliquido dies in Anacapri, Italy, at age eighty-
       eight. He had lived in Tunisia and traces of Arab popular
       music appear in his works.

1976   Lotte Lehmann dies in Santa Barbara, California, aged eighty-
       eight, remembered as one of the finest Wagnerian singers.

AUGUST 27

1521   Josquin Des Prez, greatest Flemish contrapuntist of the
       period, dies in Condé-sur-Escaut, aged about eighty-one. He
       was provost of the Cathedral Chapter there.

1611   Tomás Luis de Victoria, Spanish priest and composer of sa-
       cred music, dies in Madrid, aged about sixty-two. Most of
       his life was spent serving in Rome.

1886   Eric Coates, English composer and viola player, is born in
        Hucknall.

1900   Gabriel Fauré's lyric tragedy <u>Prométhée</u> is first produced in
        Béziers, France.

1925   Marian Anderson sings with the New York Philharmonic Orches-
        tra in Lewisohn Stadium after winning a competition over 300
        contestants.

1932   François Glorieux, Belgian pianist and composer, is born in
        Courtrai.

1937   Aaron Copland's <u>El Salon Mexico</u> receives its premiere, in
        Mexico City, Carlos Chávez conducting.

1948   Oley Speaks dies in New York City, aged seventy-four.

1953   Nicolai Berezowsky dies in New York City, aged fifty-three.
        He had played violin in the New York Philharmonic and in the
        Coolidge String Quartet.

AUGUST 28

1733   Giovanni Battista Pergolesi's opera interlude <u>La Serva padrona,</u>
        a part of his opera <u>Il Prigonier superbo</u>, is first staged, in
        Naples.

1754   Peter Winter, German composer and conductor, is baptized
        in Mannheim.

1767   Johann Schobert, German harpsichordist and keyboard com-
        poser, dies at about age thirty, along with his family, from
        eating poisonous mushrooms in Paris.

1850   Richard Wagner's opera <u>Lohengrin</u> receives its premiere, in
        Weimar; Franz Liszt conducting.

1867   Umberto Giordano, Italian opera composer, is born in Foggia.

1894   Karl Böhm, Austrian conductor, is born in Graz.

1898   Marcel Dick, Hungarian-American violinist and composer, is
        born in Miskolcz.

1913   Robert Irving, English conductor, is born in Winchester.

        Richard Tucker, American tenor and cantor, is born in
        Brooklyn.

1914   Anatol Liadov dies on his estate near Novgorod, Russia, aged
        fifty-nine. Prokofiev, Miaskovsky, and Asafiev were among
        his notable students.

1929   István Kertész, Hungarian conductor, is born in Budapest.

1932   Christina Deutekom, Dutch soprano, is born in Amsterdam.

1941   Paul Plishka, American bass, is born in Old Forge, Pennsyl-
        vania.

1949   The Aspen Music Festival is founded in Colorado on the 200th
        anniversary of Goethe's birth.

1959   Bohuslav Martinů dies in Liestal, Switzerland, aged sixty-
        eight. He taught at Princeton University during World War
        II as a visiting professor of music.

1972   René Leibowitz dies in Paris, aged fifty-nine, the foremost
        exponent of serial music in France. Among his students was
        Pierre Boulez.

AUGUST 29

1661   Louis Couperin, French organist and composer, member of
        a famed musical family, dies in Paris, aged about thirty-five.
        He was one of the first to use the basso continuo in his works
        for harpsichord.

1855   Emil Paur, Austrian conductor, is born in Bukovina.

1875   Leonardo de Lorenzo, Italian-American flutist, is born in
        Viggiano. A flute teacher at the Eastman School of Music
        in Rochester, he also played in major orchestras.

1876   Félicien-César David dies at St. Germain-en-Laye, aged
        sixty-six. He succeeded Berlioz as librarian of the Paris
        Conservatory.

        Lucien Muratore, French tenor who served as town mayor
        at Biot, is born in Marseilles.

1877   Johann Peter Müller dies in Langen, Germany, aged eighty-
        six.

1897   Helge Roswänge, Danish tenor, is born in Copenhagen.

1915   Alvinio Misciano, Italian tenor, is born in Narni.

1920   "Charlie" (Charles Christopher) Parker, American jazz saxophonist and leader of the "bebop" style, is born in Kansas City.

Lester Trimble, American composer and teacher (Juilliard School of Music in New York), is born in Bangor, Wisconsin.

1926 Raymond Lewenthal, American pianist and teacher, is born in San Antonio, Texas. He has edited a collection of Charles Alkan's piano works for G. Schirmer, Inc.

1928 Thomas Stewart, American baritone and former statistics consultant, is born in San Saba, Texas. He is married to soprano Evelyn Lear.

1943 Anne Collins, English mezzo-soprano, is born in County Durham.

AUGUST 30

1769 Bonifazio Asioli, Italian composer, teacher, and author of several music manuals, is born in Correggio.

1853 Percy Goetschius, American music theorist, is born in Paterson, New Jersey. He wrote many books on theory and composition.

1922 Regina Resnick, American soprano, is born in New York City.

1928 John Huggler, American composer, is born in Rochester, New York. Since 1974 he has taught at Harvard University.

1933 Samuel Barber's Overture to the School for Scandal (after Sheridan), has its premiere, in Philadelphia.

1949 Hans Kindler dies at Watch Hill, Rhode Island, aged fifty-seven. In 1931 he organized the National Symphony Orchestra in Washington.

1953 Gaetano Merola dies in San Francisco, aged seventy-two, while conducting a concert at Sigmund Stern Grove.

AUGUST 31

1834 Amilcare Ponchielli, Italian opera composer and professor at Milan Conservatory, is born in Cremona.

1905 Francesco Tamagno, Italian tenor, dies near Turin, aged fifty-four.

1912   Ramón Vinay, Chilean tenor, is born in Chillan.

1923   Ernest Van Dyck dies in Berlaer-lez-Lierre, Belgium, aged sixty-two. After retiring from opera he taught singing in Brussels.

1928   Kurt Weill's modern version of the Three Penny Opera, titled Die Dreigroschenoper (libretto by Bertolt Brecht), is first staged, in Berlin.

1933   Pianists Victor Babin and Vitya Vronsky are married, subsequently touring as duo-pianists.

1945   Itzhak Perlman, Israeli-American violinist, is born in Tel Aviv. Despite the polio that left his legs paralyzed, he has won prizes in competition and now tours the world as a concert artist.

1969   William Flanagan dies of a drug overdose in New York City, aged forty-six.

1970   Harrison Birtwistle's Verses for Ensembles, for twelve players, is given its premiere, in London.

SEPTEMBER 1

1653 Johann Pachelbel, German organist and composer, is baptized in Nuremberg. His Kanon in D, arranged for numerous instruments and combinations, is presently popular in the United States.

1814 Erik Tulindberg dies in Abo (Turku), Finland, aged fifty-three.

1854 Engelbert Humperdinck, German composer remembered best for his opera Hansel and Gretel, is born in Siegburg. Among his pupils was Siegfried Wagner.

1860 Cleofonte Campanini, Italian-American operatic conductor, is born in Parma, a brother of tenor Italo Campanini.

1878 Tullio Serafin, Italian conductor, is born in Venice. With A. Toni he co-authored a two-volume history of Italian opera.

1886 Othmar Schoeck, Swiss composer (especially of songs) and conductor, is born in Brunnen.

1896 Simon Barere, Russian pianist, is born in Odessa.

1912 Samuel Coleridge-Taylor dies in Croydon, England, aged thirty-seven.

1921 Matt Doran, American composer, is born in Covington, Kentucky.

1923 Frank Erickson, American composer of band music, is born in Spokane, Washington.

1935 Mario Basiola, Jr., American baritone, namesake of his baritone father, is born in Highland Park, Illinois.

Seiji Ozawa, Japanese conductor of the Boston Symphony Orchestra, the youngest ever to head it, is born in Hoten, China.

1939 Roger Soyer, French baritone, is born in Thiais.

251

1944   Leonard Slatkin, American conductor, is born in Los Angeles, the son of violinist and conductor Felix Slatkin.

1953   Jacques Thibaud dies in an air crash in the French Alps near Barcelonnette, aged seventy-two.

1957   Dennis Brain dies in an auto accident at Hatfield, England, aged thirty-six.   His father and grandfather were also French-horn performers.

1977   Ethel Waters dies at age eighty in New York City; she was the first black singer to sing with all-white bands.

SEPTEMBER 2

1661   Georg Böhm, German organist and composer of keyboard music, is born in Hohenkirchen.

1814   Mihály Mosonyi (né Michael Brandt), Hungarian composer, is born at Frauenkirchen.

1863   Isador Philipp, French pianist and professor of piano at the Paris Conservatory, is born in Paris.

1888   Friedrich Schorr, Hungarian-American baritone, is born in Nagyvarád.

1904   Set Svanholm, Swedish tenor who began his musical career as a church organist, is born in Västeras.

1915   Dai-Keong Lee, American composer, is born in Honolulu.

1917   Laurindo Almeida, Brazilian concert and jazz guitarist and composer, is born in São Paulo.

1924   Rudolf Friml's operetta Rose Marie is first staged, in New York City.

1930   Andrey Petrov, Soviet composer, is born in Leningrad.

1940   Giulio Gatti-Casazza dies in Ferrara, Italy, at age seventy-two.

1943   Gayle Smith, American cellist, is born in Los Angeles.

1945   Sona Ghazarian, Lebanese soprano, is born in Beirut.

1960   Sir William Walton's Symphony no. 2 is first performed, in Edinburgh.

1972   Krzysztof Penderecki's Cello Concerto is first performed at
        the Edinburgh Festival.

SEPTEMBER 3

1695   Pietro Locatelli, Italian virtuoso violinist and composer (a
        pupil of Corelli), is born in Bergamo. After extensive pro-
        fessional tours he eventually settled in Amsterdam.

1891   Marcel Grandjany, French-American harpist, is born in Paris.
        He taught at the Juilliard School in New York City; published
        First Grade Harp Pieces (1964).

1893   Anthony Collins, English conductor, violinist, and composer,
        is born in Hastings.

1900   Eduard van Beinum, Dutch conductor, is born in Arnhem.
        After Mengelberg's dismissal he became director of the
        Concertgebouw Orchestra in 1945. He was briefly principal
        guest conductor of the Los Angeles Philharmonic before his
        death.

1912   Arnold Schoenberg's Five Orchestral Pieces are first per-
        formed, in London.

1921   Thurston Dart, English musicologist, harpsichordist, and
        former mathematician, is born in London.

1946   Moriz Rosenthal dies in New York City, aged eighty-three,
        the "little giant of the piano."

1963   Yuri Arbatsky dies in New Hartford, New York, aged fifty-
        two. A cathedral organist in Belgrade, he also wrote arti-
        cles on the folk music of Eastern Europe; he came to the
        U.S. after World War II.

1964   Joseph Marx dies at age eighty-two in Graz, Austria, where
        he had taught at the University.

1968   Juan José Castro dies in Buenos Aires, aged seventy-three.

1974   Harry Partch dies in San Diego, California, aged seventy-
        three, an experimenter with new instruments.

SEPTEMBER 4

1824   Anton Bruckner, Austrian symphonist, composer, cathedral organist, and organ teacher, is born in Ansfelden.

1852 Edoardo Mascheroni, Italian conductor, is born in Milan.

1892 Darius Milhaud, French composer and pianist, one of "Les Six," is born in Aix-en-Provence.

1907 Edvard Grieg dies in Bergen, Norway, aged sixty-four, of heart disease. The movie Song of Norway was a story of his life.

1915 Rudolf Schock, German tenor, is born in Duisberg.

1965 Albert Schweitzer dies at his mission hospital at Lambaréné, Gabon, at the age of ninety. In his amazing career he excelled in several professions--that of medical doctor, organist, an authority on J.S. Bach, and great humanitarian--and received worldwide acclaim in all areas.

SEPTEMBER 5

1735 Johann Christian Bach, German composer (known as the "London Bach") and eleventh son of J.S. Bach, is born in Leipzig.

1781 Anton Diabelli, Austrian composer and music publisher, is born in Mattsee. His waltz theme was used by Beethoven as a basis for thirty-three variations. As publisher of Franz Schubert's works, Diabelli not only underpaid him but complained of his prolificacy.

1791 Giacomo Meyerbeer (né Jakob Beer), German composer of operas, is born in Berlin. After changing from Italian- to French-style opera, he had his greatest successes in Paris.

1803 François Devienne dies in an insane asylum at Charenton, France, at the age of forty-four.

1820 Louis Köhler, German composer of piano studies, is born in Brunswick.

1857 Franz Liszt conducts the premiere of his Faust Symphony, for chorus and orchestra, in Weimar, Germany.

1867 Amy Marcy Cheney Beach (Mrs. H. H. A. Beach), American pianist and composer, is born in Henniker, New Hampshire.

1879 Rhené-Baton (né René Baton), French conductor, is born at Courseulles-sur-Mer. From 1916 to 1932 he conducted the Concerts Pasdeloup.

1892   Joseph Szigeti, Hungarian-American violin virtuoso, is born in Budapest.

1898   Ebbe Hamerik, Danish composer, is born in Copenhagen.

1901   Mieczyslaw Kolinski, Polish-Canadian composer, music therapist and ethnomusicologist, is born in Warsaw.

1908   Joaquín Nin-Culmell, Spanish-American pianist, composer, and teacher, is born in Berlin, son of Joaquín Nin.

1910   Ralph Berkowitz, American pianist and educator, is born in New York City.

1912   John Cage, American experimental composer who uses "prepared" piano and graphic notation, is born in Los Angeles.

1914   Gail Kubik, American composer and teacher, is born in South Coffeyville, Oklahoma. His 1950 film score Gerald McBoing-Boing received a Motion Picture Academy Award.

1920   Peter Racine Fricker, English composer and teacher, is born in London. Since 1964 he has been at the University of California at Santa Barbara.

1921   György Cziffra, Hungarian pianist, is born in Budapest.

1933   Marcel Journet dies in Vittel, France, aged sixty-six.

1940   Lewis Spratlan, American composer, is born in Miami, Florida.

1941   Alexander Slobodyanik, Soviet pianist, is born in Kiev.

1943   Ellis Kohs's humorous choral work The Automatic Pistol, for men's voices a cappella, has its premiere, in Washington. The text is taken from the United States Army weapons manual.

1950   Arthur Benjamin is soloist in his Piano Concerto in its premiere in Sydney, Australia.

SEPTEMBER 6

1791   Wolfgang Amadeus Mozart's opera La Clemenza di Tito, written for the coronation of Leopold II in Prague, is produced there on the eve of the ceremony.

1882   John Powell, American pianist and composer, is born in Richmond, Virginia. An avid collector of Southern rural folksongs and organizer of regional choral festivals, he was also an amateur astronomer, discovering a comet.

1890   Manfred Gurlitt, German conductor and composer, is born in Berlin.

1891   John Charles Thomas, American baritone, is born in Meyersdale, Pennsylvania.

1910   Ralph Vaughan Williams's Fantasia on a Theme by Tallis, for strings, is first performed at the Gloucester Festival, England.

1912   Wayne Barlow, American composer, organist and faculty member at the Eastman School of Music, is born in Elyria, Ohio.

1923   William Kraft, American composer and percussionist since 1955 with the Los Angeles Philharmonic Orchestra, is born in Chicago.

1928   Eugene Svetlanov, Soviet conductor and composer, is born in Moscow.

1932   Gilles Tremblay, Canadian composer who uses graphic notation, a professor at the Montreal Conservatory, is born in Arvida, Quebec.

1937   Henry Hadley dies at age sixty-five in New York City; he had conducted his works in Europe, Japan, and South America.

1961   Elliott Carter's Double Concerto for Harpsichord and Piano with two Chamber Orchestras (called by Stravinsky the first true American masterpiece) is first performed, in New York City.

1962   Hanns Eisler dies at age sixty-four in Berlin; he had left the United States in 1948 under terms of "voluntary deportation" for his political radicalism.

1968   Anny Konetzni dies in Vienna, aged sixty-six.

1977   Thea Musgrave conducts her fourth opera, Mary, Queen of Scots, in its premiere at the Edinburgh Festival; she was also the librettist.

SEPTEMBER 7

1805   Julie Dorus-Gras, French soprano, is born in Valenciennes.

1819   Jean-Louis Duport dies in Paris, aged sixty-nine.

1902   Franz Wüllner dies at Braunfels, aged seventy, director of the
        Cologne Conservatory since 1884.

1921   Arthur Ferrante, American duo-pianist with Louis Teicher, is
        born in New York City.

1924   Hugh Aitken, American composer and teacher, is born in New
        York City. Since 1971 he has chaired the music department
        of William Paterson College, Wayne, New Jersey.

        Leonard Rosenman, American composer (including film scores),
        is born in Brooklyn.

1940   David Diamond's Concerto for Orchestra is first performed,
        in Yaddo, New York.

1954   Hershy Kay's ballet Western Symphony is given its premiere
        performance by choreographer George Balanchine with the
        New York City Ballet Company.

1971   Leonard Bernstein's Mass, "a theater piece" written for the
        opening of the John F. Kennedy Center for Performing Arts
        in Washington, is first performed there.

1977   Gustave Reese dies in Berkeley, California, at the age of
        seventy-seven. He was attending the congress of the Inter-
        national Musicological Society being held in Berkeley.

        SEPTEMBER 8

1613   Don Carlo Gesualdo, Prince of Venosa, Italian composer and
        lutenist, dies in Naples, aged about fifty-three. He had his
        wife and her lover murdered when he found her unfaithful.

1815   Giuseppina Strepponi, Italian soprano who became Giuseppe
        Verdi's second wife, is born in Lodi.

1841   Antonin Dvořák, Czech composer, violist, and organist, is
        born in Mühlhausen.

1897   Jimmie Rodgers, American country-music singer, is born in
        Mendoza, Mississippi. His was the first name in the Country
        Music Hall of Fame in Nashville, Tennessee. In 1977 a U.S.
        postage stamp honored him on his eightieth birthday.

1933   Eric Salzman, American composer who uses mixed media and
        is also a musicologist, is born in New York City.

1934   Peter Maxwell Davies, English composer, is born in Man-
        chester.

1949   Richard Strauss dies in Garmisch-Partenkirchen, Germany, aged eighty-five. A year earlier he had been acquitted of collaborating with the Nazis at a court trial in Munich.

1961   Earle Brown's Available Forms I, for eighteen players, receives its premiere, in Darmstadt, Germany.

1974   Wolfgang Windgassen dies in Stuttgart, Germany, aged sixty.

1975   Paul Chihara's Ceremony V, Symphony in Celebration has its first performance, in Houston, Texas.

SEPTEMBER 9

1583   Girolamo Frescobaldi, Italian organist and composer, is baptized in Ferrara. One of the leading composers of the Renaissance, he was organist at St. Peter's in Rome for many years.

1869   Otto Jahn dies in Göttingen, Germany, aged fifty-six. A musicologist, he had also been a professor of archaeology and a lecturer in philology.

1935   Nedda Casei, American mezzo-soprano, is born in Baltimore.

1937   Olly Wilson, American composer and composition teacher at the Oberlin Conservatory of Music, later at the University of California, is born in St. Louis.

1960   Jussi Bjoerling dies in Siarö, Sweden, aged forty-nine.

1965   Julián Carrillo dies in Mexico City, aged ninety. One of the instruments he devised for fractional tones was a harpzither, with ninety-seven strings to the octave.

1973   Frank Martin's Polyptyque, for violin and two string orchestras, receives its premiere, in Lausanne.

SEPTEMBER 10

1714   Niccolò Jommelli, Italian opera composer, is born near Naples.

1751   Bartolommeo Campagnoli, Italian violinist, is born in Cento di Ferrara.

1838   Hector Berlioz's opera Benvenuto Cellini is first staged at the Paris Opéra, but it arouses little enthusiasm.

1919   Lex Van Delden, Dutch composer who began as a medical
       student, is born in Amsterdam.

1934   Sir George Henschel dies in Scotland, aged eighty-four.   At
       the age of seventy-eight he sang in London at the Schubert
       centennial.

1939   Hans Sotin, German bass and former chemical engineer, is
       born in Dortmund.

1954   Peter Anders dies in Hamburg, Germany, at the age of forty-
       six.

1975   Hans Swarowsky dies in Salzburg, aged seventy-five.   Re-
       garded as an excellent teacher of conducting, he numbered
       Zubin Mehta and Claudio Abbado among his students.

SEPTEMBER 11

1711   William Boyce, English church composer, choral conductor,
       and organist (pupil of Maurice Green), is baptized in London.

1733   François Couperin dies at age sixty-four in Paris; he had re-
       ceived many honors from Louis XIV of France.

1786   Friedrich Kuhlau, German composer and piano teacher, is
       born in Ülzen.   Although blind in one eye, he had to flee to
       Copenhagen to avoid conscription into Napoleon's army.

1825   Eduard Hanslick, Austrian music critic and writer on music
       whom Richard Wagner caricatured as "Beckmesser" in Die
       Meistersinger von Nürnberg, is born in Prague.

1840   Robert Schumann presents his fiancée Clara Wieck with his
       Liederkreis song cycle as a gift on the eve of their wedding.

1850   Jenny Lind makes her American debut under the sponsorship
       of P. T. Barnum.

1890   Aleksander Sveshnikov, Russian conductor, is born in Kolomna.

1899   Vally Weigl, Austrian composer, pianist, and music therapist,
       is born in Vienna.

1907   Lev Oborin, Soviet pianist and teacher, is born in Moscow.

1916   Friedrich Gernsheim dies in Berlin, aged seventy-seven; he
       had numbered among his friends Johannes Brahms.

1925   Harry Stewart Somers, Canadian composer, pianist, and radio music commentator, is born in Toronto.

1926   Ernst Eulenburg dies at age seventy-eight in Leipzig, leaving
        his music-publishing business to his son Kurt.

1930   Clifford Grant, Australian bass, is born in Randwick.

1949   Henri Rabaud dies in Paris, aged seventy-five.

1951   Igor Stravinsky conducts the premiere of his opera The Rake's
        Progress, after Hogarth's engravings (libretto by W. H. Au-
        den and Chester Kallman), in Venice.

1965   Willem van Hoogstraten dies at Tutzing, Germany, aged eighty-
        one.

        SEPTEMBER 12

1764   Jean Philippe Rameau dies in Paris at age eighty. His writ-
        ings on harmony created dissension but laid the basis for mu-
        sical theory today.

1789   Franz Xaver Richter, one of the chief representatives of the
        Mannheim school, dies in Strasbourg, France, aged seventy-
        nine.

1818   Theodor Kullak, German pianist and teacher, is born in Kro-
        toschin.

1840   Robert Schumann marries Clara Wieck, daughter of his teacher,
        Friedrich Wieck (who opposed the marriage).

1842   Marianne Brandt, Austrian contralto, is born in Vienna.

1877   Julius Rietz dies in Dresden, Germany, aged sixty-four. He
        had prepared a complete edition of Mendelssohn's works for
        Breitkopf and Härtel (1874-77).

1891   Adolph Weiss, American composer and bassoonist, is born in
        Baltimore.

1898   Salvador Bacarisse, Spanish composer who moved to France
        after the Spanish Civil War, is born in Madrid.

1901   Ernst Pepping, German composer (principally of choral works)
        and teacher, is born in Duisburg.

1910   Gustav Mahler conducts his Symphony no. 8 at its premiere in
        Munich.

1930   Larry Austin, American composer, educator, and co-founder
        of the avant-garde music publication Source, is born in Dun-
        can, Oklahoma.

1932   Heitor Villa-Lobos's Bachianas Brasileiras, no. 1, for eight
        cellos, is given its first performance, in Rio de Janeiro.

1938   Tatiana Troyanos, American mezzo-soprano, is born in New
        York City.

1967   Joonas Kokonen's Symphony no. 3 is first performed, in
        Helsinki.

1969   Henri Lazerof's Cello Concerto receives its first hearing in
        Oslo.

1974   Eugene Fodor, violinist, plays at a state dinner at the White
        House during the visit of Premier Rabin of Israel.

SEPTEMBER 13

1819   Clara Schumann, pianist wife of Robert Schumann, is born in
        Leipzig.

1874   Arnold Schoenberg, Austrian-American composer and teacher,
        is born in Vienna. His twelve-tone method of composition is
        one of the strongest influences in twentieth-century music.

1894   Emmanuel Chabrier dies in Paris, aged fifty-three, remem-
        bered especially for his rhapsody España.

1903   Harold Byrns, German-American conductor, is born in Hann-
        over.

1909   Ray Green, American composer and executive secretary of the
        American Music Center in New York City (1948-61), is born
        in Cavendish, Missouri.

1914   Leonard Feather, English-American jazz encyclopedist and
        music critic, is born in London.

1917   Robert Ward, American composer and teacher at Cornell
        University, is born in Cleveland, Ohio.

1929   Nicolai Ghiaurov, Bulgarian bass who was trained in Moscow,
        is born in Velimgrad.

1932   Julius Röntgen dies in Utrecht, aged seventy-seven. A friend
        of Brahms and Grieg, he published a biography of Grieg and
        edited letters of Brahms.

1936   Werner Hollweg, German tenor, is born in Solingen.

1939   Arleen Auger, American soprano, is born in Los Angeles.

1977   Leopold Stokowski dies in Hampshire, England, aged ninety-five.

SEPTEMBER 14

1737   Michael Haydn, Austrian composer and teacher, younger brother of (Franz) Joseph Haydn, is born in Rohrau.

1760   Luigi Cherubini, Italian composer of operas and sacred works, is born in Florence.

1793   Benjamin Cooke, English organist and composer, dies in London, aged about fifty-nine.

1854   Anton Bruckner's Missa Solemnis receives its premiere, in St. Florian, Austria.

1861   Fortunato Santini dies in Rome, aged eighty-three. In 1820 he had published a catalog of music manuscripts in his library, listing over 700 composers.

1885   Vittorio Gui, Italian conductor and composer, is born in Rome.

1904   Richard Mohaupt, German composer who fled to New York City from Nazi persecution, is born in Breslau.

1936   Ossip Gabrilowitsch dies at age fifty-eight in Detroit, where he had conducted the Detroit Symphony Orchestra since 1918.

1951   Fritz Busch dies in London, aged sixty-one.

1952   Frank Martin's Concerto for Harpsichord and Small Orchestra has its premiere, in Venice.

1963   Grigori Stolyarov, a conductor of Moscow Radio Symphony Orchestra, dies in Moscow, aged seventy-one.

1964   Mary Howe, a prominent figure in Washington music circles, dies in Washington, aged eighty-two.

SEPTEMBER 15

1815   Halfdan Kjerulf, Norwegian song composer, is born in Christiania (Oslo).

1841   Alessandro Rolla, violin professor at the Conservatory of Milan, dies in Milan, aged eighty-four.

1842   Pierre Marie Baillot, aged seventy, dies in Paris. He is known for his manual L'Art du Violon (1834).

1858   Jenö Hubay, Hungarian violinist, composer, and teacher (Joseph Szigeti a student), is born in Budapest.

1863   Horatio Parker, American composer, organist, and teacher, is born in Auburndale, Massachusetts. Among his students was Charles Ives.

1876   Bruno Walter (né B. W. Schlesinger), German-American conductor, is born in Berlin.

1890   Frank Martin, Swiss composer influenced by Dalcroze and Schoenberg, is born in Geneva.

1909   Carlos Estrada, Uruguayan composer and conductor, is born in Montevideo. From 1954 to 1968 he directed the National Conservatory there.

1913   Henry Brant, American composer and teacher, is born in Montreal.

1917   Richard Arnell, English composer, is born in London.

        Hilde Gueden, Austrian soprano, is born into a musical family in Vienna.

1923   Anton Heiller, Austrian organist and composer, is born in Vienna.

1928   Julian Edwin "Cannonball" Adderley, American jazz alto saxophonist, is born in Tampa, Florida. Playing in a combo with him was his younger brother, Nat Adderley.

1933   Rafael Frühbeck de Burgos, Spanish conductor, is born in Burgos.

1945   Jessye Norman, American soprano, is born in Augusta, Georgia.

        Anton Webern accidentally violates a curfew in Mittersill, Austria, and is fatally shot by an American military policeman of the occupation forces; he was aged sixty-one.

1952   Boris Blacher's Piano Concerto no. 2 has its premiere, in Berlin.

1963   Pierre Max Dubois's Concerto for Violin, Piano, and Orchestra receives its premiere, in Bescançon, France.

SEPTEMBER 16

1685   John Gay, English librettist of The Beggar's Opera, is baptized in Barnstaple.

1782   Farinelli (Carlo Broschi) dies in his palatial home in Bologna, where he had retired after his dismissal from the Spanish court, at the age of seventy-seven.

1801   François Boieldieu's opera Le Calife de Bagdad is first produced, in Paris, and becomes one of his most enduring operas.

1844   Paul Taffanel, French flutist and conductor, co-author with Philippe Gaubert of Méthode complète de flûte, is born in Bordeaux.

1887   Nadia Boulanger, French composition teacher of many present-day American and European composers, is born in Paris. Her sister was Lili Boulanger, the composer.

1895   Karol Rathaus, Polish-American composer and teacher at Queens College, New York City, is born in Tarnopol.

1899   Hans Swarowsky, Austrian conductor and friend of Richard Strauss, is born in Budapest.

1945   John McCormack dies at age sixty-one in Glena, Ireland. In later years he toured on the concert stage, rather than in opera.

1966   Samuel Barber's opera Antony and Cleopatra, commissioned by the Metropolitan Opera House for the opening of the Lincoln Center in New York, stars Leontyne Price in its premiere.

1977   Maria Callas dies in Paris, aged fifty-three, of a heart attack. Her life was tumultuous, both professionally and personally.

SEPTEMBER 17

1711   Ignaz Holzbauer, Austrian composer and conductor of the famous Mannheim orchestra for twenty-five years, is born in Vienna.

1762   Francesco Geminiani dies in Dublin, aged seventy-four. He had settled there in 1759, serving as music master to Count Bellamont.

1795   (Giuseppe) Saverio Mercadante, Italian opera composer, is

baptized at Altamura. The last thirty years of his life he
directed the Naples Conservatory.

1884   Charles Tomlinson Griffes, American composer, teacher, and
pianist, is born in Elmira, New York.

1907   Ignaz Brüll dies in Vienna, aged sixty. From 1872 to 1878
he taught piano at Horak Institute in Vienna.

1917   Isang Yun, Korean-born teacher and composer, is born in
Tong Young. A resident of Germany, in 1970 he began teaching
at the Hochschule für Musik in Berlin.

1932   Daniel Majeske, American violinist, since 1969 concertmaster
of the Cleveland Orchestra, is born in Detroit.

1953   Henry Holden Huss dies at age ninety-one in New York City.
He had continued to compose almost to the end of his life.

1966   Fritz Wunderlich dies from a fall in his home in Heidelberg,
Germany, at age thirty-five.

1973   Hugo Winterhalter dies in Greenwich, Connecticut, aged sixty-
four.

SEPTEMBER 18

1684   Johann Gottfried Walther, German organist, composer, and
first music encyclopedist, is born in Erfurt. His <u>Musikal-
isches Lexikon oder Musikalische Bibliothek</u> was published
in Leipzig in 1732.

1693   Antonio Vivaldi is tonsured and eventually receives minor
orders in the church.

1860   Alberto Franchetti, Italian composer, is born in Turin.

1893   Arthur Benjamin, Australian composer, pianist, teacher, and
conductor, is born in Sydney.

1903   Theodor Kirchner dies in Hamburg, aged seventy-nine. He
had been encouraged and advised by both Mendelssohn and
Schumann.

1952   Frances Alda dies in Venice, aged sixty-nine. Her autobiography was titled <u>Men, Women and Tenors</u> (1937).

1954   Virgil Thomson's Concerto, written for flute, strings, and
percussion, receives its premiere, in Venice.

SEPTEMBER 19

1727   Antonio Vivaldi's music, including his <u>Te Deum,</u> is performed
        in a concert at festivities given by the French ambassador to
        honor the birth of the French royal princess.

1829   Gustav Schirmer, founder of one of the largest music publish-
        ing firms in America, is born in Königsee, Germany.

1900   Solomon Pimsleur, American pianist, composer, and scholar
        in English literature, is born in Paris.

1908   Gustav Mahler conducts the premiere of his Symphony no. 7,
        in Prague.

1911   Gustaf Allan Pettersson, Swedish composer and violist with
        the Stockholm Philharmonic Orchestra, is born in Västra Ryd.

1918   Blanche Thebom, American mezzo-soprano, is born in Mones-
        sen, Pennsylvania.   In 1968 she became director of the South-
        ern Regional Opera Company in Atlanta.

1949   Nikos Skalkottas dies in Athens, aged forty-five.   His work
        was greatly influenced by his study with Arnold Schoenberg.

1954   Tibor Harsányi dies in Paris, aged fifty-six.   A pupil of
        Kodály, he had settled in Paris in 1923.

1961   Maurice Delage dies in Paris, aged eighty-one.

1972   Robert Casadesus dies in Paris at the age of seventy-three.
        His wife, Gaby Casadesus, appeared with him and their son,
        Jean, in a concerto for three pianos and string orchestra that
        he had composed (1965).

SEPTEMBER 20

1880   Ildebrando Pizzetti, Italian composer, teacher, and writer on
        music, is born in Parma.

1885   Ferdinand "Jelly Roll" Morton, American jazz pianist and
        composer, is born in New Orleans.   He began in 1922 to re-
        cord piano rolls of Dixieland jazz; later made recordings for
        the Library of Congress, creating an aural jazz history.

1901   Leo Justinus Kauffmann, Alsatian composer, is born in Dam-
        merkirch.

1908   Pablo de Sarasate dies in Biarritz, France, at the age of
        sixty-three.   He bequeathed to his native city, Pamplona, the

gifts he had received during his career, and they were placed in a museum there.

1922   William Kapell, American concert pianist, is born in New York City.

1955   Elisabeth Schwarzkopf makes her American debut in San Francisco, starring in Der Rosenkavalier of Strauss.

1957   Jean Sibelius dies in Järvenpää, Finland, at the age of ninety-one. He drew inspiration from native legends, especially the epic Kalevala.

SEPTEMBER 21

1737   Francis Hopkinson, American statesman, signer of the Declaration of Independence, and composer, is born in Philadelphia. The Library of Congress possesses some of his manuscripts of songs.

1874   Gustav Holst, English composer, choral conductor, and teacher, is born at Cheltenham. His biographer is his daughter, Imogen Holst, a musician in her own right.

1880   The International Mozart Foundation is established in Salzburg.

1912   György Sandor, Hungarian pianist who settled in the United States after 1939, is born in Budapest. He has recorded the piano works of Bartók and Prokofiev.

1913   Vincent Duckles, American musicologist, librarian, and author of music reference books, is born in Boston.

1922   Vladimir Ruzdjak, Yugoslav baritone, is born in Zagreb.

1925   Rudolf Friml's operetta Vagabond King has its opening, in New York City.

1938   Yuji Takahashi, Japanese composer and pianist, is born in Tokyo.

1939   Philip Rehfeldt, American clarinetist and teacher, is born in Burlington, Iowa.

1942   Jill Gomez, British soprano, is born in New Amsterdam, British Guiana.

1953   Roger Quilter dies at age seventy-five in London.

SEPTEMBER 22

1737   Francesco Mancini dies in Naples, aged sixty-five.

Michel Pignolet de Montéclair dies in St. Denis, France, at
the age of sixty-nine; he was one of the earliest players of
the modern double bass.

1869   Richard Wagner's opera Das Rheingold is first produced, in
Munich; Franz Wüllner conducting.

1894   Elisabeth Rethberg, German soprano, is born in Schwarzenberg

1906   Julius Stockhausen, German baritone and teacher, dies in
Frankfurt.   A friend of Johannes Brahms, he was regarded
as one of the best interpreters of his lieder.

1918   Henryk Szeryng, Polish violinist, is born in Zelazowa Wola.

1926   William O. Smith, American composer and clarinet teacher,
is born in Sacramento, California.

1933   Leonardo Balada, Spanish composer and teacher, is born in
Barcelona.   In 1970 he joined the faculty at Carnegie-Mellon
University in Pittsburgh.

SEPTEMBER 23

1642   Giovanni Maria Bononcini, Italian composer and maestro di
cappella at various churches (father of Giovanni and Antonio
Maria), is born in Montecorone (Modena).

1777   Christoph Willibald Gluck's opera Armide is first staged, at
the Paris Opéra; since then it has been translated and performed throughout Europe and America.

1835   Vincenzo Bellini dies in Puteaux, France, aged thirty-three;
his best operas have remained in the repertory.

1836   Maria Malabran dies at age twenty-eight in a fall from a
horse, in Manchester, England.

1867   John Avery Lomax, American ethnomusicologist, is born in
Goodman, Mississippi.   With his son, Alan, he helped to
make the Archive of American Folk Song of the Library of
Congress one of the most comprehensive.

1872   Anton Rubinstein makes his American debut in New York City.

1896   Louis-Gilbert Duprez dies in Paris, aged eighty-nine.

1914   Norman Cazden, American composer, piano teacher, and
        musicologist, is born in New York City.

1915   Julius Baker, American flute virtuoso and solo flutist with the
        New York Philharmonic Orchestra, is born in Cleveland, Ohio.

1920   Alexander Arutunian, Soviet Armenian composer, is born in
        Erevan.

1926   John Coltrane, American jazz musician and tenor-saxophone
        virtuoso, is born in Hamlet, North Carolina.   His "new black
        music" reflects African resources.

1928   Robert Helps, American pianist, composer, and teacher, is
        born in Passaic, New Jersey.

1930   Ray Charles (full name Ray Charles Robinson), blind American
        jazz singer and pianist, a "soul musician," is born in Albany,
        Georgia.

1936   Igor Blazhkov, Soviet Ukrainian conductor, is born in Kiev.

1940   Rhené-Baton dies in Le Mans, France, aged sixty-one.

1958   Alfred Piccaver dies in Vienna, aged seventy-four.

1962   Aaron Copland's Connotations, an orchestral work using a
        twelve-tone technique, is first performed at the inauguration
        of Lincoln Center, in New York City.

SEPTEMBER 24

1813   André Grétry dies in Montmorency, France, aged seventy-two.
        Known as the "Molière of music" he founded the school of
        French opéra comique.

1914   Andrzej Panufnik, Polish-English composer, is born in Warsaw.

1919   Vaclav Nelhybel, Czech-American composer (principally of
        band music) and conductor, is born in Polanka.

1921   Leonard (Lopes) Salzedo, English composer and conductor,
        is born in London.

1922   Ettore Bastianini, Italian known as "a leading Verdi baritone,"
        is born in Sienna.

        Cornell MacNeil, American baritone and former machinist,
        is born in Minneapolis.

1925   Robert Shaughnessy, American composer and guitarist, is born in Worcester, Massachusetts.

1927   George Cacioppo, American avant-garde composer, is born in Monroe, Michigan.

Richard Swift, American composer, teacher, and music administrator, is born in Middlepoint, Ohio.

1938   Pablo Elvíra, American bass-baritone, is born in Santurce, Puerto Rico.

1955   André Jolivet's Suite transocéane receives its premiere, in Louisville, Kentucky.

1960   Mátyás Seiber dies in an auto crash in Krueger National Park in South Africa, aged fifty-five.

1962   Samuel Barber's Piano Concerto is first performed with the Boston Symphony Orchestra in Lincoln Center, New York City, with John Browning, soloist, and Erich Leinsdorf conducting.

1975   Lowell Cross, director of the Video/Laser Laboratory of the University of Iowa, produces Alexander Scriabin's Prometheus, James Dixon conducting, with color projections coordinated with a "color organ" in Iowa City, Iowa.

SEPTEMBER 25

1683   Jean Philippe Rameau, French composer, organist, and theorist, is born in Dijon.

1849   Johann Strauss, Sr., dies in Vienna, aged forty-five, the "Father of the Waltz."

1896   Roberto Gerhard, Spanish (Catalonian)-English composer, is born in Vails. After the Spanish Civil War he became a British citizen.

1906   Dmitri Shostakovich, Soviet composer and pianist who influenced the course of Russian music, is born in St. Petersburg.

1911   Lionel Nowak, American composer, pianist, and teacher, is born in Cleveland, Ohio.

1916   Julius Fučik dies in Leitmeritz, Czechoslovakia, aged forty-four.

1927   Colin Davis, English conductor and clarinetist, is born in Weybridge.

1932   Glenn Gould, Canadian pianist, is born in Toronto. Since 1970
he has participated in Canadian radio and television documentary
programs.

1944   Leo Justinus Kauffmann dies during a World War II air raid on
Strasbourg, France, aged forty-three.

1956   Boris Christoff makes his American debut at the San Francisco
Opera House singing Boris Godunov.

1966   Dmitri Shostakovich's Cello Concerto no. 2 is given its first
performance on the composer's sixtieth birthday, in Moscow.

1976   Dmitri Shostakovich is honored for his seventieth birthday by
the issuance of a Soviet postage stamp bearing his picture
and an excerpt from his "Leningrad Symphony."

SEPTEMBER 26

1800   William Billings dies in Boston, aged fifty-three, in abject
poverty.   His "fuging pieces" have intrigued modern American
composers; Henry Cowell's Hymn and Fuguing Tune, Nos. 1-8
are based on Billings's tunes.

1808   Paul Wranitzky, concertmaster of the Vienna Opera, dies
in Vienna, aged fifty-one.

1835   Gaetano Donizetti's opera Lucia di Lammermoor is first staged,
at the Teatro San Carlos in Naples.

1868   Henry F. Gilbert, American composer, is born in Somerville,
Massachusetts.

1877   Alfred Cortot, French pianist and conductor, is born in Nyon,
Switzerland.   He formed a trio with Jacques Thibaud and Pablo
Casals; also wrote several books on music interpretation and
technique.

1891   Charles Munch, Alsatian conductor (Boston Symphony Orchestra
1949-62), is born in Strasbourg.

1898   George Gershwin, American composer, including musical
comedies and popular songs, is born in Brooklyn.

1908   Sylvia Marlowe, American harpsichordist, is born in New York
City.

1916   Robert Kelly, American composer and teacher at the University of Illinois, is born in Clarksburg, West Virginia.

1930   Fritz Wunderlich, German tenor, is born in Kusel.

1937   Bessie Smith dies in an auto accident near Clarksdale, Mississippi, aged about forty-three.

1942   Douglas Lawrence, American bass-baritone, is born in Los Angeles.

1945   Béla Bartók dies of leukemia in New York City, aged sixty-four.

1967   Dmitri Shostakovich's Concerto no. 2 for violin and his symphonic poem October receive their premiere performances in Moscow.

1978   Seymour Shifrin dies in Boston, aged fifty-two.

SEPTEMBER 27

1879   Cyril Scott, English composer, is born in Exton.

1880   Jacques Thibaud, French violinist, is born in Bordeaux. A pupil of his father, he later played in a piano trio with Alfred Cortot and Pablo Casals.

1882   Elly Ney, German pianist, a pupil of Leschetizky, is born in Düsseldorf.

1892   Antonin Dvořák arrives in New York and is greeted by officials of the National Conservatory, which he was to head for two years.

1898   Vincent Youmans, American musical-comedy and popular-song writer, is born in New York City.

1919   Adelina Patti dies at Brecknock, Wales, aged seventy-six.

1921   Englebert Humperdinck dies in Neustrelitz, Germany, aged sixty-seven. After the success of his Hansel and Gretel he retired from teaching, devoting himself completely to composition.

1926   Fred Teschler, German baritone and former journalist, is born in Dresden.

1930   Igor Kipnis, American harpsichordist, son of singer Alexander Kipnis, is born in Berlin.

1945   Misha Dichter, American pianist who was raised in Los Angeles, is born in Shanghai.

1956   Gerald Finzi dies in Oxford, England, aged fifty-five.

SEPTEMBER 28

1834   Charles Lamoureux, French conductor and violinist, is born
in Bordeaux.

1870   Florent Schmitt, French composer and music critic, is born
in Blamont.

1913   Vivian Fine, American composer and piano teacher, is born
in Chicago.

1918   Igor Stravinsky's L'Histoire du soldat, for narrator and seven
instruments, is given its premiere, in Lausanne.

1922   Romeo Cascarino, American composer and pianist, is born in
Philadelphia.

1924   Rudolf Barshai, Soviet violist and conductor who emigrated to
Israel in 1977, is born in Labinskaya.

1926   Ferry Gruber, Austrian baritone, is born in Vienna.

1937   Edward Applebaum, American composer, is born in Los
Angeles.

1939   Harry Theyard, American tenor, is born in New Orleans.

1963   Rosa Raisa dies in Los Angeles at the age of seventy.

SEPTEMBER 29

1858   Leopoldo Mugnone, Italian opera conductor, is born in Naples.

1879   Joaquín Nin, Cuban pianist, musicologist, and composer, is
born in Havana. He was editor and performer of early
Spanish keyboard music.

1882   Emma Calvé makes her operatic debut in Brussels, starring
in Gounod's Faust.

1894   Franco Capuana, Italian conductor of opera, is born in Fano.

1918   Gustav Holst's suite The Planets, for voices and orchestra,
is given its premiere, in Queen's Hall, London.

1921   Sigmund Romberg's operetta Blossom Time is first staged, in
        New York City.

1924   Robert Nagel, American composer, trumpeter, and conductor,
        is born in Freeland, Pennsylvania.

1930   Richard Bonynge, Australian conductor, husband of singer
        Joan Sutherland, is born in Sydney.

1965   Mirella Freni and Gianni Raimondi make their American
        debuts, starring in La Bohème at the Metropolitan Opera
        House in New York City.

1968   Hans Werner Henze's Piano Concerto no. 2 is first performed,
        in Bielefeld, Germany.

1972   Richard Crooks dies in Portola Valley, California, aged
        seventy-two.

1977   Alexander Tcherepnin dies at age seventy-eight in Paris, son
        and father of composers.

SEPTEMBER 30

1791   Wolfgang Amadeus Mozart conducts his opera The Magic Flute
        in its first performance, in Vienna. His librettist, Emanuel
        Schikaneder, also plays a part in the opera.

1840   Johan (Severin) Svendsen, Norwegian composer and court
        conductor (in Copenhagen), is born in Christiania.

1863   Georges Bizet's opera Les Pecheurs de perles is first staged,
        at the Théâtre-Lyrique in Paris.

1908   David Oistrakh, Soviet virtuoso violinist and father of violinist
        Igor Oistrakh, is born in Odessa.

1919   Patricia Neway, American soprano, is born in Brooklyn.

1920   Aldo Parisot, Brazilian cellist, is born in Natal.

1925   Giuseppe Campora, Italian tenor, is born in Tortona.

1926   James Pellerite, American flutist, author of a flute manual,
        is born in Clearfield, Pennsylvania.

1935   George Gershwin's American folk opera Porgy and Bess is
        first produced, in Boston.

1971   William Mathias's Holiday Overture is first performed on a BBC
        radio broadcast.

OCTOBER 1

1708   John Blow dies in London, aged fifty-nine or sixty, and is
        buried in Westminster Abbey.

1771   Pierre Marie Baillot, French violinist, is born in Passy.

1832   Henry Clay Work, American composer of popular songs, is
        born in Middletown, Connecticut.

1865   Paul Dukas, French composer, teacher, and editor of Rameau's
        works, is born in Paris.

1876   Henri Bertini dies near Grenoble, France, at the age of
        seventy-seven.

1897   Ernst von Dohnányi plays his first independent piano recital
        in Berlin.

1904   Vladimir Horowitz, Russian-American piano virtuoso, is born
        in Berdichev. He married Wanda Toscanini, daughter of
        Arturo Toscanini.

1908   Benno Moiseiwitsch, a pupil of Leschetizky, makes his debut
        as a concert pianist in Reading, England.

1924   The Curtis Institute of Music in Philadelphia is inaugurated.

1926   Gerhard Stolze, German-Austrian tenor, is born in Dessau.

1931   Sylvano Bussotti, Italian composer whose avant-garde scores
        resemble abstract art, is born in Florence.

1945   Sandra Walker, American mezzo-soprano, is born in Rich-
        mond, Virginia.

1964   Ernst Toch dies in Los Angeles, aged seventy-six. Among
        his students was André Previn.

1975   John Tavener's Piano Concerto, with chamber orchestra, is given its premiere, in London.

1976   Antal Dorati's Cello Concerto is first performed, in Louis-
        ville, Kentucky.

1979   Roy Harris dies in Santa Monica, California, at the age of
        eighty-one. He was one of the "big five" of American com-
        posers, along with Aaron Copland, Samuel Barber, Walter
        Piston, and William Schuman.

OCTOBER 2

1704   Franz Tuma, Bohemian viola da gamba virtuoso and composer,
        is born in Kostelecz.

1854   The Academy of Music is inaugurated in New York City with
        the opera Norma.

1913   Frederick Delius's orchestral works Summer Night on the
        River and On Hearing the First Cuckoo in Spring are first
        performed, in Leipzig.

1920   Max Bruch dies in Friednau, Germany, aged eighty-two; until
        1910 he had been teaching composition at Berlin's Musikhoch-
        schule.

1930   Sir Eugene Goossens's Oboe Concerto has its premiere in
        London, with his brother, Leon Goossens, as soloist.

1935   Peter Frankl, Hungarian pianist, is born in Budapest.

1943   Robert Nathaniel Dett dies at age sixty, in Battle Creek, Mich-
        igan. He had taught in a number of Southern colleges.

1951   Nicola Rossi-Lemeni makes his American debut in Mussorg-
        sky's Boris Godunov at San Francisco Opera.

1964   The Borodin Quartet makes its New York City debut at Car-
        negie Hall.

1970   Norman Dello Joio conducts the premiere of his Evocations,
        for chorus and orchestra, in Tampa, Florida.

1971   Thea Musgrave, Scottish-born composer and composition
        teacher at the University of California in Santa Barbara,
        marries violist Peter Mark, a fellow faculty member and
        artistic director of the Norfolk, Virginia, regional opera
        company.

OCTOBER 3

1750   Georg Matthias Monn dies in Vienna, aged thirty-three.

1833   Hector Berlioz marries Irish actress Harriet Smithson, his
        inspiration for his _Symphonie fantastique_. It proved an un-
        happy union, and they later separated.

1877   Therese Tietjens dies in London, aged forty-six.

1888   Gilbert and Sullivan's operetta _Yeoman of the Guard_ is first
        staged at London's Savoy Theatre.

1900   Sir Edward Elgar's oratorio _The Dream of Gerontius_ is con-
        ducted in its premiere at Birmingham Festival by Hans Rich-
        ter. It is regarded as Elgar's masterpiece.

1923   Stanislaw Skrowaczewski, Polish-American conductor and
        composer, is born in Lwow. From 1960 to 1979 he led the
        Minneapolis Symphony Orchestra, renamed in 1970 the Min-
        nesota Orchestra.

1929   Sir William Walton's Viola Concerto is first performed, in
        London.

1930   David Epstein, American composer, conductor, and faculty
        member in music at the Massachusetts Institute of Technology,
        is born in New York.

1931   Carl Nielsen dies at age sixty-six in Copenhagen, only re-
        cently having been appointed director of the Royal Conserva-
        tory.

1934   Benjamin Boretz, American critic, teacher, composer, and
        founder of the publication _Perspectives of New Music,_ is born
        in New York City.

1936   Steve Reich, American composer, is born in New York City.

        Walter Ross, American composer and teacher, is born in
        Lincoln, Nebraska.

1941   Wilhelm Kienzl dies in Vienna, aged eighty-four. He had
        earned a doctorate in music; served as music critic and wrote
        several music biographies.

        Ruggero Raimondi, Italian bass, is born in Bologna.

1944   The New York City Opera is inaugurated.

1953   Sir Arnold Bax dies in Cork, Ireland, aged sixty-nine. His
        autobiography, _Farewell My Youth,_ was published in 1943.

1967   Woody Guthrie dies in New York City, aged fifty-five. A
        year earlier he was recognized by the government as "a poet
        of the American landscape."

        Sir Malcolm Sargent dies at age seventy-two in London. From
        1950 to 1957 he had conducted the BBC Symphony Orchestra.

        OCTOBER 4

1749   Jean-Louis Duport, foremost French cellist of his day, is
        born in Paris. His cello manual is still a standard textbook.

1768   Gaetano Brunetti's opera Jason is first produced, in Madrid.

1803   Luigi Cherubini's opera Anacréon receives its premiere at the
        Paris Opéra.

1812   Fanny Persiani, Italian coloratura soprano, a pupil of her
        father, is born in Rome.

1910   Erich Wolfgang Korngold's pantomime Der Schneemann is first
        performed, in Vienna.

1912   Alfonso Letelier, Chilean composer and teacher, is born in
        Santiago.

1916   Richard Strauss's one-act opera Ariadne auf Naxos receives
        its premiere in its revised version at the Vienna Opera.

1917   Albert de Klerk, Dutch organist and composer, is born in Haarlem

1921   The American Academy in Rome is inaugurated and grants
        the first fellowship in music to Leo Sowerby.

1934   Vladimir Pleshakov, Russian-American concert pianist, is
        born in Shanghai, China. He has studied early piano con-
        struction, playing classical music on reconstructed pianos;
        his Ph.D. is from Stanford.

1940   Alain Lombard, French conductor, is born in Paris.

1941   Manuel Ponce's Concierto del Sur, for guitar and orchestra,
        is first performed, in Montevideo.

1956   Bohuslav Martinů's Piano Concerto no. 4 has its premiere, in
        New York City.

1959   Dmitri Shostakovich's Cello Concerto no. 1 receives its first
        hearing, in Leningrad.

1964   Set Svanholm dies at age sixty in Saltsjoe-Duvnaes, Sweden.

OCTOBER 5

1707   Daniel Speer dies in Göppingen, Germany, aged seventy-one.
        Some of his humorous songs were published under an assumed
        name.

1762   Christoph Willibald Gluck's opera Orfeo ed Euridice (to a li-
        bretto by Calzabigi) is first staged, in Vienna.

1880   Jacques Offenbach dies in Paris at the age of sixty-one.

1906   Alfred Frankenstein, American music critic and writer on
        music, is born in Chicago.

1924   Matteo Manuguerra, French tenor, is born in Tunisia.

1927   John Downey, American composer, pianist, and theory pro-
        fessor, is born in Chicago.

1940   Silvestre Revueltas dies in Mexico City, aged forty, of pneu-
        monia.   In 1937 he was in Spain during the civil war, assist-
        ing the Loyalist government in cultural affairs.

1974   Ebe Stignani dies in Imola, Italy, aged seventy.

OCTOBER 6

1600   Jacopo Peri's opera Euridice, written for the wedding of Maria
        de Medici and Henry IV of France, is performed in Florence.
        Her uncle, Duke of Tuscany, acted as proxy for Henry, who
        was not allowed to leave his country.

1786   Antonio Sacchini dies in Paris, aged fifty-six.   In 1781 he
        was invited by Queen Marie Antoinette to write operas for the
        court.

1802   Ludwig van Beethoven, increasingly deaf, writes his will, the
        "Heiligenstadt Testament."

1820   Jenny Lind, Swedish soprano known as the "Swedish Nightin-
        gale," is born in Stockholm.

1868   Jacques Offenbach's operetta La Périchole is first staged at
        the Variétés, in Paris.

1873   Oscar Sonneck, American musicologist, music librarian, and
        writer on music, is born in Jersey City, New Jersey.   He
        served as head of the Music Division of the Library of Con-
        gress, editor of The Musical Quarterly, and director of G.
        Schirmer's Publication Department.

Friedrich Wieck dies in Dresden, aged eighty-eight.

1882   Karol Szymanowski, Polish composer, is born in Timoshovka, Ukraine.

1886   Edwin Fischer, Swiss pianist and teacher, is born in Basel.

1887   Maria Jeritza (real name Jedlitzka), operatic soprano, is born in Brünn, Austria.

1909   Dudley Buck dies in Orange, New Jersey, aged seventy.

Ossip Gabrilowitsch marries contralto Clara Clemens, daughter of Mark Twain. He often accompanied his wife in joint recitals.

1913   Richard Dyer-Bennett, English-American ballad singer, is born in Leicester. He has taught at Stony Brook, New York State University.

1920   Frieda Hempel impersonates Jenny Lind, singing in the first of seventy concerts in honor of the Lind Centenary.

1927   Paul Badura-Skoda, Austrian pianist and teacher, is born in Vienna. A Mozart interpreter, he has edited Mozart's piano sonatas, In 1966 he joined the faculty at the University of Wisconsin.

1935   Sir Frederic Cowen dies in London, aged eighty-five.

1939   William Schuman's American Festival Overture is first performed, in Boston.

1960   John Cage's Cartridge Music receives its premiere, in Cologne.

1962   Yoritsuné Matsudaira's Bugaku, for chamber orchestra, is first heard, in Palermo, Italy.

OCTOBER 7

1746   William Billings, early American church composer, a tanner by trade, is born in Boston. In 1770 he published the first of several songbooks, The New England Psalm Singer.

1802   Wilhelm Bernhard Molique, German violinist and composer, is born in Nuremberg.

1845   Isabella Colbran dies in Bologna, aged sixty.

1893   Gilbert and Sullivan's operetta Utopia Limited opens in the Savoy Theatre, London.

1898   Alfred Wallenstein, American cellist and conductor, is born
        in Chicago.   From 1943 to 1956 he led the Los Angeles Phil-
        harmonic Orchestra.

1905   Victor Herbert's operetta Mlle. Modiste is first produced, in
        Trenton, New Jersey.

1908   Nikolai Rabinovich, Russian conductor, is born in St. Peters-
        burg.

1909   Nicolai Rimsky-Korsakov's opera Le Coq d'or is first staged,
        posthumously, in Moscow.

1918   Sir Charles Hubert Hastings Parry dies at age seventy in Eng-
        land.

1925   Bryan Drake, New Zealand bass-baritone, is born in Dunedin.

1932   The London Philharmonic Orchestra gives its first concert,
        with Sir Thomas Beecham conducting.

1937   Silvestre Revueltas's symphonic suite Redes receives its pre-
        miere, in Barcelona.

1951   Lukas Foss is soloist in the premiere of his award-winning
        Piano Concerto no. 2, in Venice.

1955   Frieda Hempel dies in Berlin, aged seventy.

        Darius Milhaud conducts the premiere of his Symphony no. 6,
        in Boston.

1959   Mario Lanza dies in Rome, aged thirty-eight.

1976   David Del Tredici's The Final Alice, based on an episode in
        Alice in Wonderland, receives its premiere, in Chicago.

        Nikolai Lopatnikoff dies in Pittsburgh, aged seventy-three.
        He had taught composition at Carnegie Institute of Technology,
        1945-68.

        OCTOBER 8

1585   Heinrich Schütz, German composer (largely of sacred music),
        court organist, and conductor, is born in Köstritz.   He served
        as a link between Palestrina and Bach--the Italian and Ger-
        manic cultures.

1644   Alessandro Stradella, Italian composer, is born at Montefes-
        tino.

1765   The Bergen Symphony Orchestra is founded in Norway.

1834   François Boieldieu dies at age fifty-eight in Jarcy, France, of
        lung disease.

1862   Emil von Sauer, German pianist, is born in Hamburg.

1865   Heinrich Wilhelm Ernst dies in Nice, France, at the age of
        fifty-one.

1870   Louis Vierne, blind French organist and composer, is born
        in Poitiers.

1898   Musical America's first issue appears.

1903   Carl Nielsen's Helios Overture has its premiere, in Copen-
        hagen.

1929   Irene Dalis, American mezzo-soprano, is born in San Jose,
        California.

1930   Toru Takemitsu, Japanese composer, is born in Tokyo.

1939   Eugene Zador's oratorio Christopher Columbus is first per-
        formed, in New York City.

1953   Kathleen Ferrier dies of cancer in London, aged forty-one.

        OCTOBER 9

1727   Johann Wilhelm Hertel, German composer, violinist, and
        conductor, is born in Eisenach.

1826   Gioacchino Rossini's first French opera, The Siege of Corinth,
        is first staged in Paris and proves successful.

1835   Camille Saint-Saëns, French composer, conductor, and pianist
        (whose sight-reading ability impressed Richard Wagner), is
        born in Paris.

1863   Alexander Siloti, Russian pianist, conductor, and teacher, a
        cousin of Sergei Rachmaninoff, is born near Kharkov on the
        family estate.

1890   Jānis Mediņs, Latvian composer and conductor, is born in
        Riga. When the Soviet Army neared Latvia in 1944, he fled
        to Stockholm.

1891   Antonin Dvořák conducts his Requiem Mass for soli, chorus
        and orchestra at Birmingham, England. It had been com-

missioned by the Birmingham Festival Committee.

1914   Roger Goeb, American composer, director of American Com-
        posers Alliance, 1956 to 1962, is born in Cherokee, Iowa.

1919   Irmgard Seefried, German soprano, is born in Köngetried.

1921   Leoš Janáček's Slavonic rhapsody <u>Taras Bulba,</u> after Gogol,
        is first performed, in Brno.

1922   Raymond Wilding-White, American composer, is born in Cater-
        ham, England.

1940   John Lennon, English rock 'n roll star, member of The
        Beatles, is born in Liverpool during a German air raid.

OCTOBER 10

1713   Johann Ludwig Krebs, German organist and composer (a pupil
        of J. S. Bach), is born in Buttelstädt.

1806   Louis Ferdinand, Prince of Prussia, falls in battle at Saalfeld,
        aged thirty-three.   He was an excellent musician, to whom
        Beethoven dedicated his third piano concerto.

1813   Giuseppe Verdi, Italian opera composer, is born in Le Ron-
        cole.

1825   Dimitri Stepanovitch Bortniansky, Russian composer and choral
        director at the Imperial Chapel, dies in St. Petersburg, aged
        about seventy-four.

1887   Oscar Thompson, American music lexicographer, music critic,
        and editor, is born in Crawfordsville, Indiana.

1889   Adolph von Henselt dies in Warmbrunn, Silesia, aged seventy-
        five.   He composed pieces and technical studies for piano.

1893   Willi Apel, German-American musicologist and lecturer, is
        born in Konitz.   From 1950 to 1964 he taught at the University
        of Indiana.

1897   Lamar Stringfield, American composer who uses Southern
        folksongs in his works, is born in Raleigh, North Carolina.
        Conductor as well as printer, he published his own music.

1899   Margherita Grandi, Australian-born Italian soprano, is born
        in Hobart.

1903   Vernon Duke (né Vladimir Dukelsky), Russian-American composer, is born in a railway station at Parfianovka as his mother was traveling. He wrote both serious and popular music.

1906   Paul Creston (né Joseph Guttoveggio), American composer and teacher, is born in New York City.

1916   Scott Huston, American composer, conductor, and teacher at Cincinnati Conservatory, is born in Tacoma, Washington.

1919   Richard Strauss's opera Die Frau ohne Schatten, which required elaborate staging, is given its premiere at the Vienna Opera.

1931   Sir William Walton's Belshazzar's Feast, an oratorio for baritone, chorus, and orchestra, is first performed at the Leeds Festival, England.

1968   Luciano Berio's Sinfonia is first performed for the 125th anniversary of the New York Philharmonic Orchestra.

1970   Talib Rasul Hakim's Visions of Ishwara has its premiere in New York City.

1972   Yoritsuné Matsudaira's Mouvements circulatoires, for two chamber orchestra, receives its premiere at Graz Festival, Austria.

OCTOBER 11

1795   Franz Christoph Neubauer, serving as court Kapellmeister at Bückeburg, Germany, dies there at age forty-five.

1830   Frédéric Chopin is soloist in his Piano Concerto no. 1 in a Warsaw theater.

1837   Samuel Wesley dies in London, aged seventy-one. His brother Charles had been his first teacher; they were both nephews of John Wesley, founder of Methodism.

1882   Robert Nathaniel Dett, American composer, teacher, writer, and compiler of Negro spirituals, is born in Drummondville, Quebec.

1896   Anton Bruckner dies in Vienna, aged seventy-two. Only long after his death was his greatness as a symphonist recognized.

1928   Russell Oberlin, American countertenor, is born in Akron, Ohio.

1933   Stefania Malagù, Italian mezzo-soprano, is born in Milan.

1937   Isaac Stern is acclaimed in his debut as violinist in New York
        City.

1953   Olivier Messiaen's <u>Réveil des oiseaux,</u> for piano and orches-
        tra, receives its premiere, in Donaueschingen, Germany.

OCTOBER 12

1686   Sylvius Leopold Weiss, German composer and lutenist, is born
        in Breslau.

1848   Alwina Valleria (real name Schoening), American soprano, is
        born in Baltimore.

1872   Ralph Vaughan Williams, English composer and folksong col-
        lector, is born in Down Ampney, the son of a clergyman.

1880   Healey Willan, English-Canadian composer, organist, and
        teacher, is born in Balham.

1887   Nellie Melba creates a sensation in her operatic debut in
        Brussels.

1893   Páll Isólfsson, Icelandic organist and composer, is born in
        Stokkseyri.   From 1939 to 1968 he was organist at Reykjavik
        Cathedral.

1907   Wolfgang Fortner, German composer, teacher, and lecturer
        at Berkshire Music Center at Tanglewood, Massachusetts, is
        born in Leipzig.

1910   Ralph Vaughan Williams's <u>Sea Symphony,</u> for soprano, bari-
        tone, chorus, and orchestra (after Walt Whitman), is first
        heard at the Leeds Festival in England.

1935   Luciano Pavarotti, Italian tenor, is born in Modena.   A mem-
        ber of the Metropolitan Opera staff, he is acknowledged one
        of the greatest tenors of the day.

1944   Bruce Brewer, American tenor, is born in San Antonio, Texas.

1966   Gunther Schuller's opera <u>The Visitation</u> receives its premiere
        at the Hamburg Opera Festival.

1974   Joseph Frederick Wagner dies at age seventy-four in Los
        Angeles.   In addition to his compositions, he published two
        books on orchestration and band scoring.

OCTOBER 13

1694   Johann Christoph Pezel, German composer (principally for
        wind ensembles) and municipal trumpeter in Leipzig and
        Bautzen, dies in Bautzen, aged about fifty-five.

1792   Moritz Hauptmann, German music theorist and composer, is
        born in Dresden. At Mendelssohn's recommendation, he was
        appointed cantor of the Thomasschule in Leipzig in 1842, re-
        maining there until his death.

1879   Peter van Anrooy, Dutch conductor, is born in Zalt-Boomel.

1890   Gösta Nystroem, Swedish composer, is born at Silvberg.

1897   Harrison Kerr, American academician and composer, is born
        in Cleveland, Ohio.   From 1949 to 1968 he was dean of the Col-
        lege of Fine Arts, University of Oklahoma.

1909   Art Tatum, nearly blind American jazz pianist, is born in
        Toledo, Ohio.   He learned to read Braille music notation and
        developed his own style of playing.

1912   Hugo Weisgall, ˏCzech-American opera composer and teacher,
        is born in Ivancice.

1934   Theodore Baker dies in Dresden, Germany, aged eighty-three.
        His doctoral thesis was the first serious study of American
        Indian music.

1958   William Kraft's Nonet, for brass and percussion, receives its
        premiere, in Los Angeles.

1968   Gustaf Allan Pettersson's Symphony no. 7 is first performed,
        in Stockholm.

1974   Josef Krips dies in Geneva at age seventy-two, after con-
        ducting many of the major orchestras in Europe and America.

OCTOBER 14

1669   Marc' Antonio Cesti dies in Florence, aged forty-six.   Having
        been a member of the Papal choir, he stressed the importance
        of smooth-flowing melodic lines in his operas.

1771   Franz Xaver Brixi dies in Prague at the age of thirty-nine.

1859   Paul Camille Chevillard, French composer and conductor, is
        born in Paris.   He succeeded Lamoureux as conductor of the
        Lamoureux Concerts.

1891   Joseph E. Maddy, American music educator and conductor,
        is born in Wellington, Kansas. With T. P. Giddings, he
        founded the National Music Camp for high school students, at
        Interlochen, Michigan.

1898   Maurice Martenot, French inventor of the electronic instru-
        ment "Ondes Martenot," is born in Paris. A number of
        French composers have included it in their works.

1928   Gary Graffman, American pianist, is born in New York City.

1934   Berit Lindholm, Swedish soprano, is born in Stockholm.

1950   Richard Kountz dies in New York City, aged fifty-four.

        OCTOBER 15

1775   Bernhard Henrik Crusell, Finnish clarinetist, conductor, and
        composer, is born in Nystad (Uusikaupunki).

1780   (Franz) Joseph Haydn's opera La Fedelta premiata (dramma
        giocoso) is first performed in the reconstructed theater at
        Esterházy.

1818   Alexander Dreyshock, Bohemian piano virtuoso and composer,
        is born in Zak.

1839   Henriette Voigt dies in Leipzig, aged thirty.

1886   Antonin Dvořák's oratorio St. Ludmilla is first performed at
        Leeds, England.

1901   Geraldine Farrar makes her successful operatic debut at the
        Berlin Opera, starring in Gounod's Faust.

1905   Claude Debussy's La Mer receives its premiere in Paris,
        Camille Chevillard conducting.

        Dag Wirén, Swedish composer, is born in Noraberg. An
        officer of the Society of Swedish Composers, he has also
        served as a music critic.

1918   Antonio Cotogni dies in Rome, aged eighty-seven.

1923   Harold Blumenfeld, American composer and teacher, is born
        in Seattle, Washington.

1926   Karl Richter, German organist, conductor, and teacher, is
        born in Plauen.

1933   Dmitri Shostakovich's Concerto no. 1, for piano, trumpet, and
        strings, receives its first performance, in Leningrad.

1940   Elisabeth Speiser, Swiss soprano, is born in Zurich.

1943   Sir Benjamin Britten's Serenade, for tenor, horn, and string
        orchestra (written for horn player Dennis Brain), is first
        performed in London.

1950   Victoria de Los Angeles makes her American singing debut in
        Carnegie Hall in New York City.

        Gina Bachauer plays her first American piano recital in New
        York with an attendance of only thirty-five people.

1955   Iannis Xenakis's Metastasis, for sixty-one instruments, has
        its premiere in Donaueschingen, Germany.

1960   Sviatoslav Richter plays his first American concert in Chicago.

1964   Cole Porter dies in Santa Monica, California, aged seventy-
        three.   Among his most popular songs were Night and Day
        and Begin the Beguine.

1968   Franz Reizenstein dies in London, aged fifty-seven, teaching
        at the Royal Manchester College since 1964.

        OCTOBER 16

1621   Jan Pieterszoon Sweelinck, Dutch organist, composer, and
        teacher of many northern European organists, dies in Amster-
        dam, aged about fifty-nine.

1750   Sylvius Leopold Weiss dies in Dresden, aged sixty-four; he
        was regarded as one of the finest lute players of his time.

1821   Albert Franz Doppler, Polish-born composer, conductor, and
        flutist, is born in Lwow.   He lived most of his life in Vienna.

1912   Arnold Schoenberg's Pierrot Lunaire has its premiere in
        Berlin after forty some rehearsals.   The voice part, "Sprech-
        stimme," substitutes speech song, notated without pitch indi-
        cation.

1920   Alberto Nepomuceno dies in Rio de Janeiro, aged fifty-six.

1925   Richard Strauss's Parergon zur Symphonia domestica, for
        piano left hand and orchestra, is first performed in Dresden
        with Paul Wittgenstein (who commissioned the work) as soloist.

1926 Zoltán Kodály's opera <u>Háry János</u> is first staged, in Budapest.

1933 Maurice Renaud dies in Paris, aged seventy-two; he had sung in more than sixty operas.

1936 Margreta Elkins, Australian mezzo-soprano, is born in Brisbane.

Gerardo Gandini, Argentine composer and pianist, is born in Buenos Aires; since 1970 he has taught at the Juilliard School of Music.

1938 Aaron Copland's ballet <u>Billy the Kid</u> is first performed by the Ballet Caravan Company, in Chicago.

1942 Aaron Copland's one-act ballet <u>Rodeo</u> is produced in New York City by the Ballet Russe de Monte Carlo.

1946 Sir Granville Bantock dies in London, aged seventy-eight.

1949 Carl Emil Seashore dies in Lewiston, Idaho, aged eighty-three. He had served as dean at Iowa State University for many years.

1953 François d'Assise Morel's <u>Antiphonie</u> receives its premiere, in New York City under Leopold Stokowski's direction.

1958 Teresa Stratas stars in <u>La Bohème</u> in her operatic debut with the Toronto Opera.

1960 Olivier Messiaen's <u>Chronochromie</u> is first performed, in Donaueschingen, Germany.

1966 Wieland Wagner dies at age forty-nine in Munich.

1973 Gene Krupa dies in Yonkers, New York, aged sixty-four.

1975 Vittorio Gui dies in Florence, aged ninety.   From 1947 to 1965 he conducted opera in England.

OCTOBER 17

1707 Johann Sebastian Bach marries his cousin Maria Barbara Bach.

1744 Giuseppe Antonio Guarneri dies in Cremona, Italy, aged forty-six; Paganini played on one of his violins.

1761 Christoph Willibald Gluck's ballet <u>Don Juan</u> opens successfully in Vienna.

1810   Giovanni Mario, Italian tenor, is born in Cagliari.   In 1844
        he married Giulia Grisi, the singer.

1825   Peter Winter dies at age seventy-one in Munich, where he
        had been court conductor since 1798.

1831   Felix Mendelssohn's Piano Concerto no. 1 is first performed,
        in Munich.

1837   Johann Nepomuk Hummel dies in Weimar, Germany, at fifty-
        eight.   As a pianist he was considered the equal of Beethoven.

1849   Frédéric Chopin, ill for a long time with tuberculosis, dies
        in Paris, aged thirty-nine.   He was buried between Bellini
        and Cherubini.

1892   Herbert Howells, English composer and teacher, is born in
        Lydney.   He succeeded Gustav Holst as director at St. Paul's
        Girls' School.

1916   Mischa Levitzki makes his debut as concert pianist in the
        United States at Aeolian Hall, New York City.

1924   Rolando Panerai, Italian baritone, is born in Florence.

1944   Aaron Copland's Letter from Home is given its premiere on
        a radio broadcast.

1957   Mikhail Tavrizian dies in Erevan, Soviet Union, aged fifty.

1960   Carlo Maria Giulini conducts the opening performance at the
        Metropolitan Opera, and New York Times reviewer Harold
        Schonberg lauds him as "a superior technician and a first
        class interpreter."

1961   Hale Smith's Contours for Orchestra is first performed, in
        Louisville, Kentucky.

1978   Marian Anderson is presented a Congressional Gold Medal by
        President Carter at a White House ceremony in Washington.

        OCTOBER 18

1545   John Taverner, English church composer and organist who
        left music to promote Thomas Cromwell's religious persecu-
        tions, dies in Boston, England, aged about fifty-five.

1706   Baldassare Galuppi, prolific Italian opera composer, harpsi-
        chordist, and teacher (Bortniansky a pupil), is born on the
        Island of Burano, near Venice.

1817   Etienne Méhul dies in Paris, aged fifty-four. During the
        French Revolution he was most careful in his choice of sub-
        jects for his operas.

1887   Johannes Brahms conducts the premiere of his Double Con-
        certo for Violin and Cello in Cologne, with Joseph Joachim,
        violin, and Robert Hausmann, cello, as soloists. Brahms
        had written the work to heal the rift between him and Joachim.

1893   Charles Gounod dies in Paris, aged seventy-five. One of his
        best-known works is the Ave Maria set to Bach's first pre-
        lude of the Well-Tempered Clavier.

1904   Gustav Mahler conducts the premiere of his Symphony no. 5,
        "The Giant," in Cologne.

1920   Alexander Young, English tenor, is born in London.

1923   Igor Stravinsky's Octet for Wind Instruments receives its pre-
        miere, in Paris.

1930   Barry McDaniel, American baritone, is born in Topeka, Kan-
        sas.

1931   Thomas A. Edison dies in West Orange, New Jersey, aged
        eighty-four. At first, he regarded his phonograph as a "dic-
        tating machine," and his letterheads read "The Phonograph--
        The Ideal Amanuensis."

1938   Wayne Barlow's The Winter's Passed, for oboe and strings,
        has its first hearing in Rochester, New York.

1946   Aaron Copland's Symphony no. 3, in memory of Mme. Natalie
        Koussevitzky, is first performed by the Boston Symphony Or-
        chestra.

1962   Alvin Etler's Concerto for Wind Quintet and Orchestra has
        its premiere, in Tokyo.

1966   Niccolò Castiglione's Canzoni, for soprano and orchestra, is
        given its first performance in Naples.

1976   Janine Micheau dies in Paris, aged sixty-two.

        Pedro Sanjuán dies in Washington, aged eighty-nine.

        OCTOBER 19

1678   Giovanni Maria Bononcini dies in Modena, Italy, aged thirty-
        six; he is survived by his two sons, who became outstanding
        musicians.

1814   Franz Schubert writes his song <u>Gretchen am Spinnrade</u> (text from Goethe's <u>Faust</u>) in Vienna.

1845   Richard Wagner's opera <u>Tannhäuser</u> is first produced, in Dresden.

1900   Erna Berger, German soprano, is born in Dresden.

1901   Sir Edward Elgar's <u>Pomp and Circumstances Marches</u> (the first two) have their first performances, in Liverpool.

1903   Vittorio Giannini, American composer and teacher, is born in Philadelphia.

1916   Emil Gilels, Soviet pianist, is born in Odessa.

1922   Modest Mussorgsky's <u>Pictures at an Exhibition</u>, orchestrated by Maurice Ravel from the original piano suite, receives its premiere in Paris, Serge Koussevitzky (who commissioned Ravel) conducting.

1943   Robert Morris, English-American composer, pianist, and teacher (at Yale University), is born in Cheltenham.

OCTOBER 20

1842   Richard Wagner's opera <u>Rienzi</u> is first staged, at the Dresden Opera, the least popular of his major operas. Wagner's libretto is from Bulwer-Lytton's novel <u>Rienzi</u>.

1865   Lilli Lehmann makes her professional debut at age sixteen, singing in Mozart's opera <u>The Magic Flute.</u>

1870   Michael William Balfe dies at Rowney Abbey, England, aged sixty-two.

1874   Charles Ives, innovative American composer and insurance-company executive, is born in Danbury, Connecticut.

1914   Adelina Patti makes her final public appearance at a benefit concert for the Red Cross in Albert Hall, London.

1918   Alfred Cortot makes his American debut as soloist in Saint-Saëns's Piano Concerto no. 4.

1923   Robert Craft, American conductor and biographer of Igor Stravinsky (in six volumes), is born in Kingston, New York.

1940   Joanna Simon, American mezzo-soprano, is born in New York City.

1942   Frederick Stock dies in Chicago, aged sixty-nine; he had been trained in music by his German bandmaster father.

1944   William Albright, American organist and composer of the avant-garde, is born in Gary, Indiana.

OCTOBER 21

1721   Louis Nicholas Clérambault's dramatic piece Le Soleil vainqueur has its premiere, in Paris.

1784   André Grétry's opera Richard Coeur de Lion (considered his finest) opens in Paris at the Comédie-Italienne.

1858   Jacques Offenbach's operetta Orpheus in Hades is first produced at Bouffes-Parisiens, in Paris.

1879   Joseph Canteloube, French opera composer, pianist, and biographer of Vincent d'Indy, is born in Annonay. He was also an avid collector and arranger of French folksongs.

1885   Egon Wellesz, Austrian composer and authority on Byzantine music, is born in Vienna.

1908   Howard Ferguson, British composer, teacher, and music editor, is born in Belfast.

Alexander Schneider, Russian-American violinist, is born in Vilna. In 1950 he was a co-founder with Casals of the Prades Festival in France; he was also a member of the Budapest Quartet.

1912   Sir Georg Solti, Hungarian-English conductor and pianist, is born in Budapest.

1917   Dizzy (John Birks) Gillespie, American jazz-trumpet virtuoso and bandleader, is born in Cheraw, South Carolina.

1921   Malcolm Arnold, English composer, conductor, and trumpet player, is born in Northampton. His film score for Bridge on the River Kwai won an Academy Award.

1926   Carl Nielsen's Flute Concerto receives its premiere, in Paris.

1937   Julius Katchen makes his debut with the Philadelphia Orchestra as piano soloist.

1949   Shulamit Ran, Israeli composer, is born in Tel Aviv. After studying in New York City, she joined the faculty of the University of Chicago in 1973.

1955   Géza Anda makes his American piano debut with the Philadel-
        phia Orchestra.

1960   Lukas Foss's award-winning Time Cycle, for soprano and
        orchestra, with texts by Auden, Housman, Kafka, and Nietz-
        sche, is given its premiere in New York City.

OCTOBER 22

1737   Vincenzo Manfredini, Italian composer, is born in Pistoia.

1764   Jean Marie Leclair is fatally stabbed in his Paris home, aged
        sixty-seven.

1811   Franz Liszt, Hungarian piano virtuoso, improviser, composer,
        and master teacher, is born in Raiding.

1832   Leopold Damrosch, German-American conductor and violinist,
        is born in Posen. Though holding a medical degree, he chose
        a career in music, eventually emigrating to New York. His
        sons were Walter and Frank Damrosch.

1859   Ludwig Spohr dies in Kassel, Germany, aged seventy-five.
        His students included Ferdinand David and Moritz Hauptmann.

1879   Frank LaForge, American pianist, is born in Rockford, Illi-
        nois.

1881   The Boston Symphony Orchestra presents its first concert.

1883   The Metropolitan Opera House in New York City inaugurates
        its first-season, staging Gounod's Faust, Auguste Vianesi con-
        ducting.

1885   Giovanni Martinelli, Italian tenor, is born near Venice.

1922   Jacques Ibert's Ballade de la geôle de Reading (after Oscar
        Wilde), receives its premiere in Paris.

1923   Victor Maurel dies in New York City, aged seventy-five,
        active in his last year as a stage designer.

1934   Donald McIntyre, New Zealand bass, is born in Auckland.

1937   Frank Damrosch dies in New York City, aged seventy-eight.
        He had founded the Institute of Musical Art, which affiliated
        with the Juilliard School of Music in 1926. He served as
        dean until 1933.

1943   Paul Zukofsky, American violinist and teacher, is born in
        Brooklyn Heights, New York. His repertory includes the most

difficult of modern works.

1964   Marian Anderson's final concert takes place in Constitution Hall, in Washington, from which she was barred for racial reasons in 1939.

Akira Miyoshi's <u>Concerto for Orchestra</u> is given its premiere, in Tokyo.

1973   Pablo Casals dies in San Juan, Puerto Rico, at the age of ninety-six, considered the finest cellist of his generation.

1979   Nadia Boulanger, teacher and guide for many of the outstanding composers of our day, dies in Paris at age ninety-two.

OCTOBER 23

1801   Gustav Albert Lortzing, German opera composer, is born in Berlin.

Johann Gottlieb Naumann dies at age sixty in Dresden; his church music included the "Dresden Amen."

1881   Charles Lamoureux founds the Concerts Lamoureux in Paris.

1893   Jean Absil, Belgian composer, is born in Bonsecours; he was a co-founder of <u>Revue Internationale de Musique</u>.

1897   Alexander Scriabin is soloist in the premiere of his Piano Concerto, in Odessa.

1905   Alexander Melik-Pashayev, Soviet conductor, is born in Tiflis (Tbilisi).

Genia Nemenoff, French-American pianist, is born in Paris. With her husband, Pierre Luboschutz, she played in duo-piano concerts.

1906   Miriam Gideon, American composer and teacher, is born in Greeley, Colorado.

1916   Arthur Whittemore, duo-pianist with Jack Lowe, is born in Vermillion, South Dakota.

1921   Denise Duval, French soprano, is born in Paris.

1923   Ned Rorem, American composer, teacher, and writer on music, is born in Richmond, Indiana. He is regarded as one of the foremost American composers of art songs.

1931   Igor Stravinsky conducts his Violin Concerto at its premiere in Berlin, with Samuel Dushkin as soloist (whom the composer consulted in writing the violin part).

1941 Lawrence Foster, American conductor, is born in Los Angeles. In 1970 he became conductor of the Houston Symphony Orchestra.

1950 Al Jolson, the son of a Jewish cantor, dies in San Francisco at the age of sixty-four.

1969 Harold Budd's Lovely Thing, for piano, is given its premiere, in Memphis, Tennessee. Instructions to the performer read: "Select a chord--if in doubt, call me ... at 213-662-7819."

1975 Harry Stewart Somers's historical opera Louis Riel is first staged at Kennedy Center in Washington, in honor of the United States Bicentennial.

OCTOBER 24

1633 Jean Titelouze, French cathedral organist and composer, dies in Rouen, aged about seventy.

1725 Alessandro Scarlatti dies at age sixty-five in Naples.

1737 Jean Philippe Rameau's opera Castor et Pollux is first produced in Paris at the Opéra.

1799 Karl Ditters von Dittersdorf dies near Neuhaus, Austria, aged fifty-nine. He served as Kapellmeister at Johannesburg.

1811 Ferdinand Hiller, German composer, conductor, and music critic, is born in Frankfurt. He established and directed the Cologne Conservatory.

1864 Franco Leoni, Italian composer, is born in Milan.

1883 Marcella Sembrich makes her American debut at the Metropolitan Opera, starring in Lucia di Lammermoor.

1884 Florence Easton, English soprano, is born at Middlesbrough-on-Tees in Yorkshire.

1885 Johann Strauss, Jr.'s operetta The Gipsy Baron is first staged in Vienna.

1910 Victor Herbert's operetta Naughty Marietta opens in Syracuse, New York.

1912 Peter Gellhorn, German-English conductor, pianist, and composer, is born in Breslau.

1913   Tito Gobbi, Italian baritone, is born at Bassano del Grappa.

1914   Arvid Jansons, Soviet conductor, is born in Libava, Latvia.

1916   Pierre Sancan, French pianist, composer, and conductor, is
        born in Mazamet.

1918   Charles Lecocq dies at age eighty-six in Paris, having pro-
        duced more than forty operettas, many of them successful.

1919   The Los Angeles Philharmonic Orchestra begins its first
        season.

1921   Sena Jurinac, Yugoslav soprano, is born in Travnik.

1925   Luciano Berio, Italian composer, experimenter in acoustics,
        and editor, is born in Oneglia.

1929   George Crumb, American composer and innovator of sound
        effects, is born in Charleston, West Virginia.

1930   Albert Roussel's Symphony no. 3, commissioned by the Boston
        Symphony Orchestra, is first played there with Serge Kousse-
        vitzky conducting.

1946   Seth Bingham's Organ Concerto is given its premiere in
        Rochester, New York.

1948   Franz Léhar dies in Bad Ischl, Austria, aged seventy-eight.
        His music mirrored the lightheartedness of Vienna at the turn
        of the century.

1949   Joaquín Nin dies in Havana at the age of seventy. He had
        lived for many years in Paris and was known for his inter-
        pretations of early piano music.

1952   Frederick Jacobi dies at age sixty-one in New York City,
        where he had been a member of the Juilliard School of Music
        faculty, 1936-50.

1961   Teresa Stich-Randall makes her debut at the Metropolitan
        Opera in New York City.

1965   Hermann Uhde dies in Copenhagen at the age of fifty-one.

1970   Krzysztof Penderecki's Kosmogonia, for soli, chorus, and
        orchestra, commissioned by the United Nations, receives its
        premiere in the UN's New York headquarters.

1971   Carl Ruggles, at ninety-five, dies in Bennington, Vermont.
        Interest in his music revived in his later years, and most of his
        works were recorded.

1974   David Oistrakh dies in Amsterdam, aged sixty-six. Foremost
        among his pupils was his son, Igor, considered to be his
        equal in violin virtuosity.

        OCTOBER 25

1564   Hans Leo Hassler, German organist and composer, is born
        in Nuremberg.

1734   Giovanni Battista Pergolesi's opera Adriano in Siria is first
        produced in the Teatro San Bartolomeo, Naples.

1795   Francesco Antonio Uttini, Bologna-born Italian opera composer,
        dies at age seventy-two in Stockholm, where he had emigrated
        to conduct opera. His were the first operas using Swedish
        texts.

1823   Carl Maria von Weber's opera Euryanthe stars Henrietta
        Sontag at its opening, in Vienna.

1825   Johann Strauss, Jr., Austrian composer known as "The Waltz
        King," is born in Vienna.

1838   Georges Bizet, French opera composer and pianist, is born in
        Paris. In 1869 he married Geneviève Halévy, daughter of his
        composition teacher.

1864   Alexander Gretchaninov, Russian-American composer, is born
        in Moscow. His sacred works introduced a reform into Rus-
        sian church singing.

1875   Peter Ilyitch Tchaikovsky's Piano Concerto no. 1 receives its
        premiere, in Boston, with Hans von Bülow, soloist.

1885   Johannes Brahms conducts the premiere of his Symphony no.
        4 at Meinengen, Germany. Critics protested his use of the
        key of E minor for a symphony, considering it too melancholy.

1912   Richard Strauss conducts the opening of his opera Ariadne
        auf Naxos in Stuttgart.

1923   Don Banks, Australian composer influenced by Milton Babbitt,
        is born in Melbourne.

        Darius Milhaud's ballet Le Création du monde is first staged,
        in Paris.

1926   Galina Vishnevskaya, Soviet soprano and wife of cellist Mstis-
        lav Rostropovich, is born in Leningrad. In March 1978 they
        were both stripped of their Soviet citizenship and sought
        asylum in the United States.

1928   Peter Sacco, American composer, teacher, and singer, is born in Albion, New York.

1929   Werner Josten's symphonic movement <u>Jungle</u> is first played in Boston.

1949   Frank Martin's Concerto, for seven winds, strings, and percussion, receives its premiere, in Berne, Switzerland.

1952   Sergei Eduardovitch Bortkiewicz dies in Vienna, aged seventy-five.

1954   Alexander Gretchaninov is honored in New York's Town Hall on his ninetieth birthday, and hears a program of his works performed.

1965   Hans Knappertsbusch dies in Munich, aged seventy-seven. An opera conductor, he was known for his performances of the operas of Wagner and Richard Strauss.

OCTOBER 26

1685   Domenico Scarlatti, Italian composer and harpsichord virtuoso, son of Alessandro Scarlatti, is born in Naples.

1694   Johan Helmich Roman, Swedish composer known as the "father of Swedish music," is born in Stockholm.

1749   Louis Nicholas Clérambault dies in Paris, aged seventy-two. His French cantatas are the best of their period.

1873   Anton Bruckner conducts the premiere of his Symphony no. 2 in Vienna.

1874   Peter Cornelius dies in Mainz, aged forty-nine. His literary works were published by Breitkopf and Härtel.

1904   Boris Khaikin, Soviet conductor, is born in Minsk.

1908   Igor Gorin, Russian-American baritone, is born in Grodek, Ukraine.

1911   Mahalia Jackson, American gospel singer, is born in New Orleans.

1913   Netty Simons, American composer and radio scriptwriter, is born in New York City.

1917   Modest Mussorgsky's unfinished opera, <u>The Fair at Sorochinsk</u>, completed by César Cui, is first performed, in St. Petersburg.

1919   Sir Edward Elgar conducts the premiere of his Cello Concerto at Queen's Hall, London; Felix Salmond, soloist.

1927   Julian Patrick, American baritone, is born in Meridian, Mississippi.

1938   Margharita Guglielmi, Italian soprano, is born in Portovenere.

1956   Jindřich Feld's Flute Concerto is first performed on a Czech Radio broadcast.

       Walter Gieseking dies in London, aged sixty; his autobiography, So Wurde ich Pianist, was published posthumously.

1961   Robert Ward's Pulitzer Prize-winning opera The Crucible, based on the play by Arthur Miller, is first staged, in New York City.

OCTOBER 27

1771   Johann Gottlieb Graun, German composer and violinist, dies in Berlin, aged about sixty-eight. His younger brother, Karl Heinrich Graun, was also a composer.

1782   Niccolò Paganini, Italian violin virtuoso and composer, is born in Genoa.

1827   Vincenzo Bellini's opera Il Pirata is first staged, in Milan's La Scala Theater.

1864   Christine Nilsson makes her opera debut, starring in Verdi's La Traviata in Paris' Théâtre-Lyrique.

1886   Modest Mussorgsky's Night on Bald Mountain, reorchestrated by Rimsky-Korsakov, is given its first performance posthumously in St. Petersburg.

1907   Helmut Walcha, German organist and composer, is born in Leipzig.

1911   Efrem Zimbalist makes his American debut with the Boston Symphony Orchestra, performing the American premiere of Glazounov's Violin Concerto.

1912   Conlon Nancarrow, American composer, is born in Texarkana, Arkansas.

1917   Jascha Heifetz, violinist, makes his American debut at age sixteen in Carnegie Hall, New York City.

1925   Theodore Presser dies in Philadelphia, aged seventy-seven;
        he had established the Presser Foundation to assist musicians.

1927   Dominick Argento, American composer and teacher at the
        University of Minnesota, is born in York, Pennsylvania.   His
        song cycle From the Diary of Virginia Woolf won the Pulitzer
        Prize in 1975.

1938   Alma Gluck dies in New York City, aged fifty-four.   The
        novel Of Lena Geyer, written by her daughter Marcia Daven-
        port, is based on her career.

1941   Edda Moser, German soprano, is born in Berlin.

1975   Oliver Nelson dies in Los Angeles, aged forty-three; his last
        years were spent principally in composing, arranging, and
        conducting.

OCTOBER 28

1755   Joseph Bodin de Boismortier dies at age sixty-five in Roissy-
        en-Brie, France.

1768   Michel Blavet dies in Paris, aged sixty-eight.

1797   Giuditta Pasta, Italian soprano, is born in Saronno.   Bellini
        and Donizetti wrote roles in their operas to suit her voice.

1798   Henri Bertini, French pianist and composer, is born in Lon-
        don and soon taken to Paris.   He is known for his technical
        piano studies.

1803   Caroline Unger, Hungarian contralto, is born in Stuhlweissen-
        burg.   It was she who turned the deaf Beethoven's head around
        to hear applause at the performance of his Ninth Symphony.

1893   Peter Ilyitch Tchaikovsky conducts the premiere of his Sym-
        phony no. 6, "Pathétique," in St. Petersburg, only nine days
        before his death of cholera.   Oddly enough, the symphony's
        first movement contains a fragment for brass taken from the
        Russian Requiem.

1896   Howard Hanson, American composer, conductor, and educator,
        is born in Wahoo, Nebraska.   From 1924 to 1964 he directed
        the Eastman School of Music in Rochester, New York, teach-
        ing a generation of American composers.

1920   Claramae Turner, American contralto, is born in Dinuba,
        California.

1921   Alfredo Casella makes his American conducting debut with the Philadelphia Orchestra.

1924   Carroll Glenn, American violinist, is born in Chester, South Carolina. In 1943 she married pianist Eugene List.

1932   Igor Stravinsky's Duo Concertante, for violin and piano, has its premiere in Berlin with Samuel Dushkin, violin, and the composer at the piano.

1938   Laurence Lesser, American cellist and teacher, is born in Los Angeles.

1941   William Kapell makes his Town Hall debut as a concert pianist in New York City.

1943   Bohuslav Martinů's Memorial to Lidice, for orchestra, is first performed, in New York City.

1945   Alan Titus, American baritone, is born in New York City.

1952   Ben Weber's Symphony on Poems of William Blake, for baritone and chamber orchestra, receives its premiere in New York City.

1956   William Schuman's New England Triptych is given its first performance, in Miami, Florida.

1959   Teresa Stratas (née Anastasia Strataki) makes her debut with the Metropolitan Opera in New York.

1963   Leon Kirchner's Piano Concerto no. 2 has its premiere, in Seattle, Washington.

1972   Morton Feldman's Pianos and Voices receives its first hearing in the United States, in Buffalo, New York.

1975   Antal Dorati's Piano Concerto is given its premiere in Washington.

OCTOBER 29

1787   Wolfgang Amadeus Mozart's opera Don Giovanni is first produced, in Prague, where it remained a favorite for years.

1883   Robert Volkmann dies in Budapest, aged sixty-eight.

1905   The New Symphony Orchestra of London is inaugurated with a concert at the Coronet Theatre.

1926   Jon Vickers, Canadian tenor, is born in Prince Albert, Saskatch-
        ewan.

1931   Gerd Feldhoff, German bass, is born in Radevormwald.

1943   Percy Goetschius dies in Manchester, New Hampshire, aged
        ninety, resisting harmonic changes that varied from German
        tradition.

1948   Dmitri Kabalevsky's Violin Concerto is first performed, in
        Leningrad.

1953   William Kapell dies in an air crash near San Francisco as
        he is returning from an Australian concert tour.

1955   Dmitri Shostakovich's Violin Concerto no. 1 receives its pre-
        miere, in Leningrad.

1956   Maria Callas makes her Metropolitan Opera debut, starring
        in Bellini's Norma, with Fausto Cleva conducting.

1966   Darius Milhaud's Musique pour l'Indiana is first performed by
        the Indianapolis Symphony Orchestra, in Indianapolis.

1967   Vincent Persichetti's Symphony no. 8 receives its premiere,
        in Berea, Ohio.

        OCTOBER 30

1522   Jean Mouton, French composer of sacred choral music and
        church choral director, dies in St. -Quentin, aged about sixty-
        three.   Among his pupils was Flemish composer Adrian Willaert.

1854   Julie Rivé-King, American pianist, is born in Cincinnati.   Her
        first teacher was her mother; later she studied with Franz
        Liszt.

1864   Elizabeth Sprague Coolidge, American music patroness and
        composer, is born in Chicago.   In 1925 she sponsored the
        Elizabeth Sprague Coolidge Foundation in the Library of Con-
        gress to foster new compositions, concerts, festivals, and
        the like.

1875   Ethel Newcomb, American pianist, is born in Whitney Point,
        New York.

1894   Peter Warlock (pen name of Philip Heseltine), English com-
        poser and writer on music, is born in London.   He was an
        able editor of old English music.

1896   Amy March Cheney Beach's <u>Gaelic Symphony</u> has its premiere
      in Boston, the first symphonic work by an American woman.

1907   György Ránki, Hungarian composer (including eighty film
      scores), is born in Budapest.

1910   Luciano Sgrizzi, Italian composer, pianist, and harpsichordist
      is born in Bologna.

1914   Marius Flothuis, Dutch composer and artistic director of the
      Concertgebouw Orchestra (1955-74), is born in Amsterdam.
      Since 1974 he has taught musicology at the University of
      Utrecht.

1928   Oscar Sonneck dies at age fifty-five in New York City. From
      1902 to 1917 he headed the Music Division of the Library of
      Congress in Washington.

1934   Franz Brüggen, Dutch recorder virtuoso, flutist, and musi-
      cologist, is born in Amsterdam.

1944   Aaron Copland's ballet <u>Appalachian Spring</u> is first staged by
      the Martha Graham Ballet, in Washington.

1946   Aram Khachaturian's Cello Concerto is first performed, in
      Moscow.

1966   David Van Vactor's <u>Sinfonia breve</u> is given its premiere, in
      Indianapolis.

1967   Hans Theodore David dies in Ann Arbor, Michigan, aged
      sixty-five.

1969   Jacques Bondon's radio opera <u>Mélousine au rocher</u> is broad-
      cast in Luxembourg in its first performance.

1970   Luigi Dallapiccola's <u>Sicut umbra,</u> for mezzo-soprano and
      twelve instruments, receives its first hearing in Washington.

      Milko Kelemen's <u>Floreal</u> has its premiere at the Coolidge
      Festival in Washington.

OCTOBER 31

1291   Philippe de Vitry, medieval archbishop and musician, is born
      in Champagne, France. His treatise <u>Ars nova</u> interpreted a
      new theory of mensural notation and explained the various
      uses of colored notes.

1768   Francesco Maria Veracini dies in Florence, aged seventy-eight,

in great poverty. His violin works and performance greatly
influenced Giuseppe Tartini.

1825   Nicola Vaccai's opera Giulietta e Romeo (after Shakespeare)
is first produced in Milan.

1866   Jacques Offenbach's operetta La Vie parisienne opens at the
Palais Royal in Paris and proves immensely popular.

Max Pauer, English pianist and teacher, a pupil of his father,
Ernst, is born in London.

Steinway Hall is inaugurated in New York City.

1870   Mihály Mosonyi dies in Budapest, aged fifty-six. His music
emphasized Hungarian modes; he is regarded as a founder of
the Hungarian school.

1875   Camille Saint-Saëns is soloist in the premiere of his Piano
Concerto no. 4, in Paris.

1876   Georges Barrère, French flute virtuoso and editor of classical
flute music, is born in Bordeaux.

1887   Nikolai Rimsky-Korsakov's Capriccio espagnol is performed
in its premiere by the Russian Symphonic Society in St. Petersburg. Tchaikovsky wrote the composer, "Your Spanish Cap-
rice is a colossal masterpiece of instrumentation...."

1891   Pietro Mascagni's opera L'Amico Fritz is first staged at the
Teatro Costanzi in Rome.

1896   Ethel Waters, American jazz and blues singer, is born in
Chester, Pennsylvania.

1906   Louise Talma, American composer and teacher at Hunter College in New York, is born in Arcachon, France.

1908   Lucretia Bori makes her operatic debut in Rome.

1924   Nicolai Medtner makes his American debut as soloist with the
Philadelphia Orchestra in his Piano Concerto no. 1.

1934   Walter Steffans, German composer and pianist, is born in
Aachen.

1947   Carlos Chávez's Toccata, for percussion instruments, is given
its premiere, in Mexico City.

1961   Dame Myra Hess is soloist in Mozart's A major piano concerto in Festival Hall, London. It marks her last public appearance.

1968   Lukas Foss's Paradigm, for percussionist, electric guitar, and three instruments, receives its premiere at Hunter College in New York.

Lejaren Hiller's <u>An Avalanche for Pitchmen, Prima Donna, Player Piano, Percussion and Pre-recorded Playback</u> is first performed, at Hunter College in New York

1970   George Crumb's <u>Ancient Voices of Children,</u> for soprano, boy soprano, and seven instruments (to words of García Lorca) is given its first performance at the Coolidge Festival of Chamber Music in Washington.

NOVEMBER 1

1862   Alexander Lambert, Polish-American pianist, composer, and teacher, is born in Warsaw.

1877   Roger Quilter, English composer known for his settings of Shakespeare poems, is born in Brighton.

1887   Max Trapp, German composer and landscape painter, is born in Berlin.

1902   Eugen Jochum, German conductor, is born in Babenhausen.

1921   Jan Tausinger, Czech composer and music administrator, is born in Piatra Neamt, Rumania.

1923   Victoria de Los Angeles (née Victoria Gomez Cima), Spanish soprano, is born in Barcelona.

       Ernest Blanc, French baritone, is born in Sanary-sur-Mer.

1926   Louis Calabro, American composer, conductor, and teacher, is born in Brooklyn.

       Ezio Pinza makes his American debut at the Metropolitan Opera, singing in Spontini's La Vestale.

1934   William Mathias, British composer and professor at University College of North Wales, is born in Whitland, Wales.

1942   Hugo Distler dies a suicide in Berlin, aged thirty-four, unable to endure Nazi horrors any longer.

1945   John Ostendorf, American bass, is born in New York City.

1948   Aaron Copland's suite from the film The Red Pony is first performed in Houston, Texas.

1954   Maria Callas makes her American debut in Chicago, starring in Bellini's opera Norma.

1964   Virgil Thomson's _Feast of Love_, for baritone and orchestra, has its premiere in Washington.

1968   Anja Silja makes her American operatic debut in San Francisco, singing in a new version of Strauss's _Salome_ done by Wieland Wagner.

NOVEMBER 2

1739   Karl Ditters von Dittersdorf, Austrian violinist and composer, is born in Vienna.

1785   Friedrich W. Michael Kalkbrenner, German pianist and composer, is born between November 2 and 8, near Kassel. Chopin dedicated his first piano concerto to him.

1837   Auguste Vianesi, Italian conductor and voice teacher, is born in Livorno. He conducted the first performance of the Metropolitan Opera in New York in 1883.

1887   Jenny Lind dies at Malvern Wells, England, aged sixty-seven.

1904   Janis Kalniņs, Latvian-Canadian composer and conductor, is born in Riga.

1927   Richard Mayr makes his American debut at the Metropolitan Opera in New York City.

1929   Harold Farberman, American conductor and composer, is born in New York City.

1934   Kenneth Timm, American composer, arranger, and teacher, is born in San Francisco.

1939   Mario Castelnuovo-Tedesco is soloist in his Piano Concerto no. 2 with the New York Philharmonic Orchestra.

1943   Faye Robinson, American soprano, is born in Houston, Texas.

1945   Gian Carlo Menotti's Piano Concerto has its premiere in Boston.

1950   George Bernard Shaw dies in Ayot St. Lawrence, England, at age ninety-four.

        Aldo Ciccolini makes his American debut playing the Tchaikovsky Piano Concerto no. 1 with the New York Philharmonic Orchestra.

1960   Dimitri Mitropoulos dies while rehearsing Gustav Mahler's

Symphony no. 3 at La Scala in Milan; he was sixty-four.

NOVEMBER 3

1587   Samuel Scheidt, German organist and composer, is baptized
        in Halle.

1801   Vincenzo Bellini, Italian opera composer, is born in Catania,
        Sicily.

1888   Nikolai Rimsky-Korsakov's symphonic suite Scheherazade is
        given its first performance, in St. Petersburg.

1899   Nikolai Rimsky-Korsakov's opera The Tsar's Bride opens in
        Moscow.

1911   Vladimir Ussachevsky, American composer, teacher, and
        electronic-music experimenter, is born in Hailar, Manchuria.
        With Otto Luening and others, he has been associated with the
        Columbia-Princeton Electronic Music Center.

1913   Hans Bronsart von Schellendorf dies in Munich at eighty-three.

1924   Tullio Serafin makes his American conducting debut with the
        Metropolitan Opera Orchestra in New York City.

1939   Charles Tournemire dies in Arcachon, France, aged sixty-
        nine.

1958   Per Nørgaard's Constellations, a concerto for twelve solo
        strings or twelve string groups, receives its premiere, in
        Copenhagen.

1962   Aram Khachaturian's Concerto-Rhapsody, for violin and orches-
        tra, is first performed, in Moscow.

1973   Julia Smith's opera Daisy is first produced, in Miami, Florida.

NOVEMBER 4

1737   San Carlo Opera House is inaugurated in Naples.

1781   Faustina Bordoni Hasse, Italian mezzo-soprano who was
        married to Johann Adolph Hasse, dies in Venice, aged about
        eighty-one.

1783   Wolfgang Amadeus Mozart's "Linz" Symphony is first performed at Linz, hence its nickname. He had begun writing it five days earlier.

1841   Carl Tausig, Polish pianist and student of Franz Liszt, is born in Warsaw. In 1865 he opened a school for advanced pianists in Berlin.

1847   Felix Mendelssohn dies in Leipzig shortly after the death of his favorite sister, Fanny.

1876   Johannes Brahms's Symphony no. 1 is first performed at Karlsruhe, Otto Dessoff, conducting.

1883   Emmanuel Chabrier's España, based on Spanish folksongs, is first played in Paris, Charles Lamoureux conducting.

1890   Alexander Borodin's opera Prince Igor, completed posthumously by Rimsky-Korsakov and Glazounov, is first staged in St. Petersburg.

1897   Oscar Lorenzo Fernandez, Brazilian composer, conductor, and pianist, is born in Rio de Janeiro.

1906   Arnold Cooke, English composer, is born in Gomersal.

1908   Auguste Vianesi dies in New York two days after his seventy-first birthday.

1909   Sergei Rachmaninoff's initial American piano recital takes place at Smith College in Massachusetts.

1912   Titto Ruffo's first American performance is in Philadelphia with the combined Philadelphia-Chicago Opera Company.

1924   Gabriel Fauré dies in Paris at age seventy-nine; he directed the Paris Conservatory, 1905-20.

1927   Vittorio Fellegara, Italian composer, is born in Milan.

1932   Silvestre Revueltas's Ventanas, for orchestra, is first performed in Mexico City.

1944   Leon Fleisher begins his career as concert pianist at age sixteen playing with the New York Philharmonic. When his right hand became disabled years later, he turned to conducting.

1948   Arnold Schoenberg's cantata A Survivor from Warsaw, for narrator, chorus, and orchestra, has its premiere in Albuquerque, New Mexico.

1953   Elizabeth Sprague Coolidge dies in Cambridge, Massachusetts, at the age of eighty-nine.

1955   William Schuman's <u>Credendum,</u> for orchestra, receives its
       premiere in Cincinnati.

1956   André Cluytens makes his American debut in Washington as
       guest conductor of the Vienna Philharmonic Orchestra.

1957   Joseph Canteloube dies in Grigny, France, aged seventy-eight.

1961   Phyllis Curtin, American soprano, makes her Metropolitan
       Opera debut singing in Mozart's <u>Cosi fan tutte.</u>

1976   Donald Erb's Cello Concerto is given its first performance in
       Rochester, New York.

NOVEMBER 5

1494   Hans Sachs, song composer and leading poet of the Meister-
       singer, is born in Nuremberg.   Richard Wagner made him
       the principal in his opera <u>Die Meistersinger von Nürnberg.</u>

1667   Franz Tunder, German organist and composer, father-in-law
       of Dietrich Buxtehude, dies in Lübeck, aged about fifty-three.

1846   Robert Schumann's Symphony no. 2 is conducted in its pre-
       miere by Mendelssohn in Leipzig.

1884   Erminia Frezzolini, Italian opera soprano, dies in Paris, aged
       about sixty-six.

1887   Paul Wittgenstein, Austrian left-handed pianist (his right arm
       was lost in World War I at the Russian front), is born in
       Vienna.

1894   Eugene Zador, Hungarian-American composer of opera and
       film music, is born in Bátaszék.   After the Nazi annexation
       of Austria in 1938 he fled to the United States.

1895   Walter Gieseking, German pianist, son of a German doctor
       and entomologist, is born in Lyons, France.   His hobby was
       entomology and he made an extensive collection.

       Richard Strauss's tone poem <u>Till Eulenspiegel's Merry Pranks</u>
       is first performed in Cologne, Franz Wüllner conducting.

1917   Claus Adam, American cellist and composer, is born in Su-
       matra.

1918   Maria Stader, Swiss soprano, is born in Budapest.

1926   Manuel de Falla conducts the first performance of his Concerto

for Harpsichord in Barcelona.   It was commissioned and performed by Wanda Landowska.

1929   Gregor Piatigorsky makes his American debut in Oberlin,
        Ohio.

1938   Samuel Barber's Essay for Orchestra no. 1 and Adagio for
        Strings are first performed, by the NBC Symphony Orchestra
        with Toscanini conducting.   The Adagio for Strings was ar-
        ranged from the composer's String Quartet.

1942   George M. Cohan dies in New York City, aged sixty-four.
        His song Over There, popular in World War I, brought him
        a Congressional Medal.

1946   Sigismund Stojowski dies at age seventy-seven in New York
        City.

1956   Art Tatum dies in Los Angeles, aged forty-seven, one of the
        great pianists and improvisers of jazz.

1967   Ernst Krenek's Five Pieces for Trombone and Piano are first
        heard, in Buffalo, New York.

1970   Aldo Ceccato makes his American conducting debut with the
        New York Philharmonic Orchestra.

1977   Guy Lombardo dies in Houston, aged seventy-five.   His band
        had performed Auld Lang Syne for New Year's Eve in New
        York for nearly half a century.

NOVEMBER 6

1492   Antoine Busnois, Flemish contrapuntal composer and chapel
        master, dies in Bruges, age unknown; but about 1461 he wrote
        that he was a pupil of Ockeghem.

1672   Heinrich Schütz dies at age eighty-seven in Dresden, Germany.
        An important composer, he bridged the gap between Palestrina
        and Bach.

1795   Georg Benda dies in Köstritz, Germany, aged seventy-three.
        Most of his manuscripts are in the Berlin Library.

1827   Bartolommeo Campagnoli dies at age seventy-six at Neustrelitz,
        Germany, where he was maestro di capella at the court.

1828   Friedrich Kuhlau's romantic drama Elverhøj (The Fairies'
        Mound) is presented for the festivities of a royal wedding in
        Copenhagen.

1854   John Philip Sousa, American bandmaster and composer, known
        as the "March King," is born in Washington.

1855   Paul Kalisch, German tenor and husband of singer Lilli Leh-
        mann, is born in Berlin.

1875   Marietta Brambilla dies in Milan, aged sixty-eight.

1883   Hubert Bath, English composer and opera conductor, is born
        in Barnstaple.

1893   Peter Ilyitch Tchaikovsky dies of cholera after drinking un-
        boiled water during an epidemic in St. Petersburg, aged fifty-
        three.   There is some conjecture that it was a suicide.

1894   Guy Fraser Harrison, English-American conductor, is born
        in Guildford.   From 1924 to 1949 he led the Rochester (N.Y.)
        Civic Orchestra; from 1951 to 1972, the Oklahoma City Orches-
        tra.

1902   Francesco Cilèa's opera Adriana Lecouvreur (after Scribe) is
        first performed at the Teatro Lirico in Milan.

1910   Arthur Cohn, American composer, conductor, and music pub-
        lisher, is born in Philadelphia.

1911   Pavel Lisitsian, Soviet baritone, is born in Vladikavkaz, Ar-
        menia.

1912   Mykola Lysenko dies in Kiev, aged seventy, an ardent Ukrainian
        nationalist.   He made extensive collections of Ukrainian folk-
        songs.

1913   Camille Saint-Saëns's Introduction et Rondo Capriccioso, for
        violin and orchestra (arranged by Bizet for violin and piano),
        receives its premiere in Paris.

1916   Ray Coniff, American trombonist, composer and leader of
        popular vocal groups, is born in Attleboro, Massachusetts.
        In 1974 he was the first pop artist to record in the Soviet
        Union, using native musicians.

1920   Nicola Rossi-Lemeni, Italian bass, is born in Istanbul.   He
        was originally a law student before becoming a singer.

1923   Renato Capecchi, Italian baritone, is born in Cairo.

1928   Beverly Wolff, American contralto, is born in Atlanta,
        Georgia.

1941   James Bowman, English countertenor, is born in Oxford.

1950   Cesare Siepi's Metropolitan Opera debut takes place in

New York, in Verdi's <u>Don Carlos</u>.

1964   Samuel Samosud dies at age eighty in Moscow.

1965   Edgard Varèse dies in New York City, aged eighty-one. He had introduced an original principle of "organized sound," profoundly influencing the direction of new music.

1968   Charles Munch dies in Richmond, Virginia, while on tour with the Orchestre de Paris, which he had organized. He was seventy-seven.

1976   Andrew W. Imbrie's opera <u>Angle of Repose</u> (after Wallace Stegner's novel) is first staged in San Francisco.

NOVEMBER 7

1810   Ferenc Erkel, Hungarian composer of the National Hymn and creator of Hungarian national opera, is born in Gyula.

1839   Hermann Levi, German conductor, is born in Giessen.

1846   Ignaz Brüll, Austrian pianist and composer, a friend of Brahms, is born in Prossnitz.

1867   Franz Liszt's <u>Dante Symphony</u> has its premiere, in Dresden.

1898   Max Alvary dies near Gross-Tabarz, Germany, aged forty-two.

       Ernestine Schumann-Heink makes her American debut in Chicago, starring in Wagner's opera <u>Lohengrin</u>.

1900   Efrem Kurtz, Russian-American conductor, is born in St. Petersburg; he married American flutist Elaine Shaffer.

1902   Jesús Maria Sanromá, Puerto Rican pianist and teacher, is born in Carolina.

1905   William Alwyn, English composer (including film scores) is born in Northampton.

1926   Dame Joan Sutherland, Australian soprano and wife of conductor Richard Bonynge, is born in Sydney.

1928   Mattia Battistini dies in Collebaccaro, Italy, aged seventy-two.

       Sir Noel Coward's musical comedy <u>This Year of Grace</u> has its premiere in New York City.

1934   Sergei Rachmaninoff is soloist in his <u>Rhapsody on a Theme of Paganini</u> in its premiere in Baltimore. It was written for piano and orchestra.

1936   Gwyneth Jones, British soprano, is born in Pontnewynydd, Wales.

1937   Romano Emili, Italian tenor, is born in Bologna.

Mary Travers, American folksinger, composer, and arranger, is born in Louisville, Kentucky. She is a member of the folksinging trio Peter, Paul and Mary.

1951   Heitor Villa-Lobos's The Origin of the Amazon River is first performed, in Louisville, Kentucky.

1965   Vinko Globokar's Plan, for wind quartet and drum, receives its American premiere in Buffalo, New York.

Bo Nilsson's Zwanzig Gruppen, for piccolo, oboe, and clarinet, is performed in Buffalo, New York, in its American premiere.

NOVEMBER 8

1770   Friedrich Witt, German violinist and composer, is born in Hallenbergstetten.

1883   Sir Arnold Bax, English composer (knighted at George VI's coronation in 1937), is born in London. He was inspired by Celtic legends and made many settings of folksongs.

1890   César Franck dies in Paris at age sixty-seven. His string quartet was composed in his last year and his only symphony, a year earlier.

1908   Alberto Erede, Italian conductor, is born in Genoa.

1921   Jerome Hines (originally Heinz), American bass-baritone, is born in Los Angeles. During World War II he worked as a chemist.

1924   Sergey Mikhailovitch Liapunov dies at age sixty-four in Paris, where he had lived after the Russian Revolution.

1927   Ivo Vinco, Italian bass, is born in Verona.

1936   Jean Françaix's Piano Concerto is first performed, in Berlin.

1938   Juan Soumagnas, French bass, is born in Rodez.

1941   Anthony Cirone, American percussionist and educator (California State University at San Jose), is born in Jersey City, New Jersey.

1965   Nicolai Ghiaurov makes his American debut starring in Gounod's
       Faust at the Metropolitan Opera in New York.

NOVEMBER 9

1801   Karl Stamitz dies in Jena, Germany, aged fifty-six.   From
       1794 he was Kapellmeister at Jena; many of his manuscripts
       were lost after his death.

1876   Antonio Tamburini dies in Nice, aged seventy-six.

1878   The New York Symphony Society presents its first concert,
       Leopold Damrosch founder.

1881   Johannes Brahms is soloist in the premiere of his Piano Con-
       certo no. 2 at Budapest.

1888   Moriz Rosenthal makes his American debut as a concert pi-
       anist in Boston.

1901   Sergei Rachmaninoff plays the solo part in his Piano Concerto
       no. 2 in its premiere, in Moscow.

1907   Burrill Phillips, American composer and teacher, is born in
       Omaha, Nebraska.

1926   Paul Hindemith's opera Cardillac is first staged in Dresden;
       it was later revised and produced in Zurich in 1952.

1929   Piero Cappuccilli, Italian baritone, is born in Trieste.

       Alexandra Pakhmutova, Soviet composer, is born in Stalingrad
       (Volgograd).

1940   Sergio Cervetti, Uruguayan composer, is born in Dolores.

       Joaquín Rodrigo's Concierto de Aranjuez, for guitar and orches-
       tra, receives its premiere in Barcelona.

1943   Alberto Jonas dies in Philadelphia, aged seventy-five.

1951   Sigmund Romberg dies in New York City, aged sixty-four.   An
       engineer who turned to composing, he produced more than
       seventy operettas.

1957   Mario Sereni makes his debut at the Metropolitan Opera in
       New York.

1967   Toru Takemitsu's November Steps, for biwa, shakuhachi, and
       orchestra, is first performed, in New York City.

1970   Sergio Cervetti's <u>Cocktail Party</u>, for amplified instruments
        and any number of invitations, has its premiere, in Malmö,
        Sweden.

1974   Egon Wellesz dies at Oxford, England, where he had fled from
        Nazi persecution.   An authority on Byzantine music, he was
        eighty-nine.

1975   John Corigliano's Oboe Concerto is first performed, in New
        York City.

1976   Rosina Lhévinne dies in Glendale, California, aged ninety-six.

NOVEMBER 10

1668   François Couperin, French organist and composer (called le
        Grand), is born in Paris.   He followed his four-volume
        <u>Pièces de clavecin</u> by an explanatory volume, <u>L'Art de toucher
        le clavecin</u>, which greatly influenced keyboard technique.

1862   Giuseppe Verdi's opera <u>La Forza del destino,</u> which had been
        commissioned by the Russian Imperial Opera, opens in St.
        Petersburg.   Verdi was not too satisfied with this opera,
        later shortening it.

1872   Georges Bizet's <u>L'Arlésienne Suite no. 1,</u> for orchestra, is
        conducted in its premiere by Pasdeloup, in Paris.

1873   Henri Rabaud, French composer, conductor, and director of
        the Paris Conservatoire (1922-41), is born in Paris.

1888   Fritz Kreisler makes his American debut, at age thirteen, in
        Steinway Hall, New York City.

1900   Ruggero Leoncavallo's light opera <u>Zaza</u> is successfully staged
        in its premiere at the Teatro Lirico, in Milan.

1909   John McCormack makes his American opera debut at the
        Manhattan Opera House in New York, singing in Verdi's
        <u>La Traviata</u>.

1972   Francis Chagrin dies in London, aged sixty-six.

NOVEMBER 11

1767   Bernhard Romberg, German cellist and composer, is born in
        Dinklage.

1870   Rev. Edmund Horace Fellowes, English musicologist and
        editor of Elizabethan music, is born in London.

1872   Frederick Stock, German-American conductor, violinist and
        composer, is born in Jülich. For many years he directed
        the Chicago Symphony Orchestra.

1883   Ernest Ansermet, Swiss conductor and organizer of the Or-
        chestre de la Suisse Romande in 1918, is born in Vevey.

1889   Richard Strauss's tone poem Don Juan has its premiere, in
        Weimar.

1894   Aaron Avshalomov, Russian-American composer, father of
        composer Jacob Avshalomov, is born in Nikolayevsk, Siberia.

1898   Samuel Coleridge-Taylor's Hiawatha's Wedding Feast (part of
        a trilogy), for soli, chorus, and orchestra, receives its pre-
        miere in London.

1906   Dame Ethel Smyth's opera The Wreckers is first produced in
        a German version in Leipzig and titled Strandrecht.   The
        composer later translated it into English for the London per-
        formance.

1912   Lucretia Bori makes her American operatic debut at the Metro-
        politan Opera in New York, starring in Manon Lescaut.

1913   Eleanor Spencer makes her American piano debut in New
        York's Carnegie Hall.

1915   Guiomar Novaes makes her debut as concert pianist in New
        York City.

1945   Jerome Kern dies at age sixty in New York City, having pro-
        duced more than sixty musicals. He made theatrical history
        by setting literate works to music in American musicals.

1964   Edward Steuermann dies in New York City, aged seventy-two.
        An ardent supporter of Schoenberg's music, he first performed
        the composer's Piano Concerto.

1968   Jeanne Demessieux dies at age forty-seven in Paris.

        NOVEMBER 12

1833   Alexander Borodin, Russian composer and member of the group
        known as the "mighty five," is born in St. Petersburg, the
        illegitimate son of a Russian prince. He earned a doctorate in
        chemistry, spending most of his career in scientific endeavors

and instituting the first medical courses for women in Russia.

1900   Ossip Gabrilowitsch makes his American debut as a concert
       pianist in New York's Carnegie Hall.

       Alexander Semmler, German-American composer (especially
       of film scores) and arranger, is born in Dortmund.

1920   Michael Langdon, English bass, is born in Wolverhampton.

1939   Lucia Popp, Czech-Austrian soprano, is born in Bratislava.

1943   Richard Salter, English bass, is born in Hindhead.

       William Schuman's Symphony for Strings (Symphony no. 5) is
       first performed, in Boston.

1944   Edgar Stillman Kelley dies at age eighty-seven in New York
       City. From 1910 to 1944 he taught composition at the
       Cincinnati Conservatory.

1948   Umberto Giordano dies in Milan, aged eighty-one.

1956   Maureen Forrester makes her American debut in a song re-
       cital in New York City. Critics acclaimed her singing of
       German lieder.

1966   Quincy Porter dies in Bethany, Connecticut, aged sixty-nine.
       A Yale professor, he was also the son and grandson of Yale
       professors.

1972   Rudolf Friml dies in Hollywood, California, at the age of
       ninety-two.

1976   Walter Piston dies in Belmont, Massachusetts, aged eighty-
       two. He numbered Leonard Bernstein among his students.

NOVEMBER 13

1854   George Whitefield Chadwick, American composer, organist,
       and conductor, is born in Lowell, Massachusetts, and known
       as one of the "Boston Classicists."

1868   Gioacchino Rossini dies in Paris, aged seventy-six. Almost
       forty years earlier he ceased composing operas but wrote
       numerous small works and taught singing.

1879   Maurice Delage, French composer whose music reflects Ori-
       ental influences, is born in Paris.

1903   Mu Phi Epsilon, a national music sorority, is founded in
        Cincinnati.

1911   Margarete Matzenauer makes her American debut in Aïda at
        the Metropolitan Opera in New York.

1915   Heitor Villa-Lobos presents a concert of his compositions for
        the first time, in Rio de Janeiro, creating a sensation.

1921   Joonas Kokkonen, Finnish composer, is born in Iisalmi.

1925   Paul W. Whear, American composer and teacher at Doane
        College in Nebraska, is born in Auburn, Indiana.

1936   Werner Josten conducts the premiere of his Symphony in F
        with the Boston Symphony Orchestra.

1946   Martin Bresnick, American composer and teacher, is born in
        New York City.

1951   Hugo Leichtentritt dies in Cambridge, Massachusetts, aged
        seventy-seven. His manuscripts were given to the Library of
        Congress in Washington after his death.

        Nikolai Medtner dies at age seventy-one in London, where he
        had settled after leaving Russia in 1921.

1956   Carlo Bergonzi sings in Aïda in his American debut at the
        Metropolitan Opera in New York.

1959   George London makes his operatic debut with the Metropolitan
        Opera's performance of Verdi's Aïda in New York.

1966   Mario Chamlee dies in Los Angeles at age seventy-four.

1973   James Lyons dies in New York City, aged forty-seven; since
        1957 he was editor and publisher of the American Record
        Guide.

        Bruno Maderna dies in Darmstadt, Germany, aged fifty-three.
        He had become a West German citizen ten years earlier.

        NOVEMBER 14

1719   Leopold Mozart, German-Austrian composer and father of
        Wolfgang Amadeus Mozart, is born in Augsburg.

1774   Gasparo Luigi Spontini, Italian opera composer and conductor,
        is born at Majolati. His keen attention to detail in conduct-
        ing helped to establish the modern standard.

1778   Johann Nepomuk Hummel, German pianist and composer, is
        born in Pressburg.

1805   Fanny Mendelssohn Hensel, German pianist and sister of Felix
        Mendelssohn is born in Hamburg.

1831   Ignaz Pleyel dies at his estate near Paris, aged seventy-four.
        His compositions closely resemble those of his teacher, Haydn,
        but he is best known for his piano-manufacturing company.

1887   Bernhard Paumgartner, Austrian musicologist, conductor, and
        composer, is born in Vienna.

1896   Italo Campanini dies at fifty-one near Parma.

1897   Giuseppina Strepponi dies, aged eighty-two, at Busseto, Italy.

1899   Alfred Eisenstein, Polish-American composer, is born in Brody.

1900   Aaron Copland, American composer, conductor, and lecturer,
        is born in Brooklyn.   His dynamic music reflects American
        folk motives and syncopation; he has received many awards
        worldwide.

        Louise Homer first appears with the Metropolitan Opera on
        tour in San Francisco, singing in Aïda.

1908   Oscar Straus's operetta The Chocolate Soldier (based on Shaw's
        Arms and the Man) is first staged in Vienna.

1915   Theodor Leschetizky dies in Dresden, aged eighty-five.   His
        most famous pupil was Paderewski.

1918   Jean Madeira, American mezzo-soprano, is born in Centralia,
        Illinois.

1921   Amelita Galli-Curci first appears with the Metropolitan Opera,
        starring in Verdi's La Traviata.

1922   Karl Ziehrer dies in Vienna at seventy-nine.

1924   Leonid Kogan, Soviet violin virtuoso, is born in Dniepropet-
        rovsk.   He married a sister of pianist Emil Gilels; their son is
        violinist Pavel Kogan.

        Billy Jim Layton, American composer, teacher, and musi-
        cologist, is born in Corsicana, Texas.

1926   Leonie Rysanek, Austrian soprano, is born in Vienna.

1931   Yehudi Menuhin is soloist in the Mendelssohn Violin Concerto
        in Leipzig to celebrate the sesquicentennial of the Gewandhaus
        Orchestra.

1938   Nikolai Miaskovsky's Violin Concerto has its premiere in
        Leningrad.

1943   Leonard Bernstein makes his conducting debut with the New
        York Philharmonic Orchestra, substituting on short notice for
        the ailing Bruno Walter.

        Miklós Rózsa's Variations on a Hungarian Peasant Song is
        first performed in New York City.

1944   Dmitri Shostakovich's Piano Trio no. 2 receives its first
        hearing in Leningrad, the composer at the piano.

1946   Manuel de Falla dies in Alta Gracia, Argentina, aged sixty-
        nine. In 1939, at the end of the Spanish civil war, he went
        to Argentina, living in seclusion.

1959   Anna Moffo makes her initial appearance with the Metropolitan
        Opera in New York, singing in La Traviata.

NOVEMBER 15

1774   William Horsley, English organist and composer, is born in
        London.

1787   Christoph Willibald Gluck dies in Vienna, aged seventy-three,
        an invalid his last several years. He succeeded in reforming
        the opera of his day, including a new type of libretto, meant
        to focus more on drama.

1832   Felix Mendelssohn's Symphony no. 5, "Reformation," receives
        its premiere, in Berlin.

1874   Selma Kurz, Austrian soprano, is born in Bielitz.

1886   Pedro Sanjuán, Spanish-American composer and condcutor, is
        born in San Sebastian.

1905   Francis Chagrin, Rumanian-English composer and conductor,
        is born in Bucharest.

        Annunzio Paolo Mantovani, Italian-English composer and con-
        ductor of light music, is born in Venice.

1907   Dame Myra Hess makes her concert debut at age seventeen
        in London's Queen's Hall, performing Beethoven's Piano Con-
        certo in G.

1914   Jorge Bolet, Cuban-American pianist and teacher, is born in
        Havana.

1918   Rosa Ponselle makes her Metropolitan Opera debut in La
        Forza del destino in New York City.

1927   Jerome Kern's musical Show Boat opens in Washington, making
        theatrical history in the choice of serious subject matter for
        that genre.

1929   Gladys Swartout sings in Ponchielli's La Gioconda in her
        operatic debut with the Metropolitan Opera in New York.

1934   Sherwood Shaffer, American composer and teacher, is born in
        Bee County, Texas.

1942   Daniel Barenboim, Argentine-Israeli pianist and conductor, is
        born in Buenos Aires.   He married cellist Jacqueline DuPré.

1946   Set Svanholm makes his American debut at the Metropolitan
        Opera in New York City; it marks the beginning of a nine-
        year membership on the staff.

1950   Alan Rawsthorne's Symphony no. 1 is first performed, in
        London.

1951   Hilde Gueden stars in Rigoletto in making her first appearance
        with the Metropolitan Opera in New York.

1962   Jeannette Scovotti sings for the first time with the Metropoli-
        tan Opera in New York.

1963   Fritz Reiner dies at age seventy-four in New York City, a
        conductor who strived and achieved in bringing the Chicago
        Symphony Orchestra to a high point of performance.

1977   Richard Addinsell dies in London, aged seventy-three.

NOVEMBER 16

1737   Antonio Vivaldi writes to a patron: "It was twenty-five years
        ago that I said mass for what will be the last time ... on
        account of this chest ailment ... I can no longer walk. "

1801   Ludwig van Beethoven writes his famous letter to Dr. Franz
        Wegeler in which he admits his love for the young countess
        Giulietta Guiccardi (who soon married Count von Gallenberg).

1848   Frédéric Chopin, already ill, volunteers to play in London at
        a Polish benefit ball.   It is his last public appearance.

1851   Minnie Hauk, American soprano, is born in New York City.

1873   W. C. (William Christopher) Handy, American jazz musician, the "father of the blues," is born in Florence, Alabama. His Methodist minister father opposed his son's musical inclinations.

1894   Enrico Caruso's operatic debut takes place in Naples' Teatro Nuovo.

1895   Paul Hindemith, German-American composer, conductor, and lecturer at Harvard University, is born in Hanau.

1896   Lawrence Tibbett, American baritone, is born in Bakersfield, California.

1900   The Philadelphia Orchestra presents its first concert.

1908   Emmy Destinn stars in Aïda at her American debut with the Metropolitan Opera in New York.

1909   Alma Gluck appears for the first time with the Metropolitan Opera in New York, singing in Werther.

1926   Ton de Leeuw, Dutch composer and teacher who has made a study of Asian music, is born in Rotterdam.

1940   Aram Khachaturian's Violin Concerto is first performed, in Moscow.

         Slavka Taskova, Bulgarian-Italian soprano, is born in Sofia.

1945   Darius Milhaud's Suite for Harmonica and Orchestra, transcribed for violin and orchestra, is performed for the first time by Zino Francescatti, violinist, and the Philadelphia Orchestra.

1960   Emil Cooper dies at eighty-two in New York City.

1970   Kurt List dies in Milan at age fifty-seven.

NOVEMBER 17

1816   August Wilhelm Ambros, Czech music historian, is born at Mauth. His chief work is the Geschichte der Musik; he was music professor at Prague University; later at Vienna Conservatory.

1828   Louis Joseph F. Herold's ballet La Fille mal gardée is first staged at the Paris Opéra.

1839   Giuseppe Verdi's first opera, Oberto, opens at La Scala, Milan.

1866   Ambroise Thomas's opera <u>Mignon</u> (based on Goethe's <u>Wilhelm Meister</u>) is given the first of more than 2,000 performances at the Opéra-Comique, Paris.

1873   Antonin Dvořák marries contralto Anna Čermakova in Prague.

1876   Peter Ilyitch Tchaikovsky's <u>Marche Slav</u> has its premiere, in Moscow.

1888   Tchaikovsky conducts his Symphony no. 5 in its premiere in St. Petersburg.

1891   Ignace Jan Paderewski makes his American debut as concert pianist in New York City at Carnegie Hall.

1898   Umberto Giordano conducts the premiere of his opera <u>Fedora</u> in Milan's Teatro Lirico with Enrico Caruso in a leading role.

1909   Leo Slezak makes his first American appearance singing in <u>Otello</u> at the Metropolitan Opera in New York.

1913   Mathilde Marchesi dies in London, aged ninety-two.

1919   Hershy Kay, American composer and orchestrator, is born in Philadelphia.

1924   Ernst von Dohnányi conducts his <u>Ruralia Hungarica</u> in its first performance, in Budapest.

1925   Charles Mackerras, American-English conductor of Sadler's Wells Opera and later its musical director, is born in Schenectady, New York.

1930   David Werner Amram, American composer and horn player, is born in Philadelphia.

1936   Ernestine Schumann-Heink dies in Hollywood, California, at age seventy-five.

1950   Roberta Peters substitutes on short notice for her Metropolitan Opera debut in New York City, singing in <u>Don Giovanni</u>.

1959   Heitor Villa-Lobos dies in Rio de Janeiro, aged seventy-two. Although lacking formal academic training, he became one of the most original composers of this century.

NOVEMBER 18

1680   Jean-Baptist Loeillet, Flemish composer, harpsichordist, and flute player, is born in Ghent.

1772   Louis Ferdinand, Prince of Prussia and nephew of Frederick
        the Great, is born in Friedrichsfelde. He was an amateur
        musician and composer, an admirer of Beethoven.

1779   (Franz) Joseph Haydn's scores were partially lost in a fire
        at Esterházy that destroyed the large theater on the Prince's
        estate.

1786   Carl Maria von Weber, German composer who is regarded
        as the founder of the German Romantic school, is born in
        Eutin.

1836   Sir William Schwenck Gilbert, English librettist for a series
        of comic operettas with Sir Arthur Sullivan, is born in Lon-
        don.

1860   Ignace Jan Paderewski, Polish piano virtuoso, composer, and
        Prime Minister of Poland in 1919, is born in Kurylowka.

1877   Richard Mayr, Austrian bass, is born in Henndorf.

1882   Amelita Galli-Curci, Italian soprano who taught herself to sing
        by listening to her own voice recordings, is born in Milan.

1883   Antonin Dvořák's Husitska Overture is first performed at the
        gala opening of the Czech National Theater in Prague.

1891   Maria Ivogün (née Inga von Gunther), Hungarian soprano, is
        born in Budapest.

        Peter Ilyitch Tchaikovsky's symphonic ballad The Voyevode
        receives its premiere, in Moscow.

1899   Eugene Ormandy (né Blau), Hungarian-American conductor
        of the Philadelphia Orchestra since 1938, is born in Budapest.

1904   Guido Santorsola, Italian-born conductor of the Uruguayan
        Radio Symphony, composer, and violist, is born in Canosa di
        Puglia.

1907   Cilèa's opera Adriana Lecouvreur has its American premiere
        at the Metropolitan Opera in New York, but has been staged
        only once since.

1916   Amelita Galli-Curci celebrates her thirty-fourth birthday by
        making her American debut with the Chicago Opera Company.

1925   William Mayer, American composer (also for radio and thea-
        ter), is born in New York City.

1927   Lawrence Moss, American composer and Yale University pro-
        fessor, is born in Los Angeles.

1928   Otar Gordeli, Soviet composer and teacher, is born in Tbilisi.

1953   Peter Mennin's Symphony no. 6 receives its premiere in Louis-
        ville, Kentucky.

        Ruth Crawford Seeger dies in Chevy Chase, Maryland, aged
        fifty-two.

1960   Anneliese Rothenberger makes her American debut at the
        Metropolitan Opera in New York, appearing in Strauss's
        Arabella.

1968   Paul Creston's Concerto, for two pianos and orchestra, is
        first performed in Montevallo, Alabama.

1973   Alois Hába dies in Prague, aged eighty. A number of instru-
        ments were constructed for him in quarter-tones and sixth-
        tones.

NOVEMBER 19

1630   Johann Hermann Schein dies in Leipzig at age forty-four; in
        1616 he was appointed cantor at the Thomasschule, Bach's
        most famous predecessor there.

1720   Giovanni Bononcini's opera Astarto is first staged in London.

1825   Jan Hugo Voříšek dies in Vienna, aged thirty-four. His piano
        impromptus were an influence on Schubert.

1828   Franz Schubert dies at age thirty-one in Vienna from an attack
        of typhus and is buried near Beethoven

1859   Mikhail Ippolitov-Ivanov, Russian composer, is born in Gat-
        china. A collector of Caucasian folksongs, he also directed
        the Moscow Conservatory.

1875   Peter Ilyitch Tchaikovsky's Symphony no. 3, "Polish," is
        first performed in Moscow.

1884   Marianne Brandt makes her Metropolitan Opera debut, starring
        in Beethoven's Fidelio, with Leopold Damrosch conducting.

1905   Tommy Dorsey, American trombonist and bandleader, brother
        of jazz musician Jimmy Dorsey, is born in Mahoney Plains,
        Pennsylvania.

1913   Ataulfo Argenta, Spanish conductor, is born in Castro Urdiales.

1921   Géza Anda, Hungarian-Swiss pianist, is born in Budapest.

1923   Zoltán Kodály's <u>Psalmus Hungaricus</u> (based on Psalm LV),
        for tenor solo, chorus, and orchestra, has its premiere in
        Budapest.

1924   Alexander Brailowsky makes his American debut as concert
        pianist in Aeolian Hall, New York City.

        Alfredo Casella's ballet <u>La Giara</u> (called a "choreographic
        comedy") is first staged in Paris.

1944   Agnes Baltsa, Greek mezzo-soprano, is born in Lefkas.

1953   Elliott Carter's Sonata, for flute, oboe, cello, and harpsichord,
        is given its first performance in New York City.

        Wen-chung Chou's <u>Landscapes</u> has its premiere in San Fran-
        cisco.

1955   Daniel Pinkham's <u>Concerto for Celesta and Harpsichord</u> is
        first performed, in Boston.

1962   Régine Crespin makes her American debut in Strauss's <u>Der
        Rosenkavalier</u> at the Metropolitan Opera in New York.

1974   George Brunis dies in Chicago, aged seventy-four.

        NOVEMBER 20

1758   Johan Helmich Roman dies at age sixty-four in Haraldsmala,
        Sweden. His work was influenced by Handel, whom he knew
        in England.

1765   Friedrich Heinrich Himmel, German opera composer and con-
        ductor, is born in Treuenbrietzen.

1805   Ludwig van Beethoven conducts his only opera, <u>Fidelio,</u> in
        its first performance in Vienna. The audience was sparse,
        for the French army had entered the city a week before.

1827   Carl Friedrich Peters dies in Leipzig, aged forty-eight. His
        music publishing firm has continued to the present, known for
        its reliable editions and scholarly music library.

1873   Daniel Gregory Mason, American composer and teacher, son
        of piano manufacturer Henry Mason and grandson of composer
        Lowell Mason, is born in Brookline, Massachusetts.

1889   Gustav Mahler conducts his Symphony no. 1, "Titan," in its
        first performance in Budapest.

1894   Anton Rubinstein dies in Peterhof, Russia, aged sixty-two.
        He had brought to Russian musical education a more thorough
        and cosmopolitan training.

1907   Feodor Chaliapin appears in America for the first time
        singing in Mefistofele at the Metropolitan Opera in New York
        City.

1911   Gustav Mahler's Das Lied von der Erde, for soli and orchestra,
        is first performed posthumously in Munich, Bruno Walter con-
        ducting.

1914   Elisabeth Schumann makes her American debut in Strauss's
        Der Rosenkavalier at the Metropolitan Opera in New York.

1923   Wanda Landowska performs with the Philadelphia Orchestra
        in her American debut, Leopold Stowkowski conducting.

1937   René Kollo, German tenor, is born in Berlin.

1950   Francesco Cilèa dies in Varazze, Italy, aged eighty-four.

1952   Roy Harris's Symphony no. 7 is first performed, in Chicago.

1953   Irmgard Seefried sings in Mozart's The Marriage of Figaro
        in her first American appearance with the Metropolitan Opera
        in New York.

1955   David Oistrakh in the first concert of his American tour plays
        in Carnegie Hall, New York.

1957   Halsey Steven's Sinfonia Breve receives its premiere per-
        formance in Louisville, Kentucky.

NOVEMBER 21

1695   Henry Purcell, English composer and organist, dies in London,
        aged about thirty-six.   The most outstanding member of an
        English family of musicians, he is buried in Westminster
        Abbey, London.

1831   Giacomo Meyerbeer's first French opera, Robert le Diable,
        is received enthusiastically in its premiere at the Paris Opéra.

1877   Sigfrid Karg-Elert, German organ virtuoso and composer, is
        born in Oberndorf.

1904   Coleman Hawkins, American jazz tenor-saxophone virtuoso
        and bandleader, is born in St. Joseph, Missouri.

1931   Malcolm Williamson, Australian composer, is born in Sydney.

1937   Dmitri Shostakovich's Symphony no. 5 receives its premiere, in Leningrad.

1938   Leopold Godowsky dies at age sixty-eight in New York City; he had suffered a stroke in 1930.

1943   Eugene Istomin wins the Leventritt Award for his performance as soloist in Brahms's Piano Concerto no. 2 with the New York Philharmonic Orchestra.

1946   Jerome Hines makes his debut with the Metropolitan Opera in New York.

1953   James McCracken makes his Metropolitan Opera debut in New York City.

1954   Karol Rathaus dies at age fifty-nine in New York City.

1974   Frank Martin dies in Naarden, Holland, where he had lived after the end of World War II; he was eighty-four.

NOVEMBER 22

1709   Franz Benda, Bohemian violinist and composer, is baptized in Alt-Benatek.   For forty years he played in the court orchestra of Frederick the Great, frequently accompanying him.

1710   Wilhelm Friedemann Bach, German composer and organist, eldest son of Johann Sebastian Bach, is born in Weimar.

1739   George Frideric Handel's Ode for St. Cecilia's Day is first performed, in London.

1859   Cecil James Sharp, English folksong collector and founder of the English Folk Dance Society, is born in London.   He researched the English origin of Appalachian folksongs in America.

1899   Hoagy (Hoagland) Carmichael, American jazz pianist and composer, is born in Bloomington, Indiana.   He is known for his songs Stardust, Georgia on My Mind, and Rocking Chair.

1900   Sir Arthur Sullivan dies in London, aged fifty-eight.   His fame rests on the comic operas written in collaboration with librettist Sir William Gilbert.

1902   Emanuel Feuermann, Austrian virtuoso cellist, owner of a rare Stradivarius cello, is born in Kolomea.

Joaquín Rodrigo, blind Spanish composer, is born in Sagunto.

1907   Alessandro Bonci sings in <u>Rigoletto</u> in his first appearance with the Metropolitan Opera in New York.

Charles Martin Loeffler's <u>Pagan Poem</u> is first performed by the Boston Symphony Orchestra under Karl Muck's direction.

Bernard Naylor, English-Canadian composer mostly of sacred choral music, is born in Cambridge.

1908   Paul Taffanel dies in Paris, aged sixty-four.

1913   Sir Benjamin Britten, the first English composer elevated to the peerage (becoming a Lord in 1976), is born in Lowestoft.

1921   Christine Nilsson dies in Stockholm, aged seventy-eight.

1922   Fikret Amirov, Soviet Armenian composer, is born in Kirovabad.

Elisabeth Rethberg makes her Metropolitan Opera debut in <u>Aida</u>.

1923   Dika Newlin, American composer and teacher, is born in Portland, Oregon.

1925   Gunther Schuller, American composer and horn player, is born in New York City. In 1968 he published a study of early jazz development.

1928   Maurice Ravel's ballet <u>Boléro</u>, commissioned by Ida Rubinstein and first performed by her dance group, is staged at the Paris Opéra.

1931   Ferde Grofé's <u>Grand Canyon Suite</u> has its premiere performance in Chicago, Paul Whiteman conducting.

1932   Rose Bampton first sings with the Metropolitan Opera in <u>La Gioconda</u>, in New York.

Leslie Parnas, American cellist and 1962 winner of the Moscow Tchaikovsky Competition, is born in St. Louis.

1938   Risë Stevens makes her Metropolitan Opera debut singing in Strauss's <u>Der Rosenkavalier</u>, in Philadelphia.

1943   Pietro Yon dies in Huntington, Long Island, aged fifty-seven. His organ pieces include the popular <u>Gesù Bambino</u>.

1955   Guy Ropartz dies in Lanloup, France, aged ninety-one. From 1894 to 1919 he directed the Conservatory at Nancy.

1966   Alvin Brehm's overture Hephaestus has its premiere in New
        York City.

1975   Friedrich Blume dies in Schlüchtern, Germany, aged eighty-
        two; he was in the process of preparing a supplement to the
        encyclopedia Die Musik in Geschichte und Gegenwart.

1977   Paul Schoeffler dies in Amersham, England, aged eighty.

        NOVEMBER 23

1585   Thomas Tallis, English organist and church composer, dies
        in Greenwich, aged about eighty. He was one of the first to
        use English texts in rites for the Church of England.

1719   Johann Gottlob Breitkopf, son of the German publisher, is
        born in Leipzig. He devised a font with a smaller division
        of the musical elements, thus enabling piano reductions of
        scores.

1834   Hector Berlioz's symphonic work Harold en Italie (after By-
        ron's Childe Harold), for viola and orchestra, has its pre-
        miere in Paris.

1876   Manuel de Falla, Spanish composer and pianist, is born in
        Cadiz.

1878   André Caplet, French composer and opera conductor, is born
        in Le Havre.

1885   Anton Seidl makes his American conducting debut in the New
        York performance of Lohengrin at the Metropolitan Opera;
        his wife, Auguste Seidl-Kraus, sings the role of Elsa.

1899   Antonin Dvořák's opera The Devil and Kate opens in Prague.

1903   Enrico Caruso sings for the first time with the Metropolitan
        Opera, performing in Rigoletto so successfully that he re-
        mained with the company for the rest of his life.

1916   Eduard Napravnik dies at seventy-seven in St. Petersburg.

1921   Leoš Janáček's opera Katya Kabanova (after Ostrovsky) has
        its premiere in Brno.

1928   Daniel Gregory Mason's festival overture Chanticleer is first
        performed in Cincinnati.

1932   Tito Schipa first appears with the Metropolitan Opera in New
        York, starring in Donizetti's L'Elisir d'amore.

1933   Krzysztof Penderecki, Polish avant-garde composer who cre-
        ated diagrammatic notation for the performance of his works,
        is born in Debica.

1935   William Lewis, American tenor, is born in Tulsa, Oklahoma.

1939   Artur Bodanzky dies in New York City, aged sixty-one.

1950   Howard Swanson's Short Symphony receives its premiere with
        the New York Philharmonic Orchestra, Mitropoulos conducting.

1957   Werner Josten's Canzona Seria, for piano and woodwinds, is
        given its first performance in New York City.

1963   Daniel Pinkham's Symphony no. 2 has its premiere in Lan-
        sing, Michigan.

1965   Raymond Lewenthal makes his New York debut in a Town Hall
        piano recital.

1973   Jennie Tourel dies in New York City, aged seventy-three.

1974   Páll Isólfsson dies at eighty-one in Reykajavik, Iceland.

        NOVEMBER 24

1808   Henriette Voigt (née Kunze), German pianist, is born in Leip-
        zig. It was to her that Schumann dedicated his piano sonata,
        op. 22.

1839   Hector Berlioz's dramatic symphony Roméo et Juliette has its
        first performance, in Paris.

1848   Lilli Lehmann, German opera soprano, singing teacher, and
        harpist, is born in Würzburg.

1859   Adelina Patti makes her operatic debut at age sixteen in New
        York, singing in Lucia di Lammermoor.

1868   Scott Joplin, American pianist and ragtime composer, is born
        in Texarkana, Texas. In 1976 he was posthumously awarded
        the Pulitzer Prize.

1874   Antonin Dvořák's first opera, King and Collier, opens in Prague.

1897   Willie "The Lion" Smith, American jazz pianist and composer,
        is born in Goshen, New York. His autobiography, Music on
        My Mind, recounts the Harlem jazz scene.

1901   Joseph Fischer dies in Springfield, Ohio, aged sixty. With his brother Ignaz he had published music for the Roman Catholic Church.

1922   Bruce Hungerford, Australian concert pianist, is born in Korumburra.

1925   James Lyons, American music critic for the New York Herald Tribune and editor of American Record Guide, is born in Peabody, Massachusetts.

1927   Emma Lou Diemer, American composer, pianist, organist, and teacher, is born in Kansas City, Missouri.

Alfredo Kraus, Spanish tenor, is born in the Canary Islands.

1932   Hilding Rosenberg's opera Voyage to America is first staged, in Stockholm.

1938   Jussi Bjoerling makes his debut at the Metropolitan Opera in La Bohème.

1939   Maria Chiara, Italian soprano, is born in Oderzo.

1944   Anne Marie Blanzat, French soprano, is born in Neuilly.

David Diamond's Rounds, for string orchestra, is first performed, in Minneapolis.

1945   Elie Siegmeister's Western Suite is first played by the NBC Orchestra, Arturo Toscanini conducting.

1949   Carl Ruggles's Organum, for large orchestra, is given its premiere in New York City.

1972   Hall Overton dies in New York City, aged fifty-two. He was a contributor to the periodical Jazz Today.

Alexander Smallens dies in Tucson, Arizona, at the age of eighty-three. He was the original conductor of Gershwin's Porgy and Bess.

NOVEMBER 25

1847   Friedrich von Flotow's opera Martha opens in Vienna. The Irish tune The Last Rose of Summer runs throughout the opera as a theme song.

1862   Ethelbert Nevin, American composer of light popular music, is born in Edgeworth, Pennsylvania; his best-known works are The Rosary, Narcissus, and Mighty Lak' a Rose.

1881   Theobald Böhm dies in Munich at eighty-seven.

1882   Gilbert and Sullivan's operetta Iolanthe opens in London.

1885   Lilli Lehmann sings in Carmen at her Metropolitan Opera
        debut and marks her first American performance.

1895   Wilhelm Kempff, German concert pianist and composer, is
        born in Jüterbog.

1896   Virgil Thomson, American composer, conductor and music
        critic, is born in Kansas City, Missouri. From 1940 to 1954
        he wrote for the New York Herald Tribune.

1900   Tibor Serly, Hungarian-American composer, conductor, and
        violinist, is born in Losonc. In 1937 he began teaching in
        New York.

1901   Gustav Mahler conducts the premiere of his Symphony no. 4,
        in Munich.

        Josef Rheinberger dies in Munich, aged sixty-two, a re-
        nowned organ teacher whose pupils were from all over the
        world.

1907   Mary Garden stars in Thaïs in her American operatic debut
        at New York's Manhattan Opera House.

1915   Giuseppe De Luca makes his American debut at the Metro-
        politan Opera House singing in Il Barbiere di Siviglia.

1921   Charles Turner, American composer, is born in Baltimore.

1924   Paul Desmond, American jazz alto saxophonist associated
        with Dave Brubeck, is born in San Francisco.

1927   Yehudi Menuhin makes his first appearance as a violin soloist,
        performing Beethoven's Violin Concerto with the New York
        Symphony Society. He is eleven years old.

1931   Nat Adderley, American jazz cornetist, brother of "Cannon-
        ball" Adderley, is born in Tampa, Florida.

1933   Ramiro Cortés, American composer, is born in Dallas, Texas.

1940   Robert Casadesus and his wife, Gaby Casadesus, are the
        soloists in the premiere performance of his Concerto for Two
        Pianos with the New York Philharmonic Orchestra.

1946   Andrew Frank, American composer and teacher, is born in
        Los Angeles.

1958   John La Montaine's Pulitzer Prize-winning Piano Concerto is first performed, in Washington.

1965   Dame Myra Hess dies in London at age seventy-five.

NOVEMBER 26

1760   (Franz) Joseph Haydn marries Maria Anna Keller in St. Ste-
        phen's Cathedral in Vienna, but it was not a happy union.   He
        had fallen in love with her younger sister, but she had entered
        a convent.

1866   Adrien-François Servais dies in Hal, Belgium, aged fifty-nine.
        Many of his cello students became outstanding professionals.

1906   Geraldine Farrar makes her American debut starring in Roméo
        et Juliette at the Metropolitan Opera in New York.

1907   David Ewen, Polish-American writer on music, is born in
        Lwow.

1915   Earl Wild, American pianist and composer who has played for
        seven U.S. presidents, is born in Pittsburgh.

1916   Gerhard Unger, German tenor, is born in Bad Salzungen.

1920   Beniamino Gigli makes his American debut at the Metropolitan
        Opera in New York, starring in Boito's Mefistofele.

1925   Eugene Istomin, American pianist, is born in New York City.
        He married Marta Casals, widow of cellist Pablo Casals.

1932   Alan Stout, American composer, teacher, and editor, is born
        in Baltimore.

1943   Gardner Read conducts the premiere of his Symphony no. 2,
        winner of the Paderewski Fund Competition, in Boston.

1954   Witold Lutoslawski's Concerto for Orchestra has its first
        hearing, in Warsaw.

1956   Tommy Dorsey dies in Greenwich, Connecticut, aged fifty-one.

1959   Albert W. Ketèlbey dies in Cowes on the Isle of Wight, aged
        eighty-four.

1961   Dame Joan Sutherland makes her Metropolitan Opera debut in
        New York, singing in Lucia di Lammermoor.

1963   Amelita Galli-Curci dies at age eighty-one in La Jolla, Cali-
        fornia.

NOVEMBER 27

1474   Guillaume Dufay, one of the chief fifteenth-century composers, chapel master and later canon at Cambrai Cathedral, dies at Cambrai, aged about seventy-four. He is famed for his masses, motets, and three-part chansons.

1749   Gottfried Heinrich Stölzel dies in Gotha, Germany, aged fifty-nine.

1759   Franz Krommer, Austrian violinist, composer, and conductor, is born in Kamenitz.

1804   Sir Julius Benedict, German-English composer and conductor, is born in Stuttgart.

1843   Michael William Balfe's best-known opera, The Bohemian Girl, is first produced at Drury Lane Theatre, London.

1860   Victor Ewald, Russian composer and ethnomusicologist (by profession an engineer), is born in St. Petersburg.

        Ludwig Rellstab dies in Berlin at age sixty-one.

1867   Charles Koechlin, French composer, teacher, and biographer of Debussy and Fauré, is born in Paris.

1878   Mabel Daniels, American composer, is born in Swampscott, Massachusetts.

1880   Teatro Costanzi opens in Rome with the performance of Rossini's Semiramide; in 1928 it was renamed Teatro dell' Opera.

1896   Richard Strauss's tone poem Also sprach Zarathustra (after Nietzsche) is first performed, in Frankfurt, Germany.

1900   Leon Barzin, Belgian-American conductor, is born in Brussels.

1915   Victor Alessandro, American conductor who led the San Antonio Orchestra, 1952-76, is born in Waco, Texas.

1928   Walter Klien, Austrian pianist, is born in Graz.

        Igor Stravinsky conducts the premiere of his ballet Baiser de la fée (on themes of Tchaikovsky) at the Paris Opéra.

1930   Richard Crooks makes his operatic debut with the Philadelphia Grand Opera Company.

1936   Ania Dorfmann, piano recitalist, makes her first American appearance at Town Hall, New York.

1950   Mario Del Monaco makes his Metropolitan Opera debut in
        New York, starring in Puccini's Manon Lescaut.

1955   Arthur Honegger dies at age sixty-three in Paris. His can-
        tatas are considered fine examples of modern vocal writing.

1958   Artur Rodzinski dies in Boston, aged sixty-six, of a heart
        ailment.

1960   Ernest M. Skinner dies in Duxbury, Massachusetts, at age
        ninety-four. In 1932 his organ company merged with the
        Aeolian Company, becoming the Skinner-Aeolian Organ Com-
        pany.

1972   Erich Wolfgang Korngold's Symphony has its first public per-
        formance posthumously, in Munich.

1976   Victor Alessandro dies on his sixty-first birthday in San
        Antonio, Texas.

        NOVEMBER 28

1632   Jean Baptiste Lully, Italian-French composer, called the
        founder of French opera, is born in Florence.

1784   Ferdinand Ries, German composer and pianist, a pupil of
        Beethoven, is born in Bonn.

1811   Ludwig van Beethoven's Piano Concerto no. 5, "Emperor,"
        is performed by Friedrich Schneider in Leipzig's Gewandhaus.

1813   (Johann) Simon Mayr's opera Medea in Corinto opens in Naples
        in its premiere.

1829   Anton Rubinstein, Russian composer and pianist, is born in
        Vykhvatinetz. In 1862 he founded the Imperial Conservatory
        in St. Petersburg.

1856   Alexander Dmitrievitch Kastalsky, Russian conductor and com-
        poser of sacred choral music, is born in Moscow.

1895   José Iturbi, Spanish pianist and conductor, is born in Valencia.
        He and his sister, Amparo Iturbi, often gave duo-piano re-
        citals.

1905   Helen Jepson, American soprano, is born in Titusville, Pennsyl-
        vania.

1908   Rose Bampton, American soprano, wife of conductor Wilfrid
        Pelletier, is born in Cleveland.

1913   Rosa Raisa makes her American operatic debut, singing in
        Aida at the Chicago Opera.

1919   Charles Tomlinson Griffes's tone poem The Pleasure Dome of
        Kubla Khan (after Coleridge) has its premiere with the Boston
        Symphony Orchestra.

1925   Aurelio de la Vega, Cuban-American composer and teacher
        in California, is born in Havana.

1930   Howard Hanson's Symphony no. 2, "Romantic," commissioned
        for the fiftieth anniversary of the Boston Symphony Orchestra,
        is conducted in its premiere there by Serge Koussevitzky.

        Zoltán Kodály's Marosszék Dances are first performed, in
        Dresden.

1937   Josef Hofmann performs in his Golden Jubilee concert at the
        Metropolitan Opera House, celebrating his debut there as a
        child.

1954   Marcel Bitsch's Concertino, for piano and orchestra, receives
        its first performance, in Paris.

1956   Louis Kentner appears in his American debut as concert
        pianist in Town Hall, New York.

1966   Vittorio Giannini dies in New York City, aged sixty-three, a
        member of the Juilliard School of Music faculty for many
        years.

1967   Ettore Panizza dies in Milan, aged ninety-two.

1972   Havergal Brian dies in Shoreham-by-Sea, England, at the age
        of ninety-six; seven of his many symphonies were written after
        he was ninety. He was looked on as a "harmless eccentric."

        NOVEMBER 29

1643   Claudio Monteverdi dies at age seventy-six in Venice. During
        the last years of his life the first public opera house was
        opened in Venice, and he wrote two new operas for public
        performance.

1797   Gaetano Donizetti, Italian opera composer, is born in Bergamo.

1850   Sofia Scalchi, Italian mezzo-soprano, is born in Turin.

1869   Giulia Grisi dies in Berlin, aged fifty-eight.

1887   Josef Hofmann at age eleven is soloist in Beethoven's Piano
        Concerto no. 1 in New York City in his first American ap-
        pearance.

1891   Richard Donovan, American organist, composer, and professor
        at Yale University, is born in New Haven, Connecticut.

1893   Emma Calvé and Pol Plançon make their American debuts
        at the Metropolitan Opera, starring in Gounod's Faust.

1899   Gustave Reese, American musicologist, encyclopedia contribu-
        tor, music publisher administrator, and teacher, is born in New
        York City.

1915   Harold Schonberg, American music critic, is born in New
        York City; in 1971 won a Pulitzer Prize for distinguished
        criticism.

        William (Billy) Strayhorn, American jazz pianist, is born in
        Dayton, Ohio.

1916   Valentino Bucchi, Italian composer and music consultant for
        Radio Italiana, is born in Florence.

1919   Benno Moiseiwitsch appears in his first American piano re-
        cital in New York City's Carnegie Hall.

1924   Giacomo Puccini dies in Brussels, aged sixty-five.

        Erik Satie's ballet Relâche is first produced in Paris.   A
        note on the stage curtain read: "Erik Satie is the greatest
        musician in the world; whoever disagrees ... please leave
        the hall. "

1941   Jan Peerce makes his operatic debut starring in La Traviata
        at the Metropolitan Opera in New York.

1945   Marga Schiml, German contralto, is born in Weiden.

1957   Erich Wolfgang Korngold dies in Hollywood, California, aged
        sixty.   During World War II he had settled there and written
        film music.

1958   Vassily Nebolsin dies in Moscow, aged sixty.

        NOVEMBER 30

1623   Thomas Weelkes, English Elizabethan madrigalist and organist,
        dies in London, aged about forty-eight.

1703   Nicolas de Grigny, French organist at Rheims Cathedral and composer, dies at Rheims, aged about thirty-two.

1796   Karl Loewe, German song composer, is born in Lobejün.
He was also a singer and performed his dramatic ballades, a
song form that he perfected.

1813   Charles-Henri Alkan (real name Morhange), French pianist
and composer (principally for piano), is born in Paris.

1847   Ernst Eulenburg, German music publisher of miniature scores
and founder of a firm later headed by his son, is born in
Berlin.

August Klughardt, German composer and conductor, is born
in Cöthen.

1859   Sergey Mikhailovitch Liapunov, Russian pianist, composer,
and teacher, is born in Yaroslavl.

1861   Ludwig Thuille, Austrian composer, choral director, and co-
author of several music-theory texts, is born in Bozen.

1868   Ernest Newman, English music critic, is born in Liverpool.

1884   Ture Rangström, Swedish composer, conductor, and music
critic, is born in Stockholm.

1885   Jules Massenet's opera Le Cid has its premiere in Paris.

1890   Eleanor Spencer, American pianist, is born in Chicago.

1903   Claude Arrieu, French composer and pianist, is born in Paris.

1922   Robert Evett, American composer, is born in Loveland, Colorado.

1924   Klaus Huber, Swiss composer and former schoolteacher, is
born in Berne.

1930   Jacques Ibert's orchestral suite Divertissement has its premiere,
in Paris.

1937   Paul Stookey, American folksinger and guitarist, member of
the Peter, Paul and Mary trio, is born in Baltimore.

1945   Bohuslav Martinů's Symphony no. 4 is first performed, in
Philadelphia.

1954   Wilhelm Furtwängler, conductor of the Berlin Philharmonic
for many years, dies in Baden-Baden, Germany, aged sixty-
eight.

1957   Beniamino Gigli dies at age sixty-seven in Rome.   Two years
earlier he had sung on tour in the United States.

1964   Roger Matton's Concerto, for two pianos and orchestra, re-
        ceives its premiere performance in Quebec.

1967   Thea Musgrave's opera <u>The Decision</u> opens in London at Sad-
        ler's Wells.

DECEMBER 1

1709   Franz Xaver Richter, German composer and Kapellmeister at Strasbourg Cathedral, is born in Holleschau.

1847   Agathe Backer-Grøndahl, Norwegian composer and pianist (a pupil of Liszt), is born in Holmestrand.

1886   Richard Wagner's opera <u>Tristan und Isolde</u> in its American premiere proves enormously successful. Anton Seidl conducted the Metropolitan Opera in the New York opening.

1902   Carl Nielsen's Symphony no. 2, "The Four Temperaments," is given its first hearing, in Copenhagen.

1932   Richard Bonelli first sings with the Metropolitan Opera in <u>La Traviata</u> in New York City.

1935   Richard Mayr, noted operatic bass, dies in Vienna at age fifty-eight.

        Sergei Prokofiev's Violin Concerto no. 2 is first performed, in Madrid.

1937   Gordon Crosse, English composer and teacher at Essex University, is born in Bury.

1944   Béla Bartók's Concerto for Orchestra, commissioned by Koussevitzky and performed by him in Boston, has its premiere.

1945   Dorothy Kirsten stars in <u>La Bohème</u> in making her debut with the Metropolitan Opera in New York.

1950   Ernest John Moeran dies in Kenmare, Ireland, at age fifty-five.

1951   Sir Benjamin Britten conducts the premiere of his opera <u>Billy Budd</u> (the libretto by E. M. Forster after Melville) in London.

1968   Nicolae Bretan dies in Cluj, Rumania, aged eighty-one.

1977   Lukas Foss's <u>American Cantata,</u> for soli, narrators, chorus, and orchestra, receives its premiere, in New York City.

DECEMBER 2

1840   Gaetano Donizetti's opera <u>La Favorita</u> opens in Paris at the Opéra.

1845   (Johann) Simon Mayr dies in Bergamo, Italy, aged eighty-two.

1877   Camille Saint-Saëns's opera <u>Samson et Dalila</u> is first produced in Weimar in a German version after no French theater would stage it; it was Franz Liszt who assisted in bringing it to Weimar.

1879   Rudolf Friml, Bohemian-American operetta composer, is born in Prague.

1883   Johannes Brahms's Symphony no. 3 is conducted by Hans Richter in its premiere in Vienna.

1899   Sir John Barbirolli, English conductor, is born in London. From 1937 to 1943 he led the New York Philharmonic Orchestra, succeeding Arturo Toscanini.

1906   Peter Carl Goldmark, Hungarian-American electronics engineer who developed long-play (LP) records, is born in Budapest.   In 1977 in a White House ceremony President Carter awarded him the National Medal of Science for his many achievements.

1916   Sir Francesco Paolo Tosti dies at age seventy in Rome.

1919   William Wilderman, American baritone, is born in Stuttgart, Germany.

1921   Robert Moevs, American composer and Rutgers University professor, is born in La Crosse, Wisconsin.

1924   Sigmund Romberg's operetta <u>The Student Prince</u> has its premiere, in New York City.

1925   Irina Arkhipova, Soviet mezzo-soprano, is born in Moscow.

1928   Jörg Demus, Austrian concert pianist, is born in St. Poelten.

        Franz Schmidt's Symphony no. 3 is first performed, in Vienna.

Arnold Schoenberg's Variations for Orchestra receives its premiere, in Berlin.

1929   Harvey Phillips, American bass tuba virtuoso and teacher, is
        born in Aurora, Missouri.

1931   Vincent d'Indy dies in Paris, aged eighty, regarded as one of
        France's most important modern composers.

1934   Thomas Palmer, American baritone, is born in Harrisburg,
        Pennsylvania.

1949   Béla Bartók's Viola Concerto, commissioned by William
        Primrose, is performed by him at its premiere, in Minnea-
        polis.   Bartók had not finished the work before his death;
        Tibor Serly completed it.

        Olivier Messiaen's Turangalila-Symphonie is conducted in its
        premiere by Leonard Bernstein, in Boston.

1950   Dinu Lipatti dies in Chêne-Bourg, Switzerland, aged thirty-
        three.

1952   Cecil Effinger's Choral Symphony is first performed, in Den-
        ver.

1955   Goffredo Petrassi's Concerto for Orchestra, no. 5 is given its
        premiere, in Boston.

        Ernst Toch's Pulitzer Prize-winning Symphony no. 3 is first
        heard, in Pittsburgh.

1967   Emmanuel Bay dies at age seventy-six in Jerusalem.

        DECEMBER 3

1596   Nicola Amati, Italian violin maker of world-famous instruments,
        is born in Cremona.   In his workshop both Andrea Guarneri
        and Antonio Stradivari received their training.

1642   Johann Christoph Bach, German organist and composer, an
        earlier member of the extended Bach family, is born in Arn-
        stadt.

1721   Johann Sebastian Bach marries his second wife, Anna Magda-
        lena Wülken, who eventually bore him thirteen children.

1729   Padre Antonio Soler, Spanish composer and organist, a pupil
        of Domenico Scarlatti, is baptized in Olot.   A listing of his

music at El Escorial contains over 400 works.

1866   Johann Wenzel Kalliwoda dies at age sixty-five in Karlsruhe, Germany. For thirty years he conducted the court orchestra in Donaueschingen.

1876   Hermann Goetz dies in Hottingen, Switzerland, at age thirty-five.

1883   Anton Webern, Austrian composer influenced by his studies with Arnold Schoenberg, is born in Vienna.

1898   Lev Knipper, Russian composer and folksong collector of the various nationalities in the Soviet Union, is born in Tbilisi (Tiflis).

1908   Sir Edward Elgar's Symphony no. 1 has its premiere in Manchester, but it never became popular beyond England.

Halsey Stevens, American composer, is born in Scott, New York. As biographer of Béla Bartók, he learned Hungarian to research needed material.

1910   Giovanni Martinelli makes his concert debut in Milan, singing in Rossini's Stabat Mater.

1913   Franz Schmidt's Symphony no. 2 is given its premiere, in Vienna.

1914   Irving Fine, American composer and Brandeis University professor, is born in Boston.

1922   Phyllis Curtin, American soprano, is born in Clarksburg, West Virginia.

1923   Maria Callas, American soprano who studied music in Athens, is born in New York City. A temperamental diva, she made headlines with her outbursts as well as with her romance with Aristotle Onassis, the Greek shipping magnate.

Frank Guarrera, American baritone, is born in Philadelphia.

1925   George Gershwin is soloist in his Piano Concerto in F in its first performance, in Carnegie Hall, with Walter Damrosch leading the New York Symphony Society.

1929   Paul Turok, American composer, is born in New York City.

1938   José Serebrier, Uruguayan-American conductor and composer, is born in Montevideo.

1940   Salvatore Baccaloni sings in Il barbiere di Siviglia in his
        Metropolitan Opera debut in Philadelphia.

1941   Christian Sinding dies in Oslo at age eighty-five, honored by
        the Norwegian government for his musical contributions.

1943   Howard Hanson conducts the premiere of his Pulitzer Prize-
        winning Symphony no. 4, "The Requiem," with the Boston
        Symphony Orchestra.

1944   Josef Lhévinne dies in New York City, aged sixty-nine.

        Armen Tigranian's opera David-bek opens in Erivan, Ar-
        menia.

1954   Sir William Walton's opera Troilus and Cressida is first
        staged, in London's Covent Garden.

1978   William Grant Still dies in Los Angeles at age eighty-three,
        the first black musician to conduct the Los Angeles Philhar-
        monic.

        DECEMBER 4

1660   André Campra, French opera composer, is born in Aix-en-
        Provence.

1667   Michel P. de Montéclair, French composer, is baptized at
        Andelot.

1732   John Gay dies in London, aged forty-seven.

1806   Johann Friedrich Franz Burgmüller, German composer of
        piano works, is born in Regensburg.   His piano studies are
        still used.

1845   Robert Schumann's Piano Concerto in A minor is performed
        by his wife, Clara Schumann, in its premiere in Dresden.
        It was dedicated to their friend, Ferdinand Hiller, who con-
        ducted from manuscript.

1872   Charles Lecocq's operetta La Fille de Mme. Angot is first
        produced, in Brussels.

1881   Peter Ilyitch Tchaikovsky's Violin Concerto receives its pre-
        miere with the Vienna Philharmonic Orchestra, Adolf Brodsky,
        soloist.   Brodsky had agreed to perform it after Leopold
        Auer declared it "impossible to play."

1893   Nellie Melba makes her debut at the Metropolitan Opera in
        New York City, starring in <u>Lucia di Lammermoor</u>.

1909   Ermanno Wolf-Ferrari's one-act opera <u>The Secret of Suzanne</u>
        is first performed, in Munich.

1916   Claudia Muzio stars in <u>Tosca</u> in her American debut at the
        Metropolitan Opera in New York City.

1920   Erich Wolfgang Korngold's opera <u>Die tote Stadt</u> opens in its
        premiere, in Hamburg.

1935   Johan Halvorsen dies in Oslo at seventy-one.

1938   Yvonne Minton, Australian mezzo-soprano, is born in Sydney.

1943   Patrice Munsel sings a minor role at her Metropolitan Opera
        debut at age eighteen, the youngest singer ever accepted by
        the company.

1949   Luigi Dallapiccola's opera <u>Il prigioniero</u> is first heard on a
        radio broadcast.

1953   Daniel Gregory Mason dies at age eighty in Greenwich,
        Connecticut.   From 1910 to 1942 he served Columbia Univer-
        sity as professor and then as director of the Music Depart-
        ment.

1960   Walter Goehr dies in Sheffield, England, aged fifty-seven.

1976   Sir Benjamin Britten dies in Aldeburgh, England, at sixty-
        three.   A few months earlier he had been elevated to the
        peerage in recognition of his great contribution to English
        music.

        DECEMBER 5

1687   Francesco Geminiani, Italian violinist, composer, writer,
        and art dealer, is baptized in Lucca.

1749   Jean Philippe Rameau's opera <u>Zoroastre</u> opens in Paris in its
        premiere.

1758   Johann Friedrich Fasch dies in Zerbst, Germany, aged
        seventy.   His contemporary J. S. Bach held his works in
        high regard.

1791   Wolfgang Amadeus Mozart dies in Vienna, aged thirty-five.
        His last work, the Requiem, was unfinished, and his student
        Franz Süssmayr completed it.

1830   Hector Berlioz's <u>Symphonie fantastique</u> receives its premiere at the Paris Conservatoire.

1898   Grace Moore, American soprano and film star, is born in Slabtown, Tennessee.

1904   Wilhelm Ehmann, German musicologist and director of church school music in Westphalia, is born in Freistadt.

1909   Ebenezer Prout dies in London, aged seventy-four.

1916   Veronika Dudarova, Soviet woman conductor, is born in Baku.

       Hans Richter dies in Bayreuth, aged seventy-three.

1921   Louis de Froment, French conductor, is born in Paris.

1924   Toti Dal Monte makes her American debut in <u>Lucia di Lam-mermoor</u> at New York's Metropolitan Opera.

1927   Leoš Janáček's <u>Slavonic Mass</u> (<u>M'sa Glagolskaja</u>) for soli, chorus, and orchestra, is first performed, in Brno.

1930   Darius Milhaud's <u>Concerto for Percussion and Small Orchestra</u> has its first hearing, in Paris.

       Roger Sessions's symphonic suite from <u>The Black Maskers</u> receives its premiere, in Cincinnati.

1934   Pietro Bottazzo, Italian tenor, is born in Padua.

1940   Jan Kubelík, father of conductor Rafael Kubelík, dies in Prague, aged sixty.

1970   Ferdinand Grossmann dies in Vienna, aged eighty-three.

1977   Magda Olivero gives a successful song recital in Carnegie Hall in New York, a historic opera event, considering her age of sixty-five.

DECEMBER 6

1550   Orazio Vecchi, Italian priest, composer of choral music and chapel master, is baptized in Modena.

1794   Luigi Lablache, Italian bass and singing master to Queen Victoria, is born in Naples.

1804   Wilhelmine Schröder-Devrient, German soprano, is born in Hamburg.

1806   Louis Gilbert Duprez, French tenor, is born in Paris.

1833   Barbara Marchisio, Italian contralto and teacher, is born in
        Turin.

1841   Robert Schumann's Symphony no. 4 is conducted by Ferdinand
        David in its premiere at Leipzig's Gewandhaus.

1846   Hector Berlioz conducts the first performance of his "opéra
        de concert," La Damnation de Faust, at the Opéra-Comique,
        Paris.

1890   Hector Berlioz's opera La Prise de Troie (the first part of
        the two-part opera Les Troyens) is given its first production
        in Karlsruhe more than twenty years after Berlioz's death.
        He had never heard this part.

1920   Dave Brubeck, American pianist, composer, and jazz mu-
        sician, is born in Concord, California.

1927   Jacques Bondon, French composer associated with Maurice
        Martenot, is born in Boulbon.

1929   Igor Stravinsky is soloist in his Capriccio, for piano and
        orchestra, with the Paris Symphony conducted by Ernest
        Ansermet.

1937   Boris Blacher's Concertante Musik, for orchestra, is first
        performed, in Berlin.

        Arnold Schoenberg's Violin Concerto receives its premiere
        in Philadelphia.

1941   Astrid Varnay makes an unscheduled debut at the Metropolitan
        Opera, substituting without rehearsal in Die Walküre.

1944   Regina Resnick sings in Il Trovatore in her initial appearance
        with the Metropolitan Opera in New York City.

1949   Huddie "Leadbelly" Ledbetter, American folksinger and
        guitarist, jailed for murder and aided by folksong collectors
        John and Alan Lomax, dies in New York City, aged about
        sixty-four.

1960   John Boda's Sinfonia has its premiere in Knoxville, Tennessee.

        Eileen Farrell stars in Gluck's Alcestis in making her Metro-
        politan Opera bow.

1963   Gene Gutchë's symphonic poem Genghis Khan is given its
        first performance in Minneapolis.

1974   Charles Wuorinen is soloist in the premiere of his Piano

Concerto no. 2, for amplified piano and orchestra, in New York City.

1977   John Corigliano's Clarinet Concerto is first performed, in New York City.

DECEMBER 7

1840   Hermann Goetz, German composer, is born in Königsberg.

1842   The newly founded Philharmonic Society of New York presents its first concert.

1849   Carl Fischer, German-American music publisher, is born in Buttstadt.

1863   Pietro Mascagni, Italian opera composer, is born in Leghorn.

1887   Ernst Toch, Austrian-American composer and pianist, is born in Vienna.

1889   Gilbert and Sullivan's operetta The Gondoliers opens in London.

1902   Ilona Kabos, Hungarian-English pianist, is born in Budapest.

1906   Elisabeth Höngen, German contralto, is born in Gevelsberg.

1908   Frances Alda makes her first appearance with the Metropolitan Opera in New York City.

1910   Richard Franko Goldman, American bandmaster, composer, and writer on music, is born in New York City, the son of Edwin Franko Goldman.

1917   Ludwig Minkus dies at age ninety-one in Vienna.

1924   Carl Ruggles's symphonic suite Men and Mountains has its premiere in New York City.

1930   Richard Felciano, American composer credited with the introduction of electronic music in the liturgy, is born in Santa Rosa, California.

1935   Richard Cross, American bass-baritone, is born in Faribault, Minnesota.

1939   Sir William Walton's Violin Concerto, commissioned by Jascha Heifetz and performed by him in its premiere, is first performed in Cleveland, Ohio.

1940   Eleanor Steber makes her first Metropolitan Opera appearance,
        singing in <u>Der Rosenkavalier</u>.

1942   James Melton begins an eight-year association with the Metro-
        politan Opera with his New York debut.

1960   Clara Haskil dies in Brussels, aged sixty-five.

1962   Kirsten Flagstad dies at sixty-seven in Oslo.

1977   Peter Carl Goldmark dies in an auto accident near New York
        City shortly after his White House award ceremony. He was
        seventy-one.

DECEMBER 8

1562   Adrian Willaert, Flemish composer (born in Bruges) regarded
        as founder of the Venetian school of composition, dies in
        Venice, aged about seventy-two.

1813   Ludwig van Beethoven, almost totally deaf, conducts the pre-
        miere of his Symphony no. 7 in a benefit concert at the
        University of Vienna. Critics declared that he must have
        been drunk when he wrote it.

1835   Carlotta Marchisio, Italian opera soprano, is born in Turin.

1849   Giuseppe Verdi's opera <u>Luisa Miller</u> opens in Naples' Teatro
        San Carlo.

1865   Jean Sibelius, Finnish composer, the son of a doctor, is
        born in Tavastehus. His musical inspiration derived from
        native legends.

1882   Manuel Ponce, Mexican pianist and composer (known for his
        song <u>Estrellita</u>), is born in Fresnillo.

1890   Bohuslav Martinů, Czech composer, is born in Policka.

1900   Henry Russell dies in London, aged eighty-seven. His sons
        were impressario Henry Russell and composer and conductor
        Sir Landon Ronald (real name L. R. Russell).

1915   Jean Sibelius conducts the premiere of his Symphony no. 5
        in Helsinki on his fiftieth birthday.

1919   Moysey Samuilovitch Vainberg, Soviet composer, is born in
        Warsaw.

1920   Gérard Souzay (né Gérard Marcel Tisserand), French baritone,
        is born in Angers.

1924   Xaver Scharwenka dies in Berlin at age seventy-four.   He
        had published technical studies for pianists as well as con-
        cert pieces.

1928   Dominique-René De Lerma, American musicologist, writer,
        and composer, is born in Miami, Florida.

1939   James Galway, Irish flute virtuoso and briefly a teacher at
        the Eastman School of Music, is born in Belfast.   His flute
        is an 18-carat gold instrument.

        Ernest Schelling dies at sixty-three in New York City.   He
        had conducted young people's symphonic concerts throughout
        the nation.

1945   Alexander Siloti dies at age eighty-two in New York City,
        where he had taught at the Juilliard School, 1925-42.

1953   Mark Bucci has two one-act operas produced, The Dress and
        Sweet Betsy from Pike, in New York City.

1969   William Kraft's Triangles, for percussion and ten instruments,
        is first performed, in Los Angeles.

1971   Marie Collier dies in London, aged forty-five.

        DECEMBER 9

1836   Mikhail Glinka's patriotic opera A Life for the Tsar, is per-
        formed for the opening of the rebuilt Bolshoi Theater in St.
        Petersburg and becomes immensely popular until the 1917
        Revolution.

1837   Emil Waldteufel, French waltz composer known for The
        Skater's Waltz, is born in Strasbourg.

1842   Mikhail Glinka's opera Russlan and Ludmila (after Pushkin)
        is first staged in St. Petersburg despite disruptive hissing.
        It later became a popular production.

1843   David Popper, Czech cellist and composer, is born in Prague.

1882   Joaquín Turina, Spanish composer, pianist, and professor at
        the Conservatory of Madrid, is born in Seville.

1900   Claude Debussy's Nuages and Fêtes (two of the three Noc-
        turnes) are given their premieres in Paris with Camille
        Chevillard conducting at a Lamoureux concert.

1905   Richard Strauss's opera Salome (after Oscar Wilde's play) is produced by the Royal Opera in Dresden in its premiere without the notoriety that later surrounded its American performances.

1913   Franz Kullak dies at age sixty-nine in Berlin.

1915   Elisabeth Schwarzkopf, German soprano, is born in Jarolschin.

1916   Merrill Ellis, American composer, researcher in electronic music, and North Texas State University teacher, is born in Cleburne, Texas.

1921   Feodor Chaliapin returns to America after a long absence to star in Boris Godunov, singing the role of Czar Boris at the Metropolitan Opera.   The cast sang in Italian, but he sang in Russian.

1926   Darius Milhaud is soloist in the premiere of his Carnaval d'Aix, for piano and orchestra, in New York City.

1927   Hanny Steffek, Austrian soprano, is born in Bielce, Poland.

1928   Mario Castelnuovo-Tedesco's Piano Concerto no. 1 receives its first performance, in Rome.

1932   Donald Byrd, American ethnomusicologist and jazz-trumpet player, is born in Detroit.

1933   Gilbert Py, French tenor, is born in Sete.

1942   Aram Khachaturian's Stalin Prize-winning ballet Gayne is first staged in Molotov (Perm).

        George Szell conducts Salome in his Metropolitan Opera debut.

1946   Klaus Egge's Piano Concerto no. 2 is first performed, in Oslo.

1949   Samuel Barber's Piano Sonata is first performed by Vladimir Horowitz, in Havana.

1953   Issay Dobrowen dies in Oslo, aged sixty-two.

1956   Hans Barth dies at age fifty-nine in Jacksonville, Florida.

1969   Peter Maxwell Davies's Vesalii Icones (after fourteen drawings by Vesalius), for cello, winds, and piano, is given its premiere, in London.

1974   Ludwig Weber dies in Vienna, aged seventy-five.

DECEMBER 10

1800   Countess Josephine von Deym writes her sisters about a con-
        cert in her Vienna home: "Beethoven, that real angel, let
        us hear his new Quartets op. 18 which have not been engraved
        yet and are the greatest of their kind...."

1822   César Franck, Belgian-French composer, organist, and pro-
        fessor at the Paris Conservatoire, is born in Liège.

1823   Theodor Kirchner, German composer and organist who was
        encouraged by Schumann and Mendelsson, is born in Neukir-
        chen.

1825   François Boieldieu's opera La Dame blanche opens in Paris,
        eventually having more than 1,000 performances.

1854   Hector Berlioz's oratorio (sacred trilogy) L'Enfance du Christ
        receives its premiere in Paris.

1908   Mischa Elman performs the Tchaikovsky Violin Concerto with
        the Russian Symphony Society in his American debut in New
        York City.

        Olivier Messiaen, French organist and composer, is born in
        Avignon.

        Alexander Scriabin's Symphony no. 4, "Poem of Ecstasy,"
        is conducted by Modest Altschuler in its premiere by the
        Russian Symphony Society of New York.

1909   Otakar Kraus, Czech-English baritone, is born in Prague.

1910   Giacomo Puccini's opera La Fanciulla del West is conducted
        by Arturo Toscanini in its premiere, in New York City, with
        the Metropolitan Opera.

1913   Morton Gould, American composer, conductor, and radio
        pianist, is born in Richmond Hill, New York.

1919   Sesto Bruscantini, Italian operatic baritone known for his
        buffo roles, is born in Porto Civitanova.

1936   David Diamond's Psalm, for orchestra, has its premiere in
        Rochester, New York.

1938   Michael Rippon, English bass, is born in Coventry.

1950   Bernd Alois Zimmermann's Violin Concerto is first performed,
        in Baden-Baden, Germany.

1953   Cesare Valletti sings with the Metropolitan Opera in New York
        in making his American debut.

1959   Christa Ludwig stars in the <u>Marriage of Figaro</u> in her
        American debut in New York City with the Metropolitan
        Opera.

1965   Henry Cowell dies at age sixty-eight in Shady, New York.

1966   Boris Koutzen dies at age sixty-five in Mt. Kisco, New York.

1969   Franco Capuana dies in Naples, aged seventy-five.

        DECEMBER 11

1803   Hector Berlioz, French composer who instituted thematic
        repetition in program music, which he called "idée fixe," is
        born in Côte-Saint-André.

1883   Giovanni Mario dies in Rome, aged seventy-three.

1892   Giacomo Lauri-Volpi, Italian tenor, is born in Lanuvio.
        When he was eighty he sang an opera aria on a Barcelona
        stage.

        Leo Ornstein, Russian-American pianist and composer, is
        born in Kremenchug.

1908   Elliott Carter, American composer and teacher, is born in
        New York City.

        Frederick Delius's symphonic poem <u>In a Summer Garden</u> is
        given its premiere by the London Philharmonic Orchestra.

1925   Carl Nielsen's Symphony no. 6, "Sinfonia Semplice," is first
        performed, in Copenhagen.

1936   Zoltán Kodály's suite of folk dances, <u>Galanta Dances,</u> re-
        ceives its American premiere in Philadelphia. It was written
        in 1934 for the eightieth anniversary of the Budapest Phil-
        harmonic Society.

1953   Albert Coates dies in Milnerton, South Africa, at age seventy-
        one; he was conductor of the Johannesburg Symphony Orches-
        tra.

1955   Felix Labunski's <u>Elegy,</u> for orchestra, is first performed in
        Cincinnati.

1959   Henri Dutilleux's Symphony no. 2 receives its premiere, in
        Boston.

1962   Jess Thomas sings in <u>Die Meistersinger</u> in his Metropolitan
        Opera debut.

1967 Victor De Sabata dies in Santa Margherita Ligure, Italy, aged seventy-five. He was regarded as one of the finest conductors of Verdi's operas.

1969 Bernd Alois Zimmermann's <u>Requiem für einen jungen Dichter</u>, to texts of poems, articles, and news reports about suicides, is first performed in Düsseldorf. Soon after, he took his own life.

1978 Elliott Carter is honored on his seventieth birthday when New York's Mayor Edward Koch presents to him the Handel Medallion (the city's highest cultural honor).

DECEMBER 12

1857 Lillian Nordica (née Lillian Norton), American soprano, is born in Farmington, Maine. She changed her name to Nordica before her operatic debut in Italy.

1887 Kurt Atterberg, Swedish composer, is born in Göteborg. He was one of those who founded the Society of Swedish Composers, heading it from 1924 to 1947.

1903 Francisco Curt Lange, German musicologist, is born in Eilenburg. He emigrated to Uruguay, establishing the Instituto Interamericano de Música and publishing works about Latin-American music.

1909 Anatol Liadov's <u>Kikimora,</u> for orchestra, is first performed, in St. Petersburg.

1929 Constant Lambert's <u>Rio Grande,</u> for solo piano, chorus, and orchestra, is performed in Manchester, England, in its premiere.

1935 Charles Haubiel's <u>Portraits</u>, for orchestra, has its premiere, in Chicago.

1937 Roberto Benzi, French-Italian conductor and composer, is born in Marseilles.

Klaus Hirte, German bass and former toolmaker, is born in Berlin.

1938 Albert Carré dies in Paris, aged eighty-six.

1946 Vincent Persichetti's <u>The Hollow Men,</u> for trumpet and string orchestra, has its first performance, in Germantown, Pennsylvania. ("This parallels the mood of the T.S. Eliot poem ... "--Persichetti).

1948   Hans Werner Henze's Violin Concerto is first performed, in Baden-Baden, Germany.

1957   Robert Kurka dies of leukemia in New York City at age thirty-five.

1960   John Pozdro's Symphony no. 3 has its first performance, in Oklahoma City, Oklahoma.

DECEMBER 13

1785   Pauline Anna Milder-Hauptmann, soprano, the daughter of an Austrian diplomat, is born in Istanbul. Beethoven wrote the role of Leonore in Fidelio for her.

1874   Josef Lhévinne, Russian pianist, is born in Orel. Both he and his wife, Rosina Lhévinne, were distinguished teachers at the Juilliard School in New York and appeared as duo-piano recitalists.

1891   Samuel Dushkin, American violinist, is born in Suwalki, Poland. As a child he was brought to America and adopted by an American composer who trained him in music.

1895   Gustave Mahler conducts the premiere of his Symphony no. 2, "Resurrection," for soli, chorus, and orchestra, in Berlin.

1908   Victor Babin, Russian-American pianist, composer, and duo-pianist with his wife, Vitya Vronsky, is born in Moscow.

1928   George Gershwin's An American in Paris, for orchestra, is conducted in its premiere by Walter Damrosch, who commissioned the work and led the New York Philharmonic Orchestra in New York City.

1930   Igor Stravinsky's Symphony of Psalms, for chorus and orchestra, is first performed by the Société Philharmonic de Bruxelles, Ernest Ansermet conducting.

1931   Harold Owen, American composer and teacher, is born in Los Angeles.

1944   Leonard Bernstein's musical On the Town is first produced, in Boston.

1951   Selim Palmgren dies in Helsinki, aged seventy-three. From 1923 to 1926 he taught piano and composition at the Eastman School of Music in Rochester, New York.

1960   John Charles Thomas dies in Apple Valley, California, aged
        sixty-nine, a member of the Metropolitan Opera staff, 1934-
        43.

1969   Istvån Anhalt's Foci, for soprano, ten instruments, off-stage
        percussionist, and tape, is first performed, in Buffalo, New
        York.

        Arne Nordheim's Colorazione, for Hammond organ, percus-
        sion, and tape, is given its American premiere, in Buffalo,
        New York.

DECEMBER 14

1738   Johann Anton Koželuch, Bohemian composer and choirmaster
        at Prague Cathedral for thirty years, is born in Valvary.

1788   Carl Philipp Emanuel Bach dies in Hamburg, aged seventy-
        four. In 1767 he had succeeded Telemann in Hamburg's
        principal church as music director.

1829   Luigi Marchesi dies at Inzago, Italy, at age seventy-five.

1869   Ludwig Minkus's ballet Don Quixote (after Cervantes) opens
        in Moscow and proves a continuing favorite there.

1873   Joseph Jongen, Belgian composer and director of the Brussels
        Conservatory (1925-39), is born in Liège.

1914   Giovanni Sgambati dies at age seventy-three in Rome; he
        taught piano at the Liceo Musicale for many years.

        Rosalyn Tureck, American pianist and harpsichordist (a
        noted Bach exponent), is born in Chicago.

1918   Giacomo Puccini's three one-act operas, Il Tabarro, Suor
        Angelica, and Gianni Schicchi (known collectively as Il Trit-
        tico), are first staged, in New York City at the Metropolitan
        Opera.

1924   Ottorino Respighi's symphonic poem The Pines of Rome has
        its premiere, in Rome.

1925   Alban Berg's opera Wozzeck produces protests and criticism
        in its premiere, in Berlin's Staatsoper.

1927   Richard Cassilly, American tenor, is born in Washington.

1929   Ron Nelson, American composer and Brown University
        teacher, is born in Joliet, Illinois.

1944   Blanche Thebom makes her first appearance with the Metro-
        politan Opera in New York City.

1945   Tobias Matthay dies at eighty-seven in High Marley, England.

1951   Pedro Sanjuán's "ritual symphony," La Macumba, is first
        performed, in St. Louis.

1968   Margarete Klose dies in Berlin, aged sixty-six.

1975   Ruth Crawford Seeger's Suite for Piano and Woodwind Quintet
        is given its first hearing, in Cambridge, Massachusetts.

        DECEMBER 15

1567   Christoph Demantius, German composer and cantor at Zittau,
        is born in Reichenberg.

1792   Joseph Martin Kraus dies in Stockholm, aged thirty-six.
        Three years earlier he had been appointed court conductor
        there.

1858   Peter Cornelius's opera Der Barbier von Bagdad is conducted
        in its opening by Franz Liszt, in Weimar.   Cornelius com-
        posed many songs as well as writing his own opera libretti.

1889   Karl Johann Formes dies in San Francisco, aged seventy-
        four.

1893   Antonin Dvořák's Symphony no. 9, "From the New World,"
        is first performed by the New York Philharmonic Orchestra,
        Anton Seidl conducting.

1905   Ferenc Farkas, Hungarian composer and professor of com-
        position, is born in Nagykanizsa.

1910   Giulietta Simionato, Italian mezzo-soprano, is born in Forli.

1938   Silvestre Revueltas's Sensemayá, for voice and orchestra,
        receives its premiere, in Mexico City.

1940   Arnold Schoenberg's Chamber Symphony no. 2 is first per-
        formed, in New York City.

1943   "Fats" (Thomas) Waller dies in Kansas City, aged thirty-
        nine, one of the greatest pianists of the swing era.

1945   Robert Merrill begins a long association with the Metropolitan
        Opera as he makes his debut singing in Verdi's La Traviata
        in New York.

DECEMBER 16

1775   François Boieldieu, French composer of comic operas, is
        born in Rouen. His first opera was to his father's libretto.

1783   Johann Adolph Hasse dies in Venice at age eighty-four. Most
        of his manuscripts were burned in Dresden in 1760 during a
        siege, but he never ceased to compose new works.

1798   Gaetano Brunetti, Italian composer and violinist at the Royal
        Chapel in Madrid, dies in Culminal de Oreja, Spain, aged
        about fifty-four.

1877   Artur Bodanzky, Austrian conductor, is born in Vienna.

        Anton Bruckner conducts the premiere of his Symphony no.
        3, which he dedicated to Wagner, in Vienna.

1882   Zoltán Kodály, Hungarian composer, music critic, and folk-
        song collector with Béla Bartók, is born in Kecskemét.

1893   Vladimir Golschmann, French-American conductor, is born
        in Paris. From 1931 to 1958 he led the St. Louis Symphony
        Orchestra.

1894   Emil Nikolaus von Reznicek's opera Donna Diana (for which
        he wrote the libretto) opens in Prague.

1899   Sir Noel Coward, English playwright, actor, and musical-
        comedy composer, is born in Teddington. He dictated his
        songs, since he had no formal musical education.

1915   Georgy Vassilievitch Sviridov, Soviet composer, is born in
        Fatezh.

1921   Sergei Prokofiev is soloist in the premiere of his Piano Con-
        certo no. 3, in Chicago.

        Camille Saint-Saëns dies in Algiers, aged eighty-six. At
        Dieppe in August he had played a program of his piano pieces
        in the Saint-Saëns museum there.

1926   James McCracken, American tenor, is born in Gary, Indiana.

1929   Donald Grobe, American tenor, is born in Ottawa, Illinois.

1932   Rodion Shchedrin, Soviet composer who married ballerina
        Maya Plisetskaya, is born in Moscow.

1944   Glenn Miller dies in an air crash during World War II near
        England, aged forty.

1949   Bernard Wagenaar's Symphony no. 4 is first performed, in
        Boston.

1954   Daniel Pinkham's <u>Concertante no. 1</u>, for violin and harpsi-
        chord soli, strings, and celesta, is given its premiere, in
        Boston.

1965   Tito Schipa dies at age seventy-six in New York City.

1977   Thomas Schippers dies of lung cancer in New York City,
        bequeathing $5 million to the Cincinnati Orchestra, which he
        had led the seven years prior to his death; he was forty-
        seven.

DECEMBER 17

1749   Domenico Cimarosa, Italian opera composer, is born in
        Aversa.

1770   Ludwig van Beethoven, greatest of German classical com-
        posers, is baptized in Bonn; his exact birthdate is unknown.

1811   John Antes dies in Bristol, England, aged seventy-one. All
        of his manuscript compositions are in the Archives of the
        Moravian Church in Bethlehem, Pennsylvania, and Winston-
        Salem, North Carolina.

1862   Moriz Rosenthal, Polish virtuoso pianist and pupil of Liszt,
        is born in Lwow.

1865   Franz Schubert's Symphony no. 8, "Unfinished," is post-
        humously performed in its premiere, in Vienna, with Johann
        Herbeck conducting.

1870   (Giuseppe) Saverio Mercadante dies in Naples, aged seventy-
        five.

1894   Arthur Fiedler, American conductor of the Boston Pops
        (summer concerts), is born in Boston. In 1976 he was
        awarded the Presidential Medal of Freedom.

1926   Alexander Dmitrievitch Kastalsky dies in Moscow, aged
        seventy.

1930   Peter Warlock (Philip Heseltine) dies a suicide, by gas, at
        age thirty-six, in London.

1937   Zinka Milanov makes her American debut in <u>Il Trovatore</u> at
        the Metropolitan Opera in New York.

1938   Risë Stevens appears for the first time with the Metropolitan
        Opera, singing in <u>Mignon</u>.

1978   Don Ellis dies in Hollywood, California, aged forty-five.
        He had studied with Gardner Read and John Vincent.

DECEMBER 18

1737   Antonio Stradivari dies in Cremona, Italy, aged about ninety;
        he was the most celebrated of violin makers, a pupil of
        Nicola Amati.   His finest instruments were made between
        1700 and 1725.

1788   Camille Pleyel, French pianist and son of Ignaz Pleyel, is
        born in Strasbourg.   In 1821 he entered his father's piano-
        manufacturing firm.

1860   Edward MacDowell, American composer and Columbia Uni-
        versity faculty member, is born in New York City.

1869   Louis Moreau Gottschalk dies of yellow fever while on tour
        in Rio de Janeiro; his age was forty.

1880   Peter Ilyitch Tchaikovsky's Capriccio italien receives its
        premiere in Moscow.

1892   Anton Bruckner's Symphony no. 8, "Apocalyptic," is con-
        ducted by Hans Richter in its premiere, in Vienna.

        Peter Ilyitch Tchaikovsky's ballet The Nutcracker is first
        staged, in St. Petersburg.

1913   Saburo Takata, Japanese composer and teacher, is born in
        Nagoya.

1919   Horatio Parker dies in Cedarhurst, New York, aged fifty-
        six.   He was chairman of Yale University's music depart-
        ment from 1894 to his death.

1920   Rita Streich, Russian-German soprano, is born in Barnaul,
        Siberia.

1922   Cesare Valletti, Italian tenor, is born in Rome.

1929   Anton Webern's Symphony for Chamber Orchestra is first
        performed, in New York City.

1941   Darius Milhaud is soloist in the premiere of his Piano Con-
        certo no. 2, in Chicago.

1959   Birgit Nilsson stars in Tristan und Isolde in her Metropolitan
        Opera debut in New York City.

DECEMBER 19

1676   Louis Nicolas Clérambault, French composer and organist, is born in Paris.

1863   Milka Ternina, Croatian soprano, is born in Vezisče.

1888   Fritz Reiner, Hungarian conductor, is born in Budapest. From 1953 to 1962 he led the Chicago Symphony Orchestra.

1894   Paul Dessau, German composer, opera coach, and conductor, is born in Hamburg.

1900   Audrey Mildmay, English soprano, is born in Hurstmonceaux.

1902   Dusolina Giannini, American soprano, is born in Philadelphia into a musical family. Her first studies were at home.

1919   Cleofonte Campanini dies in Chicago, aged fifty-nine. He had been general director of the Chicago Opera Company since 1913.

1922   Howard Whittaker, American composer and director of Cleveland Music School Settlement, is born in Lakewood, Ohio.

1935   Charles Kullman's Metropolitan Opera debut takes place in his role as Faust.

DECEMBER 20

1738   Jean Joseph Mouret dies in Charenton, France, aged fifty-six.

1783   Padre Antonio Soler dies at the monastery of El Escorial, Spain, aged fifty-four.

1823   Franz Schubert's <u>Rosamunde: Incidental Music,</u> written in five days for the drama, accompanies its opening at Vienna's Theater an der Wien.

1871   Henry Hadley, American composer and conductor, is born in Somerville, Massachusetts.

1877   Emil Cooper, Russian conductor, is born in Kherson, Ukraine. He led opera groups throughout the world.

1928   Ernest Bloch's symphonic poem <u>America</u> is given its premiere in New York City.

1938   John Harbison, American composer and professor of music at the Massachusetts Institute of Technology in Cambridge, is born in Orange, New Jersey.

1951   Rev. Edmund Horace Fellowes dies in Windsor, England, aged eighty-one.   He published a number of works on early English music.

1973   M. William Karlins's <u>Concert Music V,</u> for orchestra, is first performed, in Chicago.

1974   André Jolivet dies at sixty-nine in Paris.   Along with Messiaen, Milhaud, and others, he wrote for the electronic instrument known as "Ondes Martenot" (named for inventor Maurice Martenot).

DECEMBER 21

1826   Ernst Pauer, Austrian pianist and arranger, is born in Vienna.   He published in English works on piano playing and musical form.

1890   Niels Gade dies at seventy-three in Copenhagen; he is regarded as the founder of the modern Scandinavian school of composition.

1896   Leroy Robertson, American composer, is born in Fountain Green, Utah.   From 1948 to 1963 he was music-department head at the University of Utah.

1899   Charles Lamoureux dies in Paris, aged sixty-five, remembered for conducting contemporary compositions.

1925   André Turp, Canadian tenor, is born in Montreal.

1928   Bruno Prevedi, Italian tenor, is born in Mantua.

1931   David N. Baker, American composer, editor, and writer, is born in Indianapolis.

1944   Michael Tilson Thomas, American conductor, is born in Hollywood, California.

1957   Eric Coates dies in Chichester, England, aged seventy-one.

DECEMBER 22

1808   Ludwig van Beethoven conducts the premieres of his Symphonies no. 5 and no. 6 "Pastoral," and his <u>Choral Fantasia,</u> and performs as soloist in his Piano Concerto no. 4 in Vienna's Theater an der Wien in a poorly attended all-Beethoven concert that lasts four hours.

1821   Giovanni Bottesini, Italian double-bass virtuoso, composer, and conductor, is born in Crema.

1853   Teresa Carreño, Venezuelan-born piano virtuoso and teacher (Edward MacDowell a pupil), is born in Caracas. One of her four brief marriages was to pianist Eugène d'Albert.

Edouard De Reszke, Polish bass, a brother to tenor Jean and soprano Josephine, is born in Warsaw.

1858   Giacomo Puccini, Italian opera composer, is born into a family of musicians in Lucca.

1874   Johann Peter Pixis dies at age eighty-six in Baden-Baden, Germany, where he had gone to teach in 1845.

Franz Schmidt, Austrian composer and cello and piano teacher, is born in Pressburg.

1875   Ignaz Brüll's opera <u>Das goldene Kreuz</u> is first staged, in Berlin.

1883   Edgard Varèse, French-American composer of electronic music who organized the New Symphony Orchestra to perform modern works, is born in Paris.

1885   Deems Taylor, American composer, music critic, writer, and president for several years of ASCAP (American Society of Composers, Authors and Publishers), is born in New York City.

1900   Alan Bush, English composer and Communist worker whose operas concern social revolt, is born in Dulwich.

1901   André Kostelanetz, Russian-American conductor and arranger, is born in St. Petersburg. He married soprano Lily Pons in 1938.

1916   Fernando Corena, Swiss bass, is born in Geneva.

1921   Robert Kurka, American composer, is born in Cicero, Illinois.

1923   Arthur Bird dies at sixty-seven in Berlin, a correspondent there for American music periodicals.

1935   Sophie Braslau dies in New York City, aged forty-three.

1941   Leopoldo Mugnone dies in Naples, aged eighty-three.

1950   Walter Damrosch dies at age eighty-eight in New York City,
        the recipient of many outstanding awards.

1965   Montserrat Caballé makes her first appearance with the Metro-
        politan Opera in New York City.

DECEMBER 23

1689   Joseph Bodin de Boismortier, French composer, is born in
        Thionville.

1806   Ludwig van Beethoven's Violin Concerto is performed in its
        premiere by violinist Franz Clement (for whom Beethoven
        wrote it), in Vienna.

1880   Antonin Dvořák's Stabat Mater, a memorial to his small
        daughter, is first performed, in Prague.

1893   Engelbert Humperdinck's fairy-tale opera Hansel and Gretel
        is first staged in Weimar.   The librettist is Adelheid Wette,
        sister of the composer.

1894   Claude Debussy's Prélude à l'après-midi d'un faune (after
        Mallarmé) is conducted in its premiere by Gustave Doret in
        Paris.

1906   Ross Lee Finney, American composer and educator who was
        awarded a Purple Heart in World War II, is born in Wells,
        Minnesota.

1911   Ermanno Wolf-Ferrari's opera The Jewels of the Madonna is
        first produced in Berlin.

1912   Josef Greindl, German bass, is born in Munich.

1924   Nicolae Bretan's opera Golem (in Hungarian) opens in Cluj,
        Rumania.

1925   Gerhard Wuensch, Austrian-Canadian composer and teacher
        at the University of Western Ontario, is born in Vienna.

1974   Gerardo Rusconi dies at age fifty-two in Milan.

DECEMBER 24

1453   John Dunstable, regarded as the most important English com-
       poser of the fifteenth century, dies in London, aged about
       sixty-five. For more than twenty years he was canon at
       Hereford Cathedral.

1773   Joseph Woelfl, Austrian pianist and composer, is born in
       Salzburg. Leopold Mozart was his mentor there.

1812   Henry Russell, English popular-song composer, singer, and
       organist, is born in Sheerness.

1824   Peter Cornelius, German composer, harmony professor, and
       writer on music, is born in Mainz.

1871   Giuseppe Verdi's opera Aïda is first produced in Cairo's
       Khedival Theater. Verdi did not attend the premiere.

1874   Adamo Didur, Polish bass, is born at Sanok.

1881   Charles Wakefield Cadman, American composer, choral con-
       ductor, and organist, is born in Johnstown, Pennsylvania. His
       best-remembered song is At Dawning.

1887   Lucretia Bori, Spanish soprano, is born in Valencia.

1920   Enrico Caruso appears in his last opera performance at the
       Metropolitan. Two weeks earlier a throat hemorrhage ne-
       cessitated efforts to arrest pleurisy, but months later he
       succumbed to the illness.

1924   Zara Nelsova, Canadian cellist and wife of pianist Grant
       Johannesen, is born in Winnipeg.

1927   Teresa Stich-Randall, American soprano, is born in West
       Hartford, Connecticut.

1929   Noel Da Costa, Nigerian-American composer, teacher, and
       violinist, is born in Lagos.

1930   Oskar Nedbal dies a suicide in Zagreb, at age fifty-six.

1931   Mauricio Kagel, Argentine-German composer and conductor,
       is born in Buenos Aires.

1935   Alban Berg dies in Vienna, aged fifty.

1951   Gian Carlo Menotti's television opera Amahl and the Night
       Visitors is first produced on NBC, becoming an annual Christ-
       mas-time event.

1961   John La Montaine's Christmas pageant Novellis, Novellis is first staged in Washington Cathedral.

1967   John La Montaine's opera The Shepherdes Playe is first per-
        formed for television, in Washington.

1975   Bernard Herrmann dies in Los Angeles, aged sixty-four.

DECEMBER 25

1583   Orlando Gibbons, English composer and organist of the
        Chapel Royal and Westminster Abbey, is baptized in Oxford.

1728   Johann Adam Hiller, German composer and singing-school
        founder, is born in Wendisch-Ossig.

1734   Johann Sebastian Bach's Christmas Oratorio is first per-
        formed in Leipzig.

1845   Wilhelm Friedrich Ernst Bach, last male descendent of
        J.S. Bach, dies in Berlin at age eighty-six.

1859   Raoul Gunsbourg, Rumanian-French impressario (with the
        Monte Carlo Opera), is born in Bucharest.

1870   Richard Wagner conducts his Siegfried Idyll in his Swiss
        villa on Christmas morning as a thirty-third birthday sur-
        prise for his wife, Cosima. It is a tribute to the birth of
        their small son, Siegfried, as well.

1874   Lina Cavalieri, Italian soprano, is born in Viterbo.

1876   Giuseppe De Luca, Italian baritone, is born in Rome.

1886   Edward "Kid" Ory, American jazz trombonist and composer,
        is born in La Place, Louisiana.

1900   Gladys Swarthout, American mezzo-soprano, is born in
        Deepwater, Missouri.

1907   Cab Calloway, American jazz singer who compiled a Hep-
        ster's Dictionary of jazz terms, is born in Rochester, New
        York.

1917   Jack Lowe, American duo-pianist with Arthur Whittemore,
        is born in Aurora, Colorado.

1923   Louis Lane, American conductor, is born in Eagle Pass,
        Texas. In 1959 he became director of Akron (Ohio) Sym-
        phony Orchestra.

1927   Bethany Beardslee, American soprano, is born in Lansing, Michigan.

1932   Bonaldo Giaiotti, Italian bass, is born in Ziracco.

1933   Morris Knight, American composer and educator, is born in Charleston, South Carolina.

1937   Arturo Toscanini conducts the inaugural concert of the NBC Symphony Orchestra, formed for him from a radio orchestra, and begins a sixteen-year directorship.

1969   John Henry Antill's opera The First Christmas, commissioned by the government of New South Wales, is first performed by the Australian Broadcasting Corporation.

1979   Hilde Somer, known for her playing of modern piano music, dies in the Bahamas, aged forty-nine.

DECEMBER 26

1696   Antonio Maria Bononcini's best-known opera, Il trionfo di Camilla, is first staged in Naples.

1709   George Frideric Handel's second Italian opera, Agrippina, brings him recognition and fortune at its premiere in Venice.

1736   Antonio Caldara, Italian cellist and composer of much sacred music, dies in Vienna, aged about sixty-six. His works also include many operas and chamber music.

        Antonio Vivaldi writes Marquis Guido Bentivoglio a letter to ask him if "His Excellency still takes pleasure in playing the mandolin." Vivaldi is the first to compose concerti for this instrument.

1767   Christoph Willibald Gluck's opera Alceste is first produced in Vienna. Gluck later acknowledged his debt to his librettist, Ranieri Calzabigi, for his inspiration.

1793   Franz Hünten, German pianist and composer of much salon music for piano, is born in Coblentz.

1830   Gaetano Donizetti's opera Anna Bolena opens in Milan's Teatro Carcano in its premiere.

1831   Vincenzo Bellini's Norma, which he considered his greatest opera, is first staged at Milan's La Scala.

1833   Gaetano Donizetti's opera Lucretia Borgia is first produced in Milan.

1867   Georges Bizet's opera La jolie fille de Perth opens at the
        Théâtre-Lyrique in Paris.

1879   Armen Tigranian, Armenian composer and pedagogue, is born
        in Alexandropol.

1926   Earle Brown, American composer, is born in Lunenburg,
        Massachusetts.

        Bain Murray, American composer, musicologist, and pro-
        fessor at Cleveland State University, is born in Evanston,
        Illinois.

        Jean Sibelius's symphonic poem Tapiola, commissioned and
        conducted by Walter Damrosch, is first performed by the
        New York Symphony Society.

1936   The Palestine Symphony Orchestra plays its inaugural con-
        cert in Tel Aviv under the direction of Arturo Toscanini.

1941   Robert Russell Bennett's Violin Concerto is first heard on
        an NBC broadcast.

1942   Adriana Maliponte, operatic soprano, is born in Italy.

1974   Robert L. Sanders dies in Delray Beach, Florida, aged
        sixty-eight.   From 1947 to 1973 he taught at Brooklyn College
        of Music.

        DECEMBER 27

1892   Felix Labunski, Polish-American composer and teacher, is
        born in Ksawerynów.   From 1945 to 1964 he taught in Cin-
        cinnati.

1899   Antonio Scotti sings in Don Giovanni in his American debut
        at the Metropolitan Opera in New York.

1906   Oscar Levant, American pianist, composer, humorous enter-
        tainer, and writer, is born in Pittsburgh.

        Florent Schmitt's Psalm XLVII, for soprano, chorus, orches-
        tra, and organ, receives its premiere in Paris.

1907   Willem van Otterloo, Dutch conductor, is born in Winter-
        swijk.

1911   Luisa Tetrazzini makes her Metropolitan Opera debut singing
        in Lucia di Lammermoor.   The famous sextet had to be re-
        peated.

1912   Frieda Hempel makes her American appearance starring in
        Les Huguenots at the Metropolitan Opera in New York.

1933   Emanuel List performs in Tannhäuser in his first Metro-
        politan Opera appearance and marks his American debut.

1944   Amy Marcy Cheney Beach (Mrs. H. H. A.) dies in New
        York City at the age of seventy-seven.

1946   Charles Munch's American conducting debut is with the Bos-
        ton Symphony Orchestra.

1954   Gian Carlo Menotti's Pulitzer Prize-winning opera The Saint
        of Bleecker Street is first produced in New York City.

1964   Cornell MacNeil leaves the stage during an opera performance
        to protest audience behavior, causing an uproar and a fight
        with the manager, in Parma, Italy.

DECEMBER 28

1812   Julius Rietz, German conductor, cellist, composer, and
        editor, is born in Berlin.

1850   Francesco Tamagno, Italian operatic tenor, is born in Turin.

1896   Roger Sessions, American composer and professor, is born
        in Brooklyn. His students include David Diamond, Milton
        Babbitt, Leon Kirchner, and Paul Bowles.

1905   Earl "Fatha" Hines, American jazz pianist with Louis Arm-
        strong's band, is born in Duquesne, Pennsylvania.

        Franz Lehár's operetta The Merry Widow is first produced
        in Vienna.

1927   Helmut Barbe, German composer (principally of sacred works)
        and choral conductor, is born in Halle.

1937   Maurice Ravel dies in Paris, at age sixty-two, following
        brain surgery. He never married, living quietly and spend-
        ing his life in composition. His ballets for Diaghilev brought
        him fame.

1939   Helen Traubel appears for the first time with the Metro-
        politan Opera in New York, singing in Die Walküre.

1944   Miklós Rózsa's Concerto for String Orchestra receives its
        premiere performance in Los Angeles.

1946   Carrie Jacobs Bond dies in Glendale, California, aged eighty-four.

1963   Paul Hindemith dies at age sixty-eight in Frankfurt, Germany. He had difficulty with Nazi authorities because his wife was part Jewish, so for many years he lived in the United States, becoming a citizen.

DECEMBER 29

1825   Giovanni Giuseppe Cambini dies in a poorhouse in Bicêtre, France, at age seventy-nine.

1876   Pablo Casals, Spanish cello virtuoso, conductor, and composer, is born in Vendrell, Catalonia. With the defeat of the Loyalists in the Spanish Civil War, he exiled himself voluntarily.

1911   The San Francisco Symphony Orchestra presents its first concert.

1912   Peggy Glanville-Hicks, Australian composer and music critic for ten years with the New York Herald Tribune, is born in Melbourne.

1919   Roman Vlad, Rumanian-Italian composer and biographer of Stravinsky, is born in Cernauti.

1921   Marcel Bitsch, French composer, twice winner of the Prix de Rome, is born in Paris.

1949   Mark Bucci's one-act opera The Boor (after Chekhov) has its premiere, in New York City.

1953   Mark Bucci's opera The Thirteen Clocks (after Thurber) opens in New York City.

1962   Hans Rosbaud, a conductor known for his performance of modern works, dies in Lugano, Italy, aged sixty-seven.

1963   John Hollingsworth dies in London at age forty-seven.

1965   Zubin Mehta conducts his first Metropolitan Opera performance.

1967   Paul Whiteman dies in Doylestown, Pennsylvania, aged seventy-seven.

1976   The Spanish Government under King Juan Carlos issues a postage stamp in honor of Pablo Casals's centenary.

DECEMBER 30

1678   William Croft, English organist at Westminster Abbey and
        composer, is baptized in Nether Ettington.

1756   Paul Wranitzky, Moravian violinist and composer, is born
        in Neureisch.

1853   André Messager, French composer and conductor, is born
        in Montluçon.

1859   Joseph Bohuslav Foerster, Czech composer and organist,
        teacher of many Czech composers, is born in Prague.

1877   Johannes Brahms's Symphony no. 2 is conducted by Hans
        Richter in its premiere in Vienna.

1880   Alfred Einstein, German-American musicologist and Smith
        College professor, is born in Munich. Scientist Albert
        Einstein was his cousin.

1884   Anton Bruckner's Symphony no. 7 has its premiere in Leip-
        zig, Arthur Nikisch conducting.

1904   Dmitri Kabalevsky, Soviet composer and pianist, is born in
        St. Petersburg. His operas follow Soviet ideology.

1910   Paul Bowles, American composer and novelist, is born in
        New York City.

1915   Alexander Borodin's opera Prince Igor is sung in Italian in
        its New York premiere.

1919   David Willcocks, English conductor and director of the Royal
        College of Music, is born in Newquay.

1921   Sergei Prokofiev conducts the premiere of his opera The Love
        for Three Oranges, in Chicago.

1943   Aram Khachaturian's Symphony no. 2 has its premiere, in Mos-
        cow.

1944   Romain Rolland dies in Vézelay, France, aged seventy-eight,
        a Nobel Prize-winner in literature and a biographer of
        Beethoven and Handel.

1946   Charles Wakefield Cadman dies at sixty-five in Los Angeles.

1969   José Echaniz dies in Pittsford, New York, aged sixty-four,
        a member of the piano faculty at the Eastman School of Mu-
        sic.

        John La Montaine's cantata Erode the Great has its premiere
        in Washington.

1973   Henri Busser dies in Paris at the age of 101.

1979   Richard Rodgers dies in New York City at the age of seventy-
        seven. Songs from his musicals are constant favorites.

DECEMBER 31

1859   Luigi Ricci dies in Prague, aged fifty-four.

1865   Nikolai Rimsky-Korsakov's Symphony no. 1 (the earliest
        Russian symphonic work) is conducted by Balakirev in its
        premiere, in St. Petersburg.

1894   Ernest John Moeran, English composer, collector, and ar-
        ranger of folksongs, is born in Heston.

1879   Gilbert and Sullivan's operetta The Pirates of Penzance
        opens in London.

1899   Silvestre Revueltas, Mexican composer, violinist, and con-
        ductor, is born in Santiago Papasquiaro. He was Carlos
        Chávez's assistant.

1904   Nathan Milstein, Russian-American violin virtuoso, is born
        in Odessa. He concertized in Russia with pianist Vladimir
        Horowitz.

1908   Marko Rothmüller, Yugoslav baritone, is born in Trnjani.

1929   Alexander Lambert dies in New York City, aged sixty-seven.
        From 1887 to 1905 he directed the New York College of Mu-
        sic.

1950   Charles Koechlin dies in Canadel, France, at age eighty-
        three, a contributor to music journals and Lavignac's
        Encyclopédie.

1954   Peter van Anrooy dies in The Hague, aged seventy-five.

1969   Salvatore Baccaloni who specialized in operatic comic roles,
        dies at age sixty-nine in New York City.

1970   Bruno Maderna's electronic ballet OEdipe-Roi is first pro-
        duced in Monte Carlo.

        Cyril Scott, who wrote that "jazz was the work of Satan,"
        dies in Eastbourne, England, aged ninety-one.

1975   Donal Michalsky dies with his family in a house fire at New-
        port Beach, California; he was forty-seven.

PERSONAL AND CORPORATE NAME INDEX

Abaco, Evaristo Fellice dall': 12 Jul 1675, 12 Jul 1742
Abbado, Claudio: 26 Jun 1933
Abravanel, Maurice: 6 Jan 1903
Absil, Jean: 23 Oct 1893, 2 Feb 1974
Académie de Musique: 19 Mar 1671
Académie des Operas: 3 Mar 1671
Academy of Music, New York: 2 Oct 1854
Adam, Adolphe-Charles: 24 July 1803, 3 May 1856
Adam, Claus: 5 Nov 1917
Adam, Theo: 1 Aug 1926
Adderley, Julian "Cannonball": 15 Sep 1928, 8 Aug 1975
Adderley, Nat: 25 Nov 1931
Addinsell, Richard: 13 Jan 1904, 15 Nov 1977
Addison, John: 16 Mar 1920
Adler, Kurt Herbert: 2 Apr 1905
Adler, Larry: 10 Feb 1914
Adler, Samuel: 4 Mar 1928, 4 Apr 1969
Adolphus, Milton: 27 Jan 1913
Agrell, Johan Joachim: 1 Feb 1701, 19 Jan 1765
Aguilar-Ahumada, Miguel: 12 Apr 1931
Aitken, Hugh: 7 Sep 1924
Aitken, Webster: 17 Jun 1908
Alain, Jehan: 3 Feb 1911, 20 Jun 1940
Alain, Marie-Claire: 10 Aug 1926
Albanese, Licia: 22 Jul 1913, 9 Feb 1940
Albéniz, Isaac: 29 May 1860, 18 May 1909
Albert, Eugène d': 10 Apr 1864, 3 Mar 1932
Albinoni, Tomaso: 8 Jun 1671, 17 Jan 1750
Alboni, Marietta: 6 Mar 1823, 23 Jun 1894
Albrechtsberger, Johann Georg: 3 Feb 1736, 7 Mar 1809
Albright, William H.: 20 Oct 1944
Alda, Frances: 31 May 1883, 15 Apr 1904, 7 Dec 1908, 3 Apr
    1910, 18 Sep 1952
Alessandro, Victor: 27 Nov 1915, 27 Nov 1976
Alexander, Boris: 4 Aug 1905
Alexander, Josef: 15 May 1907
Alfvén, Hugo, 1 May 1872, 10 May 1904, 8 May 1960
Alkan, Charles-Henri: 30 Nov 1813, 29 Mar 1888

Allen, Betty Lou: 17 Mar 1930
Almeida, Antonio de: 20 Jan 1928
Almeida, Laurindo: 2 Sep 1917
Altmeyer, Jeannine: 2 May 1948
Alva, Luigi: 10 Apr 1927
Alvary, Max: 3 May 1856, 7 Nov 1898
Alwyn, William: 7 Nov 1905
Amara, Lucine: 1 Mar 1927
Amati, Nicola: 3 Dec 1596, 12 Apr 1684
Ambros, August Wilhelm: 17 Nov 1816, 28 Jun 1876
Ambroziak, Delfina: 21 Mar 1939
Ameling, Elly: 8 Feb 1938
American Academy, Rome: 4 Oct 1921
American Composers Alliance: 16 May 1938
American Conservatory of Music, France: 24 Jun 1921
American Guild of Organists: 13 Apr 1896
American Music Center, New York: 15 Feb 1940
American Musicological Society: 3 Jun 1934
American Society of Composers, Authors and Publishers: 13 Feb
    1914, 6 Jan 1964
Amirov, Fikret: 22 Nov 1922
Amon, Johann Andreas: 29 Mar 1825
Amram, David Werner: 17 Nov 1930, 11 Apr 1965
Ančerl, Karel: 11 Apr 1908, 3 Jul 1973
Ancona, Mario: 28 Feb 1860, 22 Feb 1931
Anda, Géza: 19 Nov 1921, 21 Oct 1955, 13 Jun 1976
Anders, Peter: 1 Jul 1908, 10 Sep 1954
Anderson, Leroy: 29 Jun 1908, 18 May 1975
Anderson, Marian: 17 Feb 1902, 27 Aug 1925, 9 Apr 1939, 7 Jan
    1955, 22 Oct 1964, 17 Oct 1978
Anderson, T. J.: 17 Aug 1928
André, Maurice: 21 May 1933
Andreae, Volkmar: 5 Jul 1879, 18 Jun 1962
Andrico, Michel: 4 Jan 1895, 4 Feb 1974
Andricu, Mihail: See Andrico, Michel
Angerer, Paul: 16 May 1927
Anglebert, Jean Henri d': 23 Apr 1691
Anhalt, István: 12 Apr 1919, 13 Dec 1969
Anievas, Agustin: 11 Jun 1934
Anrooy, Peter van: 13 Oct 1879, 31 Dec 1954
Ansermet, Ernest: 11 Nov 1883, 20 Feb 1969
Antes, John: 24 Mar 1740, 17 Dec 1811
Antheil, George: 8 Jul 1900, 19 Jun 1926, 12 Feb 1959
Antill, John Henry: 8 Apr 1904, 18 Aug 1946, 25 Dec 1969
Antonini, Alfredo: 31 May 1901
Apel, Willi: 10 Oct 1893
Applebaum, Edward: 28 Sep 1937
Aragall, Giacomo: 6 Jun 1939
Arbatsky, Yury: 15 Apr 1911, 3 Sep 1963
Archer, Violet: 24 Apr 1913
Ardévol, José: 13 Mar 1911
Arditi, Luigi: 22 Jul 1822, 1 May 1903
Arel, Bülent: 23 Apr 1919

Arensky, Anton: 12 Jul 1861, 25 Feb 1906
Argenta, Ataulfo: 19 Nov 1913, 21 Jan 1958
Argento, Dominick: 27 Oct 1927
Arié, Raphäel: 22 Aug 1922
Arkhipova, Irina: 2 Dec 1925
Armstrong, Louis "Satchmo": 4 Jul 1900, 6 Jul 1971
Armstrong, Sheila: 13 Aug 1942
Arne, Thomas: 12 Mar 1710, 1 Aug 1740, 5 Mar 1778
Arnell, Richard: 15 Sep 1917
Arnold, Malcolm: 21 Oct 1921
Arrau, Claudio: 6 Feb 1903, 4 Feb 1924
Arriaga, Juan Crisóstomo: 27 Jan 1806, 17 Jan 1826
Arrieu, Claude: 30 Nov 1903
Arroyo, Martina: 2 Feb 1940
Arutunian, Alexander: 23 Sep 1920
Asafiev, Boris: 29 Jul 1884, 27 Jan 1949
Ashkenazy, Vladimir: 6 Jul 1937
Ashley, Robert: 28 Mar 1930
Asioli, Bonifazio: 30 Aug 1769, 18 May 1832
Aspen Music Festival: 28 Aug 1949
Atherton, David: 3 Jan 1944
Atlantov, Vladimir: 19 Feb 1939
Atterberg, Kurt: 12 Dec 1887, 15 Feb 1974
Atzmon, Moshe: 30 Jul 1931
Auber, Daniel-François: 29 Jan 1782, 29 Feb 1828, 12 May 1871
Auer, Leopold: 7 Jun 1845, 15 Jul 1930
Auger, Arleen: 13 Sep 1939
Auric, Georges: 15 Feb 1899, 19 Jan 1924, 17 Jun 1925, 26 May
    1926, 21 May 1929
Austin, Frederick: 30 Mar 1872, 10 Apr 1952
Austin, Larry: 12 Sep 1930
Avshalomov, Aaron: 11 Nov 1894, 26 Apr 1965
Avshalomov, Jacob: 28 Mar 1919
Ax, Emanuel: 8 Jun 1949

Babbitt, Milton: 10 May 1916, 13 Mar 1976
Babin, Victor: 13 Dec 1908, 31 Aug 1933, 1 Mar 1972
Bacarisse, Salvador: 12 Sep 1898, 7 Aug 1963
Baccaloni, Salvatore: 14 Apr 1900, 3 Dec 1940, 31 Dec 1969
Bacewicz, Grażyna: 5 May 1913, 17 Jan 1969
Bach, Carl Philipp Emanuel: 8 Mar 1714, 14 Dec 1788
Bach, Johann Christian: 5 Sep 1735, 1 Jan 1782
Bach, Johann Christoph: 3 Dec 1642, 31 Mar 1703
Bach, Johann Christoph Friedrich: 21 Jun 1732, 26 Jan 1795
Bach, Johann Sebastian: 21 Mar 1685, 14 Aug 1704, 17 Oct 1707,
    24 Mar 1721, 3 Dec 1721, 26 Mar 1723, 22 Apr 1723, 1 Jun
    1723, 23 Mar 1729, 25 Dec 1734, 7 May 1747, 28 Jul 1750
Bach, Wilhelm Friedemann: 22 Nov 1710, 1 Jul 1784
Bach, Wilhelm Friedrich Ernst: 23 May 1759, 25 Dec 1845
Bach Gesellschaft: 28 Jul 1850

Bachauer, Gina: 21 May 1913, 15 Oct 1950, 22 Aug 1976
Backer-Grøndahl, Agathe: 1 Dec 1847, 4 Jun 1907
Backhaus, Wilhelm: 26 Mar 1884, 5 Jan 1912, 5 Jul 1969
Bacon, Ernst: 26 May 1898
Bacquier, Gabriel: 17 May 1924
Badings, Henk: 17 Jan 1907
Badura-Skoda, Paul: 6 Oct 1927, 10 Jan 1953
Baez, Joan: 9 Jan 1941
Bailey, Norman: 23 Mar 1933
Bailey, Pearl: 29 Mar 1918
Baillot, Pierre Marie: 1 Oct 1771, 15 Sep 1842
Bainbridge, Elizabeth: 28 Mar 1936
Baird, Tadeusz: 26 Jul 1928
Baker, David N.: 21 Dec 1931
Baker, Janet: 21 Aug 1933
Baker, Julius: 23 Sep 1915
Baker, Theodore: 3 Jun 1851, 13 Oct 1934
Balaban, Emanuel: 27 Jan 1895, 17 Apr 1973
Balada, Leonardo: 22 Sep 1933
Balakirev, Mily: 2 Jan 1837, 2 Jan 1859, 19 Mar 1883, 29 May
    1910
Balanchine, George: 22 Jan 1904
Balbastre, Claude: 22 Jan 1727, 9 May 1799
Bales, Richard: 3 Feb 1915
Balfe, Michael William: 15 May 1808, 27 Nov 1843, 20 Oct 1870
Balsam, Artur: 8 Feb 1906
Baltsa, Agnes: 19 Nov 1944
Bampton, Rose: 28 Nov 1908, 22 Nov 1932
Banks, Don: 25 Oct 1923
Banti-Giogi, Brigida: 18 Feb 1806
Bantock, Granville: 7 Aug 1868, 16 Oct 1946
Barati, George: 3 Apr 1913
Barbe, Helmut: 28 Dec 1927
Barber, Samuel: 9 Mar 1910, 30 Aug 1933, 23 Mar 1935, 5 Nov
    1938, 16 Apr 1942, 9 Apr 1948, 9 Dec 1949, 15 Jan 1958,
    24 Sep 1962, 16 Sep 1966
Barbieri, Fedora: 4 Jun 1920
Barbirolli, John: 2 Dec 1899, 29 Jul 1970
Barenboim, Daniel: 15 Nov 1942, 15 Jun 1967
Barere, Simon: 1 Sep 1896, 2 Apr 1951
Barlow, Samuel: 1 Jun 1892, 11 Jan 1935
Barlow, Wayne: 6 Sep 1912, 18 Oct 1938
Baron, Ernst Gottlieb: 17 Feb 1696, 12 Apr 1760
Barraud, Henry: 23 Apr 1900
Barrera, Giulia: 28 Apr 1942
Barrère, Georges: 31 Oct 1876, 14 Jun 1944
Barrientos, Maria: 10 Mar 1884, 31 Jan 1916, 8 Aug 1946
Barshai, Rudolf: 28 Sep 1924
Barth, Hans: 25 Jun 1897, 9 Dec 1956
Bartók, Béla: 25 Mar 1881, 13 Jan 1904, 12 May 1917, 24 May
    1918, 1 Jul 1927, 1 Dec 1944, 26 Sep 1945, 8 Feb 1946, 2
    Dec 1949
Bartolozzi, Bruno: 8 Jun 1911

Barzin, Leon: 27 Nov 1900
Basie, William "Count": 21 Aug 1904
Basiola, Mario, Jr.: 1 Sep 1935
Bassett, Leslie: 22 Jan 1923, 6 Jul 1963
Bastianini, Ettore: 24 Sep 1922, 25 Jan 1967
Bastin, Jules: 18 Aug 1933
Bath, Hubert: 6 Nov 1883, 24 Apr 1945
Battistini, Mattia: 27 Feb 1856, 7 Nov 1928
Baudo, Serge: 16 Jul 1927
Bauer, Harold: 28 Apr 1873, 12 Mar 1951
Bauer, Marion: 15 Aug 1887, 9 Aug 1955
Baum, Kurt: 15 Mar 1908
Bavicchi, John: 25 Apr 1922
Bax, Arnold: 8 Nov 1883, 3 Oct 1953
Bay, Emmanuel: 20 Jan 1891, 2 Dec 1967
Bazelon, Irwin: 4 June 1922, 16 May 1971
Beach, Amy Marcy Cheney (Mrs. H. H. A.): 5 Sep 1867, 30 Oct
    1896, 27 Dec 1944
Beardslee, Bethany: 25 Dec 1927
Beatles, The: See Harrison, George; Lennon, J.; McCartney, P.;
    Starr, R.
Beattie, Herbert: 23 Aug 1926
Becerra, Gustavo: 26 Aug 1925
Bechstein, Friedrich Karl: 1 Jun 1826, 6 Mar 1900
Becker, John J.: 22 Jan 1886, 21 Jan 1961
Beckwith, John: 9 Mar 1927
Bedford, David: 4 Aug 1937, 11 Feb 1973
Beecham, Thomas: 29 Apr 1879, 12 Jan. 1928, 8 Mar 1961
Beeson, Jack: 15 Jul 1921, 25 Mar 1965
Beethoven, Ludwig van: 17 Dec 1770, 29 Mar 1795, 6 May 1796,
    25 Jun 1799, 2 Apr 1800, 18 Apr 1800, 10 Dec 1800, 1 Jul
    1801, 16 Nov 1801, 6 Oct 1802, 4 Apr 1803, 5 Apr 1803,
    7 Apr 1805, 20 Nov 1805, 23 Dec 1806, 15 Mar 1807, 22 Dec
    1808, 24 May 1810, 28 Nov 1811, 12 Feb 1812, 8 Dec 1813,
    27 Feb 1814, 23 May 1814, 7 May 1824, 26 Mar 1827, 29 Jun
    1830, 12 Aug 1845, 4 Feb 1846
Behrens, Jack: 25 Mar 1935
Beiderbecke, Bix: 10 Mar 1903, 6 Aug 1931
Belaieff, Mitrofan Petrovich: 22 Feb 1836, 10 Jan 1904
Bellezza, Vincenzo: 17 Feb 1888, 8 Feb 1964
Bellini, Vincenzo: 3 Nov 1801, 27 Oct 1827, 14 Feb 1829, 11 Mar
    1830, 6 Mar 1831, 26 Dec 1831, 16 Mar 1833, 24 Jan 1835,
    23 Sep 1835
Bellman, Carl Mikael: 4 Feb 1740, 11 Feb 1795
Bellson, Louis: 26 Jul 1924
Ben Haim, Paul: 5 Jul 1897
Bence, Margarethe: 13 Aug 1930
Benda, Franz: 22 Nov 1709, 7 Mar 1786
Benda, Georg: 30 Jun 1722, 6 Nov 1795
Benedict, Julius: 27 Nov 1804, 5 Jun 1885
Benelli, Ugo: 20 Jan 1935
Benjamin, Arthur: 18 Sep 1893, 5 Sep 1950, 9 Apr 1960
Bennett, Richard Rodney: 29 Mar 1936, 10 Feb 1966, 3 Apr 1966, 18
    Jan 1968

Bennett, Robert Russell: 15 Jun 1894, 26 Dec 1941
Bennett, William Sterndale: 13 Apr 1816, 1 Feb 1875
Benson, Warren: 26 Jan 1924
Benzi, Roberto: 12 Dec 1937
Berberian, Ara: 14 May 1930
Berberian, Cathy: 4 Jul 1925
Berezowsky, Nicolai: 17 May 1900; 27 Aug 1953
Berg, Alban: 9 Feb 1885, 14 Dec 1925, 19 Mar 1931, 24 Dec 1935,
    19 Apr 1936, 2 Jun 1937
Berg, Gunnar: 11 Jan 1909, 7 May 1977
Berganza, Teresa: 16 Mar 1935
Bergen Symphony Orchestra: 8 Oct 1765
Berger, Arthur: 15 May 1912
Berger, Erna: 19 Oct 1900
Berger, Karl: 30 Mar 1935
Berger, Ludwig: 18 Apr 1777, 18 Feb 1839
Bergmann, Maria: 15 Feb 1918
Bergonzi, Carlo: 13 Jul 1924, 13 Nov 1956
Bergsma, William: 1 Apr 1921, 22 Jun 1939, 1 May 1942, 20 May
    1950, 18 May 1966, 21 May 1975
Berio, Luciano: 24 Oct 1925, 10 Oct 1968, 12 Mar 1971
Berkeley, Lennox: 12 May 1903, 8 Jul 1943, 9 Aug 1963, 8 Jul
    1968, 9 Jul 1969
Berkowitz, Ralph: 5 Sep 1910
Berkshire Music Center: 8 Jul 1940
Berkshire Symphonic Festival: 23 Aug 1934
Berlin, Irving: 11 May 1888
Berlinski, Herman: 18 Aug 1910
Berlioz, Hector: 11 Dec 1803, 5 Dec 1830, 3 Oct 1833, 23 Nov
    1834, 10 Sep 1838, 24 Nov 1839, 3 Feb 1844, 6 Dec 1846, 10
    Dec 1854, 9 Aug 1862, 8 Mar 1869, 6 Dec 1890, 18 Feb 1893
Berman, Karel: 14 Apr 1919
Berman, Lazar: 26 Feb 1930, 14 Jan 1976
Bernacchi, Antonio: 23 Jun 1685, 16 Mar 1756
Bernoulli, Johann: 7 Jul 1667, 2 Jan 1747
Bernstein, Leonard: 25 Aug 1918, 14 Nov 1943, 28 Jan 1944, 18
    Apr 1944, 13 Dec 1944, 19 Aug 1957, 14 Jul 1965, 17 May
    1969, 7 Sep 1971
Berry, Wallace: 10 Jan 1928
Berry, Walter: 8 Apr 1929
Bertini, Henri: 28 Oct 1798, 1 Oct 1876
Berton, Pierre-Montan: 7 Jan 1727, 14 May 1780
Berwald, Franz: 23 Jul 1796, 3 Apr 1868
Bevan, Maurice: 10 Mar 1921
Beversdorf, Thomas: 8 Aug 1924, 9 May 1954, 17 Mar 1967, 1
    May 1971
Biber, Heinrich von: 12 Aug 1644, 3 May 1704
Biggs, E. Power: 29 Mar 1906, 10 Mar 1977
Billings, William: 7 Oct 1746, 26 Sep 1800
Billington, Elizabeth: 25 Aug 1818
Bing, Rudolf: 9 Jan 1902
Bingham, Seth: 16 Apr 1882, 24 Oct 1946, 26 Mar 1954, 21 Jun
    1972

Binkerd, Gordon: 22 May 1916, 20 Mar 1955, 13 Apr 1957, 6 Jan 1961
Bird, Arthur: 23 Jul 1856, 22 Dec 1923
Birtwistle, Harrison: 15 Jul 1934, 22 Aug 1968, 31 Aug 1970
Bitsch, Marcel: 29 Dec 1921, 28 Nov 1954
Bizet, Georges: 25 Oct 1838, 30 Sep 1863, 26 Dec 1867, 10 Nov 1872, 3 Mar 1875, 3 Jun 1875, 26 Feb 1935
Bjoerling, Jussi: 2 Feb 1911, 4 Jan 1938, 24 Nov 1938, 9 Sep 1960
Blacher, Boris: 19 Jan 1903, 6 Dec 1937, 29 Feb 1948, 15 Sep 1952, 14 Mar 1955
Blackburn, Harold: 21 Apr 1925
Blackwood, Easley: 21 Apr 1933, 18 Apr 1958, 5 Jan 1961, 7 Mar 1965, 18 Jun 1967
Blake, Eubie: 7 Feb 1883, 7 Feb 1973
Blanc, Ernest: 1 Nov 1923
Blanco, Juan: 29 Jun 1920
Blanzat, Anne Marie: 24 Nov 1944
Blavet, Michel: 13 Mar 1700, 28 Oct 1768
Blazhkov, Igor: 23 Sep 1936
Blegen, Judith: 23 Apr 1941, 19 Jan 1970
Bliss, Arthur: 2 Aug 1891, 10 Jun 1939, 11 May 1955, 24 Jun 1970, 21 Apr 1973, 27 Mar 1975
Blitzstein, Marc: 2 Mar 1905, 16 Jun 1937, 5 Jan 1941, 23 Mar 1946, 25 May 1953, 22 Jan 1964
Bloch, Ernest: 24 Jul 1880, 23 Mar 1917, 3 May 1917, 1 Jun 1925, 20 Dec 1928, 12 Jan 1934, 1 Jan 1953, 15 Jul 1959
Blom, Eric: 20 Aug 1888, 11 Apr 1959
Blow, John: 23 Feb 1648/9, 1 Oct 1708
Blume, Friedrich: 5 Jan 1893, 22 Nov 1975
Blumenfeld, Harold: 15 Oct 1923
Boccherini, Luigi: 19 Feb 1743, 28 May 1805
Boda, John: 2 Aug 1922, 6 Dec 1960
Bodansky, Artur: 16 Dec 1877, 23 Nov 1939
Boepple, Paul: 19 Jul 1896, 21 Dec 1970
Bogard, Carole: 25 Jan 1936
Böhm, Georg: 2 Sep 1661, 18 May 1733
Böhm, Karl: 28 Aug 1894, 9 Feb 1956
Böhm, Theobald: 9 Apr 1794, 25 Nov 1881
Böhme, Kurt: 5 May 1908
Boieldieu, François: 16 Dec 1775, 16 Sep 1801, 10 Dec 1825, 8 Oct 1834
Boismortier, Joseph Bodin de: 23 Dec 1689, 28 Oct 1755
Boito, Arrigo: 24 Feb 1842, 5 Mar 1868, 10 Jun 1918
Boky, Colette: 4 Jun 1935
Bolcolm, William: 26 May 1938, 2 May 1965, 9 Jan 1976
Bolet, Jorge: 15 Nov 1914
Bonci, Alessandro: 10 Feb 1870, 22 Nov 1907, 8 Aug 1940
Bond, Carrie Jacobs: 11 Aug 1862, 28 Dec 1946
Bondon, Jacques: 6 Dec 1927, 30 Oct 1969
Bonelli, Richard: 6 Feb 1887, 1 Dec 1932
Bonnet, Joseph: 17 Mar 1884, 30 Jan 1917, 2 Aug 1944
Bononcini, Antonio Maria: 18 Jun 1677, 26 Dec 1696, 8 Jul 1726
Bononcini, Giovanni: 18 Jul 1670, 19 Nov 1720, 9 Jul 1747

Bononcini, Giovanni Maria: 23 Sep 1642, 19 Oct 1678
Bonynge, Richard: 29 Sep 1930
Bordogni, Marco: 23 Jan 1789, 31 Jul 1856
Boretz, Benjamin: 3 Oct 1934
Borg, Kim: 7 Aug 1919
Borge, Victor: 3 Jan 1909
Bori, Lucrezia: 24 Dec 1887, 31 Oct 1908, 11 Nov 1912, 29 Mar
     1936, 14 May 1960
Borkh, Inga: 26 May 1921
Borodin, Alexander: 12 Nov 1833, 16 Jan 1869, 10 Mar 1877, 11
     Mar 1879, 27 Feb 1887, 4 Nov 1890, 30 Dec 1915
Borodin Quartet: 2 Oct 1964
Bortkiewicz, Sergei Eduardovitch: 28 Feb 1877, 25 Oct 1952
Bortniansky, Dimitri Stepanovitch: 10 Oct 1825
Boskovsky, Willi: 16 Jun 1909
Boston Symphony Orchestra: 22 Oct 1881
Botazzo, Pietro: 5 Dec 1934
Bottesini, Giovanni: 22 Dec 1821, 18 Jan 1871, 7 Jul 1889
Boudreau, Robert: 25 Apr 1927
Boulanger, Lili: 21 Aug 1893, 13 Mar 1918
Boulanger, Nadia: 16 Sep 1887, 22 Oct 1979
Boulez, Pierre: 26 Mar 1925, 18 Jun 1955, 13 Jun 1960, 1 May
     1964, 5 Jan 1973
Boult, Adrian: 8 Apr 1889
Bowles, Paul: 30 Dec 1910
Bowman, James: 6 Nov 1941
Boyce, William: 11 Sep 1711, 7 Feb 1779
Boykan, Martin: 12 Apr 1931
Bozza, Eugène: 4 Apr 1905
Brahms, Johannes: 7 May 1833, 22 Jan 1859, 10 Apr 1868, 3 Mar
     1870, 4 Nov 1876, 30 Dec 1877, 3 Jan 1878, 1 Jan 1879, 4
     Jan 1881, 9 Nov 1881, 2 Dec 1883, 25 Oct 1885, 18 Oct 1887,
     7 Mar 1897, 3 Apr 1897
Brailowsky, Alexander: 16 Feb 1896, 19 Nov 1924, 25 Apr 1976
Brain, Dennis: 17 May 1921, 1 Sep 1957
Brambilla, Marietta: 6 Jun 1807, 6 Nov 1875
Brandt, Marianne: 12 Sep 1842, 19 Nov 1884, 9 Jul 1921
Brannigan, Owen: 10 Mar 1908, 10 May 1973
Brant, Henry: 15 Sep 1913, 6 Feb 1933, 8 Jun 1974, 27 Apr 1977
Braslau, Sophie: 16 Aug 1892, 22 Dec 1935
Braun, Victor: 4 Aug 1935
Bream, Julian: 15 Jul 1933
Bree, Johannes Bernardus van: 29 Jan 1801, 14 Feb 1857
Brehm, Alvin: 8 Feb 1925, 22 Nov 1966
Breitkopf, Bernhard Christoph: 2 Mar 1695, 23 Mar 1777
Breitkopf, Johann Gottlob: 23 Nov 1719, 28 Jan 1794
Brendel, Alfred: 5 Jan 1931
Bresnick, Martin: 13 Nov 1946, 8 Apr 1970
Bressler, Charles: 1 Apr 1926
Bretan, Nicolae: 6 Apr 1887, 2 Feb 1921, 23 Dec 1924, 24 Jan
     1935, 24 Jan 1937, 1 Dec 1968
Brewer, Bruce: 12 Oct 1944
Brian, Havergal: 29 Jan 1876, 28 Nov 1972

Briccetti, Thomas: 14 Jan 1936
Bridge, Frank: 26 Feb 1879, 10 Jan 1941
Bright, Houston: 21 Jan 1916
Brilioth, Helge: 7 May 1931
Britten, Benjamin: 22 Nov 1913, 5 May 1941, 14 Jun 1942, 15 Oct
    1943, 7 Jun 1945, 12 Jul 1946, 20 Jun 1947, 14 Jun 1949, 1
    Dec 1951, 8 Jun 1953, 18 Jun 1958, 30 May 1962, 12 Mar
    1964, 13 Jun 1964, 9 Jun 1966, 4 Dec 1976
Brixi, Franz Xaver: 2 Jan 1732, 14 Oct 1771
Brodsky, Adolf: 2 Apr 1851, 4 Dec 1881, 22 Jan 1929
Bronsart von Schellendorf, Hans: 11 Feb 1830, 3 Nov 1913
Brott, Alexander: 14 Mar 1915, 7 Mar 1950
Brouwenstijn, Gré: 25 Aug 1915
Brown, Earle: 26 Dec 1926, 8 Sep 1961
Brown, Howard Mayer: 13 Apr 1930
Brown, Rayner: 23 Feb 1912
Brown, William: 29 Mar 1938
Browning, John: 22 May 1933
Brownlee, John: 7 Jan 1900, 17 Feb 1937, 10 Jan 1969
Brozen, Michael: 5 Aug 1934
Brubeck, Dave: 6 Dec 1920, 1 May 1971
Brubeck, Howard: 11 Jul 1916, 1 Aug 1956
Bruch, Max: 6 Jan 1838, 2 Oct 1920
Bruckner, Anton: 4 Sep 1824, 14 Sep 1854, 9 May 1868, 26 Oct
    1873, 16 Dec 1877, 20 Feb 1881, 11 Feb 1883, 30 Dec 1884,
    10 Jan 1886, 18 Dec 1892, 8 Apr 1894, 11 Oct 1896, 11 Feb
    1903
Brüggen, Franz: 30 Oct 1934
Brüll, Ignaz: 7 Nov 1846, 22 Dec 1875, 17 Sep 1907
Brün, Herbert: 9 Jul 1918
Brunetti, Gaetano: 4 Oct 1768, 16 Dec 1798
Brunis, Georg: 6 Feb 1900, 19 Nov 1974
Brunswick, Mark: 6 Jan 1902, 7 Mar 1947, 26 May 1971
Bruscantini, Sesto: 10 Dec 1919
Brustad, Bjarne: 4 Mar 1895
Brymer, Jack: 27 Jan 1915
Bucchi, Valentino: 29 Nov 1916, 9 May 1976
Bucci, Mark: 26 Feb 1924, 29 Dec 1949, 8 Dec 1953, 29 Dec 1953,
    26 Mar 1960
Buck, Dudley: 10 Mar 1839, 6 Oct 1909
Budd, Harold: 24 May 1936, 23 Oct 1969
Buketoff, Igor: 29 May 1915
Bull, John: 12/13 Mar 1628
Bull, Ole Bornemann: 5 Feb 1810, 17 Aug 1880
Bülow, Hans von: 8 Jan 1830, 18 Aug 1857, 10 Jun 1865, 12 Feb
    1894
Bumbry, Grace: 4 Jan 1937, 23 Jul 1961
Burgess, Grayston: 7 Apr 1932
Burgmüller, Johann Friedrich Franz: 4 Dec 1806, 13 Feb 1874
Burgmüller, Norbert: 8 Feb 1810, 7 May 1836
Burkhard, Willy: 17 Apr 1900, 18 Feb 1936, 18 Jun 1955
Burney, Charles: 7 Apr 1726, 12 Apr 1814
Burrows, Norma: 24 Apr 1944

Burrows, Stuart: 7 Feb 1933
Busch, Adolf: 8 Aug 1891, 9 Jun 1952
Busch, Fritz: 13 Mar 1890, 14 Sep 1951
Bush, Alan: 22 Dec 1900
Busnois, Antoine: 6 Nov 1492
Busoni, Ferruccio: 1 Apr 1866, 27 Jul 1924, 7 Feb 1966
Busser, Henri: 16 Jan 1872, 30 Dec 1973
Bussotti, Sylvano: 1 Oct 1931
Butterworth, George: 12 Jul 1885, 20 Mar 1914, 5 Aug 1916
Buxtehude, Dietrich: 3 Aug 1668, 9 May 1707
Bybee, Ariel: 9 Jan 1943
Byrd, Donald: 9 Dec 1932
Byrd, William: 27 Feb 1563, 22 Jan 1575, 4 Jul 1623
Byrns, Harold: 13 Sep 1903

Caballé, Montserrat: 12 Apr 1933, 22 Dec 1965
Cabezón, Antonio de: 26 Mar 1566
Cacioppo, George: 24 Sep 1927
Cadman, Charles Wakefield: 24 Dec 1881, 30 Dec 1946
Caffarelli: 12 Apr 1710, 31 Jan 1783
Cage, John: 5 Sep 1912, 15 May 1958, 26 Apr 1959, 6 Oct 1960
Calabro, Louis: 1 Nov 1926
Caldara, Antonio: 26 Dec 1736
Calès, Claude: 20 Apr 1934
Callas, Maria: 3 Dec 1923, 3 Aug 1947, 1 Nov 1954, 29 Oct 1956,
     16 Sep 1977
Calloway, Cab: 25 Dec 1907
Calvé, Emma: 15 Aug 1858, 29 Sep 1882, 29 Nov 1893, 2 Mar
     1904, 6 Jan 1942
Camarata, Salvador: 11 May 1913
Cambini, Giovanni Giuseppe: 13 Feb 1746, 29 Dec 1825
Campagnoli, Bartolommeo: 10 Sep 1751, 6 Nov 1827
Campanini, Cleofonte: 1 Sep 1860, 19 Dec 1919
Campanini, Italo: 30 Jun 1845, 14 Nov 1896
Campora, Giuseppe: 30 Sep 1925
Campra, André: 4 Dec 1660, 14 Jun 1744
Canadian League of Composers: 3 Feb 1951
Caniglia, Maria: 5 May 1906
Cantaloube, Joseph: 21 Oct 1879, 4 Nov 1957
Capecchi, Renato: 6 Nov 1923
Caplet, André: 23 Nov 1878, 22 Apr 1925
Capoul, Joseph Victor: 27 Feb 1839, 18 Feb 1924
Cappuccilli, Piero: 9 Nov 1929
Capuana, Franco: 29 Sep 1894, 10 Dec 1969
Cardew, Cornelius: 7 May 1936
Carewe, John: 24 Jan 1933
Carissimi, Giacomo: 18 Apr 1605, 12 Jan 1674
Carlyle, Joan: 6 Apr 1931
Carmichael, Hoagland "Hoagy": 22 Nov 1899
Carnegie Hall: 5 May 1891

Carpenter, John Alden: 28 Feb 1876, 26 Apr 1951
Carré, Albert: 22 Jun 1852, 12 Dec 1938
Carreño, Teresa: 22 Dec 1853, 12 Jun 1917
Carrillo, Julián: 28 Jan 1875, 4 Mar 1927, 9 Sep 1965
Carte, Richard D'Oyly   3 May 1844, 3 Apr 1901
Carter, Elliott: 11 Dec 1908, 27 Feb 1949, 19 Nov 1953, 6 Sep
    1961, 6 Jan 1967, 5 Feb 1970, 17 Feb 1977, 11 Dec 1978
Carulli, Ferdinando: 20 Feb 1770, 17 Feb 1841
Caruso, Enrico: 27 Feb 1873, 16 Nov 1894, 23 Nov 1903, 24 Dec
    1920, 2 Aug 1921
Casadesus, Jean: 7 Jul 1927, 20 Jan 1972
Casadesus, Robert: 7 Apr 1899, 20 Jan 1935, 25 Nov 1940, 19
    Sep 1972
Casals, Pablo: 29 Dec 1876, 3 Aug 1957, 22 Oct 1973, 29 Dec 1976
Cascarino, Romeo: 28 Sep 1922
Casei, Nedda: 9 Sep 1935
Casella, Alfredo: 25 Jul 1883, 23 Apr 1910, 28 Oct 1921, 19 Nov
    1924, 5 Mar 1947
Cassilly, Richard: 14 Dec 1927
Cassinelli, Riccardo: 27 Feb 1936
Castelnuovo-Tedesco, Mario: 3 Apr 1895, 9 Dec 1928, 12 Apr 1933,
    31 Jan 1935, 2 Nov 1939, 25 May 1961, 16 Mar 1968
Castiglioni, Niccolò: 17 Jul 1932, 18 Oct 1966, 21 May 1971
Castro, Juan José: 7 Mar 1895, 17 Mar 1952, 3 Sep 1968
Catalani, Alfredo: 19 Jun 1854, 20 Jan 1892, 7 Aug 1893
Catalani, Angelica: 10 May 1780, 12 Jun 1849
Cavalieri, Lina: 25 Dec 1874, 8 Feb 1944
Cavalli, Pier Francesco: 14 Feb 1602, 17 Jan 1676
Cazden, Norman: 23 Sep 1914
Cebotari, Maria: 10 Feb 1910, 9 Jun 1949
Ceccato, Aldo: 18 Feb 1934, 5 Nov 1970
Ceely, Robert: 17 Jan 1930
Cerha, Friedrich: 17 Feb 1926
Cervetti, Sergio: 9 Nov 1940, 9 Nov 1970, 18 May 1971
Cesti, Marc' Antonio: 5 Aug 1623, 20 Jan 1649, 14 Oct 1669
Chabrier, Emmanuel: 18 Jan 1841, 4 Nov 1883, 18 May 1887, 13
    Sep 1894
Chadwick, George Whitefield: 13 Nov 1854, 23 Apr 1904, 7 Feb
    1908, 4 Apr 1931
Chagrin, Francis: 15 Nov 1905, 10 Nov 1972
Chailley, Jacques: 24 Mar 1910
Chaliapin, Feodor: 13 Feb 1873, 20 Nov 1907, 9 Dec 1921, 14 Mar
    1929, 3 Mar 1935, 12 Apr 1938
Chambers, Paul: 22 Apr 1935, 4 Jan 1969
Chaminade, Cécile: 8 Aug 1857, 13 Apr 1944
Chamlee, Mario: 29 May 1892, 13 Nov 1966
Chanler, Theodore: 29 Apr 1902, 27 Jul 1961
Charles, Ray: 23 Sep 1930
Charpentier, Gustave: 25 Jun 1860, 2 Feb 1900, 18 Feb 1956
Charpentier, Marc-Antoine: 24 Feb 1704
Chasins, Abram: 17 Aug 1903, 18 Jan 1929, 8 Apr 1931
Chausson, Ernest: 20 Jan 1855, 4 Apr 1897, 18 Apr 1898, 10 Jun
    1899

Chávez, Carlos: 13 Jun 1899, 22 Jul 1930, 31 Mar 1932, 23 Jan
     1936, 1 Jan 1942, 31 Oct 1947, 29 Feb 1952, 11 Feb 1953,
     2 Aug 1978
Cherubini, Luigi: 14 Sep 1760, 13 Mar 1797, 16 Jan 1800, 4 Oct
     1803, 21 Jan 1816, 13 Mar 1842
Chevillard, Camille: 14 Oct 1859, 30 May 1923
Chiara, Maria: 24 Nov 1939
Chihara, Paul: 9 Jul 1938, 14 Apr 1972, 8 Sep 1975, 15 Jan 1976
Childs, Barney: 13 Feb 1926
Chopin, Frédéric: 22 Feb 1810, 17 Mar 1830, 11 Oct 1830, 26 Feb
     1832, 16 Nov 1848, 17 Oct 1849
Chou, Wen-chung: 29 Jun 1923, 19 Nov 1953
Christoff, Boris: 18 May 1914, 25 Sept 1956
Ciccolini, Aldo: 15 Aug 1925, 2 Nov 1950
Cilèa, Francesco: 26 Jul 1866, 6 Nov 1902, 18 Nov 1907, 20 Nov
     1950
Cimarosa, Domenico: 17 Dec 1749, 7 Feb 1792 11 Jan 1801
Cioni, Renato: 15 Apr 1929
Cirone, Anthony: 8 Nov 1941
Civil, Alan: 13 Jun 1929
Claflin, Avery: 21 Jun 1898, 3 Feb 1957, 9 Jan 1979
Clarke, Kenny: 9 Jan 1914
Clementi, Aldo: 25 May 1925
Clementi, Muzio: 23 Jan 1752, 10 Mar 1832
Clérambault, Louis Nicholas: 19 Dec 1676, 21 Oct 1721, 26 Oct
     1749
Cleva, Fausto: 17 May 1902, 6 Aug 1971
Cliburn, Van: 12 Jul 1934, 13 Apr 1958
Cluytens, André: 26 Mar 1905, 4 Nov 1956, 3 June 1967
Coates, Albert: 23 Apr 1882, 11 Dec 1953
Coates, Eric: 27 Aug 1886, 21 Dec 1957
Coelho, Ruy: 3 Mar 1891
Coertse, Mimi: 12 Jun 1932
Cohan, George M.: 3 Jul 1878, 5 Nov 1942, 3 Jul 1978
Cohn, Arthur: 6 Nov 1910
Colbran, Isabella: 2 Feb 1785, 7 Oct 1845
Cole, Nat "King": 17 Mar 1917, 15 Feb 1965
Coleman, Ornette: 9 Mar 1930
Coleridge-Taylor, Samuel: 15 Aug 1875, 11 Nov 1898, 1 Sep 1912
Colgrass, Michael: 22 Apr 1932
Collard, Jean-Philippe: 27 Jan 1948
Colles, Henry: 20 Apr 1879, 4 Mar 1943
Collier, Marie: 16 Apr 1926, 8 Dec 1971
Collins, Anne: 29 Aug 1943
Collins, Anthony: 3 Sep 1893
Colombo, Scipio: 25 May 1910
Coltrane, John: 23 Sep 1926, 17 Jul 1967
Como, Perry: 18 May 1913
Concertbegouw (Amsterdam): 11 Apr 1888
Coniff, Ray: 6 Nov 1916
Constant, Marius: 7 Feb 1925
Conus, Julius: 1 Feb 1869, 3 Jan 1942
Converse, Frederick Shepherd: 5 Jan 1871, 15 Apr 1927, 8 Jun 1940

Cooke, Arnold: 4 Nov 1906
Cooke, Benjamin: 14 Sep 1793
Coolidge, Elizabeth Sprague: 30 Oct 1864, 4 Nov 1953
Coolidge, Peggy Stuart: 19 Jul 1913
Cooper, Emil: 20 Dec 1877, 16 Nov 1960
Cooper, Paul: 19 May 1926
Cope, David H.: 17 May 1941
Copland, Aaron: 14 Nov 1900, 11 Jan 1925, 15 Apr 1931, 27 Aug
     1937, 16 Oct 1938, 9 Jun 1940, 28 Jan 1941, 14 May 1942,
     16 Oct 1942, 12 Mar 1943, 17 Oct 1944, 30 Oct 1944, 18 Oct
     1946, 1 Nov 1948, 1 Apr 1954, 23 Sep 1962
Coppola, Anton: 21 Mar 1917
Corder, Frederick: 26 Jan 1852, 21 Aug 1932
Cordero, Roque: 16 Aug 1917
Corelli, Arcangelo: 17 Feb 1653, 8 Jan 1713
Corelli, Franco: 8 Apr 1923, 27 Jan 1961
Corena, Fernando: 22 Dec 1916, 6 Feb 1954
Corigliano, John: 16 Feb 1938, 9 Nov 1975, 6 Dec 1977
Cornelius, Peter: 24 Dec 1824, 15 Dec 1858, 26 Oct 1874
Cortés, Ramiro: 25 Nov 1933, 9 Apr 1955
Cortot, Alfred: 26 Sep 1877, 20 Oct 1918, 15 Jun 1962
Cossa, Dominic: 13 May 1935
Cossotto, Fiorenza: 22 Apr 1935
Cossutta, Carlo: 8 May 1932
Costa, Mary: 5 Apr 1930, 6 Jan 1964
Cotogni, Antonio: 1 Aug 1831, 15 Oct 1918
Couperin, Armand-Louis: 25 Feb 1727, 2 Feb 1789
Couperin, François: 10 Nov 1668, 11 Sep 1733
Couperin, Louis: 29 Aug 1661
Coussemaker, Charles: 19 Apr 1805, 10 Jan 1876
Covent Garden (London): 15 May 1858
Coward, Noel: 16 Dec 1899, 7 Nov 1928, 10 Jun 1954, 25 Mar
     1973
Cowell, Henry: 11 Mar 1897, 11 May 1941, 10 Dec 1965, 18 May
     1978
Cowen, Frederic: 29 Jan 1852, 6 Oct 1935
Cox, Jean: 16 Jan 1932
Craft, Robert: 20 Oct 1923
Cramer, Johann Baptist: 24 Feb 1771, 16 Apr 1858
Crass, Franz: 9 Feb 1928
Crescentini, Giralamo: 2 Feb 1762, 24 Apr 1846
Crespin, Régine: 23 Feb 1927, 19 Nov 1962
Creston, Paul: 10 Oct 1906, 22 Feb 1941, 27 Jan 1944, 15 Feb
     1945, 14 Jan 1960, 18 Nov 1968, 14 Mar 1976
Cristofori, Bartolommeo: 4 May 1655, 27 Jan 1731
Croft, William: 30 Dec 1678, 14 Aug 1727
Crooks, Richard: 26 Jun 1900, 27 Nov 1930, 25 Feb 1933, 29 Sep
     1972
Cross, Lowell: 24 Jun 1938, 27 Apr 1971, 24 Sep 1975
Cross, Milton J.: 16 Apr 1897, 3 Jan 1975
Cross, Richard: 7 Dec 1935
Crosse, Gordon: 1 Dec 1937, 18 Feb 1968, 11 Jul 1972, 18 Mar
     1976

Crossley, Paul: 17 May 1944
Crumb, George: 24 Oct 1929,   26 May 1967,   31 Oct 1970,   5 May
    1977
Crusell, Bernhard Henrik: 15 Oct 1775,   28 Jul 1838
Cuénod, Hughes: 26 Jun 1902
Cugat, Xavier: 1 Jan 1900
Cui, César: 18 Jan 1835,   26 Mar 1918
Cumming, Richard: 9 Jun 1928
Curschmann, Karl Friedrich: 21 Jun 1804,   24 Aug 1841
Curtin, Phyllis: 3 Dec 1922,   4 Nov 1961
Curtis Institute of Music: 1 Oct 1924
Curzon, Clifford: 18 May 1907,   26 Feb 1939
Custer, Arthur: 21 Apr 1923,   28 Apr 1962
Cuzzoni, Francesca: 12 Jan 1723
Czerny, Carl: 20 Feb 1791,   15 Jul 1857
Cziffra, György: 5 Sep 1921

Da Costa, Noel: 24 Dec 1929
Dahl, Ingolf: 9 Jun 1912,   29 Jan 1955,   7 Aug 1970
Dale, Clamma: 4 Jul 1948
Dalis, Irene: 8 Oct 1929,   16 Mar 1957
Dallapiccola, Luigi: 3 Feb 1904,   18 May 1940,   4 Dec 1949,   7 Jun
    1954,   30 Oct 1970,   19 Feb 1975
Dal Monte, Toti: 27 Jun 1893,   5 Dec 1924,   26 Jan 1975
Damase, Jean-Michel: 27 Jan 1928,   20 Apr 1954
Damrosch, Frank: 22 Jun 1859,   22 Oct 1937
Damrosch, Leopold: 22 Oct 1832,   6 May 1871,   15 Feb 1885
Damrosch, Walter: 30 Jan 1862,   22 Dec 1950
Danco, Suzanne: 22 Jan 1911
Dandrieu, Jean François: 17 Jan 1738
Daniels, Mabel: 27 Nov 1878,   3 Jun 1931,   10 Mar 1971
Danzi, Franz: 15 Jun 1763,   13 Apr 1826
Daquin, Louis-Claude: 4 Jul 1694,   15 Jun 1772
Dargomizhsky, Alexander: 14 Feb 1813,   16 May 1856,   17 Jan 1869
Dart, Thurston: 3 Sep 1921,   6 Mar 1971
Dauprat, Louis-François: 24 May 1781,   16 Jul 1868
David, Félicien-César: 13 Apr 1810,   29 Aug 1876
David, Ferdinand: 19 Jan 1810,   18 Jul 1873
David, Hans Theodore: 8 Jul 1902,   30 Oct 1967
Davidovsky, Mario: 4 Mar 1934
Davies, Peter Maxwell: See Maxwell Davies, Peter
Davies, Ryland: 9 Feb 1943
Davis, Colin: 25 Sep 1927
Davis, Ivan: 4 Feb 1932
Davis, Meyer: 10 Jan 1895,   5 Apr 1976
Davis, Miles: 25 May 1926
Davison, "Wild" Bill: 5 Jan 1905
Dean, Stafford: 20 Jun 1937
Debussy, Claude: 22 Aug 1862,   27 Jun 1884,   23 Dec 1894,   9 Dec 1900,
    30 Apr 1902,   15 Oct 1905,   22 May 1911,   5 May 1917,   25 Mar 1918

De Fabritiis, Olivero: 13 Jun 1904
De Gaetani, Jan: 10 Jul 1933
de Klerk, Albert: 4 Oct 1917
Delage, Maurice: 13 Nov 1879, 19 Sep 1961
De Larrocha, Alicia: 23 May 1923
De Lerma, Dominique-René: 8 Dec 1928
Delibes, Léo: 21 Feb 1836, 25 May 1870, 14 Apr 1883, 16 Jan
		1891
Delius, Frederick: 29 Jan 1862, 18 Jan 1908, 11 Dec 1908, 2 Oct
		1913, 10 Jun 1934
Della Casa, Lisa: 2 Feb 1919
Deller, Alfred: 30 May 1912, 16 Jul 1979
Dello Joio, Norman: 24 Jan 1913, 13 Aug 1948, 9 May 1950, 2
		Oct 1970, 27 May 1976
Del Mar, Norman: 31 Jul 1919
Del Monaco, Mario: 27 Jul 1915, 1 Jan 1941, 27 Nov 1950
de Los Angeles, Victoria: 1 Nov 1923, 15 Oct 1950, 17 Mar 1951
Del Tredici, David: 16 Mar 1937, 7 Oct 1976
De Luca, Giuseppe: 25 Dec 1876, 25 Nov 1915, 26 Aug 1950
Demantius, Christoph: 15 Dec 1567, 20 Apr 1643
Demessieux, Jeanne: 14 Feb 1921, 11 Nov 1968
Demus, Jörg: 2 Dec 1928
Denisov, Edison: 6 Apr 1929, 14 May 1967
De Peyer, Gervase: 11 Apr 1926
De Reszke, Edouard: 22 Dec 1853, 25 May 1917
De Reszke, Jean: 14 Jan 1850, 29 Mar 1901, 3 Apr 1925
Dermota, Anton: 4 Jun 1910
Dernesch, Helga: 3 Feb 1939
Dervaux, Pierre: 3 Jan 1917
De Sabata, Victor: 10 Apr 1892, 11 Dec 1967
Desmond, Paul: 25 Nov 1924, 30 May 1977
Des Prez, Josquin: 27 Aug 1521
Dessau, Paul: 19 Dec 1894, 17 Mar 1951, 28 Jun 1979
Destinn, Emmy: 26 Feb 1878, 16 Nov 1908, 28 Jan 1930
Dett, Robert Nathaniel: 11 Oct 1882, 2 Oct 1943
Deutekom, Christina: 28 Aug 1932
Devienne, François: 31 Jan 1759, 5 Sep 1803
De Voto, Mark: 11 Jan 1940
De Waart, Edo: 1 Jun 1941
Diabelli, Anton: 5 Sep 1781, 8 Apr 1858
Diaghilev, Sergei Pavlovich: 31 Mar 1872, 19 Aug 1929
Diamond, David: 9 Jul 1915, 10 Dec 1936, 28 Apr 1938, 7 Sep 1940,
		24 Nov 1944, 29 Feb 1948, 15 Feb 1958, 1 Apr 1976
Diaz, Justino: 29 Jan 1940
Dichter, Misha: 27 Sep 1945
Dick, Marcel: 28 Aug 1898
Dickie, Murray: 2 Apr 1924
Didur, Adamo: 24 Dec 1874, 7 Jan 1946
Diemer, Emma Lou: 24 Nov 1927
Dieter, Christian Ludwig: 13 Jun 1757
Di Stefano, Giuseppe: 24 Jul 1921
Distler, Hugo: 24 Jun 1908, 1 Nov 1942
Dittersdorf, Karl Ditters von: 2 Nov 1739, 11 Jul 1786, 24 Oct 1799

Dlugoszewski, Lucia: 16 Jun 1931
Dobbs, Mattiwilda: 11 Jul 1925
Dobrowen, Issay: 27 Feb 1891, 9 Dec 1953
Döhler, Theodor: 20 Apr 1814, 21 Feb 1856
Dohnányi, Ernst von: 27 Jul 1877, 1 Oct 1897, 17 Feb 1914, 17
     Nov 1924, 26 Jan 1952, 9 Feb 1960
Doktor, Paul: 28 Mar 1919
Dolukhanova, Zara: 5 Mar 1918
Domgraf-Fassbänder, Willi: 19 Feb 1897, 13 Feb 1978
Domingo, Placido: 21 Jan 1941, 9 Aug 1966
Donath, Helen: 10 Jul 1940
Dönch, Karl: 8 Jan 1915
Donizetti, Gaetano: 29 Nov 1797, 26 Dec 1830, 12 May 1832, 26
     Dec 1833, 26 Sep 1835, 11 Feb 1840, 2 Dec 1840, 19 May
     1842, 3 Jan 1843, 8 Apr 1848
Donovan, Richard: 29 Nov 1891, 22 Aug 1970
Donzelli, Domenico: 2 Feb 1790, 31 Mar 1873
Doppler, Albert Franz: 16 Oct 1821, 27 Jul 1883
Doran, Matt: 1 Sep 1921, 12 Mar 1977
Dorati, Antal: 9 Apr 1906, 28 Oct 1975, 1 Oct 1976
Dorfmann, Ania: 9 Jul 1899, 27 Nov 1936
Dorsey, Jimmy: 29 Feb 1904, 12 Jun 1957
Dorsey, Tommy: 19 Nov 1905, 26 Nov 1956
Dorus-Gras, Julie: 7 Sep 1805, 6 Feb 1896
Dowland, John: 21 Jan 1626
Downes, Edward: 12 Aug 1911
Downes, Olin: 27 Jan 1886, 22 Aug 1955
Downey, John: 5 Oct 1927
Dragon, Carmen: 28 Jul 1914
Drake, Bryan: 7 Oct 1925
Dreyshock, Alexander: 15 Oct 1818, 1 Apr 1869
Druckman, Jacob: 26 Jun 1928, 16 May 1972
Dubois, Pierre Max: 1 Mar 1930, 15 Sep 1963
Dubois, Théodore: 24 Aug 1837, 11 Jun 1924
Duchin, Eddy: 1 Apr 1909, 9 Feb 1951
Duckles, Vincent: 21 Sep 1913
Dudarova, Veronika: 5 Dec 1916
Dufay, Guillaume: 27 Nov 1474
Dukas, Paul: 1 Oct 1865, 3 Jan 1897, 18 May 1897, 22 Apr 1912,
     17 May 1935
Duke, George: 12 Jan 1946
Duke, Vernon: 10 Oct 1903, 31 Jan 1925, 16 Jan 1969
Dukelsky, Vladimir: See Duke, Vernon
Dunn, Mignon: 17 Jun 1931
Dunstable, John: 24 Dec 1453
Duphly, Jacques: 12 Jan 1715, 15 Jul 1789
DuPlessis, Christian: 2 Jul 1944
Duport, Jean-Louis: 4 Oct 1749, 7 Sep 1819
DuPré, Jacqueline: 26 Jan 1945, 14 May 1965, 15 Jun 1967
Dupré, Marcel: 3 May 1886, 30 May 1971
Duprez, Louis-Gilbert: 6 Dec 1806, 17 Apr 1837, 23 Sep 1896
Durey, Louis: 27 May 1888
Duruflé, Maurice: 11 Jan 1902

Dushkin, Samuel: 13 Dec 1891, 23 Oct 1931, 24 Jan 1976
Dussek, Johann Ladislaus: 12 Feb 1760, 20 Mar 1812
Dutilleux, Henri: 22 Jan 1916, 7 Jun 1951, 18 Mar 1953, 11 Dec
     1959, 14 Jan 1965, 25 Jul 1970, 10 Jan 1978
Duval, Denise: 23 Oct 1921
Dvořák, Antonin: 8 Sep 1841, 9 Mar 1873, 17 Nov 1873, 24 Nov
     1874, 23 Dec 1880, 18 Nov 1883, 9 Jan 1886, 15 Oct 1886,
     1 Jan 1891, 11 Apr 1891, 18 Jun 1891, 9 Oct 1891, 27 Sep
     1892, 15 Dec 1893, 23 Nov 1899, 31 Mar 1901, 1 May 1904
Dvořáková, Ludmilla: 11 Jul 1923
Dyer-Bennett, Richard: 6 Oct 1913
Dylan, Bob: 24 May 1941

Eames, Emma: 13 Aug 1865, 13 Mar 1889, 13 Jun 1952
Easdale, Brian: 10 Aug 1909
Easton, Florence: 24 Oct 1884, 13 Aug 1955
Eben, Petr: 22 Jan 1929
Echaniz, José: 4 Jun 1905, 30 Dec 1969
Eckstine, Billy: 8 Jul 1914
Eddy, Nelson: 29 Jun 1901, 6 Mar 1967
Edelman, Otto: 5 Feb 1917
Edison, Thomas A.: 11 Feb 1847, 18 Oct 1931
Edmunds, John: 10 Jun 1913
Effinger, Cecil: 22 Jul 1914, 2 Dec 1952, 21 Jul 1965
Egge, Klaus: 19 Jul 1906, 9 Dec 1946, 7 Mar 1979
Ehlers, Alice: 16 Apr 1887, 25 Feb 1936
Ehmann, Wilhelm: 5 Dec 1904
Ehrling, Sixten: 3 Apr 1918
Eichner, Ernst: 15 Feb 1740
Einem, Gottfried von: 24 Jan 1918
Einstein, Alfred: 30 Dec 1880, 13 Feb 1952
Eisenstein, Alfred: 14 Nov 1899
Eisler, Hanns: 6 Jul 1898, 6 Sep 1962
El-Dabh, Halim: 4 Mar 1921, 5 May 1971
Eldridge, Roy: 30 Jan 1911
Elgar, Edward: 2 Jun 1857, 19 Jun 1899, 3 Oct 1900, 20 Jun 1901,
     19 Oct 1901, 3 Dec 1908, 24 May 1911, 26 Oct 1919, 23 Feb
     1934
Elias, Rosalind: 13 Mar 1933, 23 Feb 1954
Elkins, Margreta: 16 Oct 1936
Ellington, Duke: 29 Apr 1899, 29 Apr 1969, 24 May 1974
Ellinwood, Leonard: 13 Feb 1905
Ellis, Don: 25 Jul 1934, 17 Dec 1978
Ellis, Merrill: 9 Dec 1916
Elman, Mischa: 20 Jan 1891, 10 Dec 1908, 5 Apr 1967
Elmore, Robert: 2 Jan 1913, 9 Apr 1937
Eloy, Jean-Claude: 15 Jun 1938
Elvíra, Pablo: 24 Sep 1938
Elwell, Herbert: 10 May 1898, 17 Apr 1974
Emili, Romano: 7 Nov 1937

Enesco, Georges: 19 Aug 1881, 8 Mar 1903, 4 May 1955
Engel, Carl: 21 Jul 1883, 6 May 1944
Engen, Kieth: 5 Apr 1925
Enns, Harold: 29 Jul 1930
Entremont, Philippe: 6 Jun 1934, 5 Jan 1953
Epstein, David: 3 Oct 1930
Erard, Sébastien: 5 Apr 1752, 5 Aug 1831
Erb, Donald: 17 Jan 1927, 4 Nov 1976
Erede, Alberto: 8 Nov 1908
Erickson, Frank: 1 Sep 1923
Erickson, Robert: 7 Mar 1917
Erkel, Ferenc: 7 Nov 1810, 27 Jan 1844, 9 Mar 1861, 15 Jun 1893
Erlanger, Camille: 25 May 1863, 23 Mar 1906, 24 Apr 1919
Ernst, Heinrich Wilhelm: 6 May 1814, 8 Oct 1865
Escher, Rudolf: 8 Jan 1912
Essipoff, Anna: 13 Feb 1851, 18 Aug 1914
Esswood, Paul: 6 Jun 1942
Estrada, Carlos: 15 Sep 1909, 7 May 1970
Etler, Alvin: 19 Feb 1913, 18 Oct 1962, 13 Jun 1973
Eulenburg, Ernst: 30 Nov 1847, 11 Sep 1926
Evangelatos, Antiochos: 7 Jan 1904
Evangelisti, Franco: 21 Jan 1926
Evans, Bill: 16 Aug 1929
Evans, Geraint: 16 Feb 1922
Evans, Gil: 13 May 1912
Evans, Nancy: 19 Mar 1915
Evett, Robert: 30 Nov 1922, 7 May 1965, 20 May 1971, 3 Feb 1975
Ewald, Victor: 27 Nov 1860, 26 Apr 1935
Ewen, David: 26 Nov 1907

Faith, Percy: 7 Apr 1908, 9 Feb 1976
Falla, Manuel de: 23 Nov 1876, 1 Apr 1913, 15 Apr 1915, 9 Apr
      1916, 22 Jul 1919, 23 Mar 1923, 5 Nov 1926, 14 Nov 1946,
      18 Jun 1962
Farberman, Harold: 2 Nov 1929
Farinelli: 24 Jan 1705, 16 Sep 1782
Farkas, Ferenc: 15 Dec 1905
Farrar, Geraldine: 28 Feb 1882, 15 Oct 1901, 26 Nov 1906, 22
      Apr 1922, 11 Mar 1967
Farrell, Eileen: 13 Feb 1920, 6 Dec 1960
Farwell, Arthur: 23 Apr 1872, 20 Jan 1952
Fasch, Johann Friedrich: 15 Apr 1688, 5 Dec 1758
Fassbaender, Brigitte: 3 Jul 1939
Fauré, Gabriel: 12 May 1845, 21 Jun 1898, 27 Aug 1900, 10 Apr
      1919, 4 Nov 1924
Fay, Amy: 21 May 1844, 28 Feb 1928
Fayer, Yuri: 17 Jan 1890
Feather, Leonard: 13 Sep 1914
Fekete, Zoltán: 25 Jul 1900
Felciano, Richard: 7 Dec 1930

Feld, Jindřich: 19 Feb 1925, 26 Oct 1956
Feldhoff, Gerd: 29 Oct 1931
Feldman, Morton: 12 Jan 1926, 28 Oct 1972, 11 Feb 1973
Fellagara, Vittorio: 4 Nov 1927
Fellowes, Edmund Horace: 11 Nov 1870, 20 Dec 1951
Fennell, Frederick: 2 Jul 1914
Fennelly, Brian: 14 Aug 1937
Ferguson, Howard: 21 Oct 1908
Ferguson, Maynard: 4 May 1928
Fernandez, Oscar Lorenzo: 4 Nov 1897, 26 Aug 1948
Ferrante, Arthur: 7 Sep 1921
Ferrante, John: 24 Jan 1925
Ferrara, Franco: 4 Jul 1911
Ferrier, Kathleen: 22 Apr 1912, 8 Oct 1953
Fesca, Alexander Ernst: 22 May 1820, 22 Feb 1849
Festspielhaus (Bayreuth): 13 Aug 1876
Fétis, François-Joseph: 25 Mar 1784, 26 Mar 1871
Feuermann, Emanuel: 22 Nov 1902, 25 May 1942
Fiala, Joseph: 3 Feb 1748
Ficher, Jacobo: 14 Jan 1896
Fiedler, Arthur: 17 Dec 1894, 4 Jul 1978, 10 Jul 1979
Field, John: 26 Jul 1782, 23 Jan 1837
Finck, Heinrich: 9 Jun 1527
Fine, Irving: 3 Dec 1914, 23 Mar 1962, 23 Aug 1962
Fine, Vivian: 28 Sep 1913
Finney, Ross Lee: 23 Dec 1906, 5 Jan 1962
Finzi, Gerald: 14 Jul 1901, 27 Sep 1956
Firkusný, Rudolf: 11 Feb 1912, 13 Jan 1938
Fischer, Carl: 7 Dec 1849, 14 Feb 1923
Fischer, Edwin: 6 Oct 1886, 24 Jan 1960
Fischer, Johann Christian: 29 Apr 1800
Fischer, Joseph: 9 Apr 1841, 24 Nov 1901
Fischer, Ludwig: 18 Aug 1745, 10 Jul 1825
Fischer, William: 5 Mar 1935
Fischer-Dieskau, Dietrich: 28 May 1925, 2 May 1955
Fistoulari, Anatole: 20 Aug 1907
Fitelberg, Jerzy: 20 May 1903, 25 Apr 1951
Fitzgerald, Ella: 25 Apr 1918
Fizdale, Robert: 12 Apr 1920
Fjelstad, Oivin: 2 May 1903
Flack, Roberta: 10 Feb 1940
Flagello, Ezio: 28 Jan 1931
Flagello, Nicolas: 15 Mar 1928
Flagstad, Kirsten: 12 Jul 1895, 2 Feb 1935, 1 Apr 1952, 7 Dec
    1962
Flanagan, William: 14 Aug 1923, 14 Jan 1960, 31 Aug 1969
Fleisher, Leon: 23 Jul 1928, 4 Nov 1944
Flothuis, Marius: 30 Oct 1914
Flotow, Friedrich von: 26 Apr 1812, 25 Nov 1847, 24 Jan 1883
Floyd, Carlisle: 11 Jun 1926, 29 Feb 1976
Fodor, Eugene: 5 Mar 1950, 12 Sep 1974
Foerster, Joseph Bohuslav: 30 Dec 1859, 29 May 1951
Foote, Arthur: 5 Mar 1853, 8 Apr 1937

Formes, Karl Johann: 7 Aug 1815, 15 Dec 1889
Forqueray, Antoine: 28 Jun 1745
Forrester, Maureen: 25 Jul 1930, 12 Nov 1956
Fortner, Wolfgang: 12 Oct 1907
Foss, Lukas: 15 Aug 1922, 18 May 1950, 7 Oct 1951, 21 Oct 1960,
    31 Oct 1968, 1 Dec 1977
Foster, Lawrence: 23 Oct 1941
Foster, Stephen: 4 Jul 1826, 13 Jan 1864
Fournier, Pierre: 24 Jul 1906
Fox, Virgil: 3 May 1912
Frackenpohl, Arthur: 23 Apr 1924
Frager, Malcolm: 15 Jan 1935
Franc, Tugomir: 8 Feb 1935
Françaix, Jean: 23 May 1912, 8 Nov 1936
Francescatti, Zino: 9 Aug 1902
Franchetti, Alberto: 18 Sep 1860, 4 Aug 1942
Franck, César: 10 Dec 1822, 15 Mar 1885, 1 May 1886, 10 Mar
    1888, 17 Feb 1889, 8 Nov 1890
Franck, Melchior: 1 Jun 1639
Franco, Johan: 12 Jul 1908
Frank, Andrew: 25 Nov 1946
Frankel, Benjamin: 31 Jan 1906, 12 Feb 1973
Frankenstein, Alfred: 5 Oct 1906
Frankl, Peter: 2 Oct 1935
Franklin, Aretha: 25 Mar 1942
Frederick II, King of Prussia: 24 Jan 1712, 17 Aug 1786
Fredericks, Richard: 15 Aug 1933
Frémaux, Louis: 13 Aug 1921
Fremstad, Olive: 14 Mar 1871, 23 Apr 1914, 21 Apr 1951
Freni, Mirella: 27 Feb 1935, 29 Sep 1965
Frescobaldi, Girolamo: 9 Sep 1583, 1 Mar 1643
Frezzolini, Erminia: 5 Nov 1884
Fribec, Kresimir: 24 May 1908
Frick, Gottlob: 28 Jul 1906
Fricker, Peter Racine: 5 Sep 1920, 5 Jul 1950
Fricsay, Ferenc: 9 Aug 1914, 20 Feb 1963
Friedman, Ignaz: 14 Feb 1882, 7 Jan 1921, 26 Jan 1948
Friml, Rudolf: 2 Dec 1879, 2 Sep 1924, 21 Sep 1925, 12 Nov 1972
Friskin, James: 3 Mar 1886, 16 Mar 1967
Froberger, Johann Jakob: 18 May 1616, 7 May 1667
Froment, Louis de: 5 Dec 1921
Fromm, Herbert: 23 Feb 1905
Frühbeck de Burgos, Rafael: 15 Sep 1933
Fuchs, Joseph: 26 Apr 1900
Fucik, Julius: 18 Jul 1872, 25 Sep 1916
Furtwängler, Wilhelm: 25 Jan 1886, 3 Jan 1925, 30 Nov 1954
Fux, Johann Joseph: 13 Feb 1741

Gabaye, Pierre: 20 Feb 1930
Gabrieli, Domenico: 10 Jul 1690

Gabrieli, Giovanni: 1 Jan 1585, 12 Aug 1612
Gabrilowitsch, Ossip: 7 Feb 1878, 12 Nov 1900, 6 Oct 1909, 14
     Sep 1936
Gaburo, Kenneth: 5 Jul 1926
Gade, Niels: 22 Feb 1817, 21 Dec 1890
Gadski, Johanna: 15 Jun 1872, 22 Feb 1932
Gagliano, Marco da: 1 May 1582, 25 Feb 1643
Gál, Hans: 5 Aug 1890
Galindo, Blas: 3 Feb 1910, 19 Mar 1957
Galli-Curci, Amelita: 18 Nov 1882, 18 Nov 1916, 28 Jan 1918, 14
     Nov 1921, 26 Nov 1963
Galuppi, Baldassare: 18 Oct 1706, 3 Jan 1785
Galway, James: 8 Dec 1939, 21 Jul 1978
Gandini, Gerardo: 16 Oct 1936
Ganz, Rudolph: 24 Feb 1877, 2 Aug 1972
Ganzarolli, Wladamiro: 9 Jan 1939
García, Manuel del Popolo: 22 Jan 1775, 9 Jun 1832
García, Manuel Patricio: 17 Mar 1805, 1 Jul 1906
García-Morillo, Roberto: 22 Jan 1911
Garden, Mary: 20 Feb 1874, 10 Apr 1900, 30 Apr 1902, 25 Nov
     1907, 3 Jan 1908, 3 Jan 1967
Gardner, John: 2 Mar 1917
Garner, Erroll: 15 Jun 1921, 2 Jan 1977
Garrard, Don: 31 Jul 1929
Gassmann, Florian Leopold: 3 May 1729, 20 Jan 1774
Gatti-Casazza, Giulio: 3 Feb 1868, 2 Sep 1940
Gaubert, Philippe: 3 Jul 1879, 8 Jul 1941
Gauk, Alexander: 15 Aug 1893, 30 Mar 1963
Gavazzeni, Gianandrea: 25 Jul 1909
Gay, John: 16 Sep 1685, 29 Jan 1728, 4 Dec 1732
Gayarré, Julian: 9 Jan 1844, 2 Jan 1890
Gedda, Nicolai: 11 Jul 1925
Gehrkens, Karl Wilson: 19 Apr 1882, 28 Feb 1975
Gellhorn, Peter: 24 Oct 1912
Geminiani, Francesco: 5 Dec 1687, 17 Sep 1762
Genzmer, Harald: 9 Feb 1909
George, Earl: 1 May 1924
Gerhard, Roberto: 25 Sep 1896, 5 Jan 1970
Gernsheim, Friedrich: 17 Jul 1839, 11 Sep 1916
Gerschefski, Edwin: 10 Jun 1909
Gershwin, George: 26 Sep 1898, 12 Feb 1924, 3 Dec 1925, 13 Dec
     1928, 30 Sep 1935, 11 Jul 1937
Gesualdo, Don Carlo: 8 Sep 1613
Geszty, Sylvia: 28 Feb 1934
Getz, Stan: 2 Feb 1927
Ghazarian, Sona: 2 Sep 1945
Ghent, Emmanuel: 15 May 1925
Ghezzo, Dinu: 2 Jul 1941
Ghiaurov, Nicolai: 13 Sep 1929, 8 Nov 1965
Ghiuselev, Nikolai: 17 Aug 1936
Giaiotti, Bonaldo: 25 Dec 1932
Giannini, Dusolina: 19 Dec 1902
Giannini, Vittorio: 19 Oct 1903, 31 Jan 1953, 28 Nov 1966

Giardini, Felice de': 12 Apr 1716, 8 Jun 1796
Gibbons, Orlando: 25 Dec 1583, 5 Jun 1625
Gibson, Alexander: 11 Feb 1926
Gideon, Miriam: 23 Oct 1906
Giebel, Agnes: 10 Aug 1921
Gielen, Michael: 20 Jul 1927
Gieseking, Walter: 5 Nov 1895, 22 Feb 1926, 26 Oct 1956
Gigli, Beniamino: 20 Mar 1890, 26 Nov 1920, 30 Nov 1957
Gilbert, Henry F.: 26 Sep 1868, 23 Mar 1918, 19 May 1928
Gilbert, William Schwenck: 18 Nov 1836, 29 May 1911
Gilboa, Jacob: 2 May 1920, 24 Jan 1976
Gilels, Emil: 19 Oct 1916
Gillespie, John "Dizzy": 21 Oct 1917
Ginastera, Alberto: 11 Apr 1916, 12 May 1944, 19 Aug 1952, 2 Jun
    1953, 22 Apr 1961, 22 Mar 1973
Giordano, Umberto: 28 Aug 1867, 28 Mar 1896, 17 Nov 1898, 12
    Nov 1948
Giuliani, Mauro: 27 Jul 1781, 8 May 1829
Giulini, Carlo Maria: 9 May 1914, 17 Oct 1960
Glanville-Hicks, Peggy: 29 Dec 1912, 19 Aug 1961
Glass, Philip: 31 Jan 1937, 25 Jul 1976
Glazounov, Alexander: 10 Aug 1865, 19 Jan 1898, 4 Mar 1905, 21
    Mar 1936
Glenn, Carroll: 28 Oct 1924, 16 Aug 1943
Glière, Reinhold: 11 Jan 1875, 23 Mar 1912, 14 Jun 1927, 12 May
    1943, 23 Jun 1956
Glinka, Mikhail: 1 Jun 1804, 9 Dec 1836, 9 Dec 1842, 15 Feb 1857
Globokar, Vinco: 7 Jul 1935, 7 Nov 1965, 30 Apr 1972
Glorieux, François: 27 Aug 1932
Glossop, Peter: 6 Jul 1928
Gluck, Alma: 11 May 1884, 16 Nov 1909, 15 Jul 1914, 27 Oct 1938
Gluck, Christoph Willibald: 2 Jul 1714, 17 Oct 1761, 5 Oct 1762,
    26 Dec 1767, 19 Apr 1774, 23 Sep 1777, 17 May 1779, 15 Nov
    1787
Gobbi, Tito: 24 Oct 1913, 13 Jan 1956
Godard, Benjamin (Louis Paul): 18 Aug 1849, 25 Feb 1888, 10 Jan
    1895
Goddard, Arabella: 12 Jan 1836, 6 Apr 1922
Godowsky, Leopold: 13 Feb 1870, 21 Nov 1938
Goeb, Roger: 9 Oct 1914
Goehr, Alexander: 10 Aug 1932
Goehr, Walter: 28 May 1903, 4 Dec 1960
Goetschius, Percy: 30 Aug 1853, 29 Oct 1943
Goetz, Hermann: 7 Dec 1840, 3 Dec 1876
Gold, Arthur: 6 Feb 1917
Goldman, Edwin Franko: 1 Jan 1878, 21 Feb 1956
Goldman, Richard Franko: 7 Dec 1910
Goldmark, Karl: 18 May 1830, 10 Mar 1875, 2 Jan 1915
Goldmark, Peter Carl: 2 Dec 1906, 22 Nov 1977, 7 Dec 1977
Goldmark, Rubin: 15 Aug 1872, 6 Mar 1936
Goldovsky, Boris: 7 Jun 1908
Goldsand, Robert: 17 Mar 1911, 21 Mar 1927
Goldschmidt, Berthold: 18 Jan 1903

Golschmann, Vladimir: 16 Dec 1893, 1 Mar 1972
Golson, Benny: 25 Jan 1929
Goltz, Christel: 8 Jul 1912
Gomez, Jill: 21 Sep 1942
Goodman, Benny: 30 May 1909
Goodson, Katherine: 18 Jun 1872, 16 Jan 1897, 18 Jan 1907, 14
    Apr 1958
Goossens, Eugene: 26 May 1893, 2 Oct 1930, 24 Jun 1937, 13 Jun
    1962
Gordeli, Otar: 18 Nov 1928
Gorin, Igor: 26 Oct 1908
Gorodnitzki, Sascha: 24 May 1905
Gorr, Rita: 18 Feb 1926
Gossec, François Joseph: 17 Jan 1734, 16 Feb 1829
Gottschalk, Louis Moreau: 8 May 1829, 18 Dec 1869
Gould, Glenn: 25 Sep 1932, 2 Jan 1955, 28 Apr 1957
Gould, Morton: 10 Dec 1913, 9 Feb 1941, 22 Feb 1941, 13 Apr
    1952
Gounod, Charles: 17 Jun 1818, 19 Mar 1859, 28 Feb 1862, 27 Apr
    1867, 18 Oct 1893
Graf, Herbert: 10 Apr 1903, 5 Apr 1973
Graffman, Gary: 14 Oct 1928
Grainger, Percy: 8 Jul 1882, 11 Feb 1915, 20 Feb 1961
Gramm, Donald: 26 Feb 1927
Granados, Enrique: 27 Jul 1867, 28 Jan 1916, 24 Mar 1916
Grandi, Margherita: 10 Oct 1899
Grandjany, Marcel: 3 Sep 1891, 7 Feb 1924, 24 Feb 1975
Grant, Clifford: 11 Sep 1930
Grant, Parks: 4 Jan 1910
Grassini, Giuseppina: 8 Apr 1773, 3 Jan 1789, 3 Jan 1850
Grauer, Victor: 20 Mar 1977
Graun, Johann Gottlieb: 27 Oct 1771
Graun, Karl Heinrich: 7 May 1704, 6 Jan 1755, 26 Mar 1755, 8
    Aug 1759
Green, George: 23 Aug 1930
Green, Ray: 13 Sep 1909
Greenberg, Noah: 9 Apr 1919, 9 Jan 1966
Greindl, Josef: 23 Dec 1912
Gretchaninov, Alexander: 25 Oct 1864, 25 Oct 1954, 3 Jan 1956
Grétry, André: 8 Feb 1741, 21 Oct 1784, 24 Sep 1813
Grieg, Edvard: 15 Jun 1843, 3 Apr 1869, 24 Feb 1876, 4 Sep 1907
Griffes, Charles Tomlinson: 17 Sep 1884, 23 Feb 1916, 28 Nov
    1919, 8 Apr 1920
Grigny, Nicolas de: 30 Nov 1703
Grisi, Giulia: 28 Jul 1811, 29 Nov 1869
Grobe, Donald: 16 Dec 1929
Grofé, Ferde: 27 Mar 1892, 22 Nov 1931, 3 Apr 1972
Grossman, Ferdinand: 4 Jul 1887, 5 Dec 1970
Grove, George: 13 Aug 1820, 28 May 1900
Groves, Charles: 10 Mar 1915
Grüber, Ferry: 28 Sep 1926
Gruenberg, Louis: 3 Aug 1884, 7 Jan 1933, 9 Jun 1964
Grumiaux, Arthur: 21 Mar 1921

Grümmer, Elisabeth: 31 Mar 1911
Guarneri, Giuseppe Antonio: 21 Aug 1698, 17 Oct 1744
Guarnieri, Camargo: 1 Feb 1907, 7 Mar 1941
Guarrera, Frank: 3 Dec 1924
Gueden, Hilde: 15 Sep 1917, 15 Nov 1951
Guest, George: 9 Feb 1924
Guglielmi, Margharita: 26 Oct 1938
Gui, Vittorio: 14 Sep 1885, 16 Oct 1975
Guiot, Andrea: 11 Jan 1928
Guiraud, Ernest: 23 Jun 1837, 6 May 1892
Gunsbourg, Raoul: 25 Dec 1859, 31 May 1955
Gurlitt, Manfred: 6 Sep 1890, 29 Apr 1972
Gutchë, Gene: 3 Jul 1907, 29 Jul 1962, 6 Dec 1963
Guthrie, Arlo: 10 Jul 1947
Guthrie, Frederick: 31 Mar 1924
Guthrie, Woody (Woodrow Wilson): 14 Jul 1912, 3 Oct 1967

Hába, Alois: 21 Jun 1893, 18 Nov 1973
Hadley, Henry: 20 Dec 1871, 23 Aug 1934, 6 Sep 1937
Haefliger, Ernst: 6 Jul 1919
Hageman, Richard: 9 Jul 1882, 6 Mar 1966
Hahn, Reynaldo: 9 Aug 1874, 7 Apr 1923, 28 Jan 1947
Haieff, Alexei: 25 Aug 1914, 27 Apr 1952
Haitink, Bernard: 4 Mar 1929
Haken, Eduard: 28 Mar 1910
Hakim, Talib Rasul: 8 Feb 1940, 10 Oct 1970
Hale, Robert: 22 Aug 1937
Halévy, Jacques François: 27 May 1799, 23 Feb 1835, 17 Mar 1862
Halffter, Ernesto: 16 Jan 1905
Halvorsen, Johan: 15 Mar 1864, 4 Dec 1935
Hambourg, Mark: 12 Jun 1879, 26 Aug 1960
Hamerik, Ebbe: 5 Sep 1898, 11 Aug 1951
Hamilton, Iain: 6 Jun 1922, 16 Mar 1974
Hammerstein, Oscar: 8 May 1856, 1 Aug 1919
Hammerstein, Oscar, II: 12 Jul 1895, 23 Aug 1960
Hammond, Laurens: 11 Jan 1895, 1 Jul 1973
Hammond-Stroud, Derek: 10 Jan 1929
Hampton, Lionel: 12 Apr 1909
Handel, George Frideric: 23 Feb 1685, 8 Jan 1705, 26 Dec 1709,
    24 Feb 1711, 7 Jul 1713, 17 Jul 1717, 20 Feb 1724, 13 Feb
    1725, 5 May 1726, 14 Feb 1727, 16 Apr 1735, 19 Feb 1736,
    15 Apr 1738, 16 Jan 1739, 4 Apr 1739, 22 Nov 1739, 22 Aug
    1741, 13 Apr 1742, 18 Feb 1743, 10 Feb 1744, 27 Mar 1745,
    1 Apr 1747, 9 Mar 1748, 16 Mar 1750, 26 Feb 1752, 14 Apr
    1759
Handy, John: 3 Feb 1933
Handy, W.C. (William Christopher): 16 Nov 1873, 28 Mar 1958,
    17 May 1969
Hanslick, Eduard: 11 Sep 1825, 6 Aug 1904
Hanson, Howard: 28 Oct 1896, 28 Nov 1930, 3 Dec 1943, 29 Feb 1968,

Hertel, Johann Wilhelm: 9 Oct 1727, 14 Jun 1789
Hertz, Alfred: 15 Jul 1872, 17 Apr 1942
Hess, Myra: 25 Feb 1890, 15 Nov 1907, 31 Oct 1961, 25 Nov 1965
Hewitt, James: 4 Jun 1770, 1 Aug 1827
Hibbard, William: 8 Aug 1939
Hiller, Ferdinand: 24 Oct 1811, 10 May 1885
Hiller, Johann Adam: 25 Dec 1728, 16 Jun 1804
Hiller, Lejaren: 23 Feb 1924, 31 Oct 1968
Himmel, Friedrich Heinrich: 20 Nov 1765, 8 Jun 1814
Hindemith, Paul: 16 Nov 1895, 9 Nov 1926, 22 Jan 1936, 28 May
    1938, 28 Dec 1963
Hines, Earl "Fatha": 28 Dec 1905
Hines, Jerome: 8 Nov 1921, 21 Nov 1946
Hirte, Klaus: 12 Dec 1937
Hoddinott, Alun: 11 Aug 1929, 22 Jun 1969
Hodeir, André: 22 Jan 1921
Hodges, Johnny: 25 Jul 1906, 11 May 1970
Hodkinson, Sydney: 17 Jan 1934
Hoffman, Grace: 14 Jan 1925
Hoffmann, Ernst Theodor Amadeus: 24 Jan 1776, 25 Jun 1822
Hoffmann, Horst: 13 Jun 1935
Hoffmeister, Franz Anton: 12 May 1754, 9 Feb 1812
Hofmann, Heinrich: 13 Jan 1842, 16 Jul 1902
Hofmann, Josef: 20 Jan 1876, 29 Nov 1887, 28 Nov 1937, 16 Feb
    1957
Hoiby, Lee: 17 Feb 1926
Holiday, Billie: 7 Apr 1915, 17 Jul 1959
Holliger, Heinz: 21 May 1939
Hollingsworth, John: 20 Mar 1916, 29 Dec 1963
Hollreiser, Heinrich: 24 Jun 1913
Hollweg, Ilse: 23 Feb 1922
Hollweg, Werner: 13 Sep 1936
Holm, Renate: 10 Aug 1931
Holmes, Eugene: 7 Mar 1934
Holst, Gustav: 21 Sep 1874, 29 Sep 1918, 25 May 1934
Holst, Imogen: 12 Apr 1907
Holzbauer, Ignaz: 17 Sep 1711, 7 Apr 1783
Homer, Louise: 28 Apr 1871, 14 Nov 1900, 6 May 1947
Honegger, Arthur: 10 Mar 1892, 11 Jun 1921, 8 May 1924, 12 May
    1938, 27 Nov 1955
Höngen, Elisabeth: 7 Dec 1906
Hoogstraten, Willem van: 18 Mar 1884, 11 Sep 1965
Hopf, Hans: 2 Aug 1920
Hopkinson, Francis: 21 Sep 1737, 9 May 1791
Horenstein, Jascha: 6 May 1898, 2 Apr 1973
Horne, Marilyn: 16 Jan 1934, 21 Feb 1961, 3 Mar 1970
Horowitz, Vladimir: 1 Oct 1904, 12 Jan 1928, 9 May 1965, 8 Jan
    1978
Horsley, William: 15 Nov 1774, 12 Jun 1858
Horszowski, Mieczyslaw: 23 Jun 1892
Hotter, Hans: 19 Jan 1909
Hovhaness, Alan: 8 Mar 1911, 4 Feb 1945, 11 Apr 1967, 11 Jun 1970,
    20 May 1977

Howe, Mary: 4 Apr 1882, 14 Sep 1964
Howell, Gwynne: 13 Jun 1938
Howells, Anne: 12 Jan 1941
Howells, Herbert: 17 Oct 1892
Hubay, Jenö: 15 Sep 1858, 12 Mar 1937
Huber, Klaus: 30 Nov 1924
Huggler, John: 30 Aug 1928
Hughes, Edwin: 15 Aug 1884, 17 Jul 1965
Hullah, John Pyke: 27 Jun 1812, 21 Feb 1884
Hummel, Johann Nepomuk: 14 Nov 1778, 17 Oct 1837
Humperdinck, Engelbert: 1 Sep 1854, 23 Dec 1893, 27 Sep 1921
Hungerford, Bruce: 24 Nov 1922, 26 Jan 1977
Hünten, Franz: 26 Dec 1793, 22 Feb 1878
Hunter, Rita: 15 Aug 1933
Hurok, Sol: 9 Apr 1888, 5 Mar 1974
Husa, Karel: 7 Aug 1921, 10 May 1975, 26 Mar 1976
Hüsch, Gerhard: 2 Feb 1901
Huss, Henry Holden: 21 Jun 1862, 17 Sep 1953
Huston, Scott: 10 Oct 1916, 10 Aug 1972
Hutcheson, Ernest: 20 Jul 1871, 9 Feb 1951

Ibert, Jacques: 15 Aug 1890, 22 Oct 1922, 6 Jan 1924, 30 Nov
      1930, 2 May 1935, 18 Jan 1942, 5 Feb 1962
Ilosfalvy, Robert: 18 Jun 1927
Imbrie, Andrew W.: 6 Apr 1921, 22 Apr 1958, 11 May 1966, 6
      Nov 1976
Inbal, Eliahu: 16 Feb 1936
Indy, Vincent d': 27 Mar 1851, 11 Apr 1884, 20 Mar 1887, 10 Jan
      1897, 7 Mar 1899, 28 Feb 1904, 2 Dec 1931
Infante, Manuel: 29 Jul 1883, 21 Apr 1958
International Mozart Foundation: 21 Sep 1880
International Society for Contemporary Music: 11 Aug 1922, 2 Aug
      1923
Ippolitov-Ivanov, Mikhail: 19 Nov 1859, 5 Feb 1895, 28 Jan 1935
Ireland, John: 13 Aug 1879, 12 Jun 1962
Irving, Robert: 28 Aug 1913
Isólfsson, Páll: 12 Oct 1893, 23 Nov 1974
Istomin, Eugene: 26 Nov 1925, 21 Nov 1943, 15 Feb 1975
Iturbi, José: 28 Nov 1895, 28 Jun 1980
Ivanov, Konstantin: 21 May 1907
Ives, Burl: 14 Jun 1909
Ives, Charles: 20 Oct 1874, 10 Jan 1931, 20 Jan 1939, 5 Apr 1946,
      19 May 1954, 26 Apr 1965
Ivey, Jean Eichelberger: 3 Jul 1923
Ivogün, Maria: 18 Nov 1891

Jackson, Mahalia: 26 Oct 1911, 27 Jan 1972

Jackson, Milt: 1 Jan 1923
Jacob, Gordon: 5 Jul 1895
Jacobi, Frederick: 4 May 1891, 24 Oct 1952
Jadlowker, Hermann: 17 Jul 1877, 13 May 1953
Jahn, Gertrude: 13 Aug 1940
Jahn, Otto: 16 Jun 1813, 9 Sep 1869
James, Harry: 15 Mar 1916
Janáček, Leos: 3 Jul 1854, 21 Jan 1904, 9 Oct 1921, 23 Nov 1921,
     5 Dec 1927, 12 Aug 1928
Janigro, Antonio: 21 Jan 1918
Janis, Byron: 24 Mar 1928
Janowitz, Gundula: 2 Aug 1937
Jansons, Arvid: 24 Oct 1914
Janssen, Werner: 1 Jun 1899
Jaques-Dalcroze, Emile: 6 Jul 1865, 1 Jul 1950
Jarrett, Keith: 8 May 1945
Jelmoli, Hans: 17 Jan 1877, 6 May 1936
Jenkins, Newell: 8 Feb 1915
Jeppesen, Knud: 15 Aug 1892, 14 Jun 1974
Jepson, Helen: 28 Nov 1905
Jeritza, Maria: 6 Oct 1887
Joachim, Joseph: 28 Jun 1831, 24 Mar 1860, 15 Aug 1907
Jobin, Raoul: 8 Apr 1906, 13 Jan 1974
Jochum, Eugen: 1 Nov 1902
Johannesen, Grant: 30 Jul 1921
Johansen, Gunnar: 21 Jan 1906
Johnson, Hunter: 14 Apr 1906
Johnson, James Louis "J.J.": 22 Jan 1924
Johnson, Thor: 10 Jun 1913, 16 Jan 1975
Johnston, Ben: 15 Mar 1926
Jolas, Betsy: 5 Aug 1926
Jolivet, André: 8 Aug 1905, 23 Apr 1948, 30 May 1954, 24 Sep
     1955, 20 Dec 1974
Jolson, Al (Asa): 26 Mar 1886, 23 Oct 1950
Jommelli, Niccolò: 10 Sep 1714, 25 Aug 1774
Jonas, Alberto: 8 Jun 1868, 9 Nov 1943
Jones, Gwyneth: 7 Nov 1936
Jongen, Joseph: 14 Dec 1873, 12 Jul 1953
Joplin, Scott: 24 Nov 1868, 1 Apr 1917, 28 Jan 1972
Jordá, Enrique: 24 Mar 1911
Joseffy, Rafael: 3 Jul 1852, 25 Jun 1915
Josten, Werner: 12 Jun 1885, 27 Mar 1929, 25 Oct 1929, 13 Nov
     1936, 23 Nov 1957, 6 Feb 1963
Joubert, John: 20 Mar 1927, 12 Apr 1956, 11 Jan 1959
Journet, Marcel: 25 Jul 1867, 5 Sep 1933
Juilliard Musical Foundation: 30 Mar 1920
Jungwirth, Manfred: 4 Jun 1919
Juon, Paul: 6 Mar 1872, 21 Aug 1940
Jurgenson, Peter: 17 Jul 1836, 2 Jan 1904
Jurinac, Sena: 24 Oct 1921
Juyol, Suzanne: 1 Jan 1920

Kabalevsky, Dmitri: 30 Dec 1904, 12 May 1936, 22 Feb 1938, 29
    Oct 1948, 1 Feb 1953
Kabos, Ilona: 7 Dec 1902, 27 May 1973
Kagel, Mauricio: 24 Dec 1931
Kahn, Erich Itor: 23 Jul 1905, 5 Mar 1956
Kalabis, Viktor: 27 Feb 1923
Kalinnikov, Vassili Sergeievitch: 13 Jan 1886, 20 Feb 1897, 11 Jan
    1901
Kalisch, Paul: 6 Nov 1855, 27 Jan 1946
Kalish, Gilbert: 2 Jul 1935
Kalkbrenner, Friedrich W. Michael: 2 Nov 1785, 10 Jun 1849
Kalliwọda, Johann Wenzel: 21 Feb 1801, 3 Dec 1866
Kalninš, Janis: 2 Nov 1904
Kanawa, Kiri Te: 6 Mar 1944, 9 Feb 1974
Kanitz, Ernest: 9 Apr 1894, 26 Feb 1964, 7 Apr 1978
Kapell, William: 20 Sep 1922, 28 Oct 1941, 29 Oct 1953
Kapr, Jan: 12 Mar 1914, 6 Mar 1970
Karajan, Herbert von: 5 Apr 1908
Karg-Elert, Sigfrid: 21 Nov 1877, 9 Apr 1933
Karlins, M. William: 25 Feb 1932, 20 Dec 1973
Kastalsky, Alexander Dmitrievitch: 28 Nov 1856, 17 Dec 1926
Katchen, Julius: 15 Aug 1926, 21 Oct 1937, 29 Apr 1969
Katims, Milton: 24 Jun 1909
Kauffmann, Leo Justinus: 20 Sep 1901, 25 Sep 1944
Kaufmann, Walter: 1 Apr 1907
Kay, Hershy: 17 Nov 1919, 7 Sep 1954
Kay, Ulysses: 7 Jan 1917, 31 Mar 1947, 2 May 1951, 31 Mar 1964,
    8 Aug 1966, 14 Mar 1975, 10 Feb 1976
Keats, Donald: 27 May 1929, 28 Apr 1964
Kelemen, Milko: 30 Mar 1924, 30 Oct 1970
Kell, Reginald: 8 Jun 1906
Kelley, Edgar Stillman: 14 Apr 1857, 12 Nov 1944
Kellogg, Clara Louise: 9 Jul 1842, 13 May 1916
Kelly, Robert: 26 Sep 1916, 5 Feb 1963
Kempe, Rudolf: 14 Jun 1910, 11 May 1976
Kempff, Wilhelm: 25 Nov 1895
Kennan, Kent: 18 Apr 1913, 26 Feb 1943
Kentner, Louis: 19 Jul 1905, 28 Nov 1956
Kenton, Stan: 19 Feb 1912, 25 Aug 1979
Kern, Jerome: 27 Jan 1885, 15 Nov 1927, 11 Nov 1945
Kern, Patricia: 14 Jul 1927
Kerr, Harrison: 13 Oct 1897
Kertész, István: 28 Aug 1929, 16 Apr 1973
Kessler, Jerome: 13 Aug 1942
Ketèlbey, Albert W.: 9 Aug 1875, 26 Nov 1959
Khachaturian, Aram: 6 Jun 1903, 16 Nov 1940, 9 Dec 1942, 30 Dec
    1943, 30 Oct 1946, 3 Nov 1962, 1 May 1978
Khaikin, Boris: 26 Oct 1904, 11 May 1978
Khandoshkin, Ivan: 28 Mar 1804
Kibkalo, Yevgeny: 12 Feb 1932
Kielland, Olav: 16 Aug 1901
Kienzl, Wilhelm: 17 Jan 1857, 3 Oct 1941
Kiepura, Jan: 16 May 1902, 15 Aug 1966

Kim, Earl: 6 Jan 1920
Kindler, Hans: 8 Jan 1892, 30 Aug 1949
King, James: 22 May 1925
King, Terry: 20 Aug 1947
Kipnis, Alexander: 13 Feb 1891, 6 Jan 1940, 14 May 1978
Kipnis, Igor: 27 Sep 1930
Kirchner, Leon: 24 Jan 1919, 31 Jan 1952, 16 Feb 1956, 23 Feb
     1956, 28 Oct 1963, 14 Apr 1977
Kirchner, Theodor: 10 Dec 1823, 18 Sep 1903
Kirkpatrick, John: 18 Mar 1905
Kirkpatrick, Ralph: 10 Jun 1911
Kirnberger, Johann Philipp: 24 Apr 1721, 27 Jul 1783
Kirschstein, Lenore: 29 Mar 1936
Kirsten, Dorothy: 6 Jul 1917, 1 Dec 1945
Kjerulf, Halfdan: 15 Sep 1815, 11 Aug 1868
Kleiber, Erich: 5 Aug 1890, 27 Jan 1956
Klein, Lothar: 27 Jan 1932, 4 Apr 1965
Klemperer, Otto: 14 May 1885, 24 Jan 1926, 6 Jul 1973
Klerk, Albert de: See de Klerk, Albert
Kletzki, Paul: 21 Mar 1900, 5 Mar 1973
Klien, Walter: 27 Nov 1928
Klose, Margarete: 6 Aug 1902, 14 Dec 1968
Klughardt, August: 30 Nov 1847, 3 Aug 1902
Kmentt, Waldemar: 2 Feb 1929
Knappertsbusch, Hans: 12 Mar 1888, 25 Oct 1965
Kness, Richard: 23 Jul 1937
Knight, Morris: 25 Dec 1933
Kniplova, Nadezda: 18 Apr 1932
Knipper, Lev: 3 Dec 1898, 30 Jul 1974
Kodály, Zoltán: 16 Dec 1882, 19 Nov 1923, 16 Oct 1926, 28 Nov
     1930, 11 Dec 1936, 6 Mar 1967
Koechlin, Charles: 27 Nov 1867, 31 Dec 1950
Kogan, Leonid: 14 Nov 1924
Kogan, Pavel: 6 Jun 1952
Kogel, Richard: 15 Jan 1927
Köhler, Louis: 5 Sep 1820, 16 Feb 1886
Kohn, Karl: 1 Aug 1926
Kohn, Karl Christian: 21 May 1928
Kohs, Ellis B.: 12 May 1916, 5 Sep 1943, 13 Apr 1957, 19 May
     1970
Kokkonen, Joonas: 13 Nov 1921, 12 Sep 1967
Kolk, Stanley: 6 Apr 1935
Kolinski, Mieczyslaw: 5 Sep 1901
Kollo, René: 20 Nov 1937
Kolodin, Irving: 22 Feb 1908
Komlóssy, Eraszébet: 9 Jul 1933
Kondrashin, Kiril: 6 Mar 1914
Konetzni, Anny: 12 Feb 1902, 6 Sep 1968
Konetzni, Hilde: 21 Mar 1905
Kopylov, Alexander: 14 Jul 1854, 20 Feb 1911
Korngold, Erich Wolfgang: 29 May 1897, 4 Oct 1910, 4 Dec 1920,
     15 Feb 1947, 29 Nov 1957, 27 Nov 1972
Kósa, György: 24 Apr 1897

Kostelanetz, André: 22 Dec 1901, 13 Jan 1980
Kotónski, Wlodzimierz: 23 Aug 1925, 9 Jul 1960
Kountz, Richard: 8 Jul 1896, 14 Oct 1950
Koussevitzky, Serge: 26 Jul 1874, 25 Feb 1905, 23 Jan 1908, 4
    Jun 1951
Koutzen, Boris: 1 Apr 1901, 1 Apr 1927, 22 Feb 1952, 10 Dec
    1966
Koželuch, Johann Anton: 14 Dec 1738, 3 Feb 1814
Kraft, Leo: 24 Jul 1922
Kraft, William: 6 Sep 1923, 13 Oct 1958, 22 Mar 1963, 4 Apr 1968,
    8 Dec 1969
Kraus, Alfredo: 24 Nov 1927
Kraus, Joseph Martin: 20 Jun 1756, 15 Dec 1792
Kraus, Lili: 3 Apr 1905
Kraus, Otakar: 10 Dec 1909
Krause, Tom: 5 Jul 1934
Krauss, Clemens: 31 Mar 1893, 16 May 1954
Krebs, Johann Ludwig: 10 Oct 1713, 2 Jan 1780
Kreisler, Fritz: 2 Feb 1875, 10 Nov 1888, 29 Jan 1962
Krenek, Ernst: 23 Aug 1900, 10 Feb 1927, 5 Nov 1967
Krips, Josef: 8 Apr 1902, 15 Feb 1953, 19 Feb 1967, 13 Oct 1974
Kriukov, Vladimir Nikolaievitch: 22 Jul 1902, 14 Jun 1960
Krogh, Yngvar: 20 Mar 1934
Krommer, Franz: 27 Nov 1759, 8 Jan 1831
Krupa, Gene: 15 Jan 1909, 16 Oct 1973
Kubelík, Jan: 5 Jul 1880, 5 Dec 1940
Kubelík, Rafael: 29 Jun 1914
Kubik, Gail: 5 Sep 1914, 7 Jan 1952
Kucera, Václav: 29 Apr 1929
Kuhlau, Friedrich: 11 Sep 1786, 6 Nov 1828, 12 Mar 1832
Kuhnau, Johann: 6 Apr 1660, 5 Jun 1722
Kühne, Rolf: 11 Jun 1932
Kullak, Franz: 12 Apr 1844, 9 Dec 1913
Kullak, Theodor: 12 Sep 1818, 1 Mar 1882
Kullman, Charles: 13 Jan 1903, 19 Dec 1935
Kunz, Erich: 20 May 1909
Kupfermann, Meyer: 3 Jul 1926
Kurka, Robert: 22 Dec 1921, 23 Apr 1958, 12 Dec 1957
Kurtz, Efrem: 7 Nov 1900
Kurz, Selma: 15 Nov 1874, 10 May 1933

Lablache, Luigi: 6 Dec 1794, 23 Jan 1858
Labo, Flaviano: 1 Feb 1927
Labunski, Felix: 27 Dec 1892, 11 Dec 1955, 9 Feb 1961, 19 Apr
    1974
Lacerda, Francisco: 11 May 1869, 18 Jul 1934
Laderman, Ezra: 29 Jun 1924, 25 Mar 1961, 14 May 1967, 12 Jun
    1967, 10 Apr 1971
LaForge, Frank: 22 Oct 1879, 5 May 1953

Lalo, Edouard: 27 Jan 1823, 7 Feb 1875, 7 May 1888, 22 Apr 1892
Lambert, Alexander: 1 Nov 1862, 31 Dec 1929
Lambert, Constant: 23 Aug 1905, 12 Dec 1929, 29 Jan 1936, 27
    Jan 1938, 21 Aug 1951
LaMontaine, John: 17 Mar 1920, 25 Nov 1958, 24 Dec 1961, 24 Dec
    1967, 30 Dec 1969, 6 Feb 1976
Lamoureux, Charles: 28 Sep 1834, 23 Oct 1881, 21 Dec 1899
Lanchbery, John: 15 May 1923
Landon, H. C. Robbins: 6 Mar 1926
Landowska, Wanda: 5 Jul 1877, 20 Nov 1923, 16 Aug 1959
Lane, Louis: 25 Dec 1923
Langdon, Michael: 12 Nov 1920
Lange, Francisco Curt: 12 Dec 1903
Langlais, Jean: 15 Feb 1907
Lanner, Joseph: 12 Apr 1801, 14 Apr 1843
Lanza, Mario: 31 Jan 1921, 7 Oct 1959
Laredo, Jaime: 7 Jun 1941
Larrocha, Alicia de: See De Larrocha, Alicia
Larsson, Lars-Erik: 15 May 1908
Lassus, Orlandus (Roland de): 14 Jun 1594
Laubenthal, Horst: 8 Mar 1939
Lauri-Volpi, Giacomo: 11 Dec 1892, 26 Jan 1923, 17 Mar 1979
Lauro, Antonio: 3 Aug 1917, 25 Jul 1956
Lavignac, Albert: 21 Jan 1846, 28 May 1916
Lavirgen, Pedro: 31 Jul 1930
Lawes, William: 1 May 1602
Lawrence, Douglas: 26 Sep 1942
Lawrence, Marjorie: 17 Feb 1909, 13 Jan 1979
Layton, Billy Jim: 14 Nov 1924
Lazarof, Henri: 12 Apr 1932, 20 Feb 1962, 12 Sep 1969
Lear, Evelyn: 18 Jan 1927, 17 Mar 1967, 3 May 1967
Lebègue, Nicolas-Antoine: 6 Jul 1702
Leclair, Jean Marie: 10 May 1697, 22 Oct 1764
Lecocq, Charles: 3 Jun 1832, 4 Dec 1872, 24 Oct 1918
Ledbetter, Huddie "Leadbelly": 6 Dec 1949
Leduc, Alphonse: 9 Mar 1804, 17 Jun 1868
Lee, Dai-Keong: 2 Sep 1915, 14 Mar 1952
Lees, Benjamin: 8 Jan 1924, 9 Apr 1959, 22 Feb 1962, 8 Feb 1963,
    2 Mar 1977
Leeuw, Ton de: 16 Nov 1926
Leginska, Ethel: 13 Apr 1886, 20 Jan 1913, 26 Feb 1970
Lehár, Franz: 30 Apr 1870, 28 Dec 1905, 24 Oct 1948
Lehmann, Lilli: 24 Nov 1848, 20 Oct 1865, 25 Nov 1885, 16 May
    1929
Lehmann, Lotte: 27 Feb 1888, 11 Jan 1934, 26 Aug 1976
Leibowitz, René: 17 Feb 1913, 28 Aug 1972
Leichtentritt, Hugo: 1 Jan 1874, 13 Nov 1951
Leider, Frida: 18 Apr 1888, 16 Jan 1933, 3 Jun 1975
Leifs, Jón: 1 May 1899, 30 Jul 1968
Leinsdorf, Erich: 4 Feb 1912, 21 Jan 1938
Lennon, John: 9 Oct 1940
Leoncavallo, Ruggiero: 23 Apr 1857, 21 May 1892, 10 Nov 1900, 9
    Aug 1919

Leonhardt, Gustav: 30 May 1928
Leoni, Franco: 24 Oct 1864, 8 Feb 1949
Leppard, Raymond: 2 Aug 1927
Leschetizky, Theodor: 22 Jun 1830, 14 Nov 1915
Lessard, John: 3 Jul 1920
Lesser, Laurence: 28 Oct 1938
Lesure, François: 23 May 1923
Letelier, Alfonso: 4 Oct 1912, 30 Jan 1957
Levant, Oscar: 27 Dec 1906, 14 Aug 1972
Levi, Hermann: 7 Nov 1839, 13 May 1900
Levine, James: 23 Jun 1943, 5 Jun 1971
Levitzki, Mischa: 25 May 1898, 17 Oct 1916, 2 Jan 1941
Levko, Valentina: 13 Aug 1926
Levy, Marvin David: 2 Aug 1932, 17 Mar 1967
Lewenthal, Raymond: 29 Aug 1926, 23 Nov 1965
Lewis, Anthony: 2 Mar 1915
Lewis, John: 3 May 1920
Lewis, Richard: 10 May 1914
Lewis, William: 23 Nov 1935
Lhévinne, Josef: 13 Dec 1874, 27 Jan 1906, 3 Dec 1944
Lhévinne, Rosina: 28 Mar 1880, 5 Feb 1895, 9 Nov 1976
Liadov, Anatol: 10 May 1855, 18 Mar 1904, 21 Feb 1909, 12 Dec
     1909, 28 Aug 1914
Liapunov, Sergey Mikhailovitch: 30 Nov 1859, 23 Mar 1908, 8 Nov
     1924
Liberace, Walter: 16 May 1919
Lichtenwanger, William: 28 Feb 1915
Lieberson, Goddard: 5 Apr 1911, 29 May 1977
Ligabue, Ilva: 23 May 1932
Ligeti, György: 28 May 1923, 4 Mar 1965, 19 Jan 1969
Lincoln Center (New York): 23 Sep 1962
Lind, Jenny: 6 Oct 1820, 7 Mar 1838, 11 Sep 1850, 5 Feb 1852, 2
     Nov 1887
Lindholm, Berit: 14 Oct 1934
Lipatti, Dinu: 1 Apr 1917, 2 Dec 1950
Lipp, Wilma: 26 Apr 1925
Lishner, Leon: 4 Jul 1913
Lisitsian, Pavel: 6 Nov 1911
Lissenko, Nikolai: See Lysenko, Mykola
List, Emanuel: 22 Mar 1891, 27 Dec 1933, 21 Jun 1967
List, Eugene: 6 Jul 1918, 16 Aug 1943
List, Kurt: 21 Jun 1913, 16 Nov 1970
Liszt, Franz: 22 Oct 1811, 9 Mar 1831, 23 Feb 1854, 16 Feb 1855,
     7 Jan 1857, 5 Sep 1857, 7 Nov 1867, 31 Jul 1886
Litoloff, Charles Henry: 6 Feb 1818, 6 Aug 1891
Locatelli, Pietro: 3 Sep 1695, 30 Mar 1764
Loeffler, Charles Martin: 30 Jan 1861, 22 Nov 1907, 19 May 1935
Loeillet, Jean-Baptiste: 18 Nov 1680, 19 Jul 1730
Loesser, Arthur: 26 Aug 1894, 4 Jan 1969
Loesser, Frank: 29 Jun 1910, 28 Jul 1969
Loewe, Frederick: 10 Jun 1904
Loewe, Karl: 30 Nov 1796, 20 Apr 1869
Lomax, Alan: 31 Jan 1915

Lomax, John Avery: 23 Sep 1867, 26 Jan 1948
Lombard, Alain: 4 Oct 1940
Lombardo, Guy: 19 Jun 1902, 5 Nov 1977
London, Edwin: 16 Mar 1929, 26 May 1978
London, George: 30 May 1919, 13 Nov 1959
London Philharmonic Orchestra: 7 Oct 1932
London Symphony Orchestra: 9 Jun 1904
Lopantnikoff, Nikolai: 16 Mar 1903, 7 Oct 1976
Lorengar, Pilar: 16 Jan 1928, 13 Feb 1966
Lorenz, Max: 17 May 1901, 11 Jan 1975
Lorenzo, Leonardo de: 29 Aug 1875, 27 Jul 1962
Lortzing, Albert: 23 Oct 1801, 21 Jan 1851
Los Angeles Philharmonic Orchestra: 24 Oct 1919
Löschhorn, Albert: 27 Jun 1819, 4 Jun 1905
Louis Ferdinand, Prince of Prussia: 18 Nov 1772, 10 Oct 1806
Lowe, Jack: 25 Dec 1917
Loy, Max: 18 Jun 1913, 15 Feb 1977
Luboschutz, Pierre: 17 Jun 1891, 18 Jan 1937, 17 Apr 1971
Lucca, Pauline: 25 Apr 1841, 28 Feb 1908
Ludgin, Chester: 20 May 1925
Ludwig, Christa: 16 Mar 1928, 10 Dec 1959
Ludwig, Leopold: 12 Jan 1908, 25 Apr 1979
Luening, Otto: 15 Jun 1900
Lully, Jean Baptiste: 28 Nov 1632, 19 Jan 1674, 22 Mar 1687
Lutoslawski, Witold: 25 Jan 1913, 26 Nov 1954, 26 Mar 1958
Lutyens, Elisabeth: 9 Jul 1906
Luxon, Benjamin: 11 Jun 1937
Lybbert, Donald: 19 Feb 1923
Lympany, Moura: 16 Aug 1916
Lyons, James: 24 Nov 1925, 13 Nov 1973
Lysenko, Mykola: 22 Mar 1842, 6 Nov 1912

Maag, Peter: 10 May 1919
Maazel, Lorin: 6 Mar 1930
McBride, Robert: 20 Feb 1911
McCartney, Paul: 18 Jun 1942
McCauley, William: 14 Feb 1917
McCollum, John: 21 Feb 1922
McCormack, John: 14 Jun 1884, 10 Nov 1909, 16 Sep 1945
McCracken, James: 16 Dec 1926, 21 Nov 1953
McDaniel, Barry: 18 Oct 1930
McDonald, Harl: 27 Jul 1899, 3 Mar 1940, 17 Jan 1941, 30 Mar
    1955
MacDonald, Jeannette: 18 Jun 1907, 14 Jan 1965
McDonald, Susann: 26 May 1935
MacDowell, Edward: 18 Dec 1860, 5 Mar 1889, 23 Jan 1895, 23
    Jan 1908
McIntyre, Donald: 22 Oct 1934
Mackerras, Charles: 17 Nov 1925
MacNeil, Cornell: 24 Sep 1922, 21 Mar 1959, 27 Dec 1964

McPhee, Colin: 15 Mar 1901, 11 Mar 1929, 7 Jan 1964
Macurdy, John: 18 Mar 1929
Maddy, Joseph: 14 Oct 1891, 18 Apr 1966
Madeira, Francis: 21 Feb 1917, 17 Jun 1947
Madeira, Jean: 14 Nov 1918, 2 Dec 1948, 19 Mar 1956, 10 Jul 1972
Maderna, Bruno: 21 Apr 1920, 31 Dec 1970, 13 Nov 1973
Maelzel, Johannes Nepomuk: 15 Aug 1772, 21 Jul 1838
Maffeo, Gianni: 30 Mar 1936
Mahler, Fritz: 16 Jul 1901, 18 Jun 1973
Mahler, Gustav: 7 Jul 1860, 20 Nov 1889, 13 Dec 1895, 25 Nov
    1901, 9 Jun 1902, 18 Oct 1904, 27 May 1906, 1 Jan 1908, 19
    Sep 1908, 12 Sep 1910, 18 May 1911, 20 Nov 1911, 26 Jun
    1912
Majeski, Daniel: 17 Sep 1932
Malagù, Stefania: 11 Oct 1933
Malas, Spiro: 28 Jan 1933
Malcolm, George: 28 Feb 1917
Malcuzynski, Witold: 10 Aug 1914, 17 Jul 1977
Malibran, Maria Felicità: 24 Mar 1808, 7 Jun 1825, 23 Sep 1836
Malipiero, Gian Francesco: 18 Mar 1882, 27 Jan 1918, 5 Mar 1933,
    1 Aug 1973
Maliponte, Adriana: 26 Dec 1942
Mancini, Francesco: 16 Jan 1672, 22 Sep 1737
Mancini, Henry: 16 Apr 1924
Manfredini, Vincenzo: 22 Oct 1737, 16 Aug 1799
Mann, Robert: 19 Jul 1920
Mannes, David: 16 Feb 1866, 25 Apr 1959
Mantovani, Annunzio Paolo: 15 Nov 1905
Manuguerra, Matteo: 5 Oct 1924
Mara, Gertrud Elisabeth: 23 Feb 1749, 20 Jan 1833
Marais, Marin: 31 May 1656, 15 Aug 1728
Marcello, Alessandro: 24 Aug 1669, 19 Jun 1747
Marcello, Benedetto: 9 Aug 1686, 24 Jul 1739
Marchand, Louis: 2 Feb 1669, 17 Feb 1732
Marchesi, Luigi: 8 Aug 1754, 14 Dec 1829
Marchesi de Castrone, Mathilde: 24 Mar 1821, 17 Nov 1913
Marchisio, Barbara: 6 Dec 1833, 19 Apr 1919
Marchisio, Carlotta: 8 Dec 1835, 28 Jun 1872
Marinuzzi, Giuseppe Gino: 24 Mar 1882, 17 Aug 1945
Mario, Giovanni: 17 Oct 1810, 11 Dec 1883
Markevitch, Igor: 27 Jul 1912, 18 Mar 1955
Marlowe, Sylvia: 26 Sep 1908
Marriner, Neville: 15 Apr 1924, 23 Aug 1971, 15 May 1978
Marsh, Jane: 25 Jun 1945
Martenot, Maurice: 14 Oct 1898
Martin, Frank: 15 Sep 1890, 7 May 1945, 25 Oct 1949, 14 Sep 1952,
    26 Jan 1967, 27 Jun 1970, 9 Sep 1973, 21 Nov 1974
Martinelli, Giovanni: 22 Oct 1885, 3 Dec 1910, 8 Mar 1945, 31 Jan
    1967, 2 Feb 1969
Martini, Giovanni Battista: 24 Apr 1706, 3 Aug 1784
Martino, Donald: 16 May 1931
Martinon, Jean: 10 Jan 1910, 29 Mar 1957, 1 Mar 1976
Martinů, Bohuslav: 8 Dec 1890, 16 Mar 1942, 28 Oct 1943, 30 Nov

1945, 21 Jan 1947, 27 May 1947, 4 Oct 1956, 28 Aug 1959
Martirano, Salvatore: 12 Jan 1927, 24 Apr 1952
Marx, Joseph: 11 May 1882, 3 Sep 1964
Mascagni, Pietro: 7 Dec 1863, 17 May 1890, 17 Jan 1901, 31 Oct
    1891, 2 Aug 1945
Mascheroni, Edoardo: 4 Sep 1852, 4 Mar 1941
Mason, Daniel Gregory: 20 Nov 1873, 4 Mar 1921, 23 Nov 1928,
    4 Dec 1953
Mason, William: 24 Jan 1829, 14 Jul 1908
Massart, Lambert-Joseph: 19 Jul 1811, 13 Feb 1892
Massenet, Jules: 12 May 1842, 19 Jan 1884, 30 Nov 1885, 16 Feb
    1892, 16 Mar 1894, 13 Aug 1912
Matěj, Josef: 19 Feb 1922, 7 Mar 1973
Mather, Bruce: 9 May 1939
Mathias, William: 1 Nov 1934, 30 Sep 1971
Mathis, Edith: 11 Feb 1938
Matsudaira, Yoritsuné: 5 May 1907, 6 Oct 1962, 10 Oct 1972
Matthay, Tobias: 19 Feb 1858, 14 Dec 1945
Matton, Roger: 18 May 1929, 30 Nov 1964
Matzenauer, Margarete: 1 Jan 1881, 13 Nov 1911, 19 May 1963
Maurel, Victor: 17 Jun 1848, 22 Oct 1923
Maury, Lowndes: 7 Jul 1911
Maxwell Davies, Peter: 8 Sep 1934, 22 Apr 1969, 9 Dec 1969, 12
    Jul 1972
Mayer, William: 18 Nov 1925, 21 Mar 1971
Mayr, (Johann) Simon: 14 Jun 1763, 28 Nov 1813, 2 Dec 1845
Mayr, Richard: 18 Nov 1877, 2 Nov 1927, 1 Dec 1935
Mayuzumi, Toshiro: 20 Feb 1929, 2 Apr 1958, 27 Mar 1960, 12
    Jun 1962
Mazurok, Yuri: 8 Jul 1931
Medins, Janis: 9 Oct 1890, 4 Mar 1966
Medtner, Nikolai: 5 Jan 1880, 31 Oct 1924, 19 Feb 1944, 13 Nov
    1951
Mehlig, Anna: 11 Jul 1843, 16 Jul 1928
Mehta, Zubin: 29 Apr 1936, 29 Dec 1965
Méhul, Etienne: 22 Jun 1763, 28 Jan 1806, 17 Feb 1807, 18 Oct
    1817
Melba, Nellie: 19 May 1859, 12 Oct 1887, 24 May 1888, 4 Dec
    1893, 8 Jun 1926, 23 Feb 1931
Melchior, Lauritz: 20 Mar 1890, 2 Apr 1913, 17 Feb 1926, 18 Mar
    1973
Melik-Pashayev, Alexander: 23 Oct 1905, 18 Jun 1964
Melton, James: 2 Jan 1904, 22 Apr 1932, 7 Dec 1942, 21 Apr 1961
Menasce, Jacques de: 19 Aug 1905, 28 Jan 1960
Mendel, Arthur: 6 Jun 1905
Mendelssohn, Felix: 3 Feb 1809, 1 Feb 1827, 11 Mar 1829, 13 Jul
    1829, 17 Oct 1831, 14 May 1832, 15 Nov 1832, 13 May 1833,
    22 May 1836, 25 Jun 1840, 3 Mar 1842, 3 Apr 1843, 13 Mar
    1845, 26 Aug 1846, 4 Nov 1847
Mengelberg, William: 28 Mar 1871, 21 Mar 1951
Mennin, Peter: 17 May 1923, 27 Feb 1947, 18 Mar 1949, 18 Nov
    1953, 28 Mar 1976
Menotti, Gian Carlo: 7 Jul 1911, 1 Apr 1937, 2 Nov 1945, 8 May

1946, 18 Feb 1947, 15 Mar 1950, 24 Dec 1951, 27 Dec 1954, 3 Mar 1963, 7 Mar 1971
Menter, Sophie: 29 Jul 1846, 23 Feb 1918
Menuhin, Yehudi: 22 Apr 1916, 14 Nov 1931, 25 Nov 1927
Mercadante, (Giuseppe) Saverio: 17 Sep 1795, 10 Mar 1837, 10 Mar 1840, 17 Dec 1870
Merola, Gaetano: 4 Jan 1881, 30 Aug 1953
Merrill, Robert: 4 Jun 1917, 15 Dec 1945
Merriman, Nan: 28 Apr 1920, 25 Jul 1943
Merulo, Claudio: 8 Apr 1533, 4 May 1604
Mesplé, Mady: 7 Mar 1931
Messager, André: 30 Dec 1853, 24 Feb 1929
Messiaen, Olivier: 10 Dec 1908, 15 Jan 1941, 2 Dec 1949, 11 Oct 1953, 16 Oct 1960
Mester, Jorge: 10 Apr 1935
Mestres-Quadreny, José Maria: 4 Mar 1929
Metcalf, William: 12 Jan 1934
Metropolitan Opera House: 22 Oct 1883
Meyer, Kerstin: 3 Apr 1928
Meyerbeer, Giacomo: 5 Sep 1791, 21 Nov 1831, 29 Feb 1836, 16 Apr 1849, 4 Apr 1859, 2 May 1864, 28 Apr 1865
Miaskovsky, Nikolai: 20 Apr 1881, 14 Nov 1938, 15 Feb 1939, 17 Mar 1945, 8 Aug 1950
Michalsky, Donal: 13 Jul 1928, 31 Dec 1975
Micheau, Janine: 17 Apr 1914, 18 Oct 1976
Michelet, Michel: 26 Jun 1894
Migot, Georges: 27 Feb 1891, 5 Jan 1976
Milanov, Zinka: 17 May 1906, 17 Dec 1937
Milburn, Ellsworth: 6 Feb 1938
Milder-Hauptmann, Pauline Anna: 13 Dec 1785, 29 May 1838
Mildmay, Audrey: 19 Dec 1900, 31 May 1953
Milhaud, Darius: 4 Sep 1892, 21 Feb 1920, 6 Jun 1921, 25 Oct 1923, 9 Dec 1926, 5 Dec 1930, 4 Aug 1940, 18 Dec 1941, 13 Jun 1945, 16 Nov 1945, 7 Oct 1955, 29 Oct 1966, 22 Jun 1974
Miller, Glenn: 1 Mar 1904, 16 Dec 1944
Mills, Charles: 8 Jan 1914
Milnes, Sherrill: 10 Jan 1935
Milstein, Nathan: 31 Dec 1904
Mimaroglu, Ilhan Kemaleddin: 11 Mar 1926
Mingus, Charles: 22 Apr 1922, 5 Jan 1979
Minkus, Ludwig: 23 Mar 1826, 14 Dec 1869, 7 Dec 1917
Minton, Yvonne: 4 Dec 1938
Misciano, Alvinio: 29 Aug 1915
Mitchell, Howard: 11 Mar 1911
Mitropoulos, Dimitri: 1 Mar 1896, 24 Jan 1937, 2 Nov 1960
Miyoshi, Akira: 10 Jan 1933, 22 Oct 1964
Modenos, John: 16 Jun 1930
Mödl, Martha: 22 Mar 1912
Moeran, Ernest John: 31 Dec 1894, 13 Jan 1938, 19 Aug 1943, 1 Dec 1950
Moevs, Robert: 2 Dec 1921
Moffo, Anna: 27 Jun 1932, 14 Nov 1957

Mumma, Gordon: 30 Mar 1935
Munch, Charles: 26 Sep 1891, 27 Dec 1946, 6 Nov 1968
Münchinger, Karl: 29 May 1915
Munsel, Patrice: 14 May 1925, 4 Dec 1943
Muratore, Lucien: 29 Aug 1876, 16 Jul 1954
Murray, Bain: 26 Dec 1926
Murska, Ilma di: 11 May 1865, 14 Jan 1889
Musgrave, Thea: 27 May 1928, 30 Nov 1967, 5 Feb 1969, 2 Oct
    1971, 6 Sep 1977
Music Division, Library of Congress: 1 Jul 1897
Musical America: 8 Oct 1898
Musical Quarterly: 1 Jan 1915
Mussorgsky, Modest: 21 Mar 1839, 8 Feb 1874, 28 Mar 1881, 21
    Feb 1886, 27 Oct 1886, 26 Oct 1917, 19 Oct 1922
Muti, Riccardo: 28 Jul 1941
Muzio, Claudia: 7 Feb 1889, 4 Dec 1916, 24 May 1936
Mysliveczek, Josef: 9 Mar 1737, 4 Feb 1781

Nagel, Robert: 29 Sep 1924
Nancarrow, Conlon: 27 Oct 1912
Napravnik, Eduard: 24 Aug 1839, 23 Nov 1916
Nardini, Pietro: 12 Apr 1722, 7 May 1793
National Association for American Composers and Conductors: 19
    May 1933
Naumann, Johann Gottlieb: 17 Apr 1741, 23 Oct 1801
Naylor, Bernard: 22 Nov 1907
Neblett, Carol: 1 Feb 1946
Nebolsin, Vassily: 11 Jun 1898, 29 Nov 1958
Nedbal, Oskar: 26 Mar 1874, 24 Dec 1930
Nelhybel, Vaclav: 24 Sep 1919
Nelson, Oliver: 4 Jun 1932, 27 Oct 1975
Nelson, Ron: 14 Dec 1929
Nelsova, Zara: 24 Dec 1924
Nemenoff, Genia: 23 Oct 1905
Nepomuceno, Alberto: 6 Jul 1864, 16 Oct 1920
Nessler, Victor: 28 Jan 1841, 28 May 1890
Neubauer, Franz Christoph: 21 Mar 1750, 11 Oct 1795
Nevin, Ethelbert: 25 Nov 1862, 17 Feb 1901
New Symphony Orchestra (New York): 11 Apr 1919
New Symphony Orchestra of London: 29 Oct 1905
New York City Opera: 3 Oct 1944
New York Philharmonic Orchestra: 29 May 1963
New York Symphony Society: 9 Nov 1878
Neway, Patricia: 30 Sep 1919
Newcomb, Ethel: 30 Oct 1875, 28 Feb 1903, 3 Jul 1959
Newlin, Dika: 22 Nov 1923
Newman, Anthony: 12 May 1941
Newman, Ernest: 30 Nov 1868, 7 Jul 1959
Ney, Elly: 27 Sep 1882, 31 Mar 1968
Nicolai, Otto: 9 Jun 1810, 8 Mar 1849, 11 May 1849
Nicolet, Aurèle: 22 Jan 1926

Orrego-Salas, Juan: 18 Jan 1919, 3 May 1955, 17 Feb 1956
Ory, Edward "Kid"; 25 Dec 1886, 23 Jan 1973
Ostendorf, John: 1 Nov 1945
Otterloo, Willem van: 27 Dec 1907, 27 Jul 1978
Ottman, Robert W.: 3 May 1914
Overton, Hall: 23 Feb 1920, 24 Nov 1972
Owen, Harold: 13 Dec 1931
Ozawa, Seiji: 1 Sep 1935

Pachelbel, Johann: 1 Sep 1653, 3 Mar 1706
Pachmann, Vladimir de: 27 Jul 1848, 6 Jan 1933
Paderewski, Ignace Jan: 18 Nov 1860, 17 Nov 1891, 17 Jan 1919,
    29 Jun 1941
Paganini, Niccolò: 27 Oct 1782, 27 May 1840
Paillard, Jean-François: 12 Apr 1928
Paine, John Knowles: 9 Jan 1839, 25 Apr 1906
Paisiello, Giovanni: 9 May 1740, 23 Aug 1784, 5 Jun 1816
Pakhmutova, Alexandra: 9 Nov 1929, 11 Jun 1955
Paladilhe, Emile: 3 Jun 1844, 6 Jan 1926
Palau, Manuel: 4 Jan 1893, 18 Feb 1967
Palestine Symphony Orchestra: 26 Dec 1936
Palestrina, Giovanni Pierluigi da: 2 Feb 1594
Palm, Siegfried: 25 Apr 1927
Palmer, Robert: 2 Jun 1915
Palmer, Thomas: 2 Dec 1934
Palmgren, Selim: 16 Feb 1878, 13 Dec 1951
Panerai, Rolando: 17 Oct 1924
Panizza, Ettore: 12 Aug 1875, 28 Nov 1967
Panufnik, Andrzej: 24 Sep 1915, 24 Mar 1949, 26 Aug 1957, 24 May
    1970, 18 Jul 1972, 20 May 1974
Parepa-Rosa, Euphrosyne: 7 May 1836, 21 Jan 1874
Paris Conservatory: 3 Aug 1795
Parisot, Aldo: 30 Sep 1920
Parker, Charles Christopher, Jr. "Charlie": 29 Aug 1920, 12 Mar
    1955
Parker, Horatio: 15 Sep 1863, 3 May 1893, 18 Dec 1919
Parnas, Leslie: 22 Nov 1932
Parris, Robert: 21 May 1924, 25 Mar 1958
Parry, Charles Hubert Hastings: 27 Feb 1848, 7 Oct 1918
Partch, Harry: 24 Jun 1901, 22 Apr 1944, 3 Sep 1974
Pashley, Anne: 5 Jun 1937
Pasta, Giuditta: 28 Oct 1797, 1 Apr 1865
Paton, Mary Ann: 21 Jul 1864
Patrick, Julian: 26 Oct 1927
Patti, Adelina: 10 Feb 1843, 24 Nov 1859, 14 May 1861, 20 Oct
    1914, 27 Sep 1919
Patzak, Julius: 9 Apr 1898, 26 Jan 1974
Pauer, Ernst: 21 Dec 1826, 9 May 1905
Pauer, Max: 31 Oct 1866, 12 May 1945
Paul, Thomas: 22 Feb 1934

Pinza, Ezio: 18 May 1892, 1 Nov 1926, 5 Mar 1948, 9 May 1957
Pisk, Paul Amadeus: 16 May 1893
Pistocchi, Francesco Antonio: 13 May 1726
Piston, Walter: 20 Jan 1894, 6 Mar 1934, 30 May 1938, 5 Mar
   1944, 9 Jan 1948, 30 Mar 1951, 24 Feb 1956, 10 Feb 1961,
   5 Mar 1965, 12 Nov 1976
Pixis, Johann Peter: 10 Feb 1788, 22 Dec 1874
Pizzarelli, John "Bucky": 9 Jan 1926
Pizzetti, Ildebrando: 20 Sep 1880, 11 Jun 1913, 28 Feb 1929, 1 Mar
   1958, 13 Feb 1968
Plançon, Pol: 12 Jun 1851, 29 Nov 1893, 12 Aug 1914
Platti, Giovanni: 9 Jul 1697, 11 Jan 1763
Pleshakov, Vladimir: 4 Oct 1934
Pleyel, Camille: 18 Dec 1788, 4 May 1855
Pleyel, Ignaz: 18 Jun 1757, 14 Nov 1831
Plishka, Paul: 28 Aug 1941
Polacco, Giorgio: 12 Apr 1873, 30 Apr 1960
Poldini, Eduard: 13 Jun 1869, 28 Jun 1957
Pollock, Robert: 8 Jul 1946
Ponce, Manuel: 8 Dec 1882, 4 Oct 1941, 24 Apr 1948
Ponchielli, Amilcare: 31 Aug 1834, 8 Apr 1876, 16 Jan 1886
Pons, Lily: 12 Apr 1898, 3 Jan 1931, 13 Feb 1976
Ponselle, Rosa: 22 Jan 1897, 15 Nov 1918
Poot, Marcel: 7 May 1901
Popp, Lucia: 12 Nov 1939
Popper, David: 9 Dec 1843, 7 Aug 1913
Porpora, Nicola Antonio: 17 Aug 1686, 3 Mar 1768
Porter, Cole: 9 Jun 1891, 15 Oct 1964
Porter, Quincy: 7 Feb 1897, 16 May 1948, 17 Mar 1954, 18 Apr
   1958, 14 Jan 1964, 12 Nov 1966
Poulenc, Francis: 7 Jan 1899, 3 May 1929, 10 Jun 1941, 6 Jan
   1950, 13 Jun 1951, 26 Jan 1957, 20 Jan 1961, 30 Jan 1963
Pousseur, Henri: 23 Jun 1929, 17 Mar 1968
Powell, John: 6 Sep 1882, 15 Aug 1963
Powell, Maud: 22 Aug 1868, 8 Jan 1920
Powell, Mel: 12 Feb 1923
Powell, Morgan: 7 Jan 1938
Pozdro, John: 14 Aug 1923, 12 Dec 1960
Pracht, Mary: 4 Feb 1936
Praetorius, Michael: 15 Feb 1571, 15 Feb 1621
Prausnitz, Frederick: 26 Aug 1920
Presley, Elvis: 8 Jan 1935, 16 Aug 1977
Presser, Theodore: 3 Jul 1848, 27 Oct 1925
Presser, William: 19 Apr 1916
Prêtre, Georges: 14 Aug 1924
Prevedi, Bruno: 21 Dec 1928
Previn, André: 6 Apr 1929
Previtali, Fernando: 16 Feb 1907
Prey, Herman: 11 Jul 1929
Price, Leontyne: 10 Feb 1927, 27 Jan 1961, 4 Jul 1964
Price, Margaret: 13 Apr 1941
Priestman, Brian: 10 Feb 1927
Primrose, William: 23 Aug 1903

Pring, Katherine: 4 Jun 1940
Pritchard, John: 5 Feb 1921
Procter, Leland: 24 Mar 1914
Prohaska, Felix: 16 May 1912
Prokofiev, Sergei: 23 Apr 1891, 21 Apr 1918, 16 Dec 1921, 30 Dec
    1921, 1 Dec 1935, 2 May 1936, 20 Feb 1937, 17 May 1939,
    11 Jan 1940, 5 Mar 1953
Pro Musica Antiqua: 9 Apr 1919
Prout, Ebenezer: 1 Mar 1835, 5 Dec 1909
Prudent, Emile: 3 Feb 1817, 13 May 1863
Puccini, Giacomo: 22 Dec 1858, 1 Feb 1893, 1 Feb 1896, 14 Jan
    1900, 17 Feb 1904, 18 Jan 1907, 11 Feb 1907, 10 Dec 1910,
    14 Dec 1918, 29 Nov 1924, 25 Apr 1926
Purcell, Henry: 21 Nov 1695
Pütz, Ruth-Margaret: 26 Feb 1932
Py, Gilbert: 9 Dec 1933

Quantz, Johann Joachim: 30 Jan 1697, 12 Jul 1773
Querol Gavaldá, Miguel: 22 Apr 1912
Quilico, Louis: 14 Jan 1929
Quilter, Roger: 1 Nov 1877, 21 Sep 1953
Quintanar, Hector: 15 Apr 1936

Raaff, Anton: 6 May 1714, 27 May 1797
Rabaud, Henri: 10 Nov 1873, 11 Sep 1949
Rabin, Michael: 2 May 1936, 19 Jan 1972
Rabinovich, Nikolai: 7 Oct 1908
Rachmaninoff, Sergei: 1 Apr 1873, 9 Nov 1901, 1 May 1909, 4 Nov
    1909, 18 Mar 1927, 7 Nov 1934, 28 Mar 1943
Raff, Joachim: 27 May 1822, 24 Jun 1882
Ragossnig, Konrad: 6 May 1932
Raimondi, Gianni: 17 Apr 1923, 29 Sep 1965
Raimondi, Ruggero: 3 Oct 1941
Raisa, Rosa: 30 May 1893, 28 Sep 1963
Rakhlin, Nathan: 10 Jan 1906
Ralf, Torsten: 2 Jan 1901, 27 Apr 1954
Rameau, Jean Philippe: 25 Sep 1683, 23 Aug 1735, 24 Oct 1737,
    29 Feb 1748, 5 Dec 1749, 12 Feb 1760, 12 Sep 1764
Rampal, Jean-Pierre: 7 Jan 1922
Ran, Shulamit: 21 Oct 1949, 19 Jan 1970
Randall, James K.: 16 Jun 1929
Rangström, Ture: 30 Nov 1884, 11 May 1947
Ránki, György: 30 Oct 1907, 6 Jun 1953
Rankin, Nell: 3 Jan 1926
Raphling, Sam: 19 Mar 1910
Raskin, Judith: 21 Jun 1928, 23 Feb 1962
Rathaus, Karol: 16 Sep 1895, 21 Nov 1954

Riepi, Russell: 23 Feb 1945
Ries, Ferdinand: 28 Nov 1784, 13 Jan 1838
Rieti, Vittorio: 28 Jan 1898, 31 May 1924, 1 Feb 1978
Rietz, Julius: 28 Dec 1812, 12 Sep 1877
Rifkin, Joshua: 22 Apr 1944
Riley, Dennis: 28 May 1943
Riley, Terry: 24 Jun 1935
Rimsky-Korsakov, Nikolai: 18 Mar 1844, 31 Dec 1865, 21 Jan 1880,
    10 Feb 1882, 31 Oct 1887, 3 Nov 1888, 29 Jun 1889, 7 Jan
    1898, 3 Nov 1899, 21 Jun 1908, 7 Oct 1909
Rintzler, Marius: 14 Mar 1932
Rippon, Michael: 10 Dec 1938
Rivé-King, Julie: 30 Oct 1854, 24 Jul 1937
Robb, John Donald: 12 Jun 1892
Robertson, Leroy: 21 Dec 1896, 11 Dec 1947, 25 Jul 1971
Robeson, Paul: 9 Apr 1898, 23 Jan 1976
Robinson, Faye: 2 Nov 1943
Robinson, Forbes: 21 May 1926
Rochberg, George: 5 Jul 1918, 28 Mar 1958, 26 Feb 1959, 4 Apr
    1975
Rodgers, Jimmie: 8 Sep 1897, 26 May 1933, 3 Nov 1961
Rodgers, Richard: 28 Jun 1902, 30 Dec 1979
Rodrigo, Joaquín: 22 Nov 1902, 9 Nov 1940
Rodzinski, Artur: 1 Jan 1892, 27 Nov 1958
Roger-Ducasse, Jean-Jules Aimable: 18 Apr 1873, 19 Jul 1954
Rogers, Bernard: 4 Feb 1893, 3 May 1934, 4 Apr 1935, 24 May
    1968
Rogers, Nigel: 21 Mar 1935
Rohe, Robert Kenneth: 22 Aug 1916
Rolla, Alessandro: 6 Apr 1757, 15 Sep 1841
Rolland, Romain: 29 Jan 1866, 30 Dec 1944
Roman, Johan Helmich: 26 Oct 1694, 20 Nov 1758
Romberg, Bernhard: 11 Nov 1767, 13 Aug 1841
Romberg, Sigmund: 29 Jul 1887, 29 Sep 1921, 2 Dec 1924, 9 Nov
    1951
Ronald, Landon: 7 Jun 1873, 14 Aug 1938
Ronsheim, John: 17 Feb 1927
Röntgen, Julius: 9 May 1855, 13 Sep 1932
Ropartz, Guy: 15 Jun 1864, 22 Nov 1955
Rorem, Ned: 23 Oct 1923, 19 Apr 1959, 2 Feb 1977
Rosand, Aaron: 15 Mar 1927
Rosbaud, Hans: 22 Jul 1895, 29 Dec 1962
Rose, Leonard: 27 Jul 1918
Rosen, Jerome: 23 Jul 1921
Rosen, Nathaniel: 9 Jun 1948, 3 Jul 1978
Rosenberg, Hilding: 21 Jun 1892, 24 Nov 1932, 24 Jan 1952
Rosenfeld, Paul: 4 May 1890, 21 Jul 1946
Rosenman, Leonard: 7 Sep 1924
Rosenthal, Moriz: 17 Dec 1862, 9 Nov 1888, 3 Sep 1946
Rosetti, Francesco Antonio: 30 Jun 1792
Ross, Hugh: 21 Aug 1898
Ross, Walter: 3 Oct 1936, 13 Apr 1976
Rossi, Mario: 29 Mar 1902

Rossi-Lemeni, Nicola: 6 Nov 1920, 2 Oct 1951
Rossini, Gioacchino: 29 Feb 1792, 9 May 1812, 6 Feb 1813, 22
        May 1813, 20 Feb 1816, 3 Feb 1823, 9 Oct 1826, 3 Aug 1829,
        13 Nov 1868, 12 Jan 1894
Rössl-Majdan, Hilde: 21 Jan 1921
Rostropovich, Mstislav: 27 Mar 1927
·Roswänge, Helge: 29 Aug 1897, 19 Jun 1972
Rothenberger, Anneliese: 19 Jun 1924, 18 Nov 1960
Rothmüller, Marko: 31 Dec 1908
Rouleau, Joseph: 28 Feb 1929
Roussakis, Nicolas: 14 Jun 1934
Rousseau, Jean-Jacques: 28 Jun 1712, 2 Jul 1778
Roussel, Albert: 5 Apr 1869, 21 Jan 1927, 25 Apr 1929, 6 Feb 1930,
        24 Oct 1930, 23 Aug 1937
Rowicki, Witold: 26 Feb 1914
Roy, Klaus George: 24 Jan 1924
Royal Albert Hall (London): 29 Mar 1871
Royal College of Music: 28 Feb 1882
Royal Philharmonic Society of London: 24 Jan 1813
Rozhdestvensky, Gennady: 4 May 1931
Rózsa, Miklós: 18 Apr 1907, 14 Nov 1943, 28 Dec 1944, 6 Apr 1967
Rubbra, Edmund: 23 May 1901
Rubini, Giovanni Battista: 7 Apr 1794, 3 Mar 1854
Rubinstein, Anton: 28 Nov 1829, 23 Sep 1872, 20 Nov 1894
Rubinstein, Artur: 28 Jan 1887, 8 Jan 1906, 1 Apr 1976
Rubinstein, Nicholas: 14 Jun 1835, 23 Mar 1881
Rudel, Julius: 6 Mar 1921
Rudhyar, Dane: 23 Mar 1895
Rudolf, Max: 15 Jun 1902
Ruffo, Titta: 9 Jun 1877, 4 Nov 1912, 19 Jan 1922, 5 Jul 1953
Ruggles, Carl: 11 Mar 1876, 7 Dec 1924, 25 Feb 1932, 24 Nov
        1949, 24 Oct 1971
Rusconi, Gerardo: 1 Feb 1922, 23 Dec 1974
Rush, Loren: 23 Aug 1935
Russell, Henry: 24 Dec 1812, 8 Dec 1900
Russian "Mighty Five": See Balakirev, Mily; Borodin, Alexander;
        Cui, César; Mussorgsky, Modest; Rimsky-Korsakov, Nikolai
Russo, William Joseph: 25 Jun 1928, 7 Jul 1968
Rust, Friedrich Wilhelm: 6 Jul 1739, 28 Mar 1796
Ruzdjak, Vladimir: 21 Sep 1922
Rysanek, Leonie: 14 Nov 1926, 5 Feb 1959
Ryterband, Roman: 2 Aug 1914
Rzewski, Frederic: 13 Apr 1938

Sacchini, Antonio: 14 Jun 1730, 6 Oct 1786
Sacco, Peter: 25 Oct 1928
Sachs, Hans: 5 Nov 1494, 19 Jan 1576
Saeverud, Harald: 17 Apr 1897
Saint-Saëns, Camille: 9 Oct 1835, 19 Jan 1873, 24 Jan 1875, 31
        Oct 1875, 2 Dec 1877, 19 May 1886, 4 Jan 1893, 3 Jun 1896, 6
        Nov 1913, 16 Dec 1921, 26 Feb 1922

Salieri, Antonio: 18 Aug 1750, 3 Aug 1778, 7 May 1825
Sallinen, Aulis: 9 Apr 1935
Salmenhaara, Erkki: 12 Mar 1941
Salter, Richard: 12 Nov 1943
Salzedo, Carlos: 6 Apr 1885, 17 Aug 1961
Salzedo, Leonard (Lopes): 24 Sep 1921
Salzman, Eric: 8 Sep 1933
Samaroff, Olga: 8 Aug 1882, 17 May 1948
Sammartini, Giovanni Battista: 15 Jan 1775
Samosud, Samuel: 14 May 1884, 6 Nov 1964
San Carlo Opera House: 4 Nov 1737
San Francisco Symphony Orchestra: 29 Dec 1911
Sancan, Pierre: 24 Oct 1916
Sanders, Robert L.: 2 Jul 1906, 26 Dec 1974
Sandor, György: 21 Sep 1912
Sanjuán, Pedro: 15 Nov 1886, 14 Dec 1951, 18 Oct 1976
Sanromá, Jesús Maria: 7 Nov 1902
Santini, Fortunato: 5 Jan 1778, 14 Sep 1861
Santoliquido, Francesco: 6 Aug 1883, 26 Aug 1971
Santorsola, Guido: 18 Nov 1904
Sanzogno, Nino: 13 Apr 1911
Sarasate, Pablo de: 10 Mar 1844, 20 Sep 1908
Sardi, Ivan: 7 Jul 1930
Sardinero, Vincenzo: 12 Jan 1937
Sargent, Malcolm: 29 Apr 1895, 3 Oct 1967
Sáry, Lászlo: 1 Jan 1940
Sás, Andrés: 6 Apr 1900, 25 Jul 1967
Satie, Erik: 17 May 1866, 18 May 1917, 14 Feb 1920, 15 Jun 1924,
     29 Nov 1924, 1 Jul 1925
Sauer, Emil von: 8 Oct 1862, 27 Apr 1942
Sauguet, Henri: 18 May 1901, 30 Apr 1927
Sawallisch, Wolfgang: 23 Aug 1923
Sayão, Bidú: 11 May 1902, 13 Feb 1937
Scala, La (Milan): 3 Aug 1778
Scalchi, Sofia: 29 Nov 1850, 22 Aug 1922
Scarlatti, Alessandro: 2 May 1660, 24 Oct 1725
Scarlatti, Domenico: 26 Oct 1685, 23 Jul 1757
Scelsi, Giacinto: 8 Jan 1905
Schafer, R. Murray: 18 Jul 1933
Schaposhnikov, Adrian: 6 Jun 1887
Scharwenka, Philipp: 16 Feb 1847, 16 Jul 1917
Scharwenka, Xaver: 6 Jan 1850, 8 Dec 1924
Scheidt, Samuel: 3 Nov 1587, 24 Mar 1654
Schein, Johann Hermann: 20 Jan 1586, 19 Nov 1630
Schelling, Ernest: 26 Jul 1876, 8 Dec 1939
Scherchen, Hermann: 21 Jun 1891, 12 Jun 1966
Scherman, Thomas: 12 Feb 1917, 14 May 1979
Schickele, Peter: 17 Jul 1935
Schifrin, Lalo: 21 Jun 1932
Schiml, Marga: 29 Nov 1945
Schipa, Tito: 2 Jan 1889, 23 Nov 1932, 16 Dec 1965
Schippers, Thomas: 9 Mar 1930, 16 Dec 1977
Schirmer, Gustav: 19 Sep 1829, 5 Aug 1893
Schirmer, Gustave: 18 Feb 1864, 15 Jul 1907

Schmidt, Franz: 22 Dec 1874, 25 Jan 1902, 3 Dec 1913, 2 Dec
     1928, 10 Jan 1934, 11 Feb 1939
Schmidt, William: 6 Mar 1926
Schmidt-Isserstedt, Hans: 5 May 1900, 28 May 1973
Schmitt, Florent: 28 Sep 1870, 27 Dec 1906, 8 Jan 1911, 29 Feb
     1924, 17 Aug 1958
Schnabel, Artur: 17 Apr 1882, 15 Aug 1951
Schnabel, Karl Ulrich: 6 Aug 1909
Schneider, Alexander: 21 Oct 1908
Schnitger, Arp: 2 Jul 1648, 24 Jul 1719
Schnorr, Ludwig: 2 Jul 1836, 21 Jul 1865
Schobert, Johann: 28 Aug 1767
Schock, Rudolf: 4 Sep 1915
Schoeck, Othmar: 1 Sep 1886, 8 Mar 1957
Schoeffler, Paul: 15 Jul 1897, 26 Jan 1950, 22 Nov 1977
Schoenberg, Arnold: 13 Sep 1874, 18 Mar 1902, 26 Jan 1905, 8
     Feb 1907, 3 Sep 1912, 16 Oct 1912, 23 Feb 1913, 20 Jul 1924,
     2 Dec 1928, 6 Dec 1940, 15 Dec 1940, 11 Apr 1941, 6 Feb
     1944, 4 Nov 1948, 13 Jul 1951
Schonberg, Harold C.: 29 Nov 1915
Schorr, Friedrich: 2 Sep 1888, 14 Aug 1953
Schramm, Ernst Gerold: 8 Jul 1938
Schreier, Peter: 29 Jul 1935
Schreiner, Alexander: 31 Jul 1901
Schreker, Franz: 23 Mar 1878, 21 Mar 1934
Schröder-Devrient, Wilhelmine: 6 Dec 1804, 20 Jan 1821, 26 Jan
     1860
Schubert, Franz: 31 Jan 1797, 19 Oct 1814, 20 Dec 1823, 26 Mar
     1828, 19 Nov 1828, 21 Mar 1839, 17 Dec 1865
Schuller, Gunther: 22 Nov 1925, 4 Jan 1961, 12 Oct 1966, 27 Jun
     1968, 8 May 1970
Schuman, William: 4 Aug 1910, 6 Oct 1939, 13 Feb 1943, 26 Mar
     1943, 12 Nov 1943, 10 Feb 1950, 4 Nov 1955, 28 Oct 1956,
     30 Jan 1970, 15 Apr 1976
Schumann, Clara: 13 Sep 1819, 12 Sep 1840, 20 May 1896
Schumann, Elisabeth: 13 Jun 1885, 20 Nov 1914, 23 Apr 1952
Schumann, Robert: 8 Jun 1810, 11 Sep 1840, 31 Mar 1841, 6 Dec
     1841, 4 Dec 1845, 5 Nov 1846, 6 Feb 1851, 13 Jun 1852, 29
     Jul 1856
Schumann-Heink, Ernestine: 15 Jun 1861, 7 Nov 1898, 9 Jan 1899,
     11 Mar 1932, 17 Nov 1936
Schuricht, Carl: 3 Jul 1880, 7 Jan 1967
Schütz, Heinrich: 8 Oct 1585, 23 Apr 1627, 6 Nov 1672
Schwann, William: 13 May 1913
Schwantner, Joseph: 22 Mar 1943
Schwartz, Elliott: 19 Jan 1936
Schwarzkopf, Elisabeth: 9 Dec 1915, 20 Sep 1955
Schweitzer, Albert: 14 Jan 1875, 4 Sep 1965
Sciutti, Graziella: 17 Apr 1932
Scott, Cyril: 27 Sep 1879, 31 Dec 1970
Scott, Tom (Thomas Jefferson): 28 May 1912, 22 Feb 1947, 12 Aug
     1961
Scotti, Antonio: 25 Jan 1866, 27 Dec 1899, 20 Jan 1933, 26 Feb 1936

Scotto, Renata: 24 Feb 1934
Scovotti, Jeannette: 5 Dec 1936, 15 Nov 1962
Scriabin, Alexander: 6 Jan 1872, 23 Oct 1897, 10 Dec 1908, 15
     Mar 1911, 27 Apr 1915, 24 Sep 1975
Sculthorpe, Peter: 29 Apr 1929
Searle, Humphrey: 26 Aug 1915
Seashore, Carl Emil: 28 Jan 1866, 16 Oct 1949
Sébastian, Georges: 17 Aug 1903
Seefried, Irmgard: 9 Oct 1919, 20 Nov 1953
Seeger, Pete: 3 May 1919
Seeger, Ruth Crawford: 3 Jul 1901, 18 Nov 1953, 14 Dec 1975
Segovia, Andrés: 21 Feb 1893, 13 Feb 1978
Seiber, Mátyás: 4 May 1905, 11 May 1954, 24 Sep 1960
Seidl, Anton: 7 May 1850, 23 Nov 1885, 28 Mar 1898
Seixas, (José Antonio) Carlos de: 11 Jun 1704, 25 Aug 1742
Sembrich, Marcella: 15 Feb 1858, 24 Oct 1883, 6 Feb 1909, 11
     Jan 1935
Semmler, Alexander: 12 Nov 1900, 24 Apr 1977
Serafin, Tullio: 1 Sep 1878, 3 Nov 1924, 3 Feb 1968
Serebrier, José: 3 Dec 1938
Sereni, Mario: 25 Mar 1928, 9 Nov 1957
Serkin, Peter: 24 Jul 1947
Serkin, Rudolf: 28 Mar 1903
Serly, Tibor: 25 Nov 1900, 8 Oct 1978
Serocki, Kazimierz: 3 Mar 1922
Servais, Adrien-François: 6 Jun 1807, 26 Nov 1866
Sessions, Roger: 28 Dec 1896, 5 Dec 1930, 8 Jan 1940, 18 Mar
     1970, 23 May 1971, 14 Apr 1972
Sévérac, Déodat de: 20 Jul 1872, 24 Mar 1921
Sgambati, Giovanni: 28 May 1841, 14 Dec 1914
Sgrizzi, Luciano: 30 Oct 1910
Shaffer, Sherwood: 15 Nov 1934
Shankar, Ravi: 7 Apr 1920
Shapero, Harold: 29 Apr 1920, 8 Jun 1941
Shapey, Ralph: 12 Mar 1921, 26 Mar 1960, 16 May 1966, 28 Feb
     1976
Sharp, Cecil James: 22 Nov 1859, 23 Jun 1924
Shaughnessy, Robert: 24 Sep 1925
Shaw, Christopher: 30 Jul 1924
Shaw, George Bernard: 26 Jul 1856, 2 Nov 1950
Shaw, Robert: 30 Apr 1916
Shchedrin, Rodion: 16 Dec 1932, 11 Jan 1968
Shepherd, Arthur: 19 Feb 1880, 12 Jan 1958
Shifrin, Seymour: 28 Feb 1926, 8 Jan 1960, 26 Sep 1979
Shirley, George: 18 Apr 1934
Shirley-Quirk, John: 2 Aug 1931
Shostakovich, Dmitri: 25 Sep 1906, 12 May 1926, 21 Jan 1930, 15
     Oct 1933, 21 Nov 1937, 1 Mar 1942, 14 Nov 1944, 29 Oct
     1955, 10 May 1957, 4 Oct 1959, 25 Sep 1966, 26 Sep 1967,
     8 Jan 1971, 9 Aug 1975, 25 Sep 1976
Sibelius, Jean: 8 Dec 1865, 16 Feb 1893, 26 Apr 1899, 2 Jul 1900, 8
     Mar 1902, 8 Feb 1904, 4 Jun 1914, 8 Dec 1915, 24 Mar 1924, 26
     Dec 1926, 20 Sep 1957

Siegmeister, Elie: 15 Jan 1909, 24 Nov 1945, 3 Feb 1956, 8 Feb
    1959, 17 Feb 1961
Siepi, Cesare: 10 Feb 1923, 6 Nov 1950
Sigma Alpha Iota: 12 Jun 1903
Silcher, Friedrich: 27 Jun 1789, 26 Aug 1860
Silja, Anja: 3 Apr 1940, 1 Nov 1968
Sills, Beverly: 25 May 1929, 8 Apr 1975
Siloti, Alexander: 9 Oct 1863, 8 Dec 1945
Simionato, Giulietta: 15 Dec 1910
Simon, Joanna: 20 Oct 1940
Simoneau, Léopold: 3 May 1918
Simons, Netty: 26 Oct 1913
Simpson, Robert: 2 Mar 1921, 14 Mar 1963
Sims, Ezra: 16 Jan 1928
Sinding, Christian: 11 Jan 1865, 3 Dec 1941
Six, Les: See Auric, Georges; Durey, Louis; Honegger, Arthur;
    Milhaud, Darius; Poulenc, Francis; Tailleferre, Germaine
Sjögren, Emil: 16 Jun 1853, 1 Mar 1918
Skalkottas, Nikos: 8 Mar 1904, 19 Sep 1949
Skinner, Ernest M.: 15 Jan 1866, 27 Nov 1960
Skrowaczewski, Stanislaw: 3 Oct 1923
Slatkin, Leonard: 1 Sep 1944
Slenczynska, Ruth: 15 Jan 1925
Slezak, Leo: 18 Aug 1873, 17 Nov 1909, 1 Jun 1946
Slobodyanik, Alexander: 5 Sep 1941
Slonimsky, Nicolas: 27 Apr 1894
Smallens, Alexander: 1 Jan 1889, 24 Nov 1972
Smetana, Bedrich: 2 Mar 1824, 30 May 1866, 12 May 1884
Smeterlin, Jan: 7 Feb 1892, 18 Jan 1967
Smit, Leo: 12 Jan 1921
Smith, Bessie: 15 Apr 1894/5, 26 Sep 1937
Smith, Carol: 20 Feb 1926
Smith, Gayle: 2 Sep 1943
Smith, Gregg: 4 Aug 1931
Smith, Hale: 29 Jun 1925, 17 Oct 1961
Smith, Julia: 25 Jan 1911, 3 Nov 1973, 28 Feb 1976
Smith, Russell: 23 Apr 1927
Smith, William O.: 22 Sep 1926
Smith, Willie "The Lion": 24 Nov 1897, 18 Apr 1973
Smith-Brindle, Reginald: 5 Jan 1917
Smyth, Ethel: 22 Apr 1858, 11 Nov 1906, 8 May 1944
Söderström, Elisabeth: 7 May 1927
Soler, Padre Antonio: 3 Dec 1729, 20 Dec 1783
Sollberger, Harvey: 11 May 1938
Solomon (Cutner): 9 Aug 1902
Solti, Georg: 21 Oct 1912
Somer, Hilde: 11 Feb 1930, 25 Dec 1979
Somers, Harry Stewart: 11 Sep 1925, 23 Oct 1975
Sonneck, Oscar: 6 Oct 1873, 30 Oct 1928
Sontag, Henriette: 3 Jan 1806, 17 Jun 1854
Sor, Fernando: 13 Feb 1778, 8 Jul 1839
Sorell, Christiane: 13 Jan 1936
Sotin, Hans: 10 Sep 1939

Soumagnas, Juan: 8 Nov 1938
Sousa, John Philip: 6 Nov 1854, 6 Mar 1932
Southers, Leroy: 13 Jul 1941
Souzay, Gérard: 8 Dec 1920, 21 Jan 1965
Sowande, Fela: 29 May 1905
Sowerby, Leo: 1 May 1895, 4 Oct 1921, 16 Apr 1945, 7 Jul 1968
Soyer, Roger: 1 Sep 1939
Speaks, Oley: 28 Jun 1874, 17 Aug 1948
Speer, Daniel: 2 Jul 1636, 5 Oct 1707
Speiser, Elisabeth: 15 Oct 1940
Spencer, Eleanor: 30 Nov 1890, 11 Nov 1913
Spiegelman, Joel: 23 Jan 1933
Spies, Claudio: 26 Mar 1925
Spiess, Ludovic: 13 May 1938
Spivacke, Harold: 18 Jul 1904, 9 May 1977
Spohr, Ludwig: 5 Apr 1784, 28 Jul 1823, 22 Oct 1859
Spontini, Gaspare: 14 Nov 1774, 24 Jan 1851
Spratlan, Lewis: 5 Sep 1940
Sprongl, Norbert: 30 Apr 1892
Stabile, Mariano: 12 May 1888, 11 Jan 1968
Stader, Maria: 5 Nov 1918, 25 Jan 1954
Stainer, Jakob: 14 Jul 1621
Stainer, John: 6 Jun 1840, 31 Mar 1901
Stamitz, Johann Wenzel Anton: 19 Jun 1717, 27 Mar 1757
Stamitz, Karl: 8 May 1745, 9 Nov 1801
Stanley, John: 17 Jan 1713, 19 May 1786
Starer, Robert: 8 Jan 1924
Starker, Janos: 5 Jul 1924
Starr, Ringo (Richard Starkey): 7 Jul 1940
Stasevich, Abram: 10 Jan 1907
Stearns, Peter Pindar: 7 Jun 1931
Steber, Eleanor: 17 Jul 1916, 7 Dec 1940
Steffani, Agostino: 25 Jul 1654, 12 Feb 1728
Steffek, Hanny: 9 Dec 1927
Steffens, Walter: 31 Oct 1934
Steinberg, William: 1 Aug 1899, 16 May 1978
Steiner, Frances: 25 Feb 1937
Steinway, Heinrich Engelhard: 15 Feb 1797, 7 Feb 1871
Steinway Hall: 31 Oct 1866
Stella, Antonietta: 15 Mar 1929
Stern, Isaac: 21 Jul 1920, 11 Oct 1937
Stern, Robert: 1 Feb 1934
Steuermann, Eduard: 18 Jun 1892, 11 Nov 1964
Stevens, Denis: 2 Mar 1922
Stevens, Halsey: 3 Dec 1908, 3 Mar 1950, 20 Nov 1957
Stevens, Risë: 11 Jun 1913, 22 Nov 1938, 17 Dec 1938
Stewart, John: 31 Mar 1940
Stewart, Robert: 6 Mar 1918
Stewart, Thomas: 29 Aug 1928, 9 Mar 1966
Stich-Randall, Teresa: 24 Dec 1927, 24 Oct 1961
Stignani, Ebe: 10 Jul 1904, 5 Oct 1974
Still, William Grant: 11 May 1895, 3 Dec 1978
Stitt, Edward "Sonny": 2 Feb 1924

Stock, David: 3 Jun 1939
Stock, Frederick: 11 Nov 1872, 20 Oct 1942
Stockhausen, Julius: 22 Jul 1826, 22 Sep 1906
Stockhausen, Karlheinz: 22 Aug 1928, 26 May 1953, 11 Jun 1960,
    21 May 1962, 18 Jul 1976
Stojowski, Sigismund: 14 May 1869, 5 Nov 1946
Stokes, Eric: 14 Jul 1930
Stokowski, Leopold: 18 Apr 1882, 13 Sep 1977
Stoltzman, Richard: 12 Jul 1942
Stolyarov, Grigori: 20 Mar 1892, 14 Sep 1963
Stolz, Teresa: 2 Jun 1834, 30 Jun 1879, 23 Aug 1902
Stolze, Gerhard: 1 Oct 1926, 12 Mar 1979
Stölzel, Gottfried Heinrich: 13 Jan 1690, 27 Nov 1749
Stookey, Paul: 30 Nov 1937
Storchio, Rosina: 19 May 1876, 24 Jul 1945
Stout, Alan: 26 Nov 1932
Stradella, Alessandro: 8 Oct 1644, 25 Feb 1682
Stradivari, Antonio: 18 Dec 1737
Straight, Willard: 18 Jul 1930
Strandberg, Newton: 3 Jan 1921
Strang, Gerald: 13 Feb 1908
Stratas, Teresa: 26 May 1938, 16 Oct 1958, 28 Oct 1959
Straus, Oscar: 6 Mar 1870, 14 Nov 1908, 11 Jan 1954
Strauss, Franz: 26 Feb 1822, 31 May 1905
Strauss, Johann, Jr.: 25 Oct 1825, 13 Feb 1867, 5 Apr 1874, 24
    Oct 1885, 3 Jun 1899
Strauss, Johann, Sr.: 14 Mar 1804, 25 Sep 1849
Strauss, Josef: 22 Aug 1827, 21 Jul 1870
Strauss, Richard: 11 Jun 1864, 11 Nov 1889, 21 Jun 1890, 5 Nov
    1895, 27 Nov 1896, 8 Mar 1898, 3 Mar 1899, 9 Dec 1905, 22
    Jan 1907, 25 Jan 1909, 26 Jan 1911, 25 Oct 1912, 14 May
    1914, 4 Oct 1916, 10 Oct 1919, 16 Oct 1925, 8 Sep 1949
Stravinsky, Igor: 17 Jun 1882, 25 Jun 1910, 13 Jun 1911, 29 May
    1913, 26 May 1914, 28 Sep 1918, 15 May 1920, 10 Jun 1921,
    18 Oct 1923, 30 May 1927, 27 Apr 1928, 27 Nov 1928, 6 Dec
    1929, 13 Dec 1930, 23 Oct 1931, 28 Oct 1932, 27 Apr 1937,
    8 May 1938, 13 Jan 1944, 25 Mar 1946, 11 Sep 1951, 23 Aug
    1964, 6 Apr 1971
Strayhorn, Billy: 29 Nov 1915, 30 May 1967
Street, Tison: 20 May 1943
Streich, Rita: 18 Dec 1920
Strepponi, Giuseppina: 8 Sep 1815, 14 Nov 1897
Strickland, William: 25 Jan 1914
Stringfield, Lamar: 10 Oct 1897, 21 Jan 1959
Stringham, Edwin John: 11 Jul 1890, 1 Jul 1974
Subotnick, Morton: 14 Apr 1933
Suderburg, Robert: 28 Jan 1936
Suk, Josef: 4 Jan 1874, 29 May 1935
Suliotis, Elena: 28 May 1943
Sullivan, Arthur: 13 May 1842, 25 Mar 1875, 25 May 1878, 31 Dec
    1879, 25 Apr 1881, 25 Nov 1882, 5 Jan 1884, 14 Mar 1885, 22
    Jan 1887, 3 Oct 1888, 7 Dec 1889, 7 Oct 1893, 22 Nov 1900, 25
    May 1978

Suppé, Franz von: 18 Apr 1819, 24 Aug 1846, 21 May 1895
Surinach, Carlos: 4 Mar 1915
Susskind, Walter: 1 May 1913
Sutherland, Joan: 7 Nov 1926, 8 Jan 1960, 21 Feb 1961, 26 Nov 1961
Sutton, Vern: 8 Apr 1938
Svanholm, Set: 2 Sep 1904, 15 Nov 1946, 4 Oct 1964
Svendsen, Johan: 30 Sep 1840, 14 Jun 1911
Sveshnikov, Aleksander: 11 Sep 1890
Svetlanov, Eugene (Evgeny): 6 Sep 1928
Sviridov, Georgy Vassilievitch: 16 Dec 1915
Swanson, Howard: 18 Aug 1907, 23 Nov 1950, 14 Nov 1978
Swarowsky, Hans: 16 Sep 1899, 10 Sep 1975
Swarthout, Gladys: 25 Dec 1900, 15 Nov 1929, 7 Jul 1969
Sweelinck, Jan Pieterszoon: 16 Oct 1621
Swift, Richard: 24 Sep 1927
Sydeman, William: 8 May 1928
Szalowski, Antoni: 21 Apr 1907, 21 Mar 1973
Szcepanska, Krystyna: 25 Jan 1917
Szell, George: 7 Jun 1897, 9 Dec 1942, 30 Jul 1970
Szeryng, Henryk: 22 Sep 1918
Szigeti, Joseph: 5 Sep 1892, 19 Feb 1973
Szönyi, Olga: 2 Jul 1936
Szymanowski, Karol: 6 Oct 1882, 28 Mar 1937

Taddei, Giuseppe: 26 Jun 1916
Taffanel, Paul: 16 Sep 1844, 22 Nov 1908
Tagliavini, Ferruccio: 14 Aug 1913, 10 Jan 1947
Tailleferre, Germaine: 19 Apr 1892
Takahashi, Yuji: 21 Sep 1938, 29 Mar 1969
Takata, Saburo: 18 Dec 1913
Takemitsu, Toru: 8 Oct 1930, 9 Nov 1967
Tallis, Thomas: 22 Jan 1575, 23 Nov 1585
Talma, Louise: 31 Oct 1906
Talvela, Martti: 4 Feb 1935
Tamagno, Francesco: 28 Dec 1850, 24 Mar 1891, 31 Aug 1905
Tamberlik, Enrico: 16 Mar 1820, 13 Mar 1889
Tamburini, Antonio: 28 Mar 1800, 9 Nov 1876
Tansman, Alexandre: 12 Jun 1897, 5 May 1924
Tartini, Giuseppe: 8 Apr 1692, 26 Feb 1770
Taskova, Slavka: 16 Nov 1940
Tatum, Art (Arthur): 13 Oct 1909, 5 Nov 1956
Tatum, Nancy: 25 Aug 1937
Tauber, Richard: 16 May 1892, 8 Jan 1948
Taubman, Howard: 4 Jul 1907
Tauriello, Antonio: 20 Mar 1931
Tausig, Carl: 4 Nov 1841, 17 Jul 1871
Tausinger, Jan: 1 Nov 1921
Tavener, John: 28 Jan 1944, 1 Oct 1975
Taverner, John: 18 Oct 1545

Tavrizian, Mikhail: 27 May 1907, 17 Oct 1957
Taylor, Deems: 22 Dec 1885, 18 Feb 1919, 17 Feb 1927, 7 Feb
    1931, 3 Jul 1966
Tchaikovsky, Peter Ilyitch: 7 May 1840, 15 Feb 1868, 16 Mar 1870,
    7 Feb 1873, 25 Oct 1875, 19 Nov 1875, 17 Nov 1876, 4 Mar
    1877, 9 Mar 1877, 4 Mar 1878, 29 Mar 1879, 18 Dec 1880,
    4 Dec 1881, 20 Aug 1882, 17 Nov 1888, 15 Jan 1890, 18 Nov
    1891, 19 Mar 1892, 18 Dec 1892, 28 Oct 1893, 6 Nov 1893
Tcherepnin, Alexander: 20 Jan 1899, 26 Jan 1924, 20 Mar 1952,
    29 Sep 1977
Tear, Robert: 8 Mar 1939
Teatro alla Scala: 3 Aug 1778
Teatro Costanzi: 27 Nov 1880
Teatro la Fenice: 16 May 1792
Tebaldi, Renata: 1 Feb 1922, 31 Jan 1955
Teicher, Louis: 24 Aug 1924
Telemann, Georg Philipp: 14 Mar 1681, 25 Jun 1767
Templeton, Alec: 4 Jul 1909, 28 Mar 1963
Ternina, Milka: 19 Dec 1863, 18 May 1941
Teschler, Fred: 27 Sep 1926
Tesi, Vittoria: 13 Feb 1700, 9 May 1775
Tetrazzini, Luisa: 28 Jun 1871, 15 Jan 1908, 27 Dec 1911, 28 Apr
    1940
Thalberg, Sigismond: 8 Jan 1812, 27 Apr 1871
Thebom, Blanche: 19 Sep 1918, 14 Dec 1944
Theodorakis, Mikis: 29 Jul 1925
Theyard, Harry: 28 Sep 1939
Thibaud, Jacques: 27 Sep 1880, 1 Sep 1953
Thielemans, Jean "Toots": 29 Apr 1922
Thomas, Ambroise: 5 Aug 1811, 17 Nov 1866, 9 Mar 1868, 12 Feb
    1896
Thomas, Jess: 4 Aug 1927, 11 Dec 1962
Thomas, John Charles: 6 Sep 1891, 2 Feb 1934, 13 Dec 1960
Thomas, Kurt: 25 May 1904, 31 Mar 1973
Thomas, Michael Tilson: 21 Dec 1944
Thompson, Oscar: 10 Oct 1887, 3 Jul 1945
Thompson, Randall: 21 Apr 1899, 24 Mar 1932, 13 Apr 1943
Thomson, Virgil: 25 Nov 1896, 8 Feb 1934, 22 Feb 1945, 7 May
    1947, 18 Sep 1954, 1 Nov 1964
Thorne, Francis: 23 Jun 1922
Thuille, Ludwig: 30 Nov 1861, 5 Feb 1907
Tibbett, Lawrence: 16 Nov 1896, 15 Jul 1960
Tichatschek, Joseph: 11 Jul 1807, 18 Jan 1886
Tietjens, Therese: 17 Jul 1831, 3 Oct 1877
Tigranian, Armen: 26 Dec 1879, 17 Aug 1912, 10 Feb 1950, 3 Dec
    1950
Timm, Kenneth: 2 Nov 1934
Tinker, William: 16 Feb 1934
Tinsley, Pauline: 27 Mar 1938
Tippett, Michael: 2 Jan 1905, 19 Mar 1944, 27 Jan 1955, 5 Feb
    1958
Tishchencko, Boris: 23 Mar 1939
Titelouze, Jean: 24 Oct 1633

Titus, Alan: 28 Oct 1945
Toch, Ernst: 7 Dec 1887, 17 Jun 1930, 2 Dec 1955, 13 Feb 1956,
13 Mar 1964, 1 Oct 1964
Tomášek, Jan Václav: 17 Apr 1774, 3 Apr 1850
Tomasi, Henri: 17 Aug 1901, 13 Jan 1971
Topper, Hertha: 19 Apr 1924
Torelli, Giuseppe: 22 Apr 1658, 8 Feb 1709
Torkanowsky, Werner: 30 Mar 1926
Tortelier, Paul: 21 Mar 1914
Tosar, Héctor: 18 Jul 1923
Toscanini, Arturo: 25 Mar 1867, 25 Jun 1886, 25 Dec 1937, 4 Apr
1954, 16 Jan 1957
Toselli, Enrico: 13 Mar 1883, 15 Jan 1926
Tosti, Francesco Paolo: 9 Apr 1846, 2 Dec 1916
Tourangeau, Huguette: 12 Aug 1938
Tourel, Jennie: 22 Jun 1900, 23 Nov 1973
Tournemire, Charles: 22 Jan 1870, 3 Nov 1939
Tournier, Marcel: 5 Jun 1879, 12 May 1951
Tovey, Donald Francis: 17 Jul 1875, 10 Jul 1940
Town Hall (New York); 12 Jan 1921
Toye, Geoffrey: 17 Feb 1889, 11 Jun 1942
Tozzi, Giorgio: 8 Jan 1923
Trama, Ugo: 4 Aug 1932
Trampler, Walter: 25 Aug 1915
Trapp, Max: 1 Nov 1887, 31 May 1971
Traubel, Helen: 20 Jun 1899, 28 Dec 1939, 28 Jul 1972
Travers, Mary: 7 Nov 1927
Travis, Roy: 24 Jun 1922
Treigle, Norman: 6 Mar 1927, 16 Feb 1975
Tremblay, George: 14 Jan 1911
Tremblay, Gilles: 6 Sep 1932
Trimble, Lester: 29 Aug 1920
Troyanos, Tatiana: 12 Sep 1938
Trythall, Richard: 25 Jul 1939, 31 Mar 1973
Tucci, Gabriela: 4 Aug 1929
Tucker, Richard: 28 Aug 1913, 25 Jan 1945, 3 Aug 1947, 8 Jan
1975
Tuckwell, Barry: 5 Mar 1931
Tulindberg, Erik: 22 Feb 1761, 1 Sep 1814
Tuma, Franz: 2 Oct 1704, 4 Feb 1774
Tunder, Franz: 5 Nov 1667
Tureck, Rosalyn: 14 Dec 1914
Turina, Joaquín: 9 Dec 1882, 14 Jan 1949
Turner, Charles: 25 Nov 1921
Turner, Claramae: 28 Oct 1920
Turok, Paul: 3 Dec 1929, 9 Mar 1973
Turp, André: 21 Dec 1925

Uhde, Hermann: 20 Jul 1914, 24 Oct 1965
Uhl, Alfred: 5 Jun 1909

Uhl, Fritz: 2 Apr 1928
Unger, Caroline: 28 Oct 1803, 23 Mar 1877
Unger, Gerhard: 26 Nov 1916
United States Copyright Law: 1 Jan 1978
Urbaniak, Michal: 22 Jan 1943
Urbanner, Erich: 26 Mar 1936
Ursuleac, Viorica: 26 Mar 1899
Ussachevsky, Vladimir: 3 Nov 1911
Uttini, Francesco Antonio: 24 Jul 1755, 25 Oct 1795

Vaccai, Nicola: 15 Mar 1790, 31 Oct 1825, 5 Aug 1848
Vaet, Jacobus: 8 Jan 1567
Vainberg, Moysey Samuilovitch; 8 Dec 1919
Válek, Jiří: 28 May 1923
Valleria, Alwina: 12 Oct 1848, 17 Feb 1925
Valletti, Cesare: 18 Dec 1922, 10 Dec 1953
Valverde, Joaquín: 27 Feb 1846, 17 Mar 1910
Van Allan, Richard: 28 May 1935
Van Beinum, Eduard: 3 Sep 1900, 13 Apr 1959
Van Dam, José: 25 Aug 1940
Van Delden, Lex: 10 Sep 1919
Van Dyke, Ernest: 2 Apr 1861, 31 Aug 1923
Vanhal, Jan Křtitel: 12 May 1739, 20 Aug 1813
Van Kesteren, John: 4 May 1921
Van Mill, Arnold: 26 Mar 1921
Vanni, Helen: 30 Jan 1924
Van Vactor, David: 8 May 1906, 7 Feb 1938, 19 Jan 1939, 14 Mar
     1941, 3 Apr 1959, 30 Oct 1966
Van Vrooman, Richard: 29 Jul 1936
Vanzo, Alain: 2 Apr 1928
Varèse, Edgard: 22 Dec 1883, 23 Apr 1922, 9 Apr 1926, 8 Apr
     1927, 6 Mar 1933, 16 Feb 1936, 6 Nov 1965
Varesi, Felice: 13 Mar 1889
Varnay, Astrid: 25 Apr 1918, 6 Dec 1941
Varviso, Silvio: 26 Feb 1924
Vassilenko, Sergey: 30 Mar 1872, 11 Mar 1956
Vaughan, Elizabeth: 12 Mar 1936
Vaughan, Sarah: 27 Mar 1924
Vaughan Williams, Ralph: 12 Oct 1872, 6 Sep 1910, 12 Oct 1910,
     27 Mar 1914, 4 May 1920, 14 Jun 1921, 26 Jan 1922, 10 Apr
     1935, 3 May 1952, 13 Jun 1954, 26 Aug 1958
Veasey, Josephine: 10 Jul 1930
Vecchi, Orazio: 6 Dec 1550, 19 Feb 1605
Vega, Aurelio de la: 28 Nov 1925, 20 Apr 1978
Vejvanovsky, Pavel: 24 Jun 1693
Venuti, Giuseppe "Joe": 4 Apr 1898, 14 Aug 1978
Veracini, Francesco Maria: 1 Feb 1690, 31 Oct 1768
Verdi, Giuseppe: 10 Oct 1813, 17 Nov 1839, 9 Mar 1842, 11 Feb
     1843, 9 Mar 1844, 14 Mar 1847, 8 Dec 1849, 11 Mar 1851, 19
     Jan 1853, 6 Mar 1853, 13 Jun 1855, 12 Mar 1857, 17 Feb

Wakefield, John: 21 Jun 1936
Walcha, Helmut: 27 Oct 1907
Waldteufel, Emil: 9 Dec 1837, 12 Feb 1915
Walker, George: 27 Jun 1922
Walker, Sandra: 1 Oct 1945
Wallenstein, Alfred: 7 Oct 1898
Waller, Thomas "Fats": 21 May 1904, 15 Dec 1943
Walter, Bruno: 15 Sep 1876, 13 Mar 1894, 3 Mar 1909, 15 Feb
     1923, 14 Feb 1941, 17 Feb 1962
Walther, Johann Gottfried: 18 Sep 1684, 23 Mar 1748
Walton, Cedar: 17 Jan 1934
Walton, William: 29 Mar 1902, 3 Oct 1929, 10 Oct 1931, 7 Dec
     1939, 2 Jun 1953, 3 Dec 1954, 30 Jan 1958, 2 Sep 1960
Wanhal, Johann Baptiste: See Vanhal, Jan Krititel
Ward, David: 3 Jul 1922
Ward, Genevieve: 27 Mar 1833, 18 Aug 1922
Ward, Robert: 13 Sep 1917, 26 Oct 1961, 3 Jul 1964
Warfield, Sandra: 6 Aug 1929
Warfield, William: 22 Jan 1920, 19 Mar 1950
Waring, Fred: 9 Jun 1900
Warlock, Peter (Philip Heseltine): 30 Oct 1894, 17 Dec 1930
Warren, Elinor Remick: 23 Feb 1905
Warren, Leonard: 21 Apr 1911, 13 Jan 1939, 4 Mar 1960
Watanabe, Akeo: 5 Jun 1919
Watanabe, Ruth: 12 May 1916
Watanabe, Sadao: 1 Feb 1933
Waters, Ethel: 31 Oct 1896, 1 Sep 1977
Watson, Claire: 3 Feb 1927
Watts, André: 20 Jun 1946
Wa-Wan Press: See Farwell, Arthur
Weathers, Felicia: 13 Aug 1939
Weber, Ben: 23 Jul 1916, 28 Oct 1952, 19 Feb 1955 9 May 1979
Weber, Carl Maria von: 18 Nov 1786, 30 Jan 1817, 18 Jun 1821,
     25 Oct 1823, 12 Apr 1826, 5 Jun 1826
Weber, Eberhard: 22 Jan 1940
Weber, Ludwig: 29 Jul 1899, 9 Dec 1974
Webern, Anton: 3 Dec 1883, 31 Mar 1913, 23 Jun 1926, 18 Dec
     1929, 15 Sep 1945
Webster, Beveridge: 30 May 1908
Weede, Robert: 22 Feb 1903
Weelkes, Thomas: 30 Nov 1623
Weigl, Karl: 6 Feb 1881, 11 Aug 1949
Weigl, Vally: 11 Sep 1899
Weikl, Bernd: 29 Jul 1942
Weill, Kurt: 2 Mar 1900, 31 Aug 1928, 3 Apr 1950
Weinberger, Jaromir: 8 Jan 1896, 27 Apr 1927, 8 Aug 1967
Weingartner, Felix: 2 Jun 1863, 7 May 1942
Weinzweig, John: 11 Mar 1913, 3 Feb 1951
Weisgall, Hugo: 13 Oct 1912, 11 Feb 1952
Weiss, Adolph: 12 Sep 1891, 21 Feb 1930, 21 Feb 1971
Weiss, Sylvius Leopold: 12 Oct 1686, 16 Oct 1750
Weissenberg, Alexis: 26 Jul 1929
Welitsch, Ljuba: 10 Jul 1913, 4 Feb 1949

Welk, Lawrence: 11 Mar 1903
Wellesz, Egon: 21 Oct 1885, 9 Nov 1974
Welsh, Moray: 1 Mar 1947
Wernick, Richard: 16 Jan 1934, 19 Jan 1976
Wesley, Samuel: 24 Feb 1766, 11 Oct 1837
Wesley, Samuel Sebastian: 14 Aug 1810, 19 Apr 1876
Westergaard, Peter: 28 May 1931
Whear, Paul W.: 13 Nov 1925
White, Donald H.: 28 Feb 1921
Whiteman, Paul: 28 Mar 1890, 29 Dec 1967
Whitney, Robert: 9 Jul 1904
Whittaker, Howard: 19 Dec 1922
Whittemore, Arthur: 23 Oct 1916
Whittenberg, Charles: 6 Jul 1927
Widor, Charles Marie: 21 Feb 1844, 12 Mar 1937
Wieck, Friedrich: 18 Aug 1785, 6 Oct 1873
Wieniawski, Henryk: 10 Jul 1835, 31 Mar 1880
Wigglesworth, Frank: 3 Mar 1918
Wilbraham, John: 15 May 1944
Wilbye, John: 7 Mar 1574
Wild, Earl: 26 Nov 1915
Wilder, Alec: 16 Feb 1907
Wilderman, William: 2 Dec 1919
Wilding-White, Raymond: 9 Oct 1922
Wiley, Lee: 9 Oct 1915, 11 Dec 1975
Willaert, Adrian: 8 Dec 1562
Willan, Healy: 12 Oct 1880, 16 Feb 1968
Willcocks, David: 30 Dec 1919
Williams, Clifton: 26 Mar 1923
Williams, John: 24 Apr 1941
Williams, Ralph Vaughan: See Vaughan Williams, Ralph
Williamson, Malcolm: 21 Nov 1931, 22 May 1965, 4 Jan 1966
Wilson, Olly: 9 Sep 1937
Wilson, Richard: 15 May 1941
Wimberger, Peter: 14 May 1940
Windgassen, Wolfgang: 26 Jun 1914, 8 Sep 1974
Winsor, Philip: 10 May 1938
Winter, Peter: 28 Aug 1754, 17 Oct 1825
Winterhalter, Hugo: 15 Aug 1909, 17 Sep 1973
Wirén, Dag: 15 Oct 1905
Witt, Friedrich: 8 Nov 1770, 3 Jan 1836
Wittgenstein, Paul: 5 Nov 1887, 3 Mar 1961
Woelfl, Joseph: 24 Dec 1773, 21 May 1812
Wolansky, Raymond: 15 Feb 1926
Wolf, Hugo: 13 Mar 1860, 22 Feb 1903
Wolf Trap Farm: 1 Jul 1971
Wolff, Albert: 19 Jan 1884, 20 Feb 1970
Wolff, Beverly: 6 Nov 1928
Wolff, Christian: 8 Mar 1934
Wolf-Ferrari, Ermanno: 12 Jan 1876, 4 Dec 1909, 23 Dec 1911, 21 Jan 1948
Wolpe, Stefan: 25 Aug 1902, 4 Apr 1972
Wood, Henry J.: 3 Mar 1869, 19 Aug 1944

Wood, Hugh: 27 Jun 1932
Wood, Joseph: 12 May 1915
Work, Henry Clay: 1 Oct 1832, 8 Jun 1884
Workman, William: 4 Feb 1940
Wranitzky, Paul: 30 Dec 1756, 26 Sep 1808
Wuensch, Gerhard: 23 Dec 1925
Wüllner, Franz: 28 Jan 1832, 7 Sep 1902
Wüllner, Ludwig: 19 Aug 1858, 19 Mar 1938
Wunderlich, Fritz: 26 Sep 1930, 17 Sep 1966
Wuorinen, Charles: 9 Jun 1938, 4 Aug 1972, 6 Dec 1974
Wylie, Ruth Shaw: 24 Jun 1916
Wyner, Yehudi: 1 Jun 1929

Xenakis, Iannis: 29 May 1922, 15 Oct 1955, 8 Mar 1957, 20 Jul 1958,
    28 Jun 1966

Yarrow, Peter: 31 May 1938
Yon, Pietro: 8 Aug 1886, 22 Nov 1943
Youmans, Vincent: 27 Sep 1898, 21 Apr 1924, 5 Apr 1946
Young, Alexander: 18 Oct 1920
Ysaÿe, Eugène: 16 Jul 1858, 12 May 1931
Yttrehus, Rolv: 12 Mar 1926
Yun, Isang: 17 Sep 1917
Yurlov, Alexander: 11 Aug 1927

Zabaleta, Nicanor: 7 Jan 1907,
Zaccaria, Nicola: 9 Mar 1923
Zádor, Eugene: 5 Nov 1894, 8 Oct 1939, 4 Apr 1977
Zandonai, Riccardo: 30 May 1883, 19 Feb 1914, 5 Jun 1944
Zaninelli, Luigi: 30 Mar 1932
Zannini, Laura: 4 Apr 1937
Zarlino, Gioseffo: 14 Feb 1590
Zeffirelli, Franco: 12 Feb 1923
Zeisler, Fannie: 16 Jul 1863, 20 Aug 1927
Zeitlin, Denny: 10 Apr 1938
Zennatello, Giovanni: 22 Feb 1876, 11 Feb 1949
Zidek, Ivo: 4 Jun 1926
Ziehrer, Karl: 2 May 1843, 29 Jul 1899, 14 Nov 1922
Zimbalist, Efrem: 21 Apr 1889, 27 Oct 1911, 15 Jul 1914
Zimmermann, Bernd Alois: 20 Mar 1918, 10 Dec 1950, 11 Dec
    1969, 10 Aug 1970
Zinman, David: 9 Jul 1936
Zoller, Attila: 13 Jun 1927
Zukerman, Pinchas: 16 Jul 1948, 3 Apr 1971

TITLE INDEX

Abraham and Isaac (Stravinsky): 23 Aug 1964
Academic Festival Overture (Brahms): 4 Jan 1881
Achorripsis (Xenakis): 20 Jul 1958
Acta Musicologica (Jeppesen): 15 Aug 1892
Aculeo (Letelier): 30 Jan 1957
Adagio for Strings (Barber): 5 Nov 1938
Adios (Vega): 20 Apr 1978
Admeto, re di Tessaglia (Handel): 31 Jan 1729
Adriana Lecouvreur (Cilèa): 6 Nov 1902
Adriano in Siria (Pergolesi): 25 Oct 1734
Africaine, L' (Meyerbeer): 28 Apr 1865
After the Ball (Coward): 10 Jun 1954
Agrippina (Handel): 26 Dec 1709
Aïda (Verdi): 24 Dec 1871
Ain't Misbehavin' (Waller): 21 May 1904
Airborne Symphony (Blitzstein): 23 Mar 1946
Akrata (Xenakis): 28 Jun 1966
Albert Herring (Britten): 20 Jun 1947
Alceste (Gluck): 26 Dec 1767
Alceste (Lully): 19 Jan 1674
Alcina (Handel): 16 Apr 1735
Alessandro (Handel): 5 May 1726
Alessandro Stradella (Flotow): 25 Feb 1682
Alexander Nevsky (Prokofiev): 17 May 1939
Alexander's Feast (Handel): 19 Feb 1736
Alfred (Arne): 1 Aug 1740
Ali Baba (Bottesini): 18 Jan 1871
Alice in Wonderland (Del Tredici): 7 Oct 1976
Alice's Restaurant (Guthrie): 10 Jul 1947
Almira (Handel): 8 Jan 1705
Also sprach Zarathustra (Strauss): 27 Nov 1896
Amahl and the Night Visitors (Menotti): 24 Dec 1951
Amelia Goes to the Ball (Menotti): 1 Apr 1937
America (Bloch): 20 Dec 1928
American Cantata (Foss): 1 Dec 1977

American Festival Overture (Schuman):   6 Oct 1939
American in Paris, An (Gershwin):   13 Dec 1928
American Life (Weiss):   21 Feb 1930
American Popular Song (Wilder):   16 Feb 1907
American Record Guide (Lyons):   13 Nov 1973
American Requiem, An (Brant):   8 Jun 1974
Amerika (Kohs):   19 May 1970
Amériques (Varèse):   9 Apr 1926
Amico Fritz L' (Mascagni):   31 Oct 1891
Amor brujo, El (Falla):   15 Apr 1915
Amore dei tre rei, L' (Montemezzi):   10 Apr 1913, 2 Jan 1914
Anacréon (Cherubini):   4 Oct 1803
Ancient Voices of Children (Crumb):   31 Oct 1970
And David Wept (Laderman):   10 Apr 1971
And God Created Great Whales (Hovhaness):   11 Jun 1970
Andrea Chénier (Giordano):   28 Mar 1896
Angels and Devils (Brant):   6 Feb 1933
Angle of Repose (Imbrie):   6 Nov 1976
Anna Bolena (Donizetti):   26 Dec 1830
Antiphonie (Morel):   16 Oct 1953
Antony and Cleopatra (Barber):   16 Sep 1966
Anush (Tigranian):   17 Aug 1912
Aphrodite (Erlanger):   23 Mar 1906
"Apocalyptic," Symphony no. 8 (Bruckner):   18 Dec 1892
Apollo (Stravinsky):   27 Apr 1928
Appalachian Spring (Copland):   30 Oct 1944
Arcana (Varèse):   8 Apr 1927
Ariadne (Crosse):   11 Jul 1972
Ariadne (Strauss):   25 Oct 1912; 4 Oct 1916
Arianna (Monteverdi):   28 May 1608
Arkansas Traveler (McDonald):   3 Mar 1940
Arlésienne, L' (Bizet):   10 Nov 1872
Armide (Gluck):   23 Sep 1777
Ars Nova (Vitry):   31 Oct 1291
Art de toucher le clavecin, L' (Couperin):   10 Nov 1668
Art du Violon (Baillot):   15 Sep 1842
Assassinio nella cattedrale (Pizzetti):   1 Mar 1958
Astarto (Bononcini):   19 Nov 1720
At Dawning (Cadman):   24 Dec 1881
Atlántida (Falla):   18 Jun 1962
Auld Lang Syne (Lombardo):   5 Nov 1977
Automatic Pistol, The (Kohs):   5 Sep 1943
Available Forms I (Brown):   8 Sep 1961
Avalanche for Pitchmen (Hiller):   31 Oct 1968
Ave Maria (Gounod):   18 Oct 1893

Baba Yaga (Liadov):   18 Mar 1904
Babes in Toyland (Herbert):   17 Jun 1903
Bachianas Brasileira no. 1 (Villa-Lobos):   12 Sep 1932
Bachianas Brasileira no. 5 (Villa-Lobos):   25 Mar 1939

Baiser de la fée (Stravinsky): 27 Nov 1928
Baker's Biographical Dictionary of Musicians (Baker): 3 Jun 1851
Ballad of Baby Doe (Moore): 7 Jul 1956
Ballad of the Harp Weaver (Scott): 22 Feb 1947
Ballade de la geôle de Reading (Ibert): 22 Oct 1922
Ballet mécanique (Antheil): 19 Jun 1926
Ballo in maschera, Un (Verdi): 17 Feb 1859
Bánk-Bán (Erkel): 9 Mar 1861
Banks of Green Willow, The (Butterworth): 20 Mar 1914
Barber of Seville, The (Rossini): 20 Feb 1816
Barbier von Bagdad, Der (Cornelius): 15 Dec 1858
Bartered Bride, The (Smetana): 30 May 1866
Be Glad, Then, America (La Montaine): 6 Feb 1976
Beatrice di Tenda (Bellini): 16 Mar 1833
Beatrice et Benedict (Berlioz): 9 Aug 1862
Beautiful Blue Danube Waltz, The (Strauss): 13 Feb 1867
Beggar's Opera, The (Gay and Pepusch): 29 Jan 1728
Begin the Beguine (Porter): 15 Oct 1964
Belshazzar (Handel): 27 Mar 1745
Belshazzar's Feast (Walton): 10 Oct 1931
Benvenuto Cellini (Berlioz): 10 Sep 1838
Beth Alpha Mosaic (Gilboa): 24 Jan 1976
Bilby's Doll (Floyd): 29 Feb 1976
"Billy Ascends," Symphony no. 2 (Evett): 7 May 1965
Billy Budd (Britten): 1 Dec 1951
Billy the Kid (Copland): 16 Oct 1938
Biographie universelle des musiciens (Fétis): 25 Mar 1784
Black Maskers, The (Sessions): 5 Dec 1930
Blossom Time (Romberg): 29 Sep 1921
Body and Soul (Hawkins): 19 May 1969
Boeuf sur le toit Le (Milhaud): 21 Feb 1920
Bohème, La (Puccini): 1 Feb 1896
Bohemian Girl, The (Balfe): 27 Nov 1843
Boléro (Ravel): 22 Nov 1928
Boor, The (Bucci): 29 Dec 1949
Boris Godunov (Mussorgsky): 8 Feb 1874
Bridge on the River Kwai (Arnold): 21 Oct 1921
Brigg Fair (Delius): 18 Jan 1908
Bugaku (Matsudaira): 6 Oct 1962
Buona figliuola maritata, La (Piccinni): 10 Jun 1761
Burning Fiery Furnace, The (Britten): 9 Jun 1966

Calife de Bagdad, Le (Boieldieu): 16 Sep 1801
Canticle of the Sun, The (Sowerby): 16 Apr 1945
Cantique de de Noël (Adam): 3 May 1856
Canzona seria (Josten): 23 Nov 1957
Canzoni (Castiglione): 18 Oct 1966
Capriccio (Stravinsky): 6 Dec 1929
Capriccio espagnol (Rimsky-Korsakov): 31 Oct 1887
Capriccio italien (Tchaikovsky): 18 Dec 1880

Ebony Concerto (Stravinsky): 25 Mar 1946
Echoes of Time and the River (Crumb): 26 May 1967
Egmont: Incidental Music (Beethoven): 24 May 1810
8 Hitchhiker Inscriptions from a Highway Railing (Partch): 22 Apr
     1944
Eight Songs for a Mad King (Maxwell Davies): 22 Apr 1969
1812 Overture (Tchaikovsky): 20 Aug 1882
Eleanor Roosevelt Story, The (Laderman): 29 Jun 1924
Einstein on the Beach (Glass): 25 Jul 1976
Electra (Strauss): 25 Jan 1909
Elegiac Symphony (Keats): 28 Apr 1964
Elegy (Labunski): 11 Dec 1955
Elegy in Memory of Maurice Ravel (Diamond): 28 Apr 1938
Elijah (Mendelssohn): 26 Aug 1846
Elisir d'amore, L' (Donizetti): 12 May 1832
Elverhøj (Kuhlau): 6 Nov 1828
"Emancipation Symphony," Symphony no. 3 (Kelly): 5 Feb 1963
"Emperor," Piano Concerto no. 5 (Beethoven): 12 Feb 1812
Emperor Jones (Gruenberg): 7 Jan 1933
En Saga (Sibelius): 16 Feb 1893
Enchanted Lake (Liadov): 21 Feb 1909
Enchantements d'Alcine, Les (Auric): 21 May 1929
Enfance du Christ, L' (Berlioz): 10 Dec 1854
Enfant prodige, L' (Debussy): 27 Jun 1884
Enigma Variations (Elgar): 19 Jun 1899
Epiphany Variations (Crosse): 18 Mar 1976
Epitaphs (Klein): 4 Apr 1965
Ernani (Verdi): 9 Mar 1844
"Eroica," Symphony no. 3 (Beethoven): 7 Apr 1805
Eroii de la Rovine (Bretan): 24 Jan 1935
Erode the Great (La Montaine): 30 Dec 1969
Escales (Ports of Call) (Ibert): 6 Jan 1924
España (Chabrier): 4 Nov 1883
Essay for Orchestra (Barber): 5 Nov 1938
Essay no. 2 for Orchestra (Barber): 16 Apr 1942
Estancia (Ginastera): 19 Aug 1952
Estrellita (Ponce): 8 Dec 1882
Etude concrète (Kotónski): 9 Jul 1960
Eugene Onegin (Tchaikovsky): 29 Mar 1879
Euridice (Peri): 6 Oct 1600
Europa riconosciuta (Salieri): 3 Aug 1778
Euryanthe (Weber): 25 Oct 1823
Euterpe (Chadwick): 23 Apr 1904
Evocation (Shapey): 26 Mar 1960
Evocations (Dello Joio): 2 Oct 1970
. . . explosante/fixe (Boulez): 5 Jan 1973

Fabulous Dorseys, The (Dorsey): 12 Jun 1957
Fâcheux, Les (Auric): 19 Jan 1924
Fair at Sorochinsk, The (Mussorgsky): 26 Oct 1917

"From the New World," Symphony no. 9 (Dvořák): 15 Dec 1893

Gaelic Symphony (Beach): 30 Oct 1896
Galanta Dances (Kodály): 11 Dec 1936
Galileo Galilei (Laderman): 14 May 1967
Gayne (Khachaturian): 9 Dec 1942
Genghis Khan (Gutchë): 6 Dec 1963
Georgia on My Mind (Carmichael): 22 Nov 1899
Geographical Fugue (Toch): 17 Jun 1930
Gerald McBoing-Boing (Kubik): 5 Sep 1914
German Requiem (Brahms): 10 Apr 1868
Geschichte der Musik (Ambros): 17 Nov 1816
Gesicht Jesajas, Das (Burkhard): 18 Feb 1936
Gianni Schicchi (Puccini): 14 Dec 1918
"Giant," Symphony no. 5 (Mahler): 18 Oct 1904
Giants in the Earth (Moore): 28 Mar 1951
Giara, La (Casella): 19 Nov 1924
Gioconda, La (Ponchielli): 8 Apr 1876
Gipsy Baron (Strauss, Jr.): 24 Oct 1885
Giulietta e Romeo (Vaccai): 31 Oct 1825
Giuramento Il (Mercandante): 10 Mar 1837
Gloria in G (Poulenc): 20 Jan 1961
Gloriana (Britten): 8 Jun 1953
Goldene Kreuz, Das (Brüll): 22 Dec 1875
Golem (Bretan): 23 Dec 1924
Gondoliers, The (Gilbert and Sullivan): 7 Dec 1889
Good Soldier Schweik, The (Kurka): 23 Apr 1958
Gotterdämmerung (Wagner): 17 Aug 1876
Goyescas (Granados): 28 Jan 1916
Gradus ad Parnassum (Clementi): 23 Jan 1752
Grand Canyon Suite (Grofé): 22 Nov 1931
Grande Bretèche, La (Claflin): 3 Feb 1957
Grandfather's Clock (Work): 8 Jun 1884
Grass (Chihara): 14 Apr 1972
"Great, The," Symphony no. 9 (Schubert): 21 Mar 1839
Great Caruso, The (Lanza): 31 Jan 1921
Gretchen am Spinnrade (Schubert): 19 Oct 1814
Grosser Festmarsch (Wagner): 10 May 1876
Grove's Dictionary of Music and Musicians (Blom): 20 Aug 1888
Grove's Dictionary of Music and Musicians (Grove): 13 Aug 1820
Guerre-Lieder (Schoenberg): 23 Feb 1913

H. M. S. Pinafore (Gilbert and Sullivan): 25 May 1878 and 1978
Halka (Moniuszko): 4 Jun 1872
Hamlet (Thomas): 9 Mar 1868
Hansel and Gretel (Humperdinck): 23 Dec 1893
Happy Prince, The (Williamson): 22 May 1965

Harold en Italie (Berlioz): 23 Nov 1834
Harpies, The (Blitzstein): 25 May 1953
Háry János (Kodály): 16 Oct 1926
Hebrides Overture (Mendelssohn): 14 May 1832
Heldenleben, Ein (Strauss): 3 Mar 1899
Helios Overture (Nielsen): 8 Oct 1903
Hephaestus (Brehm): 22 Nov 1966
Hiawatha's Wedding Feast (Coleridge-Taylor): 11 Nov
    1898
Histoire du soldat, L' (Stravinsky): 28 Sep 1918
History of Music (Burney): 12 Apr 1814
Holiday Overture (Mathias): 30 Sep 1971
Hollow Men, The (Persichetti): 12 Dec 1946
Holy City (Hovhaness): 11 Apr 1967
Homme et son désire, L' (Milhaud): 6 Jun 1921
Hora Novissima (Parker): 3 May 1893
Horia (Bretan): 24 Jan 1937
Horoscope (Lambert): 27 Jan 1938
Horsepower (Chávez): 31 Mar 1932
Huguenots, Les (Meyerbeer): 29 Feb 1836
"Hungarian, The," Violin Concerto (Joachim): 24 Mar 1860
Hunting of the Snark, The (Laderman): 25 Mar 1961
Hunyady László (Erkel): 27 Jan 1844
Husitska Overture (Dvorák): 18 Nov 1883
Hyas Illahee (Creston): 14 Mar 1976
Hymn and Fuguing Tune, Nos. 1-8 (Cowell): 26 Sep 1800
Hymnus (Dvorák): 9 Mar 1873

I Love You Truly (Bond): 11 Aug 1862
Ideomeneo (Mozart): 29 Jan 1781
"Ilya Murometz," Symphony no. 3 (Glière): 23 Mar 1912
In a Monastery Garden (Ketèlbey): 9 Aug 1875
In a Persian Garden (Ketèlbey): 9 Aug 1875
In a Summer Garden (Delius): 11 Dec 1908
In Memoriam (Moore): 27 Apr 1944
In Praise of Shahn (Schuman): 30 Jan 1970
In Space (Bergsma): 21 May 1975
In Terra Pax (Martin): 7 May 1945
Incredible Flutist, The (Piston): 30 May 1938
Indes galantes, Les (Rameau): 23 Aug 1735
"Indian Suite," Suite no. 2 (MacDowell): 23 Jan 1895
Intolleranza 1960 (Nono): 13 Apr 1961
Introduction et Allegro (Ravel): 22 Feb 1907
Introduction et Rondo Capriccioso (Saint-Saëns): 6 Nov 1913
Investiture Dances (Hoddinott): 22 Jun 1969
Iolanthe (Gilbert and Sullivan): 25 Nov 1882
Ionisation (Varèse): 6 Mar 1933
Iphigénie en Aulide (Gluck): 19 Apr 1774
Iphigénie en Tauride (Gluck): 17 May 1779
Iris (Nørgaard): 19 May 1967

Isle of the Dead (Rachmaninoff): 1 May 1909
Israel in Egypt (Handel): 4 Apr 1739
Israel Symphony (Bloch): 3 May 1917
Istar (D'Indy): 10 Jan 1897
Italia (Casella): 23 Apr 1910
"Italian," Symphony no. 4 (Mendelssohn): 13 May 1833
Italiana in Algeri (Rossini): 22 May 1813

Jason (Brunetti): 4 Oct 1768
Jazz Singer, The (Jolson): 26 Mar 1886
Jeanne d'Arc au bûcher (Honegger): 12 May 1938
Jefferson Symphony (Ross): 13 Apr 1976
Jenufa (Janáček): 21 Jan 1904
"Jephta, Rhapsodic Poem," Symphony no. 5 (Toch): 13 Mar 1964
Jephtha (Handel): 26 Feb 1752
"Jeremiah," Symphony no. 1 (Bernstein): 28 Jan 1944
Jessonda (Spohr): 28 Jul 1823
Jeu de cartes (Stravinsky): 27 Apr 1937
Jewels of the Madonna (Wolf-Ferrari): 23 Dec 1911
Jocelyn (Godard): 25 Feb 1888
Jolie fille de Perth, La (Bizet): 26 Dec 1867
Jonny spielt auf (Krenek): 10 Feb 1927
Joseph (Méhul): 17 Feb 1807
Josephslegende (Strauss): 14 May 1914
Joshua (Handel): 9 Mar 1748
Judas Maccabaeus (Handel): 1 Apr 1747
Juive, La (Halévy): 23 Feb 1835
Julius Caesar (Handel): 20 Feb 1724
Julius Caesar Jones (Williamson): 4 Jan 1966
Jumping Frog of Calaveras County, The (Foss): 18 May 1950
Jungle (Josten): 25 Oct 1929

Kalevala (Sibelius): 20 Sep 1957
Kanon in D (Pachelbel): 1 Sep 1653
Kátya Kabanova (Janáček): 23 Nov 1921
Khovanshchina (Mussorgsky): 21 Feb 1886
Kikimora (Liadov): 12 Dec 1909
King and Collier (Dvořák): 24 Nov 1874
King Pomade's New Clothes (Ránki): 6 Jun 1953
King's Henchmen, The (Taylor): 17 Feb 1927
Knoxville: Summer of 1915 (Barber): 9 Apr 1948
Kol Nidrei (Bruch): 6 Jan 1838
Königen von Saba, Die (Goldmark): 10 Mar 1875
Kontakte (Stockhausen): 11 Jun 1960
Kontra-Punkte (Stockhausen): 26 May 1953
Kosmogonia (Penderecki): 24 Oct 1970
Kossuth (Bartók): 13 Jan 1904

Labyrinth (Menotti): 3 Mar 1963
Lady from Colorado (Ward): 3 Jul 1964
Lakmé (Delibes): 14 Apr 1883
Lament for April 15 (Claflin): 21 Jun 1898
Landscapes (Chou): 19 Nov 1953
Landstreicher, Die (Ziehrer): 29 Jul 1899
Largo (Handel): 12 Apr 1710
Lark Ascending, The (Vaughan Williams): 14 Jun 1921
Last Rose of Summer (Flotow): 25 Nov 1847
Latin American Symphonette (Gould): 22 Feb 1941
"Leningrad," Symphony no. 7 (Shostakovich): 1 Mar 1942
Letter from Home (Copland): 17 Oct 1944
Lied von der Erde, Das (Mahler): 20 Nov 1911
Liederkreis (Schumann): 11 Sep 1840
Lieutenant Kijé (Prokofiev): 20 Feb 1937
Life for the Tsar, A (Glinka): 9 Dec 1836
Lily (Kirchner): 14 Apr 1977
Lincoln Portrait (Copland): 14 May 1942
Linda di Chamounix (Donizetti): 19 May 1842
"Little Russian," Symphony no. 2 (Tchaikovsky): 7 Feb 1873
Little Sweep, The (Britten): 14 Jun 1949
Lizzie Borden (Beeson): 25 Mar 1965
"Lobgesang," Symphony no. 2 (Mendelssohn): 25 Jun 1840
Lohengrin (Wagner): 28 Aug 1850
Lombardi, I (Verdi): 11 Feb 1843
London Symphony, A (Vaughan Williams): 27 Mar 1914; 4 May 1920
Long Life (Brant): 27 Apr 1977
Louis Riel (Somers): 23 Oct 1975
Louise (Charpentier): 2 Feb 1900
Loup, Le (Dutilleux): 18 Mar 1953
Lousadzak (Hovhaness): 4 Feb 1945
Love for Three Oranges (Prokofiev): 30 Dec 1921
Lovely Thing (Budd): 23 Oct 1969
Luceafarul (Bretan): 2 Feb 1921
Lucia di Lammermoor (Donizetti): 26 Sep 1835
Lucretia Borgia (Donizetti): 26 Dec 1833
Luisa Miller (Verdi): 8 Dec 1849
Lulu (Berg): 2 Jun 1937
Lunar Laser Beam (Cross): 27 Apr 1971
Lustigen Weiber von Windsor, Die (Nicolai): 8 Mar 1849
Lyric Variations (Turok): 9 Mar 1973

M*A*S*H (Golson): 25 Jan 1929
Ma Mère l'Oye (Ravel): 11 Mar 1915
Macbeth (Verdi): 14 Mar 1847
Macumba, La "Ritual Symphony," (Sanjuán): 14 Dec 1951
Madama Butterfly (Puccini): 17 Feb 1904
Magic Flute, The (Mozart): 30 Sep 1791
Magic Prison (Laderman): 12 Jun 1967
Magic Stones, The (Martirano): 24 Apr 1952

Missa Carminum (Chihara): 15 Jan 1976
Missa solemnis (Beethoven): 29 Jun 1830
Missa solemnis (Bruckner): 14 Sep 1854
Mission Impossible (Schifrin): 21 Jun 1932
Mlle. Modiste (Herbert): 7 Oct 1905
Momente (Stockhausen): 21 May 1962
Mon ami Pierrot (Barlow): 11 Jan 1935
Mond, Der (Orff): 5 Feb 1939
Monodrama (Husa): 26 Mar 1976
Montezuma (Graun): 6 Jan 1755
Mort de Wallenstein, La (d'Indy): 11 Apr 1884
Most Important Man, The (Menotti): 7 Mar 1971
Mother, The (Nielsen): 30 Jan 1921
Mother of Us All, The (Thomson): 7 May 1947
Mourning Becomes Electra (Levy): 17 Mar 1967
Mouvements circulatoires (Matsudaira): 10 Oct 1972
"Muette de Portici," Masaniello (Auber): 29 Feb 1828
Music for a Scene from Shelley (Barber): 23 Mar 1935
Music on My Mind (Smith): 24 Nov 1897
Music Study in Germany (Fay): 21 May 1844
Musical America: 8 Oct 1898
Musical Offering (Bach): 7 May 1747
Musical Quarterly: 1 Jan 1915; 6 Oct 1873
Musik in Geschichte und Gegenwart (Blume): 5 Jan 1893; 22 Nov 1975
Musik-Lexikon (Riemann): 18 Jul 1849
Musikalische Opfer, Das (Bach): 7 May 1747
Musikalisches Lexikon (Walther): 18 Sep 1684
Musique funèbre (Lutoslawski): 26 Mar 1958
Musique pour l'Indiana (Milhaud): 29 Oct 1966
My Fair Lady (Loewe): 15 Mar 1956; 26 Jul 1856

Nabucco (Verdi): 9 Mar 1842
Nachtschwalbe, Die (Blacher): 29 Feb 1948
Narcissus (Nevin): 25 Nov 1862
Naughty Marietta (Herbert): 24 Oct 1910
Nausicaa (Glanville-Hicks): 19 Aug 1961
Neue Zeitschrift für Musik: 3 Apr 1834
New England Episodes (Porter): 18 Apr 1958
New England Psalm Singer (Billings): 7 Oct 1746
New England Triptych (Schuman): 28 Oct 1956
New Methods of Measuring Sound (McDonald): 30 Mar 1955
Night and Day (Porter): 15 Oct 1964
Night Flight (Read): 27 Apr 1944
Night on Bald Mountain (Mussorgsky): 27 Oct 1886
Night Soliloquy (Kennan): 26 Feb 1943
"Night Swallow, The," Nachtschwalbe (Blacher): 29 Feb 1948
Nights in the Gardens of Spain (Falla): 9 Apr 1916
Nine-minute Overture (Shapero): 8 Jun 1941
Nirvana-Symphonie (Mayuzumi): 2 Apr 1958
No for an Answer (Blitzstein): 5 Jan 1941

No, No Nanette (Youmans): 21 Apr 1924
Nocturnes (Debussy): 9 Dec 1900
Norma (Bellini): 26 Dec 1831
Novellis, Novellis (La Montaine): 24 Dec 1961
November Steps (Takemitsu): 9 Nov 1967
Noye's Fludde (Britten): 18 Jun 1958
Nuages (Debussy): 9 Dec 1900
Nutcracker Suite, The (Tchaikovsky): 18 Dec 1892

O the Chimneys (Ran): 19 Jan 1970
Oberon (Weber): 12 Apr 1826
Oberto (Verdi): 17 Nov 1839
Oceanides (Sibelius): 4 Jun 1914
Octagon (Mayer): 21 Mar 1971   .
Ode for St. Cecilia's Day (Handel): 22 Nov 1739
OEdipe-Roi (Maderna): 31 Dec 1970
Oedipus Rex (Stravinsky): 30 May 1927
Of Lena Geyer (Gluck): 27 Oct 1938
Offrandes (Varèse): 23 Apr 1922
Omaggio alla tromba (Kapr): 6 Mar 1970
On Hearing the First Cuckoo in Spring (Delius): 2 Oct 1913
On the Town (Bernstein): 13 Dec 1944
Once Upon a Time, Five Fairy Tales (Rogers): 4 Apr 1935
Opera Flies (El-Dabh): 5 May 1971
Oracle (Bolcom): 2 May 1965
Orfeo (Monteverdi): 24 Feb 1607
Orfeo ed Euridice (Gluck): 5 Oct 1762
"Organ" Symphony no. 3 (Saint-Saëns): 19 May 1886
Organum (Ruggles): 24 Nov 1949
Origin of the Amazon River (Villa-Lobos): 7 Nov 1951
Orontea (Cesti): 20 Jan 1649
Orpheus in Hades (Offenbach): 21 Oct 1858
Otello (Verdi): 5 Feb 1887
Our Town (Copland): 9 Jun 1940
Ouverture de fête (Ibert): 18 Jan 1942
Over There (Cohan): 5 Nov 1942
Overture on the Theme of Three Russian Songs (Balakirev): 2 Jan
    1859
Overture to a Comedy, no. 2 (Van Vactor): 14 Mar 1941
Overture to a Midsummer Night's Dream (Mendelssohn): 1 Feb
    1827
Overture to the Creole Faust (Ginastera): 12 May 1944
Overture to the School for Scandal (Barber): 30 Aug 1933
"Oxford," Symphony no. 92 (Haydn): 8 Jul 1791

PCOMP (Bresnick): 8 Apr 1970
Pacific 231 (Honegger): 8 May 1924

Pagan Poem (Loeffler): 22 Nov 1907
Pageant (Persichetti): 7 Mar 1953
Pageant of P.T. Barnum (Moore): 15 Apr 1926
Pagliacci (Leoncavallo): 21 May 1892
Paladins, Les (Rameau): 12 Feb 1760
Palestrina (Pfitzner): 12 Jun 1917
Parade (Satie): 18 May 1917
Paradigm (Foss): 31 Oct 1968
Pardon de Ploërmel, Le (Meyerbeer): 4 Apr 1859
Parergon zur Symphonia domestica (Strauss): 16 Oct 1925
Parsifal (Wagner): 26 Jul 1882
Partita for Orchestra (Walton): 30 Jan 1958
Passion According to St. Matthew (Bach): 11 Mar 1829
"Pastoral," Symphony no. 6 (Beethoven): 22 Dec 1808
"Pastoral," Symphony no. 3 (Vaughan Williams): 26 Jan 1922
Pastorale, La (Auric): 26 May 1926
"Pathétique," Symphony no. 6 (Tchaikovsky): 28 Oct 1893
Patience (Gilbert and Sullivan): 25 Apr 1881
Paul Bunyan (Bergsma): 22 Jun 1939
Paul Bunyan (Britten): 5 May 1941
Pause del silenzio (Malipiero): 27 Jan 1918
Pêcheurs de perles, Les (Bizet): 30 Sep 1863
Peer Gynt (Grieg): 24 Feb 1876
Pelléas et Mélisande (Debussy): 30 Apr 1902
Pelléas et Mélisande (Fauré): 21 Jun 1898
Pelleas und Melisande (Schoenberg): 26 Jan 1905
Perfect Day, A (Bond): 11 Aug 1862
Péri, La (Dukas): 22 Apr 1912
Périchole, La (Offenbach): 6 Oct 1868
Perspectives of New Music: 3 Oct 1934
Peter and the Wolf (Prokofiev): 2 May 1936
Peter Grimes (Britten): 7 Jun 1945
Peter Ibbetson (Taylor): 7 Feb 1931
Peter Pan (Toch): 13 Feb 1956
Petit elfe ferme-l'oeil, Le (Schmitt): 29 Feb 1924
Petite suite (Roussel): 6 Feb 1930
Petrouchka (Stravinsky): 13 Jun 1911
Philador's Defense--A Musical Chess Game (Reif): 10 Apr 1965
Piano and Voices (Feldman): 28 Oct 1972
Piccola musica notturna (Dallapiccola): 7 Jun 1954
Pictures at an Exhibition (Mussorgsky): 19 Oct 1922
Pièces de clavecin (Couperin): 10 Nov 1668
Pierrot Lunaire (Schoenberg): 16 Oct 1912
Pines of Rome, The (Respighi): 14 Dec 1924
Pirata, Il (Bellini): 27 Oct 1827
Pirates of Penzance, The (Gilbert and Sullivan): 31 Dec 1879
Pisanella, La (Pizzetti): 11 Jun 1913
Pithoprakta (Xenakis): 8 Mar 1957
Plan (Globokar): 7 Nov 1965
Planets, The (Holst): 29 Sep 1918
Pleasure Dome of Kubla Khan (Griffes): 28 Nov 1919
Plexus (Cervetti): 18 May 1971
Pli selon pli (Boulez): 13 Jun 1960

Poebells (London):   26 May 1978
"Poem of Ecstasy, " Symphony no. 4 (Scriabin):   10 Dec 1908
Poème (Chausson):   4 Apr 1897
Poème symphonique (Ligeti):   4 Mar 1965
Poet and Peasant (Suppé):   24 Aug 1846
Polifonica, Monodia, Ritmica (Nono):   10 Jul 1951
"Polish, " Symphony no. 3 (Tchaikovsky):   19 Nov 1875
Polovtsian Dances (Borodin):   11 Mar 1879
Polyhyperchord (Grauer):   20 Mar 1977
Polyptyque (Martin):   9 Sep 1973
Pomp and Circumstances Marches (Elgar):   19 Oct 1901
Porgy and Bess (Gershwin):   30 Sep 1935
Portraits (Haubiel):   12 Dec 1935
Ports of Call (Ibert):   6 Jan 1924
Praise (Shapey):   28 Feb 1976
Praise the Lord and Pass the Ammunition (Loesser):   28 Jul 1969
Prajna Paramita (Takahashi):   29 Mar 1967
Prayer in Time of War (Schuman):   13 Feb 1943
Prélude à l'après-midi d'un faune (Debussy):   23 Dec 1894
Prelude and Fugue (Mason):   4 Mar 1921
Prelude and Passacaglia (Weber):   19 Feb 1955
Préludes, Les (Liszt):   23 Feb 1854
Prigonier superbo, Il (Pergolesi):   28 Aug 1733
Prigioniero, Il (Dallapiccola):   4 Dec 1949
Primavera (Labunski):   19 Apr 1974
Prince Igor (Borodin):   4 Nov 1890; 30 Dec 1915
Princess Ida (Gilbert and Sullivan):   5 Jan 1884
Principles of Pianoforte Practice (Friskin):   16 Mar 1967
Prise de Troie, La (Berlioz):   6 Dec 1890
Pro Musica Antiqua (Greenberg):   9 Apr 1919
Prologue, Capriccio and Epilogue (Lees):   9 Apr 1959
Prométhée (Fauré):   27 Aug 1900
Prometheus (Scriabin):   24 Sep 1975; 15 Mar 1911
Prophète, Le (Meyerbeer):   16 Apr 1849
"Prophets, The, " Violin Concerto no. 2 (Castelnuovo-Tedesco):   12
     Apr 1933
Prosperina y el extranjero (Castro):   17 Mar 1952
Psalm (Diamond):   10 Dec 1936
Psalm XLVII (Schmitt):   27 Dec 1906
Psalm 80 (Roussel):   25 Apr 1929
Psalmus Hungaricus (Kodály):   19 Nov 1923
Psyché (Franck):   10 Mar 1888
Pulcinella (Stravinsky):   15 May 1920
Punch and Judy (Birtwistle):   22 Aug 1968
Puritani, I (Bellini):   24 Jan 1835

Quaker Reader, A (Rorem):   2 Feb 1977
Quartet Romantic (Cowell):   18 May 1978
Quatuor pour la fin du temps (Messiaen):   15 Jan 1941
Quiet City, A (Copland):   28 Jan 1941

Rake's Progress, The (Stravinsky): 11 Sep 1951
Rape of Lucretia, The (Britten): 12 Jul 1946
Rapsodie espagnole (Ravel): 15 Mar 1908
Raymonda (Glazunov): 19 Jan 1898
Re pastore, Il (Uttini): 24 Jul 1755
Re Teodoro in Venezia, Il (Paisiello): 23 Aug 1784
Red Pony, The (Copland): 1 Nov 1948
Red Poppy, The (Glière): 14 Jun 1927
Redes (Revueltas): 7 Oct 1937
"Reformation," Symphony no. 5 (Mendelssohn): 15 Nov 1832
Reine de Saba, La (Gounod): 28 Feb 1862
Relâche (Satie): 29 Nov 1924
"Requiem," Symphony no. 4 (Hanson): 3 Dec 1943
"Requiem for Manon," Violin Concerto (Berg): 19 Apr 1936
Requiem für einen jungen Dichter (Zimmermann): 11 Dec 1969; 10
    Aug 1970
Requiem Mass (Dvořák): 9 Oct 1891
"Resurrection," Symphony no. 2 (Mahler): 13 Dec 1895
Retablo de Maese Pedro (Falla): 23 Mar 1923
Réveil des oiseaux (Messiaen): 11 Oct 1953
Revue Internationale de Musique (Absil): 23 Oct 1893
Rhapsody for Orchestra (Panufnik): 26 Aug 1957
Rhapsody for Orchestra (Sessions): 18 Mar 1970
Rhapsody for Piano and Orchestra (Moeran): 19 Aug 1943
Rhapsody in Blue (Gershwin): 12 Feb 1924
Rhapsody on a Theme of Paganini (Rachmaninoff): 7 Nov 1934
Rhapsody on Ukrainian Themes (Liapunov): 23 Mar 1908
Rheingold, Das (Wagner): 22 Sep 1869
"Rhenish," Symphony no. 3 (Schumann): 6 Feb 1851
Richard Coeur de Lion (Grétry): 21 Oct 1784
Rienzi (Wagner): 20 Oct 1842
Rigoletto (Verdi): 11 Mar 1851
Rinaldo (Handel): 24 Feb 1711
Ring des Nibelungen (Wagner): 13 Aug 1876
Rituals (Shapey): 16 May 1966
Robert le Diable (Meyerbeer): 21 Nov 1831
Rocking Chair (Carmichael): 22 Nov 1899
Rodelinda (Handel): 13 Feb 1725
Rodeo (Copland): 16 Oct 1942
Rodgers and Hart Songbook (Rodgers): 28 Jun 1903
Roger Young (Loesser): 28 Jul 1969
Roi, David, Le (Honegger): 11 Jun 1921
Roi d'Ys, Le (Lalo): 7 May 1888
Roi malgré lui, Le (Chabrier): 18 May 1887
Romance (Vaughan Williams): 3 May 1952
"Romantic," Symphony no. 2 (Hanson): 28 Nov 1930
"Romantic," Symphony no. 4 (Bruckner): 20 Feb 1881
Romeo and Juliet (Prokofiev): 11 Jan 1940
Romeo and Juliet (Tchaikovsky): 16 Mar 1870
Roméo et Juliette (Berlioz): 24 Nov 1839
Roméo et Juliette (Gounod): 27 Apr 1867
Rondine, La (Puccini): 27 Mar 1917
Rosamunde: Incidental Music (Schubert): 20 Dec 1823

Sesame Street (Thielemans): 29 Apr 1922
Shéhérazade (Ravel): 17 May 1904
Sheherazade (Rimsky-Korsakov): 3 Nov 1888
Shepherdes Playe, The (La Montaine): 24 Dec 1967
Short Overture (Kay): 31 Mar 1947
Short Symphony (Swanson): 23 Nov 1950
Showboat (Kern): 15 Nov 1927; 23 Aug 1960
Sicut umbra (Dallapiccola): 30 Oct 1970
Siege of Corinth (Rossini): 9 Oct 1826
Siegfried (Wagner): 16 Aug 1876
Siegfried Idyll (Wagner): 25 Dec 1870; 6 Jun 1869
Simon Boccanegra (Verdi): 12 Mar 1857
Sinfonia (Berio): 10 Oct 1968
Sinfonia (Boda): 6 Dec 1960
Sinfonia (Kirchner): 31 Jan 1952
Sinfonia breve (Stevens): 20 Nov 1957
Sinfonia breve (Van Vactor): 30 Oct 1966
Sinfonia Concertante (Panufnik): 20 May 1974
Sinfonia de Madrid (Custer): 28 Apr 1962
"Sinfonia espansiva," Symphony no. 3 (Nielsen): 28 Feb 1912
Sinfonia in Do (Castiglioni): 21 May 1971
Sinfonia in E (Kay): 2 May 1951
Sinfonia India (Chávez): 23 Jan 1936
Sinfonia romantica (Chávez): 11 Feb 1953
Sinfonia Sacra (Cortés): 9 Apr 1955
Sinfonia semplice (Rosenberg): 24 Jan 1952
"Sinfonia semplice," Symphony no. 6 (Nielsen): 11 Dec 1925
Sinfonietta giocosa (Martinů): 16 Mar 1942
Sirius (Stockhausen): 18 Jul 1976
Six Pieces for Orchestra (Webern): 31 Mar 1913
Skater's Waltz (Waldteufel): 9 Dec 1837
Slavonic Mass, "M'sa Glagolskaja," (Janáček): 5 Dec 1927
Sleeping Beauty (Tchaikovsky): 15 Jan 1890
Snow Maiden (Rimsky-Korsakov): 10 Feb 1882
So Wurde ich Pianist (Gieseking): 26 Oct 1956
Socrate (Satie): 14 Feb 1920
Soleil vainqueur, Le (Clérambault): 21 Oct 1721
Solitude (Koutzen): 1 Apr 1927
Some Times (Ogerman): 14 Jul 1972
"Sommermorgentraum, Ein," Symphony no. 3 (Mahler): 9 Jun
    1902
Sonata quasi una fantasia (Perle): 19 Mar 1972
Song of Norway (Grieg): 4 Sep 1907
Sonnambula, La (Bellini): 6 Mar 1831
Sorcerer's Apprentice (Dukas): 18 May 1897
Source (Austin): 12 Sep 1930
Southern Harmony (Kay): 10 Feb 1976
Spirituals for Orchestra (Gould): 9 Feb 1941
"Spring," Symphony no. 1 (Schumann): 31 Mar 1841
Stabat Mater (Dvořák): 23 Dec 1880
Stabat Mater (Poulenc): 13 Jun 1951
Stadtfpeifermusik (Mohaupt): 7 Jul 1946

Telephone, The (Menotti): 18 Feb 1947
Ten Pieces for Wind Quintet (Ligeti): 19 Jan 1969
Tender Land (Copland): 1 Apr 1954
Tenor, The (Weisgall): 11 Feb 1952
Testament of Freedom, A (Thompson): 13 Apr 1943
Thaïs (Massenet): 16 Mar 1894
Theodora (Handel): 16 Mar 1750
Thirteen Clocks, The (Bucci): 29 Dec 1953
This Year of Grace (Coward): 7 Nov 1928
Three Chinese Pieces (Chasins): 8 Apr 1931
Three-Cornered Hat (Falla): 22 Jul 1919
Three Japanese Pieces (Rogers): 3 May 1934
Three Penny Opera (Weill): 31 Aug 1928
Three Pieces for Blues Band and Orchestra (Russo): 7 Jul 1968
Three Pieces for Orchestra (Shifrin): 8 Jan 1960
Three Places in New England (Ives): 10 Jan 1931
Three Russian Songs (Rachmaninoff): 18 Mar 1927
Threnody in Memory of Victims of Hiroshima (Penderecki): 31 May
    1961
Through the Looking Glass (Taylor): 18 Feb 1919
Till Eulenspiegels lustige Streiche (Strauss): 5 Nov 1895
Timbres, espace, mouvement (Dutilleux): 10 Jan 1978
Time Cycle (Foss): 21 Oct 1960
"Titan," Symphony no. 1 (Mahler): 20 Nov 1889
Toccata (Chávez): 31 Oct 1947
Toccata (Kirchner): 16 Feb 1956
Toccata e due canzone (Martinů): 21 Jan 1947
Tod Jesu (Graun): 26 Mar 1755
Tod und Verklarung (Strauss): 21 Jun 1890
Tosca (Puccini): 14 Jan 1900
Tote Stadt, Die (Korngold): 4 Dec 1920
Tout un monde lointain (Dutilleux): 25 Jul 1970
Tower of Saint Barbara, The (Dahl): 29 Jan 1955
Tragédie de Salomé, La (Schmitt): 8 Jan 1911
Tragic Overture (Brahms): 4 Jan 1881
Tragic Overture (Panufnik): 24 Mar 1949
Trauermusik (Hindemith): 22 Jan 1936
Traviata, La (Verdi): 6 Mar 1853
Treemonisha (Joplin): 28 Jan 1972; 17 Aug 1928
Trial by Jury (Gilbert and Sullivan): 25 Mar 1875
Triangles (Kraft): 8 Dec 1969
Trio Concertante (Klein): 4 Apr 1965
Trionfo di Camilla, Il (Bononcini): 26 Dec 1696
Tristan und Isolde (Wagner): 10 Jun 1865; 1 Dec 1886
Trittico, Il (Puccini): 14 Dec 1918
Triumph of Saint Joan, The (Dello Joio): 9 May 1950
Troilus and Cressida (Walton): 3 Dec 1954
Trois poèmes juifs (Bloch): 23 Mar 1917
Trovatore, Il (Verdi): 19 Jan 1853
Truth Has Fallen (Brubeck): 1 May 1971
Tsar's Bride (Rimsky-Korsakov): 3 Nov 1899
Turandot (Puccini): 25 Apr 1926
Turangalila-Symphonie (Messiaen): 2 Dec 1949

Umbrian Scene (Kay): 31 Mar 1964
"Unfinished," Symphony no. 8 (Schubert): 17 Dec 1865
Universal Prayer (Panufnik): 24 May 1970
Utopia Limited (Gilbert and Sullivan): 7 Oct 1893

Vagabond King, The (Friml): 21 Sep 1925
Valley Forge (Elmore): 9 Apr 1937
Vanessa (Barber): 15 Jan 1958
Variaciones Concertantes (Ginastera): 2 Jun 1953
Variants (Schuller): 4 Jan 1961
Variations (Bliss): 21 Apr 1973
Variations for Orchestra (Bassett): 6 Jul 1963
Variations for Orchestra (Bennett): 3 Apr 1966
Variations for Orchestra (Schoenberg): 2 Dec 1928
Variations on a Hungarian Peasant Song (Rózsa): 14 Nov 1943
Variations on a Nursery Song (Dohnányi): 17 Feb 1914
Ventanas (Revueltas): 4 Nov 1932
Verhör des Lukullus, Das (Dessau): 17 Mar 1951
Verklärte Nacht (Schoenberg): 18 Mar 1902
Verses for Ensembles (Birtwistle): 31 Aug 1970
Vesalii Icones (Maxwell Davies): 9 Dec 1969
Vespri Siciliani, I (Verdi): 13 Jun 1855
Vestale, La (Mercadante): 10 Mar 1840
Vida breve, La (Falla): 1 Apr 1913
Vie parisienne, La (Offenbach): 31 Oct 1866
Vision of Christ (Beversdorf): 1 May 1971
Vision of Isaiah, The (Burkhard): 18 Feb 1936
Visions at Midnight (Kanitz): 26 Feb 1964
Visions of Ishwara (Hakim): 10 Oct 1970
Visions of Terror and Wonder (Wernick): 19 Jul 1976
Visitation, The (Schuller): 12 Oct 1966
Voices (Mennin): 28 Mar 1976
Voices and Instruments II (Feldman): 11 Feb 1973
Volo di notte (Dallapiccola): 18 May 1940
Vor deinen Thron tret' ich hiermit (Bach): 28 Jul 1750
Votre Faust (Pousseur): 17 Mar 1968
Vox Humana (Pettersson): 19 Mar 1976
Voyage into the Golden Screen (Nørgaard): 24 Mar 1969
Voyage to America (Rosenberg): 24 Nov 1932
Voyevode, The (Tchaikovsky): 18 Nov 1891

Walküre, Die (Wagner): 26 Jun 1870
Wally, La (Catalani): 20 Jan 1892
War Requiem (Britten): 30 May 1962
Warsaw Concerto (Addinsell): 13 Jan 1904
Water Music (Handel): 17 Jul 1717
Wa-Wan Press (Farwell): 23 Apr 1872